Probate Records

Sonoma County, California

Index for

1847 to 1959

Volume 1: A-K

Sonoma County Genealogical Society

HERITAGE BOOKS
2014

HERITAGE BOOKS
AN IMPRINT OF HERITAGE BOOKS, INC.

Books, CDs, and more—Worldwide

For our listing of thousands of titles see our website
at
www.HeritageBooks.com

Published 2014 by
HERITAGE BOOKS, INC.
Publishing Division
5810 Ruatan Street
Berwyn Heights, Md. 20740

International Standard Book Numbers
Paperbound: 978-0-7884-5590-2
Clothbound: 978-0-7884-6055-5

Probate Records, Sonoma County, California
Index for 1847 to 1959

The Sonoma County, California, Superior Court currently archives a probate index for the years 1847 through 1959 and contains 28,765 records. The index is also available at the Local History and Genealogy Annex of the Sonoma County Library in Santa Rosa.

Probate records generally relate to the disposition of an estate after the owner's death. However, the records found in the Sonoma County Index also contain a number of additional types of records including adoption, conservatorship, establishing identity, homestead, incompetency, insanity, and others. The names of minors frequently, but not always, appear. The type of file is identified in the last column of the tables that follow and is abbreviated as follows:

a (adoption)
con (conservatorship)
d (deceased)
don (donor)
ei (establishing identity)
m (minor)
g (guardian)
h (homestead)
inc (incompetent)
ins (insane)
jt (joint tenancy)
mp (missing person)
o (orphan)
p (petition or petitioner)
res (restoration to capacity)
t (trustee)

Surname Spelling Variations
We have adhered as closely as possible to the spellings given in the index and this may cause some anomalies in the sequence of surnames. For example, surnames such as DeCarli, McKean, etc., are sometimes spelled with a space separating the parts, as De Carli or Mc Kean and therefore will not be listed next to each other alphabetically. In addition, occasionally the first part may be excluded and placed with the given name. For example, Carli may be indexed with the Cs instead of the Ds. The researcher is advised to be aware of these anomalies and search accordingly.

Condition of Index
The index from which these data were read was copied onto a DVD from microfilm which, in many cases, varied from difficult to impossible to read. A sample is given here:

If the entry on this index could not be determined, SCGS volunteers went to the Sonoma County Court House to gather what information they could from the actual filmed probate records, which are filed by file number.

It was discovered that some file numbers were missing from the index. Many of these were recovered from the probate register book which is kept in the Sonoma County Archives. For whatever reason some case numbers appear not to have ever been assigned. No cases were filed under these numbers: 874, 1787, 1953, 2112, 2593, 2594, and 2656.

Acknowledgments

This project was prepared using a multi-step process. First, microfiche from the Superior Court Office were transformed to PDF files on a DVD. Appreciation is expressed to The Friends of Santa Rosa Libraries who funded this step of the process. Next, volunteers of the Sonoma County Genealogical Society produced hard copy and then entered the data into a spreadsheet format. The data were then sent online to a person who acted as the central data collector. The data were printed and proofread against either hard copy or the PDF files or a combination of both. In a considerable number of cases, the information contained on the files was illegible and those cases were referred to a SCGS volunteer for verification against the archival files in the Superior Court Records Office. Persons contributing to this effort include the following:

Project Coordinator
Carmen Finley

Hard Copy Production
Shirley Flick
Sue Guerra
Jeremy Nichols
Joe Panaro

Data Entry
Shirley Flick
Sue Guerra
Joseph Panaro

Proof Reading
Kurt Boldt
Anna Conley
Doris Dickenson
Carmen Finley
Lois Nimmo
Marie Nottingham

Verification
Kurt Boldt
Ray Owen

Final Copy
Carmen Finley

Month	Day	Year	File No.	Surname	Given Name	Type
May	15	1958	25628	Abaya	Hilaron	d
		1873	594	Abbelbeck	F. D.	d
		[1904-1906]	3868	Abbey	Alfred B.	m
Feb.	15	1954	22916	Abbey	Lynn	m
		1860	170	Abbey	Wm. C.	d
July	25	1927	9615	Abbott	G. Frank	d
Jan.	27	1946	17537	Abbott	H. A.	d
Jan.	5	1951	20134	Abbott	Mary L., etc.	d
		1884	1388	Abbott	Minerva	d
Oct.	5	1941	14630	Abel	Almina, etc.	d
Mar.	23	1939	13540	Abel	Almira	inc
Jan.	5	1951	20586	Abel	Gary	m
Sept.	5	1951	20586	Abel	Michal	m
		1955	23235	Abele	Meta	d
Apr.	9	1915	5977	Abels	Coard	d
Nov.	18	1931	11033	Abels	Ihak	d
Nov.	2	1956	24306	Abildgaard	Walter E., etc.	d
Nov.	18	1940	14243	Ables	Richard	d
Dec.	10	1920	7571	Ables	Zilla I.	m
		1892	2238	Abraham	Isidora	d
		[1910-1911]	4883	Abraham	Peter	d
Apr.	6	1957	24571	Abraham	Sigrid M.	d
		1893	2322	Abraham	Sophia	d
Dec.	22	1950	20114	Abraio	Leonie	d
Sept.	30	1944	16147	Abraio	Mary	d
Apr.	24	1943	15323	Abrais	Mary	d
Nov.	22	1947	18011	Abrams	James O.	d
June		1923	8328	Abramsky	Bernard	d
June	3	1949	19050	Abshire	Alfred Cecil, etc.	d
		[1907-1908]	4375	Abshire	Dorlesca	d
Aug.	7	1954	22570	Abshire	F. A., etc.	d
Aug.	17	1915	6042	Abshire	James H.	d
		1903	3531	Abshire	Jas. H.	i
Feb.	22	1921	7654	Abshire	Lily B.	d
Dec.	9	1939	13800	Acken	Charles S.	d
June	12	1915	6017	Ackerman	B. D.	d
		1870	460	Ackerman	B. H.	d
		1877	884	Ackerman	Harriet B.	m
		1871	494	Ackerman	Lewis D.	m
		1865	288	Ackerman	Mary	d
		1877	884	Ackerman	Mary E.	m
		1911	5190	Ackerman	Mary Edith	d

Month	Day	Year	File No.	Surname	Given Name	Type
		1875	754	Ackerman	N. A.	d
		1877	884	Ackerman	Rebecca J.	m
Feb.	27	1920	7623	Ackroyd	Charles	d
July	24	1957	24827	Ackroyd	Lucille	d
June	4	1954	22513	Acme	Macy, etc.	inc
Aug.	18	1952	21254	Acorne	John Burton	d
		1935	12297	Acquistapace	Battista	d
		[1917-1918]	6608	Acquistapace	Bernardo	d
Dec.	16	1920	7565	Acquistapace	Caesar	d
Oct.	3	1912	5407	Acquistapace	Camillo	m
Oct.	4	1957	25063	Acquistapace	Charles, etc.	d
May	1	1952	21095	Acquistapace	Edward J.	d
Nov.	19	1955	23491	Acquistapace	Frank, etc.	d
Mar.	25	1929	10471	Acquistapace	Giovanni, etc.	d
Jan.	3	1912	5407	Acquistapace	James	m
Sept.	23	1934	12010	Acquistapace	James	d
Feb.	16	1932	11196	Acquistapace	Jas., etc.	inc
Nov.	18	1932	11413	Acquistapace	Joe, etc.	d
Mar.	8	1946	16999	Acquistapace	Maria	d
July	19	1952	21124	Acquistapace	Maria	d
Oct.	4	1956	24252	Acquistapace	Ronald	m
		1911	5043	Acquistepace	J. A.	d
		1874	697	Acton	Martha	d
		1887	1635	Adair	Agnes	d
Sept.	3	1957	24993	Adami	Phillip Frederich	d
Apr.		1955	23050	Adamis	Joseph, etc.	d
Oct.	3	1958	25976	Adams	Alice J.	d
Apr.	8	1953	21753	Adams	Amelia	d
May	21	1915	6183	Adams	Ann	d
Oct.	2	1940	14206	Adams	Anna Margaret	d
		1892	2233	Adams	Bertha P.	m
		1911	5127	Adams	Bertha P.	d
July	12	1949	19166	Adams	Carol Jean	m
Nov.	4	1955	23514	Adams	Charles D.	d
Feb.	28	1958	25331	Adams	Charles, etc.	d
July	19	1938	13380	Adams	Clara C.	d
Apr.	12	1954	22448	Adams	Clara E.	d
Mar.	5	1946	17047	Adams	Clarence E.	d
Mar.	5	1946	17049	Adams	Clarence E.	d
		1893	2325	Adams	Colin C.	d
Feb.	21	1946	16951	Adams	Elisha W.	d
Nov.	28	1939	13771	Adams	Elmer C.	d

Month	Day	Year	File No.	Surname	Given Name	Type
		[1897-1898]	2708	Adams	Eva G.	d
Aug.	7	1939	13717	Adams	Franklin L., etc.	d
Mar.	30	1942	14799	Adams	Fred Luther	d
Feb.	20	1914	5698	Adams	Gilbert K.	d
Dec.	24	1944	16289	Adams	Harold A.	d
		1896	2648	Adams	John	d
		1926	9312	Adams	John Quincy	d
Jan.	17	1948	18742	Adams	Joseph	d
		1886	1597	Adams	Joshua	d
July	21	1949	19138	Adams	Leonard Oliver, etc.	d
		[1890-1892]	2213	Adams	Levi Carter	d
July	12	1949	19166	Adams	Loretta	m
Apr.	3	1953	21624	Adams	Mabel	d
July	15	1953	21946	Adams	Marcia Raye	m
		1892	2233	Adams	Mary E.	m
July		1947	17818	Adams	Nellie, etc.	d
Apr.	14	1944	15928	Adams	Robert M.	m
May	1	1936	12603	Adams	Robert S.	d
July	12	1949	19166	Adams	Shirley	m
Dec.	8	1941	14735	Adams	Thomas Allan, etc.	d
July	12	1949	19166	Adams	Virgil	m
		1918	6646	Adams	William	d
Oct.	20	1938	13439	Adams	Wilma Margaret	m
Jan.	31	1942	15130	Adams	Winfield	d
		1867	343	Adams	Samuel	d
Dec.	7	1952	21437	Adamson	Clara	d
Dec.	19	1956	24338	Adamson	Ida Lawrence, etc.	d
		1890	1925	Adamson	James	d
		1890	2002	Adamson	James T. et al	m
		1890	1926	Adamson	Mary	d
		1861	186	Adamson	Mary E.	m
Sept.	17	1954	22701	Adamson	Rosina M.	d
Oct.	10	1958	25990	Adcock	Catherene Lee	m
Oct.	10	1958	25990	Adcock	Chesley Roscoe	m
Oct.	10	1958	25990	Adcock	Larry	m
Oct.	10	1958	25990	Adcock	William Roy	m
Oct.	25	1944	16186	Addmis	Maria Clotilde, etc.	d
Apr.	17	1944	15930	Adler	Adam Winkle, etc.	d
		1956	24061	Adler	Charles David, etc.	d
July	3	1928	9962	Adler	David	d
Sept.		1920	7440	Adler	Irma	m
	19	1956	24060	Adler	Johanna M.	d

Month	Day	Year	File No.	Surname	Given Name	Type
Sept.		1920	7440	Adler	Leland	m
		1896	2641	Adler	Lewis	d
		1923	8524	Adler	Martha	d
Mar.		1921	7930	Adroin	Adolphe	d
Aug.	7	1954	22564	Adsit	Horace C.	d
Jan.	27	1949	19279	Agastinho	Janet L.	d
Jan.	24	1943	15734	Agastini	Felix	d
May	8	1944	15963	Agastini	Maria, etc.	d
May	8	1944	15964	Agastini	G. D.	d
		1958	26023	Agee	Fred L.	d
May	2	1949	19044	Aggi	Anita Louise	m
		[1919-1920]	7107	Aggio	Pietro etc.	d
Dec.	21	1941	14712	Agius	Francis	m
Dec.	21	1941	14712	Agius	James	m
Oct.	11	1951	20667	Agius	Phyllis J.	m
Nov.	21	1941	14712	Agius	Ruth	m
Nov.	21	1941	14712	Agius	Thomas	m
Apr.	19	1932	11234	Agler	James A., etc.	d
Sept.	13	1945	16644	Agnew	Asahel Warren, etc.	d
		1890	1930	Agnew	Clairrissa A.	m
		1890	1930	Agnew	Richard A.	m
Apr.	5	1949	19001	Agostinho	Hazel M.	d
May	27	1928	9891	Agostini	Davide aka D., etc	d
Nov.	17	1928	10022	Agostini	Elizabeth, etc.	m
May	15	1937	12925	Aguallo	Pete, etc.	d
		1923	8530	Aguillon	Bertha	d
		1908	4501	Aguillon	Camille F.	d
Apr.	19	1944	15793	Aguillon	Elise	d
Sept.	15	1949	19172	Aguirre	Evelyn E.	d
Feb.	3	1941	14376	Aguis	Angelo, etc.	d
Aug.	14	1944	16080	Aguis	John, etc.	d
Feb.	21	1915	5944	Ah	Wah	d
		1885	1455	Ah Duck	White Child	m
		1894	2446	Ah Kay		d
Oct.	17	1958	26010	Ahern	Earl Joseph, etc.	d
Oct.	21	1953	22025	Ahern	George F.	d
Mar.	8	1951	20262	Ahern	Mary	d
Aug.	3	1943	15540	Ahern	Nicholas P.	inc
Nov.	27	1944	16235	Ahern	Nicholas P.	d
Mar.	19	1919	7002	Aherns	Albert N.	d
Jan.	28	1944	16293	Aherns	George W.	d
Mar.	20	1936	12559	Ahl	Jacob	d

Month	Day	Year	File No.	Surname	Given Name	Type
		1937	13080	Ahl	Raymond	d
		1937	13108	Ahl	Wilmer P.	m
June	25	1941	14492	Ahlborn	Hazel J.	d
		1925	8846	Ahlstedt	Gustave, etc.	d
May	11	1946	17133	Ahlstrom	Elis W.	d
June	18	1953	21895	Ahner	Ruth Esther, etc.	d
Jan.	14	1955	23654	Aho	Eugene M., etc.	d
		[1937-1938]	13185	Aho	Matt	d
July	21	1930	10582	Ahonen	Emil	d
Nov.	8	1954	22799	Ahonen	Fanny	d
Nov.	16	1953	22121	Ahrendsen	John	d
		1886	1585	Ahrens	Jacob	d
		1888	1747	Aiken	Della	m
Dec.	13	1927	9720	Aiken	Squire J.	d
		1923	8254	Aikin	Robert L.	d
Feb.	24	1936	12840	Aimd	Joe, etc.	d
Sept.	6	1934	11990	Aimisegger	Conrad	d
Jan.	15	1945	16886	Aimonetti	Anton, etc.	d
		[1898-1899]	2843	Aitken	James	d
		[1898-1899]	2847	Aitken	James	d
Dec.	23	1955	23609	Aitken	William, etc.	d
Jan.	12	1950	20101	Akena	John D.	d
Apr.	12	1956	23856	Akers	Archie A.	d
Apr.	5	1952	20898	Akers	Edwin W.	d
Nov.	3	1942	15001	Akers	Medora	d
June	13	1942	14983	Akers	Medora M.	d
June	6	1931	10903	Akers	Montgomery P.	d
June	13	1942	14983	Akers	Montgomery P.	d
Sept.	21	1917	6425	Akers	Stephen	d
Aug.	11	1932	11334	Akers	Stephen	d
Mar.	5	1932	11219	Akers	William Arden	m
		1887	1665	Akins	Thomas	d
Feb.	30	1919	6976	Alamada	Manuel	d
Oct.	10	1958	25991	Alaman	Joseph	d
May	5	1956	23905	Alasaari	Aurora, etc.	d
		1883	1291	Albee	Aurel	d
July	28	1912	5423	Alber	Ernest Emire	d
Oct.	13	1943	15594	Albera	Marie	d
July	7	1950	19803	Albera	Michele	d
Jan.	14	1958	25286	Alberigi	Jennie	d
		[1904-1906]	3903	Alberigi	Mary	d
		1903	3577	Alberigi	Pietro	d

Month	Day	Year	File No.	Surname	Given Name	Type
Dec.	9	1950	19960	Alberigi	Silvio Anthony	d
		[1908-1910]	4737	Alberloni	Abbondio	d
July	11	1950	19807	Albers	Dedrick E.	d
Sept.	10	1941	14544	Albert	Carl	d
Jan.	27	1938	13446	Alberti	Charles M.	d
Aug.	6	1954	22680	Alberti	John	d
		1926	9281	Albertoni	Abondio	m
Apr.	21	1919	7031	Albertoni	Albert	m
Mar.	21	1919	7031	Albertoni	Corina	m
July	2	1922	8057	Albertoni	D.	d
July		1926	9281	Albertoni	Edwin	m
		1926	9281	Albertoni	Elsie	m
Mar.	21	1919	7031	Albertoni	Elvi	m
Mar.	21	1919	7031	Albertoni	Evelina	m
May		1918	6701	Albertoni	John	d
		1912	5255	Albertoni	John C.	d
Mar.	21	1919	7031	Albertoni	Lella	m
Mar.	21	1919	7031	Albertoni	Linda	m
June	6	1910	4877	Albertoni	Marguerita	d
		1919	7031	Albertoni	Rosa	m
		1926	9281	Albertoni	Victor	m
Feb.		1925	9091	Albertson	James Henry	d
July	16	1939	13701	Albertson	Jessie	d
Dec.	13	1916	6367	Albertson	Mary Elizabeth	d
Apr.	30	1925	9102	Albertson	William G.	d
		1923	8289	Albertz	Ferdinand, etc.	d
Nov.	6	1946	17330	Albini	Adele	d
		[1937-1938]	13338	Albini	Amadeo	m
		[1937-1938]	13338	Albini	Amados	m
Apr.	25	1935	12239	Albini	Annunziata	d
Feb.	16	1915	6069	Albini	Aumenziata	i
Apr.	6	1953	21629	Albini	Caterina	d
Aug.	5	1933	11630	Albini	Domenico	d
Jan.		1913	5600	Albini	Donato	d
		[1937-1938]	13338	Albini	Edward	m
June	3	1946	17230	Albini	Edward Richard, etc.	d
Nov.	13	1957	25139	Albini	Emilia, etc.	d
Dec.	17	1927	9745	Albini	George	d
Aug.	7	1937	13024	Albini	Helen, Jane, Emma, Edw	m
Dec.	28	1947	18068	Albini	John	d
Dec.	30	1936	12820	Albini	John B.	d
June	17	1946	17258	Albini	John C.	d

Month	Day	Year	File No.	Surname	Given Name	Type
Sept.	22	1944	16183	Albini	Lucille H., etc. (Dean)	inc
Apr.	29	1952	20951	Albini	Mario P.	d
Sept.	22	1935	12383	Albini	Mervyn H.	m
May	21	1932	11446	Albini	Paulo, etc.	d
Sept.	25	1944	16139	Albini	Peter C.	d
June	26	1950	19774	Albini	Peter D., etc.	d
Sept.	22	1935	12383	Albini	Ronaldo C.	m
Mar.	28	1958	25432	Albouze	Maria	d
June	30	1953	21815	Albrecht	Fred	d
June	6	1937	12987	Albright	Charles M.	ins
Nov.	30	1944	16197	Alcalde	Della Sandra	m
Apr.	9	1954	22334	Aldamar	Balbino A., etc.	d
Apr.	20	1927	9610	Alden	Annie F.	d
Aug.	15	1929	10308	Alderman	Keith	m
Aug.	15	1929	10308	Alderman	Roger Lee	m
Apr.	30	1951	20301	Aldinger	Albert	d
Oct.	29	1958	25891	Alessandri	Lelio	d
Dec.	27	1958	26036	Alessi	Grace	d
Oct.	12	1932	11361	Alessi	Valentino	d
Oct.	3	1940	14226	Alexander	Ada	d
June	27	1935	12313	Alexander	Albert E.	d
Mar.	28	1947	17669	Alexander	Alonzo Carleton, etc.	d
		[1897-1898]	2769	Alexander	Charles	d
		[1900-1901]	3306	Alexander	Chas. Rufus	m
		1872	589	Alexander	Cyrus	d
	13	1917	6561	Alexander	Cyrus	d
Nov.	13	1934	12049	Alexander	Dell T.	d
Feb.	12	1951	20153	Alexander	Elizabeth	inc
Jan.	30	1931	11150	Alexander	Elizabeth R., etc.	d
Apr.	18	1941	14441	Alexander	Geo. E., etc.	d
		1886	1598	Alexander	George Cyrus	m
May		1918	6723	Alexander	Joseph	d
May	14	1932	11252	Alexander	Julius M.	d
		1898	2835	Alexander	Levi	d
Feb.	13	1916	6368	Alexander	Lucille E.	i
		[1900-1901]	3306	Alexander	Lue Melissa	m
Feb.	15	1940	14274	Alexander	M. Maude, etc.	d
Jan.	8	1946	17474	Alexander	Martha	d
		[1900-1901]	3306	Alexander	Mary Ida	m
Jan.	10	1951	20148	Alexander	Max, etc.	d
		[1900-1901]	3306	Alexander	Samuel	m
Oct.	7	1950	19912	Alexander	Samuell R.	d

Month	Day	Year	File No.	Surname	Given Name	Type
July	9	1934	11970	Alexander	Thomas	d
Jan.	19	1949	19269	Alexander	Walter C.	d
Sept.	25	1957	24910	Alexander	William G., etc.	d
Feb.	1	1926	9325	Alexander	William John	d
		[1890-1892]	2162	Alexander	Wm.	d
Apr.	16	1915	5960	Alfieri	Joseph	d
Jan.	1	1923	8201	Alger	William I.	d
		[1919-1920]	7248	Alietti	Joseph	i
Oct.	24	1933	11673	Alietti	Joseph, etc.	d
		1913	5472	Aljets	Philip	m
July	25	1946	17279	Alkire	Edwin C., etc.	d
		[1899-1900]	3065	Alkire	Jackson	d
		1906	4192	Alkire	Martha E.	d
June	8	1952	21106	Alladio	Frank Sylvester, etc.	d
July	1	1958	25751	Alladis	Anna Lucia, etc.	d
		1921	7819	Allan	Allis	d
Oct.	9	1957	25070	Allan	Bertha	d
Jan.	17	1957	25222	Allan	Bertha	d
Jan.	17	1941	14746	Allard	Ellen C.	d
		[1907-1908]	4456	Allegrini	Julius	d
		[1904-1906]	3881	Alleman	Arzola Lee	m
		1903	3719	Alleman	Jacob	d
July		1955	23273	Allen	Anna	d
		1889	1890	Allen	B. B.	d
Aug.	13	1927	9699	Allen	Carrie May	d
July	13	1957	24733	Allen	Charles Jas.	d
Apr.	30	1945	16388	Allen	Dick	d
Aug.	16	1927	9673	Allen	E. R.	d
Oct.	15	1958	25927	Allen	Earl	d
Mar.		1926	9454	Allen	Edward Nacy	d
July	20	1952	21210	Allen	Elizabeth	d
Nov.	25	1957	25102	Allen	Emelia Emma	d
May	6	1951	20316	Allen	Frank L.	d
Nov.	28	1934	12064	Allen	Frank Z.	inc
		1955	23231	Allen	Grant	d
Jan.	12	1948	18168	Allen	John F.	d
Apr.	13	1951	20275	Allen	John P.	d
Dec.	16	1956	24331	Allen	Lillie L.	d
Jan.	25	1914	5808	Allen	Luella L.	d
Mar.	15	1936	12551	Allen	Lynn D.	d
		1899	2997	Allen	Mary C.	m
June	12	1928	9908	Allen	Mary Mildred	m

Month	Day	Year	File No.	Surname	Given Name	Type
Jan.	16	1942	14775	Allen	Mollie L.	inc
		[1898-1899]	2867	Allen	Otis	d
June	15	1931	10945	Allen	Robert	d
Feb.		1913	5613	Allen	Samuel	d
May	10	1933	11739	Allen	Samuel G.	d
		[1910-1911]	4920	Allen	Samuel S.	i
		[1910-1911]	4935	Allen	Samuel Strong	d
Oct.	29	1940	13976	Allen	Virgina Lee	d
		1890	2140	Allen	William T.	d
Jan.	30	1948	18759	Allenden	Gerald Young	d
		1911	5201	Allenden	John	d
Nov.	16	1940	14242	Allenden	Myrtle Lee	d
Nov.	21	1941	14684	Allenden	Myrtle Lee	d
Mar.	10	1938	13454	Allenden	Ruth	d
		1922	7975	Allenden	Gerald Y.	m
June	6	1922	7975	Allenden	Clarence A.	m
Sept.	26	1955	23388	Allens	Mario	d
		1867	336	Alley	C. W. & Starr	m
Nov.	18	1954	22871	Allig	Josef, etc.	d
Aug.	10	1951	20477	Allik	Rose	d
Apr.	29	1943	15740	Allingham	Ray	d
July	18	1958	25712	Allison	John B.	inc
Apr.	22	1954	22304	Allison	Louise P.	d
Feb.	24	1940	13908	Allison	Perry L., etc.	d
Nov.	8	1932	11384	Allison	William Delray	m
		[1907-1908]	4367	Allman	Elizabeth	m
		[1907-1908]	4367	Allman	Frederick Peter	m
Apr.	17	1941	14438	Allman	Helene Anna	d
		[1907-1908]	4367	Allman	Henry	m
		[1908-1910]	4507	Allman	Margaret	d
Jan.	5	1934	12091	Allvenn	Edward	d
Mar.	17	1919	6998	Almada	Manuel	d
Oct.		1923	8365	Almazza	Lorenzo Manesco, etc.	d
		[1901-1902]	3377	Almeida	Geo. S.	d
Apr.	14	1946	17072	Almeida	M. S., etc.	d
Nov.	29	1956	24299	Almeida	Maria S., etc.	d
Feb.	21	1958	25306	Alovey	Horace Herman	d
June	24	1953	21908	Alpha	Jean	d
		1947	17720	Alten	John H.	d
		1918	6682	Alten	Martha	d
Mar.	10	1941	14391	Alten	Mary E.	inc
Sept.	3	1943	15544	Alten	Mary E.	inc

Month	Day	Year	File No.	Surname	Given Name	Type
Sept.	8	1947	17989	Alten	Mary E.	d
Aug.		1956	24071	Altenreuther	Leopold C., etc.	d
Nov.	12	1954	22857	Altenreuther	Vincent L.	d
	4	1955	23019	Alth	Aline	d
Mar.	13	1940	13932	Altherr	Augustine	ins
Feb.	27	1956	23755	Altherr	Augustine	d
June	16	1950	19702	Altman	Charles G.	d
Mar.	7	1958	25437	Altman	Genevieve Sterling	d
		1911	5108	Alto	Arthur	d
		1893	2363	Alton	Anna (adoption)	m
		[1907-1908]	4391	Alton	Catherine	d
Jan.	1	1922	8089	Alton	Henry	d
		1926	9262	Alton	Louie Frances	d
Mar.		1957	24449	Alujevich	Martin	d
May	29	1958	24931	Alvarez	Lola, etc.	d
July	1	1916	6241	Alvernas	Maria	i
Apr.	20	1940	13969	Alvernez	Manuel B., etc.	d
Jan.	25	1918	6795	Alves	Joseph	d
May	4	1952	21034	Alvord	Vernon M.	d
		[1919-1920]	7292	Amadon	Ernestine	d
		1907	4234	Amana	Minnie etc.	d
Aug.	28	1953	21976	Amaral	Anthony	d
		[1907-1908]	4450	Amaral	de Mary Jose Francisca	i
Dec.	14	1943	15685	Amaral	John	d
July	11	1958	25776	Amaral	Marianna	d
June	26	1947	17713	Amaral	Theresa Antonia, etc.	d
		1911	5103	Amaral	Maria Jose	d
Oct.	30	1940	14017	Amarel	Margaret	m
		1921	7828	Ambrogiani	Enrico	d
Oct.	14	1953	22112	Ambrogio	Giovanna, etc.	d
Apr.	12	1943	15275	Ambuehl	Benjamin Harrison	d
Feb.	17	1942	14782	Amedeo	Josephine	d
Feb.	18	1923	8251	Ames	Addie F.	d
		1923	8403	Ames	Eddella L.	d
Sept.	22	1958	25874	Ames	Grace, etc.	d
Feb.	4	1952	20827	Ames	Mamie C.	d
Nov.	8	1944	16249	Ames	Richard George	d
Jan.	15	1919	6949	Ames	Gwen E.	d
		[1904-1906]	3767	Amesbury	Carl	m
		[1904-1906]	3767	Amesbury	Herbert	m
Aug.	7	1951	20531	Ammann	Eliza	d
Aug.	10	1944	16126	Ammann	John	d

Month	Day	Year	File No.	Surname	Given Name	Type
Apr.	1	1935	12215	Amoral	Jesse	d
May	11	1958	25547	Amouh	Phillip	con
Jan.	3	1958	25249	Amsberry	Franklin Blaine	d
Sept.	12	1932	11360	Amstalden	Theodore	d
Sept.	19	1950	19877	Andeoud	Victor T.	d
		1877	879	Anderline	Charles	d
May	13	1948	18341	Andersen	A. W., etc.	d
Mar.	17	1934	12103	Andersen	Anders R.	d
July	20	1958	25722	Andersen	Andreas	d
Feb.	15	1940	13933	Andersen	Eleanore Meir, etc.	d
June	9	1942	14973	Andersen	Johannas, etc.	d
Jan.	7	1956	24376	Andersen	Karoline	d
Feb.	25	1956	23745	Andersen	Lilli Marie, etc.	d
Jan.		1924	8791	Andersen	Marie F.	d
May	12	1935	12269	Andersen	Mary Madsen	d
Mar.	29	1921	7834	Andersen	Peter C.	d
Nov.	14	1942	15146	Andersen	Sophus	d
Apr.	21	1929	10189	Anderson	Aaron	d
Nov.	31	1957	25118	Anderson	Ada D.	d
Jan.	6	1957	25194	Anderson	Alexander C. Alexander	d
Sept.	28	1941	14496	Anderson	Alexander W., etc.	d
May	16	1954	22462	Anderson	Alfred	d
May	3	1937	12985	Anderson	Amanda E.	d
Feb.	27	1914	5888	Anderson	Amanda I.	d
Apr.	3	1932	11431	Anderson	Andrew	d
July	15	1934	11974	Anderson	Andrew	d
Apr.	4	1958	25519	Anderson	Andrew Louis, etc.	d
June	12	1942	14942	Anderson	Andrew T., etc.	d
Dec.		1958	26039	Anderson	Anna H.	d
Feb.	8	1945	16354	Anderson	Arthur W.	d
Dec.	22	1954	22879	Anderson	Ashley D.	d
June	8	1942	14970	Anderson	August	d
Dec.	7	1939	13777	Anderson	August T.	d
June	28	1950	19785	Anderson	B. A.	d
Mar.	3	1956	23777	Anderson	Bernadina	d
May	18	1916	6198	Anderson	Catherine V.	d
June	12	1953	21889	Anderson	Charles G.	d
Aug.	2	1937	13079	Anderson	Charley E.	d
Jan.	20	1958	25300	Anderson	Christian	d
Sept.	11	1947	17886	Anderson	Clara B.	d
Jan.	9	1952	21509	Anderson	Clarence E.	d
Apr.	14	1953	21768	Anderson	Clarence E.	d

Month	Day	Year	File No.	Surname	Given Name	Type
June	17	1953	21894	Anderson	Clarence E.	d
Feb.	2	1959	26184	Anderson	Clarence J.	d
Oct.	5	1952	21284	Anderson	Daisy	d
Mar.	10	1949	18819	Anderson	David P., etc.	d
Apr.	16	1926	9201	Anderson	Delbert A.	m
Jan.	2	1920	7595	Anderson	Ella M.	d
Aug.	12	1949	19169	Anderson	Ellen	d
July	7	1932	11271	Anderson	Eric O., etc.	d
Sept.	30	1951	20571	Anderson	Eva	d
Oct.	27	1957	25043	Anderson	Frank M.	d
Apr.	21	1927	9573	Anderson	Frank W.	d
Sept.	10	1925	8851	Anderson	George H.	d
Aug.	22	1935	12365	Anderson	Gussie	inc
Aug.	9	1957	24863	Anderson	Gussie B.	d
		[1919-1920]	7099	Anderson	Hans	d
Aug.	13	1932	11296	Anderson	Harold, etc.	d
Sept.	13	1948	18579	Anderson	Harrison M.	d
July		1918	6776	Anderson	Hazel	d
July	28	1950	19785	Anderson	Helen	d
Aug.	24	1921	7687	Anderson	Helen Elizabeth	m
July	5	1931	10992	Anderson	Henry	d
Feb.	7	1940	14266	Anderson	Henry	d
May	25	1944	15947	Anderson	Herman	d
Aug.	21	1943	15393	Anderson	Hild, his wife	p
June	18	1944	15991	Anderson	J. H.	d
Sept.	10	1954	22688	Anderson	Jake W.	d
Mar.	7	1941	14383	Anderson	Jennie P.	ins
Mar.	15	1941	14433	Anderson	Johanna	d
Jan.	6	1950	19446	Anderson	Johanna Gabriella	d
		[1908-1910]	4568	Anderson	John	d
Apr.	16	1948	18232	Anderson	John	d
		[1908-1910]	4541	Anderson	John A.	d
Jan.	11	1918	6787	Anderson	John Frederick	m
		[1907-1908]	4272	Anderson	John H.	d
Apr.	4	1949	18933	Anderson	John V.	d
Apr.	16	1948	18231	Anderson	John, etc.	d
Aug.	29	1948	18489	Anderson	Joseph A.	d
Feb.	20	1947	17584	Anderson	Joseph Edward	d
		1918	6743	Anderson	Josephine	d
June	6	1957	24714	Anderson	Julia	d
Apr.	8	1946	17130	Anderson	Leslie R.	d
May	2	1958	25490	Anderson	Louise, etc.	d

Month	Day	Year	File No.		Surname	Given Name	Type
Jan.	8	1939	13860		Anderson	Lydia C.	d
May	29	1949	19041		Anderson	M. E., etc.	d
Mar.	11	1949	18944		Anderson	Mary Belle	d
Mar.	6	1930	10753		Anderson	Mathilda	d
Jan.	18	1958	26161		Anderson	Mattie R.	d
June	21	1948	18401		Anderson	Nels	d
Jan.	7	1947	17552		Anderson	Olga, etc.	inc
July	24	1953	21909		Anderson	Oscar Theodore	d
		1890	1951		Anderson	Paul J. et al	m
Oct.	17	1954	22761		Anderson	Pearl, etc.	d
Nov.	27	1952	21309		Anderson	Peter A.	d
Oct.	19	1941	14645		Anderson	Peter C.	d
May	2	1942	14837		Anderson	Rasmus	d
Feb.	11	1931	11162		Anderson	Richard	d
Mar.	2	1951	20193		Anderson	Sam	d
June	3	1914	5709		Anderson	Sarah J.	d
Sept.	13	1957	25019		Anderson	Sofia, etc.	d
Mar.	14	1956	23789		Anderson	Stephen, etc.	m
Aug.	21	1943	15393		Anderson	Sven	p
July		1955	23238		Anderson	Theodore M.	d
		1929	10279		Anderson	Thomas J.	d
		1957	24447		Anderson	Victor	d
Nov.	23	1952	21415		Anderson	William	d
July	5	1957	24850		Anderson	William B.	d
June	13	1944	16035		Anderson	A. J. F.	d
		1913	5570		Anderson	Albert G.	d
June	28	1953	21812		Anderson	Edith M.	d
May	16	1926	9255		Anderson (formerly An	Nellie M.	d
Dec.	13	1943	15717		Anderton	Annie	d
Jan.	5	1945	16349		Anderton	Daniel	d
Aug.	22	1945	16620		Anderton	Daniel	d
July	25	1915	6044		Anderton	Margaret E.	d
Feb.	11	1933	11688		Andrade	Cecilia Juanita	m
Aug.	25	1950	19834		Andrade	Sarah Jane	m
Aug.	25	1950	19834		Andrade	Thomas David	m
		1892	2268		Andrazzi	Charles	d
Oct.	21	1953	22069		Andre	Antone	d
Oct.	13	1948	18626		Andreasen	Hazel H., etc.	d
		1954	22945		Andreaux	Josephine S., etc.	d
Jan.	18	1946	16947		Andresen	Carl A.	d
		[1908-1910]	4530		Andresen	Jann Diedrich	d
		[1908-1910]	4530		Andresen	John Diedrich	d

Month	Day	Year	File No.	Surname	Given Name	Type
June	1	1954	22556	Andresen	Julius T., etc.	d
Dec.	28	1947	18108	Andresen	Theodora E., etc.	d
Jan.	23	1941	14749	Andrews	Alice F.	d
		1890	1952	Andrews	Amasa B.	d
		1878	966	Andrews	Anton	d
		1910	4800	Andrews	Charles S.	d
		1955	23046	Andrews	Clara Lopes, etc.	d
Oct.	18	1914	5718	Andrews	Elizabeth Frances	d
June	8	1948	18381	Andrews	Elizabeth Jane	d
Sept.	24	1921	7853	Andrews	Flora	d
Jan.	5	1951	20129	Andrews	George W.	d
		1956	24025	Andrews	Harry Delahunt, etc.	d
Nov.	15	1948	18677	Andrews	Helmig	d
June	23	1958	25647	Andrews	Isabelle B.	d
Aug.	29	1927	9618	Andrews	John H.	d
May	23	1937	12970	Andrews	John W.	d
May	24	1930	10560	Andrews	Laverna	m
May	2	1952	21099	Andrews	Lydia, etc.	d
		[1904-1906]	3842	Andrews	Mary	d
June	13	1934	11864	Andrews	Mary E.	d
July		1922	8046	Andrews	Melissa Ann	d
		[1910-1911]	4897	Andrews	Robert C.	m
		1955	23207	Andrews	Tony	d
Nov.	15	1948	18732	Andrews	Vernon A., etc.	d
Nov.	15	1929	10437	Andrews	W. J., etc.	d
Apr.	28	1958	25501	Andrews	William A., etc.	d
		1901	3361	Andrews	Wm. C.	d
Jan.	9	1956	23708	Andrieux	Emile	d
July	24	1945	16543	Andrieux	Karen Louise	m
Apr.	18	1929	10247	Andrus	Frank E.	d
Dec.	30	1931	11039	Angeli	Americo	ins
		[1937-1938]	13190	Angeli	Rappello	d
Oct.	14	1953	22115	Angelini	F., etc,	d
Feb.	3	1953	22158	Angelini	Giuseppe	d
May	2	1957	24710	Angell	Catherine	d
June	6	1942	14844	Angell	Otis B., etc.	d
		1920	7414	Angostus	Lottie B.	d
Apr.	20	1953	21784	Anker	Susan Lee	m
Jan.	16	1953	22122	Anker	Thomas G.	d
Apr.	20	1953	21784	Anker	William Roger	m
July	22	1928	10003	Annand	Danl	d
Feb.	28	1927	9817	Annett	Americus F., etc.	d

Month	Day	Year	File No.	Surname	Given Name	Type
Nov.	11	1954	22803	Annett	Blanche E.	d
		[1900-1901]	3212	Annis	Elizabeth Ann	d
Nov.	23	1936	12639	Anradou	Jules L.	d
Sept.	14	1948	18606	Anthenien	Agatha	d
		1920	7419	Anthony	Edward A.	d
		[1890-1892]	2179	Anthony	John	d
May	15	1949	19020	Antognini	Arthur	d
Feb.	27	1935	12501	Antognini	Joseph	d
		1919	7044	Antoniazzi	Peter	d
Jan.	21	1917	6590	Antonieth	Peter	d
Aug.	15	1955	23370	Antonietti	Carlo, etc.	d
June	4	1946	17187	Antonini	Joe	d
Dec.	7	1945	16866	Antonioli	Lodovias	d
June	22	1943	15487	Antonovich	Mike	d
Jan.	14	1945	16880	Antossi	Luis	d
		1955	23032	Apons	Etienne	d
Sept.	3	1949	19204	Apostal/Andreadis	Yocovos/James, etc.	d
May	2	1957	24632	Appel	Martha	d
		1890	2089	Appleby	Robert	d
		1920	7334	Appleby	William	d
Sept.	3	1943	15581	Appleton	Ben	d
Sept.	3	1943	15584	Appleton	Ben	d
		1890	2029	Appleton	Caroline S.	m
		1888	1724	Appleton	Eliza	d
		1887	1640	Appleton	Eliza G.	m
Oct.	28	1930	10638	Appleton	Hannah Spring, etc.	d
Dec.	10	1936	12772	Appleton	Jessie L.	d
		[1901-1902]	3468	Appleton	Wellington	d
		1887	1640	Appleton	William G.	m
Apr.	29	1946	17114	Aprile	Salvatore	d
Dec.	7	1936	12826	Aquistapace	John	d
Dec.	18	1945	16776	Aquistapace	Luigi, etc.	d
		1911	5094	Arata	Angelo	d
		[1937-1938]	13147	Arata	Francisco	d
Nov.	29	1929	10395	Arata	Giobatta, etc.	d
		[1908-1910]	4769	Arata	Giovanni	d
July	29	1953	21912	Arbaugh	Willa M.	m
		[1901-1902]	3478	Arbuckle	James C.	d
Sept.	29	1948	18490	Arbunich	Tony, etc.	d
		1920	7404	Archambeau	Alice	m
		[1900-1901]	3119	Archambeau	Anna	d
June	27	1915	6011	Archambeau	John B.	i

Month	Day	Year	File No.	Surname	Given Name	Type
		1917	6412	Archambeau	John B.	d
		1920	7404	Archambeau	Jos. K.	m
May	15	1915	5997	Archambeau	Matilda	d
Dec.	28	1916	6282	Archambeau	Melvyn J.	m
		1876	838	Archambeau	P. T.	d
Mar.	1	1935	12214	Archer	Anna C., etc.	d
Dec.	19	1957	25154	Archer	Aranda, etc.	d
July	6	1944	16066	Archer	Ella M.	inc
July	7	1944	16069	Archer	Genevra	d
July	30	1950	19790	Archer	H. E.	d
		1916	6248	Archer	John H. etc.	d
Mar.		1935	12214	Archer	Mrs Allison M., etc.	d
Jan.	2	1927	9797	Archer	Myrtle	d
Nov.	6	1935	12397	Archer	Nettie A.	inc
July	13	1918	6768	Archer	Ray E.	d
July	25	1951	20409	Archer	W. J.	d
July	13	1933	11611	Archer	Warren O.	d
Feb.	11	1952	20846	Archer	William Creed, etc.	d
Aug.	10	1925	9033	Archer	William H., etc.	d
		1868	369	Archer	Winston	d
Oct.	18	1945	16695	Archer	Ella M.	d
June	19	1953	21899	Archinal	Louis, etc.	d
Apr.	14	1949	18900	Ardenghi	Emil, etc.	d
Jan.	30	1928	10047	Arderson	Herbert A, etc.	d
May	23	1954	22483	Ardito	Santino	d
June	4	1954	22537	Ardito	Silvio	d
		[1908-1910]	4634	Arey	Thomas	d
		1890	2027	Arfort	Sophronia	d
June	14	1918	6739	Arfsten	Arfrs J.	d
July	9	1942	14975	Arfsten	Ben T.	d
Oct.	12	1955	23429	Arfsten	C. H., etc.	d
Dec.	25	1923	8481	Arfsten	Caroline	d
Jan.	12	1943	15222	Arfsten	Esther L. et al	d
		1911	5207	Arfsten	William	d
Mar.	30	1951	20185	Arfsten	William Arthur	d
Apr.	9	1937	12887	Arghittu	Giovanni	d
Dec.		1916	6295	Ariasi ?	Albina	i
Sept.	17	1939	13726	Arishita	Henry	m
Oct.	10	1958	25994	Arishita	Kozue	d
June	29	1934	11964	Arishita	Masaki	m
		1957	24437	Arke	Lenore	d
Apr.		1957	24480	Arke	Lenore	d

Month	Day	Year	File No.	Surname	Given Name	Type
		[1904-1906]	3867	Arlington	Ella L.	d
Mar.	29	1936	12843	Arlington	William	d
July	11	1949	19162	Armenskis	James	d
Sept.	6	1957	25001	Armfield	Maria G.	d
Sept.	6	1957	25006	Armfield	Maria, etc.	d
Apr.	11	1944	15922	Armfield	William A., etc.	d
Oct.	1	1954	22725	Armi	F. P., etc.	d
Aug.	16	1928	10020	Arminino	Annie	d
July	24	1949	19098	Armour	Mary D.	d
Jan.	15	1951	20155	Armout	Alvina W.	d
		[1899-1900]	3086	Armstrong	A. E.	d
		[1900-1901]	3298	Armstrong	Albert	m
		1923	8597	Armstrong	Anna	d
Apr.	5	1936	12572	Armstrong	Anna A.	inc
Dec.	12	1935	12458	Armstrong	Cassie	inc
Dec.	6	1946	17385	Armstrong	Clara J.	d
		1879	1015	Armstrong	David	d
July	24	1950	19830	Armstrong	Donald H.	d
		[1900-1901]	3298	Armstrong	Earl N.	m
		[1907-1908]	4305	Armstrong	Eleanor	d
Jan.	13	1947	18133	Armstrong	Emma C.	d
July	16	1944	16039	Armstrong	Eva E.	d
		[1900-1901]	3298	Armstrong	Frank L.	m
Aug.	16	1946	17297	Armstrong	George J., etc.	d
Oct.	15	1942	14984	Armstrong	George R.	d
Jan.	7	1946	16916	Armstrong	George R.	d
		[1900-1901]	3298	Armstrong	Hazel	m
Dec.	18	1955	23599	Armstrong	J. C., etc.	d
July	27	1912	5350	Armstrong	James B.	d
Mar.	19	1928	10118	Armstrong	James C.	d
		1956	24421	Armstrong	Johanna	d
		[1898-1899]	2922	Armstrong	Kate	d
		[1904-1906]	3799	Armstrong	Katharine M.	d
		[1900-1901]	3298	Armstrong	Lewis A.	m
May	6	1956	23909	Armstrong	Mabel	inc
		1872	578	Armstrong	Rosanna	m
		[1900-1901]	3298	Armstrong	Roy V.	m
		[1900-1901]	3298	Armstrong	Ruby A.	m
		1920	7342	Armstrong	Sarah	i
Jan.	22	1955	23675	Armstrong	Sarah J.	d
Feb.		1929	10453	Armstrong	Walter	inc
Apr.	21	1944	15940	Armstrong	Walter et al	d

Month	Day	Year	File No.	Surname	Given Name	Type
		1923	8574	Armstrong	William	d
Aug.	15	1958	25786	Armstrong	William C., etc.	d
Mar.	29	1946	16977	Armstrong	William C., etc.	d
Dec.	22	1957	25163	Arndt	Mary	d
Nov.	5	1945	18663	Arndt	Nellie M., etc.	d
Nov.	1	1940	14257	Arndt	Paul M.	d
		1921	7739	Arnhart	W. H.	d
Mar.	15	1939	13611	Arning	Christoph	d
		[1904-1906]	3780	Arnold	Catharine	d
Aug.		1956	24072	Arnold	Esther	d
		1859	152	Arnold	G. W.	i
		1885	1499	Arnold	George W.	i
June	11	1937	12993	Arnold	Harry B.	d
May	6	1944	15962	Arnold	Helen P.	m
Feb.	24	1950	19475	Arnold	Henry H., etc.	d
Aug.	7	1937	13025	Arnold	Hobart L.	d
June	10	1947	17740	Arnold	Jerold	d
		[1908-1910]	4783	Arnold	Judson	d
Oct.		1917	6512	Arnold	Julia M.	d
Aug.	23	1935	12366	Arnold	Mattie A.	d
Aug.	8	1958	25834	Arnold	Minnie I.	d
Dec.	23	1954	22883	Arnold	Oliver L., etc.	d
		1903	3704	Arnold	William J.	d
July	25	1946	17273	Arras	Helene	d
Nov.	19	1954	22875	Arrascada	G. F., etc.	d
Dec.	10	1935	12399	Arrighi	C.	d
Nov.	21	1941	14683	Arrigoni	Zaneris	d
Sept.	23	1947	17862	Art	John	d
		[1901-1902]	3454	Artara	Alexander	d
June	20	1950	19572	Arthur	Craig H., etc.	d
		[1907-1908]	4492	Artnar	John	d
May	11	1958	25542	Arughi	Mario	d
		[1907-1908]	4437	Arvidson	John A.	d
May	24	1944	15942	Arwine	James Tevis, etc.	inc
Sept.	18	1944	16176	Arwine	James Tevis, etc.	d
		1924	8739	Asaia	G. B.	d
Apr.	7	1936	12576	Asbell	Leona E.	d
Feb.	25	1919	6970	Asbury	B.	d
		1912	5250	Aschereman	Charles F.	d
Aug.	30	1912	5388	Ascherman	Arthur	m
Oct.	30	1912	5388	Ascherman	Calvin	m
Aug.	30	1912	5388	Ascherman	Charlotte	m

Month	Day	Year	File No.	Surname	Given Name	Type
Oct.	30	1912	5388	Ascherman	Dorothy	m
Aug.	30	1912	5388	Ascherman	Lewis	m
Jan.	4	1951	20127	Ascoop	Hortense	d
Oct.	17	1958	26006	Asdell	Earl R., etc.	d
Oct.	19	1929	10383	Asedo	Ramon D., etc.	m
Oct.	18	1925	9059	Asedo	Ramon D., Jr.	m
Dec.	31	1950	20016	Ash	Arethusa	inc
July	15	1951	20444	Ash	Arethusa	d
Oct.	21	1948	18637	Ash	Emerson F.	d
Sept.	11	1938	13370	Ash	I., etc.	d
		1935	12155	Ash	Mary Elizabeth, etc.	d
Feb.	11	1938	13245	Ash	Sarah	d
Aug.	14	1952	21247	Ashdown	C. L.	d
		1890	1983	Ashley	Martha E.	m
Mar.	26	1958	25422	Aslin	Colleen	d
May	13	1948	18344	Asman	Margaret E., etc.	d
Oct.	28	1956	24243	Aspenwall	Earl, etc.	d
Mar.	14	1939	13607	Asplund	Kristine	d
Apr.	8	1915	5989	Asprooch	O. W. etc.	d
Oct.	4	1936	12629	Assin/Assien	Annie/Anna May	d
Sept.	29	1946	17315	Assini	Joseph	d
May	8	1929	10275	Asti	Joseph	d
July	20	1931	11009	Asti	Paul, etc., et al	d
Sept.	17	1957	25026	Asti	Victoria	inc
		1902	3491	Aston	George Peter	d
		[1916-1917]	6370	Aston	Edna, Julian, Wilbert, E	m
Apr.	30	1956	23899	Asturias	Ramiro	d
Oct.	12	1947	17992	Atchison	Charles, etc.	d
June	17	1944	15988	Atchison	John B.	d
		1876	794	Atherton	Albert W.	m
		1876	794	Atherton	D. W. C.	m
		[1890-1892]	2170	Atkins	Nancy J.	d
		1904	3754	Atkins	Pohatan Alfred Peyton	d
		1883	1290	Atkins	W. G.	d
Sept.	16	1920	7522	Atkinson	Clair	m
Jan.	25	1952	21477	Atkinson	Clarence L.	d
Mar.		1912	5266	Atkinson	Dewey T.	d
Mar.	30	1928	9846	Atkinson	Ednad	d
Mar.	11	1942	14814	Atkinson	George E.	d
Mar.	15	1940	13960	Atkinson	Hiram V.	d
		1924	8771	Atkinson	Joseph, etc.	d
Nov.	16	1920	7522	Atkinson	Lawrence	m

Month	Day	Year	File No.	Surname	Given Name	Type
Aug.		1921	7824	Atkinson	Lettie	d
Oct.	5	1954	22788	Atkinson	Orrill E.	d
		1911	5085	Atkinson	Sarah J. E.	d
Mar.	24	1950	19530	Atkinson	William K., etc.	d
Oct.	25	1957	25039	Attaberry	John M.	d
May	8	1950	19555	Attwell	James Walter	m
Aug.	5	1912	5373	Atwater	Addie A.	d
		[1897-1898]	2774	Atwater	Henry H.	d
		[1904-1906]	4040	Atwood	George	d
Dec.	23	1945	16827	Atwood	Mary, etc.	d
		1887	1601	Augsburg	Peter George	d
Aug.	22	1912	5385	Aulich	Charles J.	d
Aug.	22	1912	5381	Aulich	Chas. J.	d
		1869	432	Aull	A. B.	d
		1870	436	Aull	Geo. & Laura	m
		1875	765	Aultenberger	Henry	d
July	11	1958	25775	Auradon	Laura	d
Jan.	20	1958	25297	Auradon	Laura P.	inc
Mar.	1	1946	17038	Auradou	John G., etc.	d
June	22	1939	13617	Aurel	Germain	d
July	15	1912	5361	Ausseresses	Louis F.	inc
Apr.	7	1921	7671	Ausseresses	Louis Florentine, etc.	d
June	10	1933	11585	Ausseresses	Paul Robert	d
Sept.	7	1956	24150	Austen	Donna	d
		1900	3111	Austin	Anna	d
		1894	2431	Austin	Charles	d
		1895	2537	Austin	Charles A.	m
		1895	2537	Austin	Emile W.	m
Apr.	26	1958	25494	Austin	Evelyn Ruth	m
		1927	9529	Austin	Herbert Warren	d
		1884	1396	Austin	Howard J.	d
		1894	2381	Austin	James	d
		1884	1397	Austin	James Howard	m
June	30	1946	17176	Austin	Jewell S.	d
		1894	2419	Austin	John	d
Nov.	1	1943	15657	Austin	Julia C.	d
Oct.	6	1953	22099	Austin	Mary E.	d
Sept.	31	1953	21987	Austin	Mervin N., etc.	d
June	17	1945	16422	Austin	Sewell S.	d
June	12	1951	20394	Austin	William E., etc.	d
Oct.	31	1927	9716	Autrim	Sarah Ella	d
		1920	7383	Avellar	Adolph	m

Month	Day	Year	File No.	Surname	Given Name	Type
		1920	7358	Avellar	Alfred	m
		1920	7358	Avellar	Alice	m
		1920	7358	Avellar	Arthur	m
		1920	7358	Avellar	Carrie	m
		1920	7360	Avellar	Francesca	d
		1920	7358	Avellar	George	m
		1920	7359	Avellar	Joe	d
		1920	7358	Avellar	Joseph	m
Aug.	25	1927	9709	Avery	James M.	d
June		1912	5270	Avery	James W.	d
Sept.	25	1927	9710	Avery	Matthew T.	d
Feb.	30	1958	26180	Avery	Ruby Kizziah	d
Jan.	27	1951	20636	Avila	Antonio	d
Dec.	9	1955	23641	Avila	Antonio, etc.	d
May	8	1935	12264	Avila	C.	d
Mar.	6	1947	17683	Avila	Isabel, etc.	d
Jan.	9	1930	10673	Avila	John J.	d
May		1955	23064	Avila	John M.	d
Mar.	27	1947	17606	Avila	Joseph	d
Feb.	21	1953	21596	Avila	Mary	d
Apr.	16	1931	10839	Avila	Vernon J.	m
		[1904-1906]	4015	Avilla	Anton	m
		[1904-1906]	4015	Avilla	Frank	m
Oct.	18	1950	19881	Avilla	John Silveira	inc
Sept.	30	1951	20573	Avilla	John Silveira	d
Nov.	26	1956	24297	Avoorys	Dennis	d
Oct.	24	1956	24181	Avsoorys	Spiros, etc.	d
June	22	1956	24001	Ayer	Charlotte C., etc.	d
Aug.	21	1958	25799	Ayer	Hazel H.	d
		1903	3650	Ayer	Isaac	d
Aug.	6	1951	20469	Ayers	Anna E.	d
Jan.	13	1923	8248	Ayers	Clarence Leonard	d
July	8	1912	5357	Ayers	David	d
July	27	1944	16056	Ayers	G. L., etc	d
Feb.	3	1935	12480	Ayers	George W.	d
Aug.	30	1912	5371	Ayers	Helen Ruth	m
July	24	1939	13621	Ayers	John C.	d
Mar.	2	1915	5951	Ayers	John Henry	d
Apr.	19	1927	9570	Ayers	Marua	m
Jan.	18	1944	16332	Ayers	Myron P.	d
Aug.	30	1912	5371	Ayers	Samuel Talmadge	m
		[1899-1900]	3072	Ayers	William	d

Month	Day	Year	File No.	Surname	Given Name	Type
July	18	1912	5287	Aylsworth	Sarah L.	d
		1877	910	Aynsley	John	d
May	15	1952	21060	Azevedo	Evelyn E.	m
May	27	1951	20369	Azevedo	Joe S., etc.	d
Jan.	5	1950	20079	Azevedo	John	d
Nov.	7	1945	16713	Azevedo	John Machado, etc.	d
May	24	1936	12622	Azevedo	Joseph L.	d
Mar.	27	1950	19480	Azevedo	Mariana T.	d
Feb.	26	1953	21608	Azevedo	Mary O.	d
Jan.	6	1947	18123	Azevedo	Pedro J., etc.	d
Feb.	14	1939	13865	Azevedo	Peter J., etc.	ins
Jan.	13	1948	18123	Azevedo	Rose, etc.	d
May	6	1952	21102	Azzarelli	Celestine M.	d
Sept.	23	1957	24977	Azzari	Genevieve F., etc.	d
Nov.	29	1948	18757	Azzari	James	d
May	12	1957	24662	Azzari	Joseph	d
Feb.	4	1949	18847	Azzasi	James	d

Month	Day	Year	File No.	Surname	Given Name	Type
		[1918-1919]	6845	Baagoe	Andrew	d
Nov.	1	1945	16799	Baalke	Edith Y.	d
Oct.	16	1937	13096	Babbini	Armando	d
Jan.	8	1951	20137	Babbini	Beverley	m
Aug.	18	1954	22703	Babbini	Emelio, etc.	d
Nov.	14	1939	13840	Babbini	Ernesto, etc.	d
Oct.	29	1921	7856	Babbino	Elaine	m
Feb.	7	1915	5932	Babbino	Michael	d
		[1919-1920]	7330	Babbino	Thomas	d
Mar.	28	1945	16444	Babcock	Alfred C.	d
July	26	1943	15494	Babcock	Fred D., etc.	d
Mar.	13	1934	11890	Babcock	Joseph L.	d
Mar.	8	1941	14427	Babcock	Libbie M.	d
		[1919-1920]	7452	Babcock	Lillie	d
Feb.	20	1950	19466	Babcock	Mamie C.	d
May	18	1948	18392	Babcock	Tell W.	d
		1906	4143	Baccala	Della	m
		1906	4143	Baccala	Henry	m
Mar.	9	1956	23846	Baccala	Josephine	d
		1906	4141	Baccala	Peter	d
		1906	4141	Baccala	Peter, Jr.	m
June	7	1946	17238	Baccala	Peter	d
		1922	8171	Bacchini	Romeo	inc
Oct.	14	1946	17439	Bacci	Alcide, etc.	d
		1908	4427	Bacci	Antonietti	d
Mar.	23	1943	15318	Bacci	Correna	jt
May	27	1933	11597	Bacci	Ettore	m
Apr.	6	1956	23907	Bacci	Eva	d
Dec.	13	1945	16879	Bacci	Joseph	d
Mar.	27	1948	18258	Bacci	Natale	inc
Sept.	27	1948	18601	Bacci	Natale	d
Aug.	29	1957	24916	Bacci	Roberto	d
Oct.	3	1921	7859	Bacci	Vincenzo	d
Mar.	1	1946	17037	Baccola	Peter	d
Oct.	26	1933	11724	Bach	Eva Rosa	d
		1874	674	Bach	Frederick	d
		1870	440	Bacharino	Juan	d
Jan.	6	1930	10513	Bache	Elizabeth	m
Jan.	6	1930	10513	Bache	Elsie	m
Jan.	6	1930	10513	Bache	Jean	m
Jan.	6	1930	10513	Bache	Robert	m
Jan.	6	1930	10513	Bache	Ruth	m

Month	Day	Year	File No.	Surname	Given Name	Type
		1896	2617	Bachelder	Joseph E.	d
		1896	2620	Bachelder	Joseph E.	d
		1898	2972	Bachelder	Marie Louise	d
Jan.	10	1958	25284	Bachman	Arthur M.	d
		1908	4435	Bachman	Herman	d
		1894	2397	Bachman	John	d
		[1908-1911]	4544	Bachman	Julia	m
		1908	4436	Bachman	Mary	d
Apr.	21	1958	25566	Bacigalupi	Carmela	d
		1900	3161	Bacigalupi	G.	d
Mar.	7	1949	18938	Bacigalupi	Virginia	d
Dec.	23	1951	20759	Bacigalupi	Maria	d
July	9	1951	20473	Backelmann	Fernando G. C.	d
May	12	1958	25618	Backus	Clarence James, etc.	d
Mar.	18	1952	20927	Bacon	Alice, etc.	inc
Oct.	14	1935	12439	Bacon	Edwin H.	d
July	5	1940	14092	Bacon	Edwin S.	ins
Aug.	23	1955	23455	Bacon	Frances	d
Nov.	17	1934	12080	Bacon	William	d
Feb.	27	1941	14415	Badano	Antonio C., etc.	d
Mar.	12	1952	20976	Badeau	Charles	d
Aug.		1928	9995	Baden	Henry	d
Mar.	28	1950	19593	Badger	Alice M.	d
Feb.	13	1924	8570	Badger	Douglas	g
Aug.	8	1927	9643	Badger	Douglas	inc
Nov.	7	1927	9764	Badger	Douglas	d
Jan.	21	1937	13176	Badger	Ephrain	d
		1886	1575	Badger	Francis Ann	d
May	11	1955	23228	Badger	Frank Hamilton, etc.	d
Oct.	23	1932	11393	Badger	John F.	d
Sept.	3	1932	11381	Badger	Laura Ellen	d
Nov.	19	1951	20686	Badger	Marlene E.	m
Feb.	19	1946	17012	Baebe	Thomas E.	d
Jan.	10	1915	6155	Baer	Elizabeth T.	m
Nov.	27	1942	15122	Baer	Helen I.	d
Jan.	10	1915	6155	Baer	Herman L.	m
Sept.	3	1954	22733	Baeuerlein	Augusto L., etc.	d
May	26	1917	6475	Bagley	Herbert Lincoln	d
June	10	1955	23312	Bagley	Lorabelle King	d
		[1918-1919]	6924	Bagley	Robert Wayland	d
Oct.	5	1953	22094	Bagley	Weaver T., etc.	d
Feb.	3	1958	25349	Bagley	William Charles, etc.	d

Month	Day	Year	File No.	Surname	Given Name	Type
Dec.	19	1930	10738	Bahnsen	Emilie J.	d
Oct.	19	1956	24284	Bahnsen	Henry Mae	d
		1883	1344	Bahr	Albert F.	m
Feb.		1917	6402	Bahrs	Herman	inc
Apr.		1917	6440	Bahrs	Herman	d
Apr.	9	1934	11919	Baier	Kate, etc.	ins
		1859	146	Bailee	George H.	d
June	11	1954	22583	Bailey	Alban L.	d
Aug.	3	1954	22675	Bailey	Alban L.	d
		[1922-1923]	8233	Bailey	Charles E.	d
Oct.	24	1948	18693	Bailey	Eugene R.	d
Mar.	1	1933	11525	Bailey	George C.	d
Nov.	9	1939	13802	Bailey	Gertrude V.	d
		1900	3118	Bailey	John H.	d
Jan.	24	1945	16900	Bailey	Kitty, etc.	d
		[1908-1911]	4596	Bailey	Mary A.	d
Sept.	22	1942	15058	Bailey	Mary K.	d
		1907	4302	Bailey	Michael C.	d
		1905	3975	Bailey	Rachael Elizabeth	d
		1898	3015	Bailey	Samuel N.	d
		1898	3068	Bailey	Sarah A.	d
June	17	1946	17215	Bailey	Stephen	d
Mar.	23	1929	10219	Bailhache	Dora	inc
Mar.	21	1955	23125	Bailhache	Vina	d
Oct.	5	1940	14170	Bailhache	Winona	d
		1900	3255	Bailiff	John	d
Sept.	13	1913	5620	Bailly	Albert Jules	d
Nov.	16	1956	24332	Bain	Agnes Maria, etc.	inc
		[1908-1911]	4725	Bain	Ann	d
Mar.	10	1953	21687	Bain	Charles	d
Oct.	16	1952	21405	Bain	Arthur Lee	d
Jan.	18	1954	22290	Bainbridge	C. E., etc.	d
Mar.	7	1931	10864	Bainchi	Francisco, etc.	d
July	25	1914	5755	Baines	Doris Ann	m
May	12	1950	19695	Baines	Henry Alfred, etc.	d
Feb.	19	1948	18244	Baines	James	d
Oct.	27	1956	24237	Baines	Jane West	d
Nov.	29	1948	18706	Baines	Margaret	d
Oct.	16	1952	21404	Baines	Minnie A.	d
Dec.		1917	6628	Baines	Sarah	d
Aug.	13	1934	12020	Baines	Thomas H., etc.	d
July		1919	7130	Baiocchi	Angelo	d

Month	Day	Year	File No.	Surname	Given Name	Type
Nov.	5	1934	12092	Baiocchi	Rosa	d
Dec.	6	1935	12481	Baiosahi	Frank	m
Dec.	4	1942	15180	Baird	Emma	d
Jan.	20	1958	25299	Baird	William H.	con
		[1908-1911]	4851	Baitinger	John Adam	d
Apr.	25	1955	23139	Bak	Gabriel, etc.	d
		1922	8030	Baker	A. M.	d
Aug.	21	1946	17362	Baker	Albert F.	d
Aug.	13	1928	10034	Baker	Alfred	d
Jan.	28	1954	22947	Baker	Catherine A.	d
June	3	1912	5332	Baker	Christian J.	d
		1902	3558	Baker	Clara	d
Mar.	18	1944	15845	Baker	Clara E.	d
Nov.	27	1929	10419	Baker	Clare I.	d
June	2	1916	6253	Baker	Elvira J.	d
May	14	1948	18391	Baker	Florence E.	d
July	26	1949	19185	Baker	George M., etc.	d
		1906	4095	Baker	George W.	d
Jan.	10	1958	25278	Baker	Harold P., etc.	d
June	12	1945	16569	Baker	Henry	d
July	24	1913	5564	Baker	Henry E.	d
		1862	205	Baker	Isaac	d
Jan.	19	1946	16945	Baker	Jack Daniel	d
Jan.	19	1946	16948	Baker	Jack Daniel	d
Feb.	29	1913	5481	Baker	James M.	d
Jan.	28	1946	16967	Baker	Joseph A.	d
Dec.	30	1949	19395	Baker	Josephine	d
May	14	1931	10966	Baker	Julia R.	d
May	27	1954	22499	Baker	Lillie M.	d
Aug.	16	1917	6532	Baker	Lorin G.	m
		1893	2298	Baker	Mary B.	d
Nov.	2	1935	12451	Baker	Mary E. & Sheridan, Jr.	m
July	13	1934	11997	Baker	Meliasa D.	d
July	2	1951	20463	Baker	Minnie Y.	d
May	16	1940	13997	Baker	Robert	d
		1891	2049	Baker	Roxie Dell	m
June	28	1941	14534	Baker	Sophia	d
Jan.	7	1955	22963	Baker	Theron H., etc.	d
Jan.	16	1951	20158	Baker	William Ernest	d
Feb.	1	1929	10196	Baker	William H.	d
Jan.	9	1953	21563	Baker	William W.	d
Sept.	12	1951	20598	Bakori	Steve	d

Month	Day	Year	File No.	Surname	Given Name	Type
July	26	1948	18534	Balan	Louis Ellena	d
		1906	4069	Balbi	Giacomo	d
June	16	1933	11616	Balbi	Joseph	d
Mar.	27	1946	17031	Bald	Lawrence A., etc.	d
Mar.	18	1954	22398	Baldam/Baldan	William	d
Feb.	21	1958	25404	Balderi	Vittorio	d
June	1	1935	12245	Balderston	Jeanne	d
Apr.	30	1955	23146	Baldi	Bartolomeo	d
Apr.	2	1957	24639	Baldi	Cesare	d
Aug.	6	1942	15036	Baldi	Isabella	d
Apr.	29	1937	12949	Baldo	Benjamin	d
Aug.	17	1941	14552	Baldocchi	Eugene	m
July	28	1932	11325	Baldocchi	Henry	d
July	7	1938	13368	Baldocchi	Peter, etc.	d
June	5	1941	14540	Baldocchi	Romeo P.	d
Dec.	16	1947	18138	Baldwin	Albert Francis, etc.	d
Apr.	19	1940	13967	Baldwin	Clara S.	d
		1905	3894	Baldwin	Hiram F.	d
Feb.	1	1952	20894	Baldwin	Myrtle, etc.	d
Feb.	4	1949	18883	Baldwin	O. T.	d
Oct.	27	1929	10418	Baldwin	Oliver C.	d
Feb.	1	1935	12176	Bale	Ernest	ins
Nov.	7	1952	21438	Bales	Marion A.	d
Apr.	17	1956	23933	Baley	Della, etc.	inc
Sept.	17	1934	12023	Balgart	Grace N.	d
July	20	1939	13705	Balish	Charles	d
Oct.	20	1941	14681	Ball	Frederick W., etc.	d
		[1919-1920]	7396	Ball	Mary Elizabeth, etc.	d
Feb.	1	1952	20893	Ball	Noah	d
May	25	1957	24690	Ballani	Attilio, etc.	d
July		1925	8972	Ballard	Bernice ?	m
Jan.	30	1933	11806	Ballard	Floyd D., etc.	d
Oct.	8	1934	12045	Ballard	Howard B., etc.	d
June	7	1955	23302	Ballard	Irene B.	d
June	7	1955	23303	Ballard	Irene B.	d
June	7	1955	23304	Ballard	Irene B.	d
June	7	1955	23305	Ballard	Irene B.	d
Nov.	18	1955	23538	Ballard	Irene B.	d
		[1908-1911]	5172	Ballard	J. H., Sr.	d
		[1908-1911]	5107	Ballard	Rachel	d
Nov.	22	1944	16285	Ballard	Byron	d
Nov.	22	1944	16285	Ballard	Eva H.	d

Month	Day	Year	File No.	Surname	Given Name	Type
Mar.	27	1934	11881	Ballard	Margaret	d
Apr.	1	1947	17723	Ballard	Sheridan E., etc.	d
Sept.	5	1952	21321	Ballatore	Esther	d
July	22	1948	18506	Ballauri	Felice, etc.	d
Sept.	15	1933	11716	Ballinger	Herbert Reed	m
Nov.		1922	8174	Ballou	Arthur M.	d
July	20	1904	3821	Ballou	Eunice	inc
Oct.	27	1958	26037	Ballou	Ralph, etc.	d
		1903	3723	Ballou	Rosa A.	d
		1877	902	Ballou	V. J.	d
July	7	1940	14066	Ballou	Volney T.	d
Oct.	11	1952	21328	Balocci	Antone	d
July	9	1934	11993	Balooca	Angelina	inc
Apr.	25	1958	25492	Baltzer	Clarinda T., etc.	d
Dec.	16	1934	12100	Balzari	James A.	inc
Nov.	9	1939	13799	Balzari	James A.	d
Oct.	1	1938	13448	Balzari	Rosa	d
		1907	4396	Bamberger	Catherine, etc.	d
Feb.	7	1952	20908	Bamhoff	Florence	d
July	2	1949	19111	Banchero	Charles S.	d
May	12	1950	19694	Bandiera	Liduena	d
July	17	1919	7113	Bandini	Mary B. E.	d
Oct.	13	1923	8476	Bandini	Titus M.	d
		1898	2926	Bane	David C.	d
Oct.	19	1951	20678	Banelli	Aladino	d
July	14	1929	10338	Banes	Frederica, etc.	d
Oct.	6	1944	16201	Bangor	Hans A.	d
July	23	1936	12686	Bank	Alva R.	d
Mar.	2	1956	23824	Banks	Ansel W., etc.	d
Nov.	5	1958	26060	Banks	Harriet A.	d
Oct.	22	1939	13764	Banks	Ida E.	d
		1900	3223	Banks	L. I.	d
Jan.	17	1944	16363	Banks	Ruth E.	d
Jan.	26	1930	10822	Bankson	John E., etc.	d
Mar.	21	1958	25406	Bankson	Margaret, etc.	d
Mar.	21	1958	25478	Bankson	Margaret, etc.	d
Feb.	8	1957	24524	Bankston	Hugh	d
Mar.	12	1929	10239	Bannean	Thomas S.	d
July	16	1956	24098	Bannerman	Laura	d
Sept.	30	1946	17375	Banness	Richard O.	d
		1892	2146	Bannon	John	d
Dec.	30	1955	23618	Banse	Albert	d

Month	Day	Year	File No.	Surname	Given Name	Type
Feb.	7	1946	16993	Bante	Eduardo	d
June	3	1935	12322	Banton	John	d
Nov.	26	1956	24298	Banzet	Josephine	d
		1922	8193	Baptista	Anna	inc
		1923	8447	Baptista	Anna, etc.	d
		1902	3469	Baptista	Lena	m
		1902	3469	Baptista	Mary	m
Feb.	27	1912	5479	Baptista	Mary	d
		1902	3469	Baptista	Rosie	m
July	7	1939	13716	Baracchi	Mary	d
		[1908-1911]	5075	Baralli	Joseph	d
		1894	2461	Barbarin	Augustina	m
		1898	2941	Barbarin	Augustinio	d
		1898	2894	Barbarin	Jean Baptiste	d
Mar.	7	1947	17687	Barbee	Kathryn	d
		1908	4477	Barber	Andrew Jackson	d
		1907	4280	Barber	Arthur John	d
Sept.	12	1941	14635	Barber	Elizabeth	d
Apr.	29	1950	19596	Barber	John H.	d
Jan.	21	1954	22933	Barber	Lewis Edward	m
May	10	1943	15421	Barber	Lewis Ransome	d
July	27	1950	19778	Barber	Louise E.	d
Jan.	23	1947	17593	Barber	Orles, etc.	d
Dec.	23	1927	9786	Barber	Sarah E.	d
June	12	1956	24040	Barber	W. E., Jr.	d
June	11	1917	6483	Barbera	Matilda	d
Aug.	20	1946	17304	Barbera	Pauline	d
Dec.	2	1952	21492	Barbettini	Maurice A., etc.	d
		[1918-1919]	7050	Barbieri	Italo	d
Dec.	2	1925	9103	Barbo	Rosie	d
		1892	2165	Barborin	Gratien	inc
		1893	2296	Barborin	Gratien	d
Oct.	18	1949	19324	Barbour	Gertrude D.	d
Mar.	7	1930	10549	Barcaglia	D. G., etc.	d
Aug.	7	1951	20528	Barcaglia	Marie, etc.	d
Feb.	3	1948	18202	Barcaglia	Peter	d
May	6	1941	14508	Bardellini	Lorenzo, etc.	d
Aug.	4	1953	21993	Bardini	Joseph J.	d
Apr.	1	1958	25511	Bardsley	Mayme S.	d
Feb.	13	1958	25377	Bardsley	Mayme Sophie, etc.	con
May	17	1955	23241	Bardsley	William W.	d
June	3	1955	23294	Bardsley	William W., etc.	d

Month	Day	Year	File No.	Surname	Given Name	Type
Mar.	20	1934	11876	Bardy	Estelle J.	d
Oct.	23	1927	9727	Bare	Frank P.	d
Feb.	8	1940	13927	Barelli	Matteo, etc.	d
		1906	4123	Barenchi	Charles	d
Mar.	31	1941	14369	Barenchi	Emilia	d
Mar.	27	1945	16495	Barenchi	Fred T.	d
Dec.		1913	5649	Bargagliotti	Vitorio, etc.	d
Aug.	17	1946	17354	Bargiani	Bessie	d
Nov.	16	1933	11742	Barham	Charles A., etc.	inc
		1928	10103	Barham	John A., etc.	d
		1883	1341	Barich	Herman	d
Jan.	30	1942	15204	Barich	John	d
		1924	8766	Baridon	Joseph	d
Nov.	20	1946	17489	Barilla	Mary	d
July	26	1957	24833	Barindelli	Abbie	d
May	21	1931	10949	Barindelli	Giuseppe	d
Jan.	5	1953	21555	Barior	Louise	d
Feb.		1921	7663	Barker	C. B.	d
Mar.	26	1927	9550	Barker/Baker	William R./W. R.	d
Dec.	5	1950	20089	Barkway	Mary Frances	d
Feb.	14	1953	21579	Barletta	Matteo	d
Jan.	4	1928	9824	Barley	Andrew J.	d
		1895	2597	Barlow	Anna D.	d
Apr.	7	1938	13239	Barlow	Charles A.	d
Sept.	21	1936	12711	Barlow	Charlotte	m
		1895	2565	Barlow	S. I.	d
		1904	3845	Barlow	Thomas E.	d
		[1919-1920]	7379	Barlow	Thomas E.	d
July	24	1944	16052	Barmin	Lucretia E.	d
Mar.	25	1935	12206	Barnard	Carl	d
July	21	1913	5578	Barndt	Julius	d
July	23	1913	5579	Barndt	Julius Marion	m
Dec.	24	1958	26100	Barndt	Juluis M.	d
July	23	1913	5579	Barndt	Leo Raymond	m
Jan.	17	1931	11167	Barndt	Ruby Laura	d
June	10	1958	25688	Barndt	Ruby Laura	con
July	23	1913	5579	Barndt	Winslow Frederick	m
		[1908-1911]	4906	Barnedt	Grace R.	d
		1897	2734	Barnes	Aaron	d
		1888	1789	Barnes	Aaron, Jr.	d
		1908	4520	Barnes	Alisson	d
Jan.	7	1947	17553	Barnes	Annabella P.	d

Month	Day	Year	File No.	Surname	Given Name	Type
		1903	3668	Barnes	Arthur	m
Oct.		1921	7861	Barnes	Arthur	d
Dec.	14	1933	11761	Barnes	Ben H.	d
		1898	3096	Barnes	Benny F.	d
Mar.	3	1941	14421	Barnes	Beverly Nell	d
Dec.	30	1956	24354	Barnes	Cap, etc.	d
Aug.	24	1955	23345	Barnes	Clifford S., etc.	d
Apr.	18	1956	23935	Barnes	Connie B., etc.	d
Apr.	13	1916	6212	Barnes	Cynthia	d
Apr.	1	1958	25514	Barnes	Debra	m
		1898	2901	Barnes	Dora Harlan	d
		1898	2933	Barnes	Edwin R.	d
Apr.	9	1941	14470	Barnes	Elizabeth L.	d
Oct.	13	1953	22111	Barnes	Elizabeth Tracey	d
Feb.	7	1944	15822	Barnes	Elsie J.	m
Sept.	6	1930	10722	Barnes	Emmarene	d
Apr.	3	1956	23903	Barnes	Ethel	d
		1898	2901	Barnes	Etta Ella	d
		[1918-1919]	6960	Barnes	Eunice Daisy	d
May	24	1953	21806	Barnes	Floyd W., etc.	d
May	3	1948	18370	Barnes	Guy L.	d
July	22	1937	13047	Barnes	Henry	inc
Mar.	1	1948	18262	Barnes	Henry	d
Mar.	1	1948	18263	Barnes	Henry	d
		1903	3682	Barnes	Ivan Aaron	m
Dec.	30	1956	24354	Barnes	Ivan Morris, etc.	d
Feb.	21	1925	9148	Barnes	J. A.	d
	17	1921	7705	Barnes	James A.	d
		1887	1625	Barnes	Jannett	m
		1897	2761	Barnes	Jehu	d
Nov.	1	1946	17464	Barnes	Jennie	d
		1877	867	Barnes	John J.	d
Sept.	8	1948	18616	Barnes	Joseph, etc.	d
		1902	3578	Barnes	Lawrence J.	d
Apr.	1	1958	25514	Barnes	Lee	m
Jan.	8	1948	18161	Barnes	Lillie Dale, etc.	d
Dec.	15	1937	13166	Barnes	Louis G.	d
Apr.	1	1958	25514	Barnes	Randolph	m
		1887	1662	Barnes	Ruth	d
		1902	3540	Barnes	Samuel L.	d
		1898	3062	Barnes	Samuel L. (absentee)	d
Aug.	18	1947	17895	Barnes	Talton T.	d

Month	Day	Year	File No.	Surname	Given Name	Type
Feb.	29	1948	18190	Barnes	W. G.	d
May	21	1931	10962	Barnes	William	d
Mar.	20	1930	10580	Barnes	William G.	inc
Jan.	7	1944	15750	Barnes	William O., etc.	d
		1928	10116	Barnes	William P.	d
		1923	8377	Barnes		d
July	10	1958	25767	Barnet	John Peter	m
Dec.	4	1933	11783	Barnett	Agnes	d
Nov.	22	1927	9784	Barnett	Albert	d
July	15	1931	11002	Barnett	Charles D.	d
Aug.	5	1952	21287	Barnett	Ellsworth Lansing, etc.	d
Sept.	15	1931	11054	Barnett	Emma F.	d
June		1947	17865	Barnett	Evageline C., etc.	d
Dec.	19	1958	26166	Barnett	Florence L.	d
May	21	1915	6003	Barnett	George W.	d
		1908	4403	Barnett	J. D.	d
Aug.	2	1946	17326	Barnett	James	d
Jan.	6	1956	23700	Barnett	Janie	inc
Feb.	31	1958	25342	Barnett	John	d
Dec.	4	1942	15178	Barnett	John Whitely	d
Apr.	24	1958	25575	Barnett	Lester H.	d
Jan.		1917	6391	Barnett	Marion L .R.	d
Sept.	23	1929	10386	Barnett	Mary M.	d
		1902	3570	Barnett	Wilson	d
Oct.	17	1931	11082	Barney	Alyce	m
Apr.	26	1931	10925	Barney	Charles Elmer	d
Dec.	15	1954	22865	Barney	Edna Locke	d
Oct.	5	1931	11095	Barney	Ellen	d
Feb.	1	1954	22317	Barnhart	Caroline E.	d
May	18	1950	19639	Barnhart	George H. W.	d
Dec.	12	1947	18090	Barnhart	William T.	d
June	17	1947	17801	Barnstorf	Frank	d
Sept.	18	1951	20611	Barnum	Arlie D.	d
July	26	1922	8082	Barnum	Elizabeth	d
Sept.	26	1952	21307	Barnum	Gladys A.	d
Apr.	9	1928	9928	Baron	Arvilla	d
July	15	1934	11975	Barr	Ernest	d
Nov.	4	1947	18081	Barr	Ethel H., etc.	d
Jan.	12	1927	9494	Barr	Frank	d
Jan.	20	1947	17582	Barr	Frank Enoch, etc.	d
Apr.	10	1943	15376	Barr	John	d
Mar.	27	1954	22363	Barr	Stanley J.	d

Month	Day	Year	File No.	Surname	Given Name	Type
Oct.	18	1944	16174	Barr	F. M.	d
Jan.	11	1955	22969	Barrachi	Andrea	d
Apr.	1	1953	21739	Barre	O. J.	d
Aug.	14	1919	7164	Barrett	Charles	d
July	26	1953	21910	Barrett	Eilden C.	d
		1926	9343	Barrett	Manuel, etc.	d
June	7	1912	5281	Barrett	Mary Etta	d
		[1908-1911]	4797	Barrett	Mary Etta	inc
Jan.	4	1944	15746	Barrett	N. Edward	inc
Sept.		1926	9367	Barrett	Namie L.	d
Jan.	14	1955	22982	Barrett	Nora L.	d
Apr.	11	1952	21051	Barrett	Jessie M.	d
Oct.	10	1944	16204	Barrett	Rae M., etc.	d
		1926	9379	Barretto	Joe	m
May	22	1948	18357	Barretto	John, etc.	d
		1926	9379	Barretto	Manuel	m
Sept.		1926	9379	Barretto	Mary	m
Sept.		1926	9379	Barretto	Peter	m
Mar.	26	1932	11238	Barri/Berri	Beniamino/Benjamin, et	d
July	13	1934	11999	Barrieros	John T., etc.	d
Feb.	20	1951	20225	Barringer	Thomas	d
May	12	1935	12357	Barron	Alice	d
Sept.	23	1957	25033	Barron	Alice E., etc.	d
Dec.	19	1951	20749	Barros	Manuel	d
Feb.	10	1944	16411	Barrow	Jennie E.	d
Apr.	22	1957	24685	Barrows	Gordon L., etc.	d
		1873	641	Barry	Ellen Agnes	m
Feb.	9	1945	16409	Barry	Gertrude	d
		1873	641	Barry	Julia	m
Sept.		1907	4324	Barry	Julia A.	inc
		[1908-1911]	5086	Barry	Julie/Julio/Julia	d
Nov.	25	1956	24295	Barry	Mary A.	inc
July	16	1957	24883	Barry	Mary A.	d
		1873	641	Barry	Mary E.	m
		1872	521	Barry	Richard	d
Apr.	29	1950	19598	Barry	S. B.	d
Feb.	2	1954	22320	Barry	Simon John	d
		1873	641	Barry	Susan A.	m
		1873	641	Barry	Thomas	m
Jan.	21	1934	12136	Barry	Thomas	inc
Apr.	7	1939	13598	Barry	Thomas	d
		1906	4079	Barry	W. J.	d

Month	Day	Year	File No.	Surname	Given Name	Type
		1873	641	Barry	William	m
Apr.	12	1949	19015	Barsante	Michele	d
May	9	1957	24723	Barsanti	Lottie U.	d
Oct.		1923	8465	Barsi	Abram	d
May	24	1934	11934	Barsi	Alibrando	d
June	29	1942	14963	Barsi	Alibrando	d
June	3	1955	23288	Barsi	Caterina, etc.	d
Sept.	25	1958	25952	Barsi	Clara	d
Oct.	28	1947	18067	Barsi	Egist	d
Oct.	28	1947	18069	Barsi	Egisto	d
Jan.	30	1931	11180	Barsi	Fortunato	d
		1924	8604	Barsi	Fred	d
July	30	1913	5582	Barsi	Lorenzo	d
Aug.	30	1913	5582?	Barsi	Lorenzo	d
Mar.	11	1932	11225	Barsi	Martina	d
Mar.	18	1946	17650	Barsi	Nichol	d
Feb.	31	1925	8868	Barsi	Pasquale	d
		1924	8622	Barsi	Santi	d
		1903	3647	Barsotti	Antonio	d
June	17	1937	12999	Barsuglia	Antoniette	d
Apr.	18	1926	9206	Barsulia	Susie	d
Apr.	7	1950	19618	Bartell	Louis	d
		1919	7135	Bartels	Harry	d
Dec.	5	1947	18118	Bartelt	Catharina	d
		[1919-1920]	7422	Barth	Adolph	d
Feb.	8	1932	11186	Barth	Babette	d
June	1	1951	20371	Bartle	Henry M., etc.	d
July	21	1945	16611	Bartleson	William H.	d
Feb.	31	1946	16978	Bartlett	Allen William	m
		1879	1021	Bartlett	Caleb	d
Oct.	26	1947	18024	Bartlett	Effa Constance, etc.	d
		1896	2626	Bartlett	Ella	m
		1896	2626	Bartlett	George R.	m
Sept.	19	1929	10384	Bartlett	George W.	d
		1905	3914	Bartlett	Harris	d
Sept.	8	1941	14631	Bartlett	Iva	d
Feb.	31	1946	16978	Bartlett	Jacqueline Lee	m
		1880	1095	Bartlett	John	m
Sept.	19	1954	22705	Bartlett	Joyce	m
		1880	1114	Bartlett	Lydia A.	d
		1896	2626	Bartlett	Theresa	m
June	25	1954	22547	Bartlow	James M.	d

Month	Day	Year	File No.	Surname	Given Name	Type
July	30	1944	16061	Bartoli	Enrico	d
May	20	1954	22541	Bartolomei	Victor, etc.	d
		1898	3014	Barton	Archa	m
		1885	1459	Barton	Charles Henry	d
May	7	1942	14889	Barton	Elizabeth Ann, etc.	d
Dec.	10	1951	20791	Barton	Lottie V., etc.	d
Aug.	15	1929	10358	Barton	Thomas F.	d
July-Nov.		1914	5818	Bartsch	Charles	d
Jan.	18	1952	20861	Basagia	Peter, etc.	d
Dec.	17	1943	15724	Basaglia	Egata	d
Apr.	25	1949	19035	Bascom	Harvey W.	d
Jan.	22	1958	25313	Basford	Louise	inc
Apr.	18	1957	24676	Bashkov	Nick	d
Dec.	10	1946	17523	Basilan	Angelina	inc
Feb.	9	1944	16382	Basloni	Pasquale, etc.	d
Aug.	31	1951	20514	Bassett	Blanche I., etc.	d
Sept.	13	1943	15560	Bassett	Fred L.	d
July	21	1937	13044	Bassett	Marie	inc
July	9	1940	14097	Bassett	Marie	d
		[1908-1911]	4747	Bassett	Ralph T.	m
Oct.	15	1942	15081	Bassett	Ruth M.	d
Oct.	15	1927	9722	Bassett	William David, etc.	d
Feb.	4	1955	23024	Bassett	William Hudson, etc.	d
July	4	1955	23024	Bassett	William Theodore, etc.	d
Jan.	14	1951	20802	Bassetti	Carolina, etc.	d
Oct.	9	1951	20656	Bassetti	Caroline	inc
Apr.	19	1931	10917	Bassi	Angelina Pinoli	d
Apr.		1908	4452	Bassi	Antonio	d
Feb.	15	1957	24539	Bassi	Della	d
Aug.	9	1954	22630	Bassi	Giovanni G., etc.	d
Jan.	15	1954	22283	Bassi	Mary Ann	d
Dec.	5	1950	20090	Bassi	Paul	d
June	5	1957	24770	Bassi	Rocco, etc.	d
Apr.	27	1939	13623	Bassignani	Antonio, etc.	d
Apr.	12	1957	24660	Bassignani	Michele Sabotino, etc.	d
May		1921	7726	Bassignani	Sebastina	d
Nov.	7	1956	24317	Basso	Louis Fred, etc.	d
Dec.	14	1945	16874	Bastas	Marie	d
Aug.	26	1958	25883	Bastas	Mario E.	d
Aug.	30	1957	24919	Bastas	Victor	d
Sept.	8	1947	17987	Bastoni	Delio, etc.	d
Aug.	18	1947	17916	Bastoni	Frank, Sr.	d

Month	Day	Year	File No.	Surname	Given Name	Type
Mar.	26	1952	20946	Bastoni	Luigi	d
July	3	1956	24086	Bastow	Herbert	d
Aug.	4	1950	19853	Bataeff	Katherine, etc.	d
Feb.	31	1931	10855	Batchelder	Elmer E.	d
Jan.	18	1951	20810	Batchelder	Ernest A., etc.	d
		1863	231	Batchelder	Ezra D.	d
		1863	229	Batchelder	Ira (no papers)	d
Feb.	17	1950	19520	Batchellor	Stillman	d
Sept.	2	1915	6085	Batchelor	Elsie	m
Sept.	2	1915	6085	Batchelor	Irene	m
Sept.	2	1915	6085	Batchelor	Lawrence	m
Nov.		1926	9399	Bates	Amelia H.	d
Apr.	24	1943	15326	Bates	Andrew	d
		[1908-1911]	5099	Bates	E. F.	d
		1890	1949	Bates	G. W.	d
Mar.	7	1952	20967	Bates	George W..	d
Feb.	23	1945	16432	Bates	Hazel G.	d
Mar.		1933	11556	Bates	Henrietta	m
July	28	1932	11323	Bates	Henry F.	d
		1893	2289	Bates	Henry Frederick	d
Oct.		1907	4327	Bates	J. L.	d
July	19	1956	24110	Bates	Joseph Frank	m
		1877	911	Bates	Laura	m
		1871	483	Bates	Lydia J.	d
Dec.	14	1920	7611	Bates	Mary M.	d
		1877	911	Bates	Neely	m
Mar.	7	1933	11556	Bates	Pauline Cottle	m
		1879	993	Bates	Samuel	d
		1893	2303	Bates	Theodore J. K. P.	d
		1926	9267	Bates	Zoe R.	d
July	10	1939	13720	Bath	Fred	d
Mar.	20	1937	12897	Bath	Grace	d
		1926	9382	Bathmet	K. L.	d
		1926	9392	Bathurst	Arch	m
		1926	9392	Bathurst	Kent	m
Sept.	20	1913	5603	Batkin	Leonard Charles	m
Aug.	23	1928	10004	Batkin	Leonard Stanley, etc.	d
Apr.	22	1953	21793	Batsford	Sterling B.	d
		1924	8658	Batt	Alice E., etc	d
		1918	6844	Batt	George Ray	d
Jan.	11	1957	24450	Battaglia	Deanne, etc.	d
		1907	4249	Battaglia	Guiseppe	d

Month	Day	Year	File No.	Surname	Given Name	Type
Apr.	24	1921	7716	Battaglia	L. Olinto	d
		1907	4283	Battaglia	Vitoria	d
July	8	1919	7127	Battan	John W.	m
Dec.	9	1935	12486	Batten	Helen	d
Mar.	10	1950	19556	Batten	William Albert, etc.	d
Jan.	8	1946	16919	Battistesa	Carl	d
Apr.	22	1954	22477	Battistessa	Moss, etc.	d
Dec.	15	1920	7575	Batto	Evelyn & Francis	m
Feb.		1918	6656	Batton	Maggie	d
May	3	1926	9272	Batts	John	d
May	11	1938	13288	Batts	Rosa	d
Aug.	18	1958	25861	Bauder	Ira J.	d
Apr.	12	1949	19011	Bauder	Jean	d
May	19	1951	20345	Baudino	Michele	d
Apr.	28	1949	18985	Bauer	Fred	d
Nov.	21	1946	17490	Bauer	Helen Josephine	d
		1925	8942	Bauer	Henri J.	d
		1898	3090	Bauer	Lena	d
Nov.	24	1952	21418	Bauer	Russell, etc.	d
		1903	3744	Bauer	aka Ludwig)	d
Dec.	24	1941	14713	Bauer	Amanda Belle, etc.	d
Dec.	7	1940	14260	Bauermeister	Ernest, etc.	d
May	29	1941	14498	Baugh	Joseph	d
		1908	4467	Baugh	Ralph W.	m
Mar.	15	1957	24596	Baughman	Horace Ray, etc.	d
Feb.	18	1928	9840	Bauir	Ernest William, etc.	d
June	24	1939	13649	Baukson	May, etc.	d
		1890	2032	Baum	August	d
		1895	2586	Baum	John	d
Oct.	5	1931	11094	Baum	Thomas J., etc.	d
July	17	1913	5531	Bauman	Charles H.	d
Oct.	3	1952	21377	Bauman	Charles H.	d
June	27	1913	5516	Bauman	Jacob	d
		[1918-1919]	7065	Bauman	Peter, etc.	d
Aug.	20	1951	20555	Baumann	Edwin P.	d
Aug.	13	1946	17343	Baumann	Esther R., etc.	d
Aug.	13	1948	18580	Baumeister	William Henry, etc.	d
July	13	1951	20478	Baumgartner	John	d
Oct.	15	1958	26002	Baumgartner	Veneda	d
Jan.	14	1944	15770	Baur	Dora	d
Aug.	13	1923	8412	Bauumeister	Frank	d
Sept.	14	1953	22058	Bava	Bernerdo	d

Month	Day	Year	File No.	Surname	Given Name	Type
Feb.	12	1942	14764	Bavarsky	Paul	d
Dec.	23	1943	15691	Baxie	Myrtle, etc.	d
June	14	1916	6232	Baxman	Angie	m
Aug.	10	1915	6065	Baxman	Eliza Jane	d
June	14	1916	6232	Baxman	Gussie	m
Apr.	14	1916	6232	Baxman	Herbert	m
Oct.	23	1925	9062	Baxmann	Louis J., etc.	d
Jan.	21	1922	7933	Baxter	Charles P.	m
Mar.	9	1943	15268	Baxter	Joseph	d
		1902	3481	Baxter	Lillie C.	d
Jan.	21	1922	7933	Baxter	Marion C.	m
Dec.	14	1912	5418	Baxter	Shirley R.	m
Nov.	28	1940	14247	Bay	Henry	d
June	2	1950	19739	Bayer	Annie May, etc.	inc
Oct.	14	1952	21400	Bayer	Annie May, etc.	d
		[1908-1911]	4918	Bayer	Herman	d
Feb.	25	1954	22307	Bayer	Hermina, etc.	d
		1902	3428	Bayler	Caroline	d
		[1919-1920]	7471	Bayler	Cerescentea A.	d
		[1908-1911]	4674	Bayless	Charles	m
		[1908-1911]	4674	Bayless	Dayton Raymond	m
Oct.	11	1946	17434	Bayless	Fred B.	d
Dec.	7	1945	16864	Bayley	John Cox	d
		1880	1120	Baylis	Honora	d
		1873	615	Baylis	Thomas F.	d
		1873	608	Bayliss	T. H.	m
		1867	364	Bayliss	Thomas F.	d
		1908	4418	Baylor	John	d
		[1908-1911]	4601	Baylor	John Paul	m
Apr.	22	1915	5984	Bayly	Henry P. F.	d
Sept.	19	1957	24961	Bazeley	Mabel R.	d
		[1908-1911]	4896	Bazzano	Giovanni B.	d
Aug.	27	1938	13390	Beach	Dorothy	d
Aug.	16	1955	23440	Beach	Helen H., etc.	d
Oct.	6	1933	11738	Beach	Lillie M., etc.	d
		1892	2264	Beacom	Mary	d
		1900	3264	Beadle	Louis	d
Sept.	31	1954	22722	Beagles	Hettie	d
Aug.	26	1949	19190	Beagles	Robert Lee, etc.	d
Nov.	30	1951	20707	Beagles	Robert Lee, etc.	d
July	9	1918	6784	Beal	Elizabeth R.	d
		1894	2473	Beal	Kirk S.	m

Month	Day	Year	File No.	Surname	Given Name	Type
Feb.	25	1917	6408	Beal	Silas	d
May	2	1958	25593	Beal	William H.	d
Mar.	20	1950	19573	Beale	Elsie	d
Jan.	24	1927	9510	Beale	Lora Merrill	d
		1921	7777	Beall	Fredericka	d
		1890	2020	Beall	Mary F.	m
Feb.	16	1934	11871	Beals	A. C., etc.	d
Mar.	14	1939	13575	Beals	Tammy May Hosmer	d
		1885	1483	Beam	Jeremiah	d
		1885	1484	Beam	Mary	d
Feb.	1	1957	24504	Beame	Jacob	d
Sept.	8	1928	10054	Beamer	George	d
Sept.	11	1957	25012	Bean	Catherine Nelligan	d
Aug.	8	1958	25837	Bean	Ethel R.	d
Dec.	4	1930	10799	Bean	J. W.	d
		1884	1381	Bean	Joseph M.	m
Oct.	25	1957	25041	Bean	Katherine Nelligan	d
Jan.	6	1942	14761	Bean	Laura P., etc.	d
		1882	1255	Bean	Mary	d
		1884	1381	Bean	Mary Francis	m
Apr.	13	1916	6231	Bean	Maybell Iris	m
Apr.	13	1916	6231	Bean	Sharon Philander	m
Apr.	13	1916	6231	Bean	Ulysses S.	m
Aug.	29	1956	24186	Bear	Catherine, etc.	d
Aug.	25	1939	13737	Bear	Don E.	d
Nov.	16	1951	20742	Bear	Frank L.	d
May	13	1944	15982	Beard	Inez	d
June	3	1955	23287	Beard	John	d
		[1919-1920]	7372	Beardin	Blanche D.	d
Apr.	27	1947	17714	Beardon	Ethel	d
July	27	1949	19147	Bearse	James Miles, etc.	d
July	5	1947	17834	Bearse	Mary A.	d
Apr.	19	1941	14443	Beasley	John, etc.	d
Feb.	1	1957	24506	Beasley	Lauretta	inc
Dec.	28	1940	14248	Beasley	Lucy	d
June	5	1938	13311	Beasley	Spencer, etc.	d
Sept.	10	1930	10726	Beason	Edward	d
Jan.	9	1940	13883	Beattie	A.	d
Sept.	17	1958	25934	Beattie	Arthur W.	d
Feb.	6	1951	20200	Beattie	Effie R.	d
Aug.	1	1952	21280	Beattie	Margaret	d
Jan.	9	1940	13883	Beattie	Susan C.	d

Month	Day	Year	File No.	Surname	Given Name	Type
Aug.	5	1946	17283	Beattie	Susan C.	d
Jan.	22	1958	25310	Beatty	Laura	inc
May	7	1949	19066	Beaty	George Benjamin, etc.	d
Aug.	4	1915	6061	Beau	John	d
Dec.	3	1915	6119	Beau	Ulysses Socrates	d
	16	1923	8280	Beauchamp	Charlotte Elizabeth	d
Oct.	8	1950	19918	Beaudry	Minnie M.	d
		[1919-1920]	7484	Beaumont	William H.	d
		1854	26	Beaver	Henry	g
		1896	2689	Beaver	Henry	inc
		1897	2747	Beaver	Henry	d
		1905	4010	Beaver	Henry	d
		1900	3233	Beaver	Mary J.	d
Feb.	4	1929	10191	Beaver	Sarah Jane	d
Dec.	19	1957	25156	Becchetti	Fiorenzo	d
		1904	3837	Bech	Nelson A.	d
Sept.	5	1952	21322	Bechetti	Amelia	d
Oct.	10	1950	19967	Bechtel	Mollie T.	d
		1900	3107	Beck	Anna H.	d
Sept.	19	1957	25030	Beck	Asta	d
July	14	1915	6038	Beck	Chester	m
July	16	1933	11641	Beck	Chris	d
Nov.	7	1956	24316	Beck	Christian Herman	d
July	14	1915	6038	Beck	Frederick	m
Dec.	9	1947	18129	Beck	Hermann Heinrich	d
Dec.	6	1956	24371	Beck	Leah	d
Sept.	12	1944	16163	Beck	Mary C., etc.	d
Apr.	17	1934	11925	Beck	Matthew Clayton, etc.	m
	15	1933	11542	Beck	Peter	d
Jan.	14	1947	17570	Beck	Roy O., etc.	d
July	21	1946	17263	Beck	William J.	d
Oct.	12	1944	16164	Beck	William N., etc.	d
June	14	1915	6038	Beck	Woodley	m
Nov.	6	1944	16245	Beck	Woodley E.	d
Jan.	27	1926	9479	Beckemeier	William H.	d
June		1918	6699	Becker	Adam	d
		[1918-1919]	7047	Becker	Adam	d
		1881	1201	Becker	Anna	m
		1922	7939	Becker	Charles C.	d
		1881	1201	Becker	Elizabeth	m
May	26	1958	25650	Becker	Glenn A.	d
Oct.	17	1938	13410	Becker	Mary L., etc.	d

Month	Day	Year	File No.	Surname	Given Name	Type
		1924	8729	Beckert	Nettie	d
Aug.	30	1937	12980	Beckett	John	d
May	30	1956	23959	Beckman	August C., etc.	d
Feb.	7	1944	15823	Beckman	Donald W.	m
		[1919-1920]	7353	Beckman	Gus	d
Oct.	14	1952	21403	Beckman	Gustav	d
June	16	1922	8072	Beckmann	Caroline F.	d
Feb.	6	1956	23778	Beckmann	Johanna	inc
Oct.		1921	7843	Beckmann	William	d
July	10	1951	20475	Becknell	Ralph W., etc.	d
Oct.	9	1917	6577	Beckner	Adam	inc
Nov.	18	1927	9782	Becks	Warren Chester	g
June	17	1954	22599	Bedeau	Jeanne	inc
Oct.	29	1958	25962	Bedeau	Jeanne	d
Aug.	22	1958	25870	Bedford	Arthur	d
		1886	1593	Bedwell	Franklin	d
		1860	93	Bedwell	James	m
		1860	93	Bedwell	John	m
		1860	93	Bedwell	Nancy	m
		1903	3797	Bee	Emile A.	d
Mar.	15	1949	18957	Beebe	Mary J.	d
Mar.	11	1946	17062	Beebe	Mary O., etc.	d
Feb.	19	1946	17013	Beebe	Thoma E.	d
Dec.	16	1955	23662	Beecher	Frances M.	d
Feb.	19	1916	6178	Beedie	Edward John	m
Feb.	19	1916	6178	Beedie	Gladys Gray	m
Jan.	19	1916	6178	Beedie	Ivy Hope	m
Mar.	15	1916	6178	Beedie	William LeRoy	m
		[1908-1911]	4884	Beedle	Charlotte	d
Apr.	26	1943	15400	Beedle	Louis S.	d
		1890	1980	Beeson	Caroline	d
Sept.	29	1951	20570	Beeson	Everett V.	ins
		1877	885	Beeson	Isaac	d
Jan.	19	1944	16334	Beeson	Isaac R.	d
		1875	732	Beeson	J. B.	d
		1901	3378	Beeson	Mary	d
		1880	1102	Beeson	Robert	d
Mar.	5	1946	17047	Beeson	William Ira	d
June	10	1915	6015	Beeson	William J.	inc
		1902	3573	Beeson	William Sanders	d
Nov.		1926	9406	Beffa	Alice	m
Oct.	10	1950	19961	Beffa	Antione	d

Month	Day	Year	File No.	Surname	Given Name	Type
Apr.	4	1950	19612	Beffa	Ceasar F,, etc.	d
Aug.	4	1943	15542	Beffa	James	d
Dec.	5	1943	15667	Beffa	James	d
May	10	1944	15977	Beffa	Louis	d
		1919	7175	Beffa	Mary	g
June	9	1950	19747	Beffa	Mary	d
Mar.	19	1915	5966	Beffa	Monair	d
Apr.	13	1948	18340	Beffa	Tony, Jr.	d
Oct.	12	1918	6804	Beggs	Elrose	m
Sept.		1921	7795	Beggs	Margaret J., etc.	d
		1893	2369	Behler	Charles	d
June	8	1953	21884	Behling	Fred W.	d
Oct.	8	1917	6545	Behling	Herman	d
June	1	1940	14053	Behmer	Cornelius	d
May	20	1940	14039	Behmer	Elsie	d
		1897	2817	Behrens	Albert	m
		1897	2817	Behrens	Carl	m
		1897	2817	Behrens	Dora	m
Feb.	24	1921	7655	Behringer	Elsie	m
		[1919-1920]	7354	Behringer	Rudolph J.	d
Jan.	13	1956	23722	Behrs	Johanna	d
Sept.	21	1948	18639	Beichen	L. W.	d
June	18	1952	21200	Beickin	Vera	inc
		[1919-1920]	7313	Beins	J. W.	d
May	15	1957	24737	Beisel	Bert C.	d
		[1908-1911]	4843	Belcher	Frederic Parsons	d
Apr.	27	1928	9917	Belden	Charles C.	d
Dec.	20	1935	12467	Belden	Frances E.	d
Jan.	17	1956	23730	Belden	Ralph A.	d
Nov.	15	1936	12776	Belden	Sylvania P.	d
July	18	1951	20447	Beliaev	Peter	d
Aug.	31	1913	5583	Belknap	I(?) E.	inc
Dec.	24	1939	13850	Bell	Ada May	d
		1858	132	Bell	Albert K.	m
Mar.	21	1918	6671	Bell	Albert K.	d
Sept.	15	1958	25926	Bell	Amelia Ann, etc.	d
May	28	1941	14495	Bell	Anna	d
		1902	3455	Bell	Annie B.	d
Mar.	1	1934	11884	Bell	Bettilou	m
		[1908-1911]	4579	Bell	Charles K.	ins
		[1918-1919]	6897	Bell	Charles K.	d
Apr.	28	1958	25504	Bell	Charley/Charles	d

Month	Day	Year	File No.	Surname	Given Name	Type
Mar.	18	1954	22400	Bell	Doretta	d
Nov.	16	1944	16218	Bell	Estella, etc.	d
		1858	132	Bell	Henry H.	m
Aug.	14	1957	24949	Bell	Huldah, etc.	d
		1898	3020	Bell	J. S.	d
June	28	1958	25655	Bell	John H., etc.	d
		1858	132	Bell	John W.	m
Mar.	18	1955	23069	Bell	Lou Alice	d
		1858	132	Bell	Louisa F.	m
May		1922	8011	Bell	Martha Ellen	d
May	16	1928	9936	Bell	Mary Ardell Burneson	d
July	2	1948	18493	Bell	Noah, etc.	inc
		1897	2827	Bell	Rosa E.	m
Jan.	5	1934	11817	Bell	Thomas F.	d
Aug.	1	1958	25826	Bell	Tryphena F.	d
Oct.	28	1946	17418	Bell	William	d
		[1918-1919]	7055	Bellatia	John	d
Oct.		1936	12734	Belli	Angelo	d
Feb.	27	1939	13548	Belli	Caesar A.	d
Dec.	6	1935	12482	Belli	Eustaquis	d
Nov.	8	1950	20033	Belli	Leonie N.	d
May	17	1947	17800	Belli	Santi	d
Apr.	20	1953	21786	Belli	Umberto, etc.	d
Dec.	19	1955	23668	Belloir	Edward Fredrick	d
		[1919-1920]	7193	Bellone	Mary	m
July	15	1952	21249	Bellows	Alonzo C.	d
Dec.	3	1947	18115	Bellport	Herbert S., etc.	d
Apr.	31	1942	14880	Bellport	Walter Joseph	inc
Oct.	17	1932	11390	Belluomini	Matteo	d
Dec.	21	1939	13848	Belluomini	Frances	d
May	1	1956	23961	Belmondo	Charles	inc
May	11	1956	23982	Belmondo	Charles, etc.	d
May	25	1944	15944	Belser	George	d
Nov.	6	1951	20719	Beltrami	Adelia Z., etc.	d
Apr.	10	1944	15917	Beltrami	Sero	d
Apr.	10	1944	15917	Beltrami	Seroaka	d
Aug.	11	1947	17938	Beltran	Lorenzo	d
Apr.	7	1941	14466	Beluel	Parthenia	d
May	16	1932	11297	Belvail	Emma C.	d
Aug.	26	1932	11349	Belvail	John H., etc.	d
Aug.	12	1949	19211	Belveal	Minnie	d
June	5	1958	25670	Benamy	Solomon, etc.	d

Month	Day	Year	File No.	Surname	Given Name	Type
Dec.	23	1932	11451	Benardi	Carrie	d
Oct.	22	1953	22072	Benda	Adelbert, etc.	d
Mar.	23	1929	10220	Benda	Maria	d
Apr.	14	1952	21052	Bender	Grace A.	d
Oct.	3	1949	19292	Benecke	Herman A.	d
Apr.	13	1945	16521	Benedetti	Dante	d
		[1918-1919]	6993	Benedetti	Gilade	d
June	21	1950	19768	Benedetti	Ralph J., etc.	d
Oct.	11	1940	14238	Benedetto	Jennie	d
Mar.	9	1942	14848	Benedetto	John, etc.	d
Aug.		1922	8104	Beneker	Frederick W.	d
Aug.		1919	7144	Benelli	Ferdinando	d
July	16	1930	10655	Benelli	Govini	d
Apr.	16	1934	11893	Benelli	Lena, etc.	m
Mar.	16	1934	11893	Benelli	Leo, etc.	m
Dec.	28	1933	11799	Benelli	Luccia	d
June	3	1947	17829	Benelli	Rosa, etc.	d
Jan.	25	1957	24483	Benepe	Agnes	inc
May	7	1942	14887	Benepe	Martha L.	d
Oct.	11	1950	19971	Benepe	Wesley L., etc.	d
Nov.	19	1951	20748	Benguerel	Marie Indart	d
Dec.	6	1952	21501	Benian	Carl A.	d
		1897	2772	Benitz	William	d
		1897	2773	Benitz	William	d
		[1908-1911]	4980	Benjamin	A. M.	d
June	21	1957	24825	Benjamin	David Marshall	d
Jan.	5	1945	16352	Benjamin	Frank E., etc.	d
Oct.	23	1917	6535	Benjamine	(name not given)	m
Dec.		1917	6621	Benjamine	Mariah	d
Sept.	10	1948	18621	Benneche	Gertrude	d
Sept.	10	1948	18621	Benneche	Krist	d
Jan.	30	1943	15741	Bennesen	Nora M.	d
Feb.	13	1942	14766	Bennett	August P., etc.	d
		1896	2618	Bennett	Charles K.	d
		1884	1379	Bennett	Daniel	d
Oct.	7	1943	15632	Bennett	Effie Howard	d
Mar.	14	1930	10557	Bennett	Elizabeth	d
Nov.	31	1958	26050	Bennett	Elmer J.	d
		1902	3465	Bennett	Fannie	d
May	4	1927	9588	Bennett	George F.	m
Apr.	13	1953	21764	Bennett	Grace Edna, etc.	d
Oct.	10	1950	19968	Bennett	Ida May	inc

Month	Day	Year	File No.	Surname	Given Name	Type
Feb.		1923	8513	Bennett	Jacob D. A.	d
		[1919-1920]	7418	Bennett	John	d
Oct.	24	1943	15609	Bennett	John C., etc.	d
Mar.	19	1914	5721	Bennett	Joseph	m
June	28	1939	13655	Bennett	Josephine May	d
Feb.	5	1926	9191	Bennett	Katherine, etc.	d
		[1908-1911]	4854	Bennett	Nellie Florence	m
Dec.	5	1950	20099	Bennett	Newton N.	d
Feb.	19	1939	13537	Bennett	Nora	d
June	1	1936	12656	Bennett	Q.	d
Dec.		1924	8806	Bennett	Rose E.	d
		[1918-1919]	6945	Bennett	Sedonaha, etc.	d
		1882	1223	Bennett	Silas F.	d
Nov.	17	1958	26084	Bennett	Vivian, etc.	d
Apr.	4	1927	9588	Bennett	Walter C.	m
		1925	8883	Bennyhoff	Deloria A.	d
Oct.		1925	9044	Bennyhoff	John William, Ethel, Ja	m
July	14	1932	11339	Bennyhoff	William F.	d
Feb.	14	1947	17645	Benoit	Lillian Louise, etc.	d
June	23	1944	15995	Bensen	Marie	d
June	25	1936	12640	Bensing	Charles A.	d
July	5	1942	14969	Benson	Augusta	d
Jan.	6	1950	19445	Benson	Carl A.	inc
		1892	2159	Benson	Charlotte Psyche	d
Aug.	28	1958	25813	Benson	Clarence	d
		1895	2566	Benson	Eliza J.	d
Feb.	15	1946	17009	Benson	Emil S.	d
Jan.	23	1947	18143	Benson	Harold M.	d
		1872	530	Benson	Henry	m
Aug.	26	1938	13387	Benson	Henry	d
		1872	530	Benson	Josiah	m
		1896	2630	Benson	Josiah H.	d
Apr.	9	1943	15374	Benson	Josiah H., etc.	d
		1872	530	Benson	Laura	m
		1872	530	Benson	Louis E.	m
		[1908-1911]	4608	Benson	Mabel A. E.	m
		1872	530	Benson	Martha E.	m
		1872	530	Benson	Nathaniel	m
July	21	1934	11957	Benson	Nathaniel W.	d
May	15	1950	19698	Benson	O. A., etc.	d
Mar.	18	1929	10246	Benson	Roy D.	d
		1872	530	Benson	William	m

Month	Day	Year	File No.	Surname	Given Name	Type
		[1908-1911]	4608	Benson	William A. S.	m
May	17	1946	17150	Benson	William Kosta, etc.	d
Feb.	29	1954	22313	Bent	Leticia A., etc.	d
Oct.	2	1933	11731	Bente	Fred H.	d
Jan.	22	1950	20118	Bentley	Harriet A.	d
		[1918-1919]	6902	Bento	Antone M.	d
		1888	1795	Benton	A. S.	d
Apr.	21	1937	12968	Benton	George Ulysses	d
June	20	1942	14955	Benton	Winifrid	inc
Oct.	3	1940	14223	Bentzen	Lars	d
June	13	1958	25703	Benzon	Dane Allen	m
May	7	1933	11582	Beoletto	Spirito	d
		[1908-1911]	4881	Berbossi	Joseph	d
Apr.	20	1956	23943	Berchtold	Louis	d
July	3	1946	17281	Berchtold	Sharasia	d
Aug.	15	1932	11342	Berdie	M. G., Mrs., etc.	d
Apr.	14	1941	14437	Berenchi	John	d
June		1922	8061	Beretta	Mario	m
		[1919-1920]	7448	Beretta	Mary	d
Mar.	14	1956	23866	Berettini	Elisa	d
Aug.	16	1957	24956	Berettini	Luigi	d
Aug.	30	1937	12978	Berge	Max William	d
		[1908-1911]	5155	Berger	B. Frank	m
June	11	1948	18450	Berger	Bernard F., etc.	d
Apr.	25	1946	17098	Berger	Caroline	d
June	11	1948	18450	Berger	Frank, etc.	d
Apr.	14	1953	21770	Berger	Hertha A.	inc
Dec.	7	1953	22215	Berger	William	d
Apr.	27	1940	13974	Berges	Edmond R.	d
Mar.	17	1942	14821	Bergfried	Carl, etc.	d
		1860	165	Berggren	John F.	d
May	29	1958	25588	Bergh	William	d
Sept.	5	1947	17985	Bergreen	Catherine, etc.	d
July	21	1944	16091	Bergstidt	John J.	d
Nov.	3	1950	20022	Berizzi	John J.	d
Feb.	27	1930	10535	Berka	Frank, etc.	d
Sept.	25	1956	24227	Berka	Mabel B.	d
Mar.	5	1951	20251	Berka	Polly Ann, etc.	d
Feb.		1923	8545	Berli/Berlin	Enie	d
		1884	1423	Bermel	J. G.	d
Jan.	18	1956	23733	Bermingham	Eva May, etc.	d
Mar.	27	1953	21671	Bermoder	Mary, etc.	d

Month	Day	Year	File No.	Surname	Given Name	Type
May	23	1928	9953	Bermudez	Manuel	d
Sept.	13	1915	6091	Bern	Vittore	d
		1925	8940	Bernard	Alphonse Stanislaus	d
Apr.	27	1933	11571	Bernard	John	d
		1893	2366	Bernardi	De Maria	d
May	20	1952	21130	Bernardi	Peter	d
June	9	1954	22578	Bernardo	Re, etc.	d
Sept.	15	1947	17994	Bernett	Adelina M.	d
Apr.	31	1942	14877	Bernett	George, etc.	d
		1955	23012	Bernicke	Otto	d
Feb.	27	1958	25327	Berning	Maude	inc
		1904	3833	Bernstein	Josephine	d
Oct.	28	1948	18649	Berrettini	Pietro, etc.	d
July	17	1913	5576	Berri	Bartholomew	d
July		1918	6777	Berri	Bartolomeo, etc.	d
Aug.	28	1937	13073	Berri	Catherine B.	d
June	1	1949	19110	Berri	Ernest Alfred, etc.	d
Dec.	2	1907	4379	Berri	Joseph	d
Jan.	20	1930	10819	Berri	Marianna	d
Oct.	13	1954	22751	Berringer	Catherine Bell	inc
Feb.	8	1952	20914	Berruto	Otto	d
June	14	1955	23320	Berry	Anna May, etc.	d
Aug.	5	1955	23414	Berry	Anna May, etc.	d
		1892	2205	Berry	B. B.	d
Feb.	3	1921	7665	Berry	Charles	d
		1896	2628	Berry	Elizabeth P.	d
Mar.	1	1949	18925	Berry	Elmer I.	inc
Apr.	29	1949	18988	Berry	Elmer I.	d
Aug.	31	1939	13745	Berry	Frances J.	d
July	7	1933	11659	Berry	George C.	d
		1902	3539	Berry	Harrison	d
June	19	1953	21847	Berry	Jack C.	d
		1901	3375	Berry	Joseph	ins
Aug.	7	1944	16117	Berry	Joseph P.	d
Dec.	6	1943	15710	Berry	Lillie	d
Feb.	3	1921	7664	Berry	Lucinda	d
		1926	9336	Berry	Lucinda M.	d
Feb.	3	1921	7666	Berry	Oliver	d
	13	1926	9337	Berry	Richard D.	d
May	16	1947	17798	Berry	Russell L.	d
		1908	4451	Berry	S. B.	d
Feb.	3	1921	7667	Berry	Vivian	d

Month	Day	Year	File No.	Surname	Given Name	Type
Dec.	2	1932	11460	Berry	William R.	d
Dec.	14	1951	20799	Berry	Willmina	inc
Sept.	25	1947	18020	Berscaker	Alta	d
Sept.	14	1946	17398	Berta	John	d
May	13	1932	11274	Bertani	Enrico, etc.	d
Dec.	17	1940	14308	Bertelli	Lucy	d
		[1919-1920]	7355	Bertellotti	Edourdo	d
		1924	8596	Bertellotti	Gilda	m
		1923	8347	Bertellotti	Mario	d
Nov.	31	1957	25116	Bertellotti	Pio, etc.	d
Nov.	23	1945	16782	Bertelsen	Christian, etc.	d
Feb.	4	1958	25351	Berti	Cristofors Chris, etc.	d
Apr.	22	1953	21795	Berti	Elvira, etc.	d
June	13	1950	19756	Bertilsen	Svend, etc.	d
June	15	1954	22595	Bertini	Giuseppe	d
Sept.		1935	12369	Bertino	Junie B.	d
July	8	1947	17884	Bertocchini	Palmira	d
		1928	10111	Bertola	Marie	d
Mar.	6	1951	20257	Bertolaccini	Amadeo	d
		1908	4470	Bertolani	Pietro	d
Sept.	23	1958	25947	Bertoldi	Candido	d
Oct.	1	1958	25968	Bertoldi/Bartoldi	Candido, etc.	d
Feb.	29	1957	24494	Bertoli	Charles, etc.	inc
Feb.		1925	9142	Bertoli	David J., Jr.	d
Oct.	23	1955	23500	Bertoli	Felix, etc.	d
		1908	4408	Bertoli	Giovanni	d
May	15	1956	23993	Bertoli	Irene	d
Oct.	3	1958	25979	Bertoli	John, etc.	d
Mar.		1925	8894	Bertoli	Paul	d
July	3	1945	16632	Bertoli	Mary	d
May	5	1942	14925	Bertolini	Angelo	d
Dec.	14	1942	15190	Bertolini	Angelo	d
Feb.	3	1939	13552	Bertolini	Christoforo	d
June	6	1944	16019	Bertolini	Elsie, etc.	d
Jan.	14	1942	15190	Bertolini	Ernest	d
Dec.	14	1942	15190	Bertolini	James	d
Feb.	3	1939	13553	Bertolini	Julia, etc.	d
Dec.	14	1942	15190	Bertolini	Louisa	d
		[1918-1919]	7004	Bertolino	Giuseppe	d
Apr.	2	1929	10269	Bertolone	August	d
Oct.	19	1935	12411	Bertolone	Charles	d
Dec.	4	1933	11781	Bertolone	Parla	d

Month	Day	Year	File No.	Surname	Given Name	Type
Apr.	28	1945	16506	Bertoloni	Pietro, etc.	d
		[1908-1911]	5037	Bertolotti	Joseph	inc
Dec.	4	1912	5445	Bertolucci	Angelo	d
		1922	8094	Bertolucci	Antonio	d
Nov.	2	1943	15661	Bertolucci	Dario	d
Mar.	10	1943	15270	Bertolzzi	Rosa, etc.	d
		1903	3635	Berton	Flavien	d
		1903	3742	Berton	Germien Mais Just	m
		1903	3742	Berton	Xavier Mars	m
Apr.	6	1916	6227	Bertoni	Agostino	d
Jan.	3	1941	14322	Bertoni	Albina	d
June	29	1958	25661	Bertoni	Guido	d
July	11	1956	24095	Bertoni	Louis, etc.	d
July-Nov.		1914	5817	Bertossi	Beatrice	m
July-Nov.		1914	5817	Bertossi	Estella	m
July	6	1918	6782	Bertossi	Carlo	d
Jan.	9	1956	23712	Bertozzi	Pietro	d
July	22	1953	21900	Bertozzi	Santi	d
Sept.	26	1958	25957	Bertrad	Jame I., etc.	d
Nov.	22	1944	16223	Bertram	Frederick W.	d
Sept.	26	1958	25957	Bertram	James Ignatius, etc.	d
Oct.	10	1950	19962	Bertram	Maitland A.	d
Mar.	4	1942	14842	Bertrand	John	d
Nov.	10	1920	7570	Bertrand	Joseph	d
Oct.	14	1943	15644	Berwich	Clemence	d
June	9	1944	16028	Besaglia	Louis	d
Oct.	20	1950	19994	Besio	Marta, etc.	d
Jan.	13	1931	10835	Best	Ethel, etc.	ins
Jan.	13	1917	6399	Best	Mary Ellen	d
Dec.	16	1955	23659	Bethanis	Basil, etc.	d
June	3	1945	16600	Betscher	Ludwina, etc.	d
Nov.		1942	15142	Bettega	Guiseppe, etc.	d
Sept.	8	1944	16161	Bettencourt	Donald Leroy	m
Nov.	6	1950	20026	Bettencourt	Joe E.	d
Aug.	18	1958	25793	Bettencourt	Maria L.	d
Sept.	23	1950	19941	Bettencourt	Marie	d
Sept.	2	1952	21313	Bettendorff	John	d
Nov.	19	1951	20745	Bettiga	Bruno J.	d
Apr.	31	1947	17719	Bettiga	Joe, etc.	d
Mar.	12	1946	17068	Bettigu	Caterine	d
Oct.	5	1945	16750	Bettinelli	Antonio, etc.	d
Jan.	2	1917	6385	Bettinelli	Filippo	d

Month	Day	Year	File No.	Surname	Given Name	Type
Feb.	2	1956	23767	Bettini	A. J.	d
Mar.	12	1956	23853	Bettini	Alessio J., etc.	d
Aug.	13	1958	25849	Bettini	Emma	d
Apr.	19	1954	22404	Betz	Dora .	d
Sept.	3	1946	17378	Beughill	Elmer M.	d
Aug.	28	1924	8720	Beut	Minnie E.	d
Oct.	8	1935	12432	Beute	Beryl Louise	m
Oct.	7	1935	12429	Beute	Nellie L.	d
Oct.	3	1943	15623	Beutel	Gottlieb	d
Feb.	24	1949	18855	Bevens	William Riley, Jr.	d
		1906	4081	Bew	Caroline	d
		1892	2278	Bew	George	d
		1923	8448	Bezal	Joe	d
June	12	1946	17248	Biagi	Nicola, etc.	d
July	3	1940	14058	Bianaschi	Bernard, etc.	d
Aug.	21	1939	13762	Bianaschi	Celestino, etc.	d
July	2	1940	14090	Bianaschi	Ida	ins
July	11	1958	25780	Bianchi	Anna Emma, etc.	d
July	9	1930	10620	Bianchi	Bruno	d
May	27	1956	23956	Bianchi	Domenico	d
Jan.	7	1938	13211	Bianchi	Elia	d
Jan.	3	1928	10136	Bianchi	Felice	d
Feb.	29	1934	11844	Bianchi	Giuseppina, etc.	d
Feb.	15	1944	16417	Bianchi	Jemma	m
Sept.	5	1952	21319	Bianchi	Julia	d
Apr.	9	1948	18327	Bianchi	Leandro	d
Feb.	15	1944	16417	Bianchi	Louise	m
Nov.	20	1950	19994	Bianchi	Marta, etc.	d
Jan.	31	1916	6374	Bianchi	Peter/Pietro	d
July	16	1956	24102	Bianchi	Pietro, etc.	d
May	5	1945	16561	Bianchi	Rose	d
June	25	1937	13008	Bianchi	V.	d
Sept.	11	1947	17939	Bianchini	A. J., etc.	d
		[1919-1920]	7469	Bianchini	Amadio	d
Apr.	9	1954	22446	Bianchini	Bruno	d
Feb.	8	1939	13567	Bianchini	Elisa, etc.	d
June	6	1945	16603	Bianchini	Emilio	d
Oct.	16	1941	14642	Bianchini	M. G, etc.	d
		1926	9470	Bianchini	Mario	d
Jan.	16	1941	14742	Bianchini	Mario	d
Dec.	5	1930	10800	Bianchini	Rose	d
May	17	1934	11954	Bianchini	Sarah	d

Month	Day	Year	File No.	Surname	Given Name	Type
Mar.	20	1945	16484	Bianconi	Joseph	d
Dec.	13	1954	22912	Biasotti	Louis, etc.	d
Feb.	1	1951	20192	Biasotti	Robert Ernest	m
June	27	1958	25743	Biavaschi	E. A.	d
June	27	1958	25743	Biavaschi	Emil	d
June	9	1938	13312	Bice	Charles A.	d
		1891	2073	Bice	Frank S.	m
		1890	1935	Bice	Mary A. M.	d
Oct.	15	1915	6098	Bice	Mary J.	d
		[1908-1911]	4693	Bice	Mary Jane	inc
		1883	1352	Bicigalupi	Louis	d
Nov.		1916	6284	Bick	Israel Wolf	d
June	18	1951	20445	Bickelhaupt	Harry L.	d
		1873	652	Bicknell	Anna	m
		1860	183	Bicknell	C. J.	d
		1873	652	Bicknell	Charles	m
		1873	652	Bicknell	Ida	m
		1908	4484	Bidaux	Joseph	d
		[1908-1911]	4816	Bideaux	Bertha	inc
June	27	1929	10320	Bidia	Aninta Della	d
Jan.	19	1924	8828	Bidwell	Herman	d
		1892	2239	Bidwell	Ira	d
Sept.	19	1941	14581	Bidwell	John N.	d
Apr.	22	1949	19031	Biedermann	Winifred, etc.	d
July-Nov.	30	1914	5783	Bierce	Albert S.	d
Apr.	4	1928	9925	Biffa	Quillie William	d
July	19	1957	24888	Bigelow	Albert C., etc.	d
May	16	1936	12615	Bigelow	Frank L.	d
Aug.	3	1923	8424	Biggins	James	d
Apr.	27	1937	12974	Biggio	Maria	d
May	27	1937	12974	Biggis/Cereghino	Maria	d
July	26	1957	24912	Biggs	Cleo C., etc.	d
Nov.	15	1946	17478	Biggs	Genevieve	d
Oct.	10	1938	13399	Biggs	Leland Stuart	d
Aug.	7	1934	12016	Bigler	William	d
Mar.	7	1947	17684	Bignell	James	d
Sept.	8	1950	19916	Bignell	Josephine, etc.	d
Feb.	7	1957	24517	Bigos	Stephen J.	d
		1896	2650	Bihler	William	d
Sept.	5	1952	21316	Bihn	Cyril J., etc.	mp
Dec.	24	1952	21476	Bihn	Cyril J., etc.	d
Dec.	28	1952	21483	Bihn	Joan A.	m

Month	Day	Year	File No.	Surname	Given Name	Type
Jan.	30	1935	12496	Bihn	William Henry	d
Feb.	11	1958	25372	Bilello	Charles	d
Aug.	25	1930	10693	Billaria	Pietro	d
Mar.	10	1913	5492	Billett	Frederick James	d
May	16	1929	10285	Billings	Angeline Olive	d
		1926	9453	Billings	Anglina Olive	inc
		[1908-1911]	4746	Billings	Elizabeth	d
		1880	1112	Billings	Sylvesta	d
Aug.	19	1946	17357	Billman	Gladys K., etc.	d
July	17	1934	12004	Billon	Ada M.	m
July	17	1934	12004	Billon	Clara J.	m
Aug.	17	1934	12004	Billon	Edward C.	m
Oct.	8	1952	21391	Bills	Carrie Eliza	d
Oct.	3	1952	21378	Bills	Lemuel J., etc.	d
		1872	561	Bills	Sherman	d
		[1908-1911]	4821	Bills	Walter E.	d
Jan.		1921	7911	Bilstein	Eliza	d
July	18	1926	9316	Bilstern	Hazel	inc
Dec.	8	1953	22222	Bily	Frank	d
Oct.	10	1944	16208	Bin	Giacomo	d
Dec.	8	1931	11159	Bindi	Achils	d
Feb.	3	1935	12145	Bindi	Luisa, etc.	d
		1881	1136	Bingham	Alpheous W.	d
		1895	2500	Bingham	Ann	d
Sept.		1924	8741	Bingham	Octena	d
		1907	4252	Bink	Conrad	d
Nov.	21	1954	22816	Binkelman	Fred	d
Nov.	9	1954	22855	Binkleman	Paulina	inc
Apr.	10	1925	8902	Binkley	Morley B.	d
Oct.	13	1925	9082	Bino	Anna	d
Jan.	22	1951	20167	Biocca	Agnes	d
Sept.	10	1957	25003	Biocca	William	mp
Sept.		1924	8749	Biogotte	Charles	d
Aug.	3	1951	20524	Bionda	Emilio	d
May	18	1940	14038	Bionda	Emily Agnes, etc.	d
Mar.	9	1954	22384	Birch	Nellie K., etc.	d
Jan.	18	1914	5901	Bird	Edward	d
Apr.	24	1956	23947	Bird	Fronz D.	d
Jan.		1917	6387	Bird	James	d
Jan.	15	1916	6347	Bird	Jesse	d
		1922	8123	Bird	Phebe	d
May	8	1944	15965	Birdsall	Florence	d

Month	Day	Year	File No.	Surname	Given Name	Type
Sept.	22	1947	18013	Birdsall	Sara	d
Feb.	20	1953	21655	Birge	Marguerite S., etc.	d
Feb.	9	1959	26194	Birkhofer	Emil Jacob, etc.	d
Aug.	31	1950	19844	Birkhofer	Fred J., etc.	d
Nov.	28	1952	21428	Birkhofer	Oscar G., etc.	d
Oct.	11	1951	20666	Bisagno	Salvatore	d
		1857	32	Bischoff	Frederick	d
Mar.	20	1951	20224	Biscioni	Francis, etc.	d
Dec.	5	1950	20085	Biscioni	Francisco, etc.	d
Oct.	27	1949	19278	Biscioni	John	d
Aug.	13	1951	20542	Biseioni	Joseph	inc
Jan.	15	1934	12127	Biset	Jane	inc
Apr.	1	1949	18991	Bishop	Alexander Melrose, etc.	d
Apr.	25	1952	21007	Bishop	Beulah	d
Sept.		1915	6071	Bishop	John	d
		[1908-1911]	4766	Bishop	John T.	d
Dec.	28	1941	14726	Bishop	Orpheus, etc.	d
		1888	1803	Bishop	T. C.	d
Mar.	6	1950	19551	Bisinius	W. P.,etc.	d
July	18	1948	18465	Bisordi	Bertha	d
Jan.	24	1957	24479	Bisordi	Emma	d
Mar.	27	1950	19537	Bisordi	Eugenio, etc.	d
Feb.	6	1933	11492	Bisordi	Pete	d
June		1917	6501	Bisordi	Terrisa	d
Oct.	19	1956	24287	Bispham	Eldora J.	d
Oct.	8	1956	24260	Bispham	Harvey E.	d
July	24	1957	24829	Bispham	Harvey E.	d
Feb.	11	1935	12192	Bisset	Jane	d
June	8	1948	18443	Bisso	Luigi, etc.	d
		[1908-1911]	4949	Bittner	F. R.	d
Oct.	27	1928	10078	Bittner	Helene, etc.	d
Apr.	18	1950	19640	Bivens	Leo G.	d
July	9	1938	13369	Bixby	Wilfred Everett	d
		1897	2764	Bizzini	Julius	d
Jan.	23	1958	26173	Bjorge	Jacob Godfrey, etc. ?	d
Mar.	14	1936	12549	Black	Alexander Duncan	d
Sept.	14	1941	14609	Black	Annabell	inc
Aug.	24	1944	16093	Black	Celia Annie	d
May	2	1955	23208	Black	Charles A.	d
Jan.	9	1939	13528	Black	Charles W.	d
Nov.	2	1943	15658	Black	Claude H., etc.	d
Sept.	29	1958	25888	Black	Duncan	d

Month	Day	Year	File No.	Surname	Given Name	Type
Nov.	3	1955	23572	Black	Elizabeth Jane, etc.	d
Aug.	2	1915	6049	Black	George H.	d
Oct.	7	1915	6105	Black	George J.	m
Jan.	20	1941	14353	Black	Harry E., etc.	d
		1873	610	Black	Henry	d
Mar.	6	1945	16456	Black	James S., etc.	d
		1871	514	Black	Joseph L	d
July	16	1951	20488	Black	Lora L.	d
Mar.	25	1955	23138	Black	Mae	d
		[1919-1920]	7184	Black	Margaret Anna	d
Dec.	7	1922	8214	Black	Marion Melba	m
Mar.	2	1956	23825	Black	Martin L.	d
Nov.	7	1915	6105	Black	Mary	m
July	10	1935	12329	Black	Norah E.	d
Dec.	28	1955	23682	Black	Shirley	inc
Feb.	9	1959	26198	Black	Shirley R.	d
		1921	7879	Black	Wilbur C.	d
		[1919-1920]	7409	Black	William A.	d
Dec.	15	1955	23657	Black	William Earl, etc.	d
		[1908-1911]	4555	Black	William H.	d
		[1908-1911]	4788	Black	William H.	m
		1922	8214	Black	William Woodrow	m
		1897	2805	Blackburn	Charles	d
Dec.	11	1916	6346	Blackburn	Charles W.	d
Sept.	3	1945	16682	Blackburn	Emma Eleanor	d
Aug.		1923	8417	Blackburn	Emma Harriett	d
July	16	1936	12681	Blackburn	Frank L.	d
Feb.	3	1940	13916	Blackburn	George	d
Jan.		1905	4022	Blackburn	Jemima J.	d
		1903	3649	Blackburn	John S.	d
Feb.	17	1948	18241	Blackburn	Margaret	d
May	7	1934	11947	Blackburn	Maude	d
May	2	1936	12605	Blackford	Emma F.	d
Apr.	3	1936	12570	Blackford	Ernest F., etc.	d
Feb.	3	1947	17616	Blackford	Lottie E.	inc
Feb.	3	1947	17646	Blackford	Lottie E.	inc
Feb.	4	1949	18886	Blackford	Lottie E.	d
Jan.	2	1958	25248	Blackman	A. Z., etc.	d
		[1919-1920]	7500	Blackman	George M.	d
		[1919-1920]	7502	Blackman	Holder	d
Jan.	18	1940	14312	Blackman	Marcus	d
Oct.	4	1915	6102	Blackman	William	d

Month	Day	Year	File No.	Surname	Given Name	Type
		[1919-1920]	7501	Blackman	William, Jr.	d
		1905	3896	Blackmon	Nathan L.	d
Mar.	22	1943	15315	Blackney	Charles William	d
Feb.	21	1943	15243	Blackney	Inez	d
Mar.	7	1952	20970	Blackstock	Barbara	d
		1883	1332	Blackwell	A. J.	d
		1918	6706	Blacow	Wilson	m
Dec.	6	1932	11465	Blair	Courtland	m
Apr.	20	1945	16537	Blair	Duke R.	d
May	30	1945	16553	Blair	Duke R.	d
		1884	1422	Blair	Frank P.	m
		[1908-1911]	4772	Blair	Friderike	d
Aug.	2	1937	13078	Blair	George Franklin	d
Dec.	6	1932	11466	Blair	Harold E.	d
		1895	2554	Blair	Mary	d
Feb.	15	1954	22343	Blair	Ollie D., Sr.	d
July	1	1958	25747	Blair	Orval	d
Feb.	26	1946	17027	Blake	C. A., etc.	d
May	27	1955	23202	Blake	Elvina, etc.	d
Sept.	1	1950	19903	Blake	George	d
		1892	2141	Blake	Hiram	d
June	4	1951	20382	Blake	Isabel	d
Apr.	17	1944	15931	Blake	James	d
Mar.	23	1949	18977	Blake	John L.	d
Apr.	18	1931	10947	Blake	John Robert	d
Mar.	28	1948	18259	Blake	Lorraine	d
Dec.	4	1942	15179	Blake	William L.	d
Sept.	24	1955	23459	Blakeley	Charles W.	d
Jan.	25	1957	24485	Blakeley	Elizabeth Frances, etc.	d
		1877	912	Blakely	Eugene	m
		1877	912	Blakely	M. L.	m
		1877	912	Blakely	Unity	m
Sept.	8	1950	19916	Blanc	Josephine Marie, etc.	d
July	1	1949	19157	Blanc	Marie	d
Oct.	27	1957	25046	Blanchard	Alexander	d
Jan.	10	1958	25282	Blanchard	Alexander	d
Jan.	19	1939	13868	Blanchard	Annette	m
Aug.	20	1919	7171	Blanchard	Eleanor	g
Jan.	18	1944	15786	Blanchard	Frances Josephine	d
Mar.	23	1937	12942	Blanchard	Mary T., etc.	d
Jan.	17	1937	13192	Blanchard	Olive P.	d
Jan.	20	1921	7651	Blanchet	Emile	d

Month	Day	Year	File No.	Surname	Given Name	Type
Apr.	4	1957	24645	Blancoe	Albert	d
Jan.	31	1958	26181	Blaney	Besse Anabell, etc. ?	d
Nov.	9	1951	20727	Blaney	Ellen F., etc.	d
Aug.	14	1933	11690	Blaney	J. W.	d
June	3	1947	17825	Blank	Amy T.	d
Sept.	31	1956	24190	Blank	George	d
		1922	7990	Blank	John	d
Sept.	15	1928	10035	Blank	John, Jr.	d
Aug.	29	1948	18547	Blank	Louis	d
Apr.	23	1917	6468	Blankenberger	Adam	d
Jan.	13	1947	17563	Blankenship	Blanch Minetta, etc.	d
Jan.	21	1948	18177	Blankenship	Robert P.	d
Aug.	6	1943	15505	Blasi	Antims	d
Nov.	28	1932	11425	Blay	Ernest B.	d
June	29	1953	21874	Blay	Mary Ann	d
June	28	1943	15453	Blazer	Adelia B., etc.	d
Dec.	27	1957	25169	Blazer	Alfreda, etc.	d
		1922	8152	Blazer	C. N.	d
Feb.	18	1944	15789	Blazer	Carl Lloyd	d
Dec.	23	1907	4364	Blazer	Carl Loyd	m
Dec.	3	1945	16856	Blazer	Forrest J.	d
Mar.	25	1955	23085	Blecha	Conrad	d
		1897	2752	Bledsoe	Anthony C.	d
Dec.	18	1944	16294	Bledsoe	E. Wayne	d
Mar.		1924	8586	Bledsoe	Ernest	d
July		1918	6781	Bledsoe	J. C.	d
Apr.	9	1931	10940	Bledsoe	Louisa F., etc.	d
		1919	7097	Bledsoe	Margaret	d
		[1918-1919]	6918	Bledsoe	Margaret	inc
		1900	3116	Bledsoe	Sophia	d
		[1918-1919]	6919	Bledsoe	Vesta	m
		[1918-1919]	6919	Bledsoe	Winifred	m
		1891	2133	Bledsoe	Zurithy	d
Mar.	9	1956	23843	Bles	John L.	d
Mar.	10	1942	14850	Blewett	Laura F.	d
Aug.	12	1929	10353	Blim	Peter J., etc.	d
Dec.	25	1942	15167	Blinklors	James Alfred	d
		1902	3409	Blish	Bessie	m
		1898	2845	Bliss	Alexander	d
Jan.	11	1944	15758	Bliss	Carol	m
Feb.	26	1956	23751	Bliss	Dwight M., etc.	d
Sept.	18	1949	19219	Bliss	Elizabeth Bancroft	d

Month	Day	Year	File No.	Surname	Given Name	Type
Jan.	11	1944	15758	Bliss	Martha	m
		1886	1588	Bliss	William D.	d
Aug.	18	1949	19218	Bliss	William J. A.	d
Dec.	26	1949	19387	Bloch	Harold W.	d
Feb.	4	1958	25353	Bloch	Harold W.	d
Nov.	14	1937	13142	Block	Albert	d
July	30	1958	25745	Block	Duncan	con
Oct.	7	1949	19303	Block	Harold W.	d
Dec.	28	1950	20073	Blocklinger	Charles H.	d
Apr.	28	1945	16520	Blodgett	Stuart M.	d
May	9	1952	21114	Blohm	Rudolf	d
Jan.	22	1949	19417	Bloise	Joseph	d
June	4	1936	12630	Blom	Charles	d
Mar.	4	1954	22378	Blom	Victor Lincoln	d
July	8	1929	10348	Blomme	Dezer, etc.	d
Mar.	21	1940	13940	Blomquist	Aina Marie, etc.	inc
Oct.	7	1935	12430	Blomstrom	Charles	d
Dec.	28	1915	6116	Blood	Betsy	d
Dec.	9	1949	19409	Blood	Harold	d
Jan.	9	1941	14335	Bloom	A. E., etc.	d
Nov.	5	1937	13136	Bloom	Adolph John	d
May	27	1951	20364	Bloom	Eva H.	d
Aug.	21	1927	9656	Bloom	Joseph	d
Apr.	8	1931	10938	Bloom	Lucia M.	d
July	25	1939	13735	Bloom	Romilda	d
June	16	1927	9628	Blossfeldt	Herman Eugene	d
Aug.	8	1915	6050	Blossom	Marcus	d
		1882	1217	Blucher	Lillie (alias Lillie Peter	m
July	1	1949	19156	Blue	Ralph L.	d
Sept.	31	1933	11703	Blum	Jacob	d
		1906	4100	Blum	Louis	d
		1890	2009	Blume	F. G.	d
		1888	1798	Blume	Julius	d
Aug.	2	1957	24926	Blunt	Naomi Corrine, etc.	d
Jan.	10	1957	24441	Blut	M. J., etc.	d
Dec.	17	1948	18782	Blutt	Jacob	d
		1853	23	Boake	S. A.	d
Jan.	11	1946	16920	Board	Horace D., etc.	d
Sept.	13	1941	14638	Board	Ida F.	d
Feb.	8	1949	18894	Board	M. E., etc.	d
		1905	3953	Board	William	d
Feb.	6	1958	25362	Bobb	Ida, etc.	d

Month	Day	Year	File No.	Surname	Given Name	Type
Nov.	20	1945	16821	Bobb	Charles A.	d
May	28	1953	21814	Bobbett	Augusta L., etc.	d
Nov.	31	1935	12448	Bobbini	Guiseppi	d
Jan.	11	1943	15220	Bobbino	Marin	d
Aug.	14	1913	5602	Bocca	Francisco	d
Mar.	7	1913	5505	Bocca	Giovanni	d
July	11	1917	6509	Bocca	Guiseppe	d
Dec.	27	1934	12109	Boccaleoni	Mae	inc
Mar.	24	1958	25412	Bocchi	Charles	d
Dec.	13	1944	16326	Boccoli	Meri	d
June	20	1955	23257	Boccoli	Pietro	d
Feb.	21	1929	10186	Boch	Louis	d
Aug.	20	1942	15013	Bochow	Clara A., etc.	d
Sept.		1921	7798	Bochroeder	Catherine	d
Jan.	13	1956	24393	Bociarini	Louis, etc.	d
Apr.	3	1926	9218	Bock	Blanche E.	d
		1887	1652	Bock	David	d
Oct.	19	1956	24283	Bock	Elizabeth	d
Apr.	1	1954	22426	Bock	Ernest M.	d
Mar.	1	1928	9862	Bock	John P.	ins
Apr.	21	1928	9914	Bock	John P.	d
Aug.	20	1937	13067	Bock	Josephine	inc
Feb.	6	1939	13564	Bock	Josephine, etc.	d
		1896	2646	Bock	Lucy	d
Feb.	19	1948	18246	Bock	Mathias	d
July	30	1951	20462	Bockee	Harold Young, etc.	d
		1878	972	Bocock	James	d
June	29	1911	5217	Bodalla	Mary Ann	d
		1896	2670	Bodemer	Michael	d
June	2	1952	21162	Boden	Berenise O.	d
Apr.	25	1952	21006	Bodenhamer	Dona F.	d
Nov.	22	1953	22131	Bodine	Guy Franklin, etc.	d
Oct.	1	1948	18653	Bodwell	C. A., etc.	d
Mar.	3	1927	9553	Body	Mary A.	d
Sept.	5	1958	25899	Boe	Norman Joe	d
Feb.	19	1940	13936	Boedocchi	Anna	d
		1921	7660	Boegler	F.	d
Aug.	30	1948	18548	Boehm	Katherine	d
		[1908-1911]	5110	Boehm	Oscar	d
		[1918-1919]	6849	Boehmer	John	d
Aug.	11	1944	16119	Boenneck	August P.	d
Aug.	14	1958	25851	Boerstler	Tracy	d

Month	Day	Year	File No.	Surname	Given Name	Type
June	24	1956	24010	Boes	Axel	d
Oct.	15	1915	6093	Boettcher	Louise J.	d
Feb.	9	1951	20209	Bogani	Angelo	d
Mar.	26	1949	18919	Bogdin	John	d
Sept.	25	1944	16141	Bogdonaff	John, Jr.	d
Feb.	10	1956	23784	Bogdonoff	John K.	d
		1873	606	Boggs	A. B.	d
		1879	1001	Boggs	Joseph O.	d
		1889	1902	Boggs	Joseph O.	d
Apr.	10	1944	15885	Bogh	Anton	d
June	8	1955	23307	Boglio	Paolina	d
		[1908-1911]	4822	Bognuda	Natale (aka N.)	d
Feb.	14	1958	25389	Bogue	Donovan K.	d
Feb.	14	1958	25388	Bogue	John Eugene	d
		[1918-1919]	6899	Bohan	Catherine Elizabeth	inc
		[1918-1919]	6892	Bohan	Elizabeth	d
		[1918-1919]	6898	Bohan	Elizabeth	d
		[1918-1919]	6893	Bohan	Elizabeth Catherine	inc
Feb.	13	1948	18224	Bohan	James R.	d
Sept.	14	1956	24206	Bohan	Michael	d
Apr.	12	1914	5740	Bohan	Miles	d
Aug.	31	1956	24138	Bohlen	Carolyn	m
June	8	1956	24035	Bohling	Herman D., etc.	d
Jan.	30	1933	11807	Bohn	Ann	d
Nov.	16	1956	24335	Bohn	Edward J., etc.	d
		[1908-1911]	4869	Bohnenberger	Charles U.	d
		[1908-1911]	5114	Bohnonberger	Charles H.	m
June	26	1941	14530	Bohnser	Emily, etc.	d
		[1908-1911]	4824	Boice	Mary L.	d
Dec.	7	1931	11126	Boiocchi	Quido	d
Dec.	10	1951	20794	Boissonneau	Louis	d
Feb.	11	1955	23047	Boitano	Fortunato John, etc.	d
May	29	1958	25583	Boland	Anna M., etc.	d
Jan.	1	1927	9796	Bolaten	William	d
Mar.	10	1950	19558	Boler	Wonotee	d
Mar.	20	1953	21656	Bolgard	William H.	d
Dec.		1926	9451	Bolin	Johannes Waldemer	d
May	7	1957	24716	Boling	Melville James	d
		1854	27	Bolio	Mary	d
June	17	1926	9282	Bolla	Amedeo, etc.	d
Aug.	31	1945	16676	Bolla	Antonio, etc.	inc
Sept.	14	1945	16720	Bolla	Antonio, etc.	d

Month	Day	Year	File No.	Surname	Given Name	Type
		[1919-1920]	7282	Bolla	Constantino	d
		1896	2665	Bolla	Elvezio	m
		1881	1170	Bolla	Giacondo	d
		1896	2665	Bolla	Ida	m
Dec.	2	1947	18112	Bolla	Luisa Saldate, etc.	d
		1896	2665	Bolla	Olivia	m
		1896	2665	Bolla	Olympio	m
		1896	2661	Bolla	Peter	d
June	20	1949	19092	Bollenbach	Aramonta	d
		[1908-1911]	4999	Bolles	Walter A.	d
Mar.	12	1942	14854	Bolli	Battista	d
Feb.	14	1952	20848	Bollinger	Floyd F.	d
Jan.	24	1952	21536	Bolman	Marlene E.	m
Nov.	1	1934	12066	Bologna	Domenico, etc.	d
Dec.		1928	10125	Bologna	Louisa	d
Aug.	24	1955	23344	Bolton	Esta	d
Sept.	6	1912	5334	Bolton	Estes, Jr.	inc
Oct.	6	1912	5335	Bolton	Ogden J.	inc
Apr.	29	1946	17110	Bolzari	Lidwina M.	d
Mar.	16	1925	8885	Bomhoff	F. W.	d
		1900	3113	Bonacich	Marco	d
Oct.	4	1935	12423	Bonades	John (Giovanni)	d
Mar.	6	1944	15874	Bonanazon	Clarence	d
Jan.	29	1947	18148	Bonansen	Giovanni Pietro, etc.	d
Jan.	10	1929	10172	Bonar	Renben M., etc.	d
Oct.	13	1949	19255	Bonardi	Joe	d
		1908	4508	Bonbeer	Anna	d
		1908	4493	Bond	Carl W.	d
		1881	1144	Bond	Ellen (formerly Blakely	d
		1900	3159	Bond	J. W.	d
		1873	625	Bond	Joshua L.	d
		1896	2632	Bond	Martha M.	d
		1901	3357	Bond	Moses	d
Sept.	14	1951	20600	Bond	Nelson	d
Aug.	4	1948	18564	Bond	Pearl, etc.	d
		1876	837	Bond	Rezuba	d
		1880	1064	Bond	Richard L.	d
Mar.	14	1958	25464	Bondi	Paolo/Paul/Paul, Sr./P. /	d
June	1	1956	24027	Bondietti	Ella, etc.	d
Feb.	21	1944	15795	Bondietti	F., etc.	d
		1926	9424	Bondietti	Frances	d
Mar.	2	1914	5726	Bondietti	Frank	d

Month	Day	Year	File No.	Surname	Given Name	Type
Oct.	8	1957	25068	Bone	Lancelot, etc.	d
May	16	1941	14518	Bones	Ethel H.	d
Nov.	19	1948	18745	Bones	Ethel H.	d
Apr.	24	1944	15897	Bones	Howard L.	d
		1881	1177	Bones	James C.	d
June	1	1937	13016	Bones	Lester B.	d
Feb.	11	1944	15837	Bones	Morley Elbert, etc.	d
		1898	2976	Bones	Sarah Eliza	d
Feb.	3	1930	10542	Bones	W. H., etc.	d
		1893	2387	Bones	William	inc
Oct.	3	1937	13081	Bones	William R.	d
		1923	8477	Bonetti	Annette	d
Feb.	5	1954	22112	Bonetti	Giovanni	d
Sept.	3	1930	10721	Bonetti	Joseph Roberto, etc.	d
Aug.	29	1952	21273	Bonetti	Lester	d
		1903	3803	Bonetti	Luca	d
Mar.	13	1930	10574	Bonfigli	Aloise, etc.	d
		[1908-1911]	4899	Bonfigli	Joseph	d
Dec.	6	1934	12120	Bonham	Ella, etc.	d
Nov.		1917	6582	Bonham	Henry Ernest	d
May	6	1946	17188	Bonham	Jeanne Frances	m
Jan.	8	1949	18817	Boni	Guido, etc.	d
Mar.	22	1937	12937	Bonino	Bartolomer	d
Nov.	4	1947	18076	Bonino	Emanuel	d
Feb.	13	1934	11866	Bonis	Albert Edward, etc.	d
Mar.	5	1929	10228	Bonman	Jacob	d
		1890	2031	Bonneau	Louis	d
		1908	4455	Bonneau	Louis Keith	m
Sept.	10	1954	22743	Bonnel	Maurice J., etc.	d
Mar.	3	1947	17672	Bonnell	Willard T.	d
		1882	1246	Bonner	John	d
Sept.	26	1915	6081	Bonney	Daniel Allen	d
Oct.	15	1931	11079	Bono	Antonio	d
Mar.	21	1949	18913	Bonsignore	Agastino, etc.	d
		1925	9017	Bonta	Martino	d
Apr.	6	1942	14885	Bontecon	Daniel, etc.	inc
Mar.	28	1935	12211	Bontin	Alfred	d
		1890	1936	Bonton	Andrew	d
Feb.	2	1954	22323	Bontrager	Joseph A., etc.	d
Mar.	11	1942	14815	Bonugli	Giulia	d
June	2	1936	12658	Bonugli	Pietro	d
Apr.	13	1955	23172	Bonvecchio	Leon P.	d

Month	Day	Year	File No.	Surname	Given Name	Type
Aug.	14	1950	19869	Bookee	Ollie A., etc.	d
Mar.	9	1942	14846	Booker	Alex Arthur	d
Oct.	23	1946	17409	Boolsen	Sophia, etc.	d
Sept.	2	1958	25892	Boomsma	Henrika C.	d
		1921	7906	Boone	Reunette E., etc.	d
Sept.	26	1958	25954	Boone	Thomas C.	d
		1893	2370	Booth	Jesse	d
Jan.	14	1946	16935	Boothe	Edwin J.	d
Jan.	22	1948	18178	Borba	Frank	d
May	8	1940	13990	Borba	Joseph W.	d
June	12	1950	19754	Borba	Louis Anthony, etc.	d
Feb.	9	1940	13884	Borba	Manuel, etc.	d
Dec.		1922	8208	Borba	Regina	m
Feb.	8	1954	22332	Borden	Alice Ada	d
Jan.	26	1922	7938	Borden	Charles L.	m
Jan.	26	1922	7938	Borden	Joe R.	m
Jan.	26	1922	7938	Borden	Leroy E.	m
Feb.	26	1922	7938	Borden	Loretta C.	m
Jan.	26	1922	7938	Borden	Naomi I.	m
Jan.	26	1922	7937	Borden	Rescomb Eldred	d
Jan.	26	1922	7938	Borden	Rescome E.	m
Jan.	26	1922	7938	Borden	Ruth G.	m
Feb.	9	1940	13885	Borden	William L.	d
May	14	1953	21840	Bordessa	Antonio	d
Dec.	9	1920	7603	Bordessa	Galdino	m
May	14	1953	21839	Bordessa	Guiliana. etc.	d
		1894	2426	Borer	Eliza A.	d
		1896	2640	Borer	John	d
July	2	1939	13688	Boretti	Aquiliro	d
Aug.	9	1943	15550	Borga	Luigia, etc.	d
June	12	1922	8041	Borger	Willis E.	ins
		1906	4129	Borges	Manuel S.	d
Oct.	9	1942	15105	Borghino	Clementina/Clementino	d
Aug.	29	1952	21272	Borghino	Mike	d
Mar.	10	1954	22386	Borgwart	Fred, etc.	d
Dec.	16	1948	18738	Borheris	Tarsilla	d
Dec.	13	1929	10491	Bori	A. J., etc.	d
Mar.	7	1958	25441	Boris/Bories/Borris	Charles	d
		1904	3854	Bork	Alice	m
		1902	3492	Bork	Elise Sophie	d
Mar.	15	1937	12892	Bork	Jacob C.	d
		1904	3854	Bork	Jennie	m

Month	Day	Year	File No.	Surname	Given Name	Type
		1904	3854	Bork	Julia Molly	m
		1904	3854	Bork	Lizzie Sophia	m
		1904	3854	Bork	Sophia	m
Nov.	15	1957	25143	Bork	William E., etc.	d
		1904	3854	Bork	William Ehlert	m
June	26	1931	10975	Borkowski	Helena	d
Jan.	31	1929	10507	Born	Charles F.	d
Jan.	3	1927	9484	Born	John	d
June	18	1927	9629	Born	John J.	d
Apr.	22	1957	24684	Bornwasser	Mayme Lowder	d
Oct.	3	1940	14225	Borogino	Giovoni	d
		[1919-1920]	7472	Borradori	A.	d
July	24	1952	21212	Borrell	Floyd Allen	d
Feb.	8	1949	18892	Borsanti	Michele	inc
		1918	6820	Borshen	Roxana	d
Mar.	18	1952	20995	Borst	Gladys, etc.	d
Nov.	8	1931	11099	Borst	Helen Brayton, etc.	d
May	13	1958	25621	Borstnar	John, etc.	inc
June	2	1958	25664	Borstnar	John, etc.	d
Oct.	2	1950	19953	Bortans	Lucille A.	d
Jan.	16	1953	22235	Bortolussi	Fedele	d
May	5	1938	13310	Borzone	Guiseppe	d
Apr.	12	1944	15924	Boscacci	John, etc.	d
Aug.	6	1946	17333	Bosch	John D.	d
Feb.	16	1951	20219	Bosch	Louise	inc
Oct.	9	1952	21394	Bosch	Louise	d
Aug.	1	1951	20521	Boschen	Marie E.	d
Feb.	11	1946	17000	Boschen	Mary Ellen	d
June	18	1935	12274	Boschetti	Mary	d
July	26	1933	11651	Boschetti	Pietro, etc.	d
Mar.	15	1957	24598	Boschi	Charles	d
June	27	1952	21145	Bosio	John, etc.	d
May	30	1954	22509	Boss	Joseph J.	d
Mar.	17	1944	15842	Bossa	Albert J., etc.	d
		1926	9376	Bossa	Battista	d
Dec.	16	1958	26156	Bossa	Margherita, etc.	d
		[1918-1919]	6940	Bosse	C.	d
		1923	8346	Bosse	Marie	d
Mar.	2	1934	11885	Bossert	John	d
Dec.	5	1933	11785	Bostrom	Gustav	inc
		1901	3342	Bostwick	Guadalupe I. C.	m
Apr.	5	1957	24648	Boswell	William T.	d

Month	Day	Year	File No.	Surname	Given Name	Type
		1879	1009	Bosworth	Albert H.	m
		1902	3587	Bosworth	Amy A.	d
		[1908-1911]	4880	Bosworth	Calvin M.	d
		1879	1009	Bosworth	Climena D.	m
		1879	1009	Bosworth	Fannie L.	m
		1878	975	Bosworth	James O.	d
		1879	1009	Bosworth	James O.	m
		1879	1009	Bosworth	Lorinda W.	m
		1879	1009	Bosworth	Viola	m
Feb.	21	1935	12202	Botcher	Aimee Ella	d
Oct.	30	1951	20617	Boto	Andrew, etc.	d
Oct.	30	1958	25963	Bottini	Alberto, etc.	d
July	18	1952	21255	Bottini	Jim	d
		1904	3877	Bottini	Louis	m
May	28	1952	21089	Bottini	Maria	inc
July	18	1952	21255	Bottini	Maria	d
		1902	3559	Bottini	Santo	d
		[1918-1919]	7032	Botto	Arthur	d
		1872	537	Bottrell	Elizabeth	d
Mar.	12	1931	10900	Botts	Eliza D.	d
July		1917	6510	Botts	Junius	inc
Oct.		1917	6581	Botts	Junius	d
Sept.	28	1944	16142	Boubright	Elizabeth C.	d
Nov.	17	1946	17486	Bouchat/Banchat	Anna/Hannah	d
Nov.		1917	6588	Bouches	Jules	d
Oct.	19	1952	21355	Bouchovitz	William Z, etc.	d
Dec.	22	1950	20117	Boughton	Richard C.	m
Dec.	22	1950	20117	Boughton	Ronald C.	m
		1925	8968	Bouham	Mary E.	d
Oct.	28	1957	25107	Bouk	Amelia A.	inc
Nov.	8	1947	18086	Boumgarten	Walter	d
Oct.	17	1949	19320	Boumley	Joseph aka Boumeller, J	d
Feb.	12	1937	12858	Bounemagou	Clarence	inc
Apr.	9	1946	17131	Bouras	Stota	d
June	11	1946	17245	Bouras	Stotos	d
Mar.	14	1950	19561	Bourbeau	Joseph	d
July		1903	3812	Bourdens	Pierre	d
Feb.	27	1949	18866	Bourdette	Isabel H.	d
Oct.	25	1955	23461	Bourg	Victor Antone	d
Sept.	8	1954	22740	Bourke	Leo A.	d
Dec.	3	1913	5651	Bourke	William	d
Apr.	26	1911	5090	Bourns	Mary A.	d

Month	Day	Year	File No.	Surname	Given Name	Type
		[1908-1911]	5091	Bourns	Mary A.	d
Feb.	31	1951	20190	Bourry	Selma C.	d
Mar.	18	1958	25471	Bouscal	August Marie, etc.	d
Dec.	27	1945	16837	Bouscal	Henri	d
Nov.	10	1950	20039	Bousguet	Edward S.	d
		1849	4	Bousse	Frederick (no papers)	d
Jan.	21	1947	17588	Bowden	Alfreda	d
Jan.	24	1948	18797	Bowden	Arthur R.	d
Jan.	13	1947	17569	Bowden	Freda G., etc.	d
		1884	1377	Bowden	Isaac	d
Sept.	26	1958	25885	Bowden	Viola Frances	d
		1903	3775	Bowen	Ezra	d
		1903	3734	Bowen	John D.	d
Aug.	8	1958	25840	Bower	Francis Eugene	m
June	6	1933	11632	Bower	Fred	d
Oct.	6	1958	25981	Bower	Mamie P.	d
Mar.	29	1924	8588	Bowers	Albert, etc.	d
Sept.	31	1956	24193	Bowers	Anna Marea	inc
Jan.	11	1957	24456	Bowers	Anna Maria	d
Oct.	24	1943	15612	Bowers	Emelia L., etc.	d
Jan.	27	1949	19425	Bowers	Fannie E.	d
Oct.	25	1956	24294	Bowers	Florence	inc
Oct.	24	1956	24293	Bowers	Frank L.	inc
Sept.	11	1944	16162	Bowers	Henry P.	d
Feb.	7	1944	15825	Bowers	Joseph E.	d
Jan.	14	1946	17528	Bowers	Russell	d
		1917	6613	Bowers	Stella M.	d
Nov.	13	1956	24326	Bowers/Bauer	Frank Louis/Frank L., e	d
June	16	1933	11613	Bowhay	Marion Nancy	m
Nov.	13	1958	26076	Bowie	Francis Douglas	d
Dec.	12	1932	11472	Bowker	Wm. H., etc.	d
Aug.	31	1918	6799	Bowles	Elizabeth	d
		1850	8	Bowles	J.	d
		1902	3498	Bowles	Joseph M.	d
		[1919-1920]	7306	Bowles	Scott	d
Dec.	23	1952	21530	Bowman	Alexander, etc.	d
Apr.	30	1936	12592	Bowman	Ben F.	d
May	29	1947	17768	Bowman	Harry	d
		1883	1349	Bowman	Hattie P.	m
		1894	2424	Bowman	John	d
June	6	1952	21174	Bowman	John	d
		1882	1271	Bowman	John H.	d

Month	Day	Year	File No.	Surname	Given Name	Type
		1883	1349	Bowman	John P.	m
May	12	1953	21831	Bowman	Lloyd Russell, etc.	d
June	24	1943	15492	Bowman	Marjorie K.	d
		1883	1349	Bowman	Robert B.	m
Dec.	23	1952	21531	Bowman	Rose, etc.	inc
Apr.	22	1954	22473	Bowman	Roy H.	d
		1905	3949	Bowman	W. K.	d
		1894	2425	Bowman	Zilpha	d
		1895	2580	Box	Lucy	d
		1902	3526	Boyce	John E.	m
		1900	3138	Boyce	John F.	d
		1900	3109	Boyce	L. Dwight	d
		1902	3526	Boyce	Ruth A.	m
May	14	1948	18388	Boyd	Alfred H., etc.	d
		1925	8930	Boyd	Anna	ins
Sept.	3	1945	16680	Boyd	Daisy M.	d
		[1908-1911]	4768	Boyd	Elmer	m
Apr.	9	1957	24655	Boyd	Frederick, etc.	m
June	1	1956	24026	Boyd	George W.	d
		1880	1087	Boyd	James	d
		1894	2444	Boyd	Jennie (Jennie Watson)	d
		[1908-1911]	5161	Boyd	Jesse	m
June	26	1952	21141	Boyd	Jesse Poff	d
Nov.	20	1950	19997	Boyd	Margaret J.	inc
Jan.	14	1958	25287	Boyd	Marian, etc.	d
		1923	8285	Boyd	Samuel	d
		1898	2830	Boyden	Alonzo	d
		1854	29	Boyden	C. W.	d
		1925	9021	Boye	Louise	d
Aug.	1	1918	6800	Boyen	Clayton, etc.	d
Sept.	10	1948	18622	Boyer	Ernest	d
May	20	1932	11303	Boyer	Josephine	m
June	20	1932	11303	Boyer	Marion	m
June	20	1932	11303	Boyer	Nadine	m
Oct.	5	1948	18661	Boyer	R. M.	d
Mar.		1921	7686	Boyer	Sidney Roswell	d
Aug.	29	1956	24187	Boyes	Antoinette Charlotte, et	d
May	13	1926	9280	Boyes	Cora E.	d
Dec.	8	1938	13452	Boyes	Oliver	d
July		1918	6775	Boylan	Ann	d
Feb.	29	1932	11208	Boylan	Maggie	d
		[1908-1911]	4756	Boylan	Maggie, etc.	ins

Month	Day	Year	File No.	Surname	Given Name	Type
Mar.	3	1913	5484	Boylan	Mathew J.	d
		1882	1241	Boylan	Terrance	d
		[1908-1911]	4709	Boylan/Boylen	James	d
		[1908-1911]	4709	Boylan/Boylen	Jennie M.	d
		[1908-1911]	4697	Boylan/Boylen	Mary	d
Mar.	28	1945	16498	Boyle	Cora M., etc.	d
July	24	1956	24120	Boyle	Edith M.	d
Mar.	5	1935	12219	Boyle	Peter	d
Oct.	6	1941	14669	Boyle	Samuel Saffell	d
		[1908-1911]	4709	Boylen	James	d
Apr.	20	1917	6452	Boynton	Florence S.	d
		[1919-1920]	7348	Boynton	Fred Whiting	d
Dec.	14	1936	12829	Boynton	Harry E.	d
Nov.	10	1958	26070	Boys	Helene A.	d
Nov.		1920	7550	Boyse	Alexander E.	d
Jan.	21	1948	18794	Boysen	Frederick B.	d
Jan.	12	1949	18830	Boysen	Frederick B.	d
		1923	8410	Boysen	Lucy	d
June	10	1944	16032	Brabaw	Frederick A., etc.	d
July	2	1956	24085	Brabaw	Johanna	d
Jan.	16	1939	13532	Braccialini	Florindo	d
Jan.	13	1938	13506	Brack	Fred	d
Dec.	5	1944	16303	Brack	Harrry	d
Nov.	17	1936	12754	Bracket	Stanley W.	m
Dec.	20	1931	11141	Brackett	Catherine Ann	d
Mar.	10	1921	7676	Brackett	Jacob	d
		1921	7675	Brackett	Joanna	d
		1888	1712	Brackett	Joshua	d
Apr.	29	1937	12946	Brackett	Lillian	d
Dec.	11	1934	12123	Brackett	Percival, etc.	d
Mar.	11	1958	25452	Bradberry	Herbert Trevor, etc.	d
		1863	232	Bradbury	J. C.	d
Aug.	27	1949	19193	Bradford	Daniel B.	d
Dec.	13	1944	16322	Bradford	Flora	d
		1880	1066	Bradford	Joseph	d
Apr.	22	1956	23878	Bradford	Yewell M.	d
July	21	1939	13730	Bradlee	Arthur Seawell, etc.	d
		1907	4314	Bradlee	Stephen H.	d
May	20	1934	11929	Bradley	Alma E.	d
June	18	1952	21198	Bradley	Bettie Lou	inc
June	17	1957	24801	Bradley	Bryan	d
Oct.	5	1955	23518	Bradley	Chester T.	d

Month	Day	Year	File No.	Surname	Given Name	Type
		1896	2662	Bradley	Daniel H.	d
Feb.	28	1947	17607	Bradley	Estelle C., etc.	d
Nov.	25	1943	15652	Bradley	Hannah, etc.	d
Mar.	14	1928	9878	Bradley	James Edward	d
Dec.	24	1952	21535	Bradley	Martha H.	d
Apr.	16	1946	17144	Bradley	Minnie	d
June	21	1955	23334	Bradley	Perry T., etc.	d
Nov.	25	1935	12444	Bradley	Sarah E.	d
Aug.	7	1952	21288	Bradley	Wilbur Squire, etc.	d
		1887	1676	Bradshaw	Arthur	m
		1894	2466	Bradshaw	Frances B.	d
May	11	1929	10270	Bradshaw	Frederich	d
		1880	1130	Bradshaw	J. A.	d
Feb.	18	1952	20926	Brady	Charles E., etc.	d
Feb.	6	1936	12513	Brady	Mary	d
		1923	8353	Brady	Patrick	d
Oct.	8	1947	18038	Braendle	John	d
Mar.	8	1949	18940	Braga	John, etc.	d
July	9	1952	21244	Braga	Margarita, etc.	d
July	29	1943	15497	Braga	Margherita, etc.	ins
Oct.	6	1953	22098	Braga	Mary, etc.	d
Dec.		1914	5887	Bragagliotti	Amelia M.	m
		[1918-1919]	6933	Braghero	John (Giovanni)	inc
Aug.	9	1918	6785	Braham	Newton F.	d
Nov.	28	1955	23562	Brain	Hester	d
		1878	953	Brain	Samuel	d
		1893	2297	Brain	Sarah	d
Feb.	31	1930	10538	Brainard	Edward Wilson	d
Oct.	13	1935	12403	Brainard	Jessie E.	d
		1900	3150	Brainerd	H. P. (trustee of the esta	t
June	26	1915	6009	Brainerd	Henry P.	d
Feb.	29	1931	10851	Brake	Frank	ins
		1907	4303	Braman	C. E.	d
Nov.	25	1943	15646	Braman	Lillian	d
Apr.	19	1954	22403	Brambani	Martin	d
June	4	1948	18435	Bramhall	Bernard	d
Oct.	3	1947	18032	Bramham	John W., etc.	d
Dec.	6	1936	12791	Branard	Junie	d
Mar.	24	1941	14409	Brand	Fred, etc.	d
June	10	1915	6035	Brand	John	d
Mar.	18	1957	24541	Brand	John	d
		1896	2601	Brandon	James E.	m

Month	Day	Year	File No.	Surname	Given Name	Type
June		1919	7105	Brandon	John Dodson, etc.	d
July	17	1919	7114	Brandon	John Dodson, etc.	d
Jan.	3	1956	23692	Brandon	Mynta S.	d
Aug.	11	1933	11687	Brandon	William J.	d
		[1919-1920]	7329	Brandt	Alonzo B.	d
		1923	8480	Brandt	Antonia	inc
Aug.	7	1930	10678	Brandt	Antonia, etc.	d
		[1918-1919]	6846	Brandt	August	d
Aug.	19	1946	17355	Brandt	Bertha	d
Nov.	2	1956	24305	Brandt	Ellen Augusta	inc
Oct.	10	1957	25077	Brandt	Ellen Augusta, etc.	d
		[1918-1919]	6907	Brandt	F. O., etc.	d
Jan.	14	1956	24397	Brandt	Fred J.	d
Dec.	2	1912	5443	Brandt	H. P., etc.	d
		1919	7174	Brandt	John	d
Sept.	11	1957	25011	Brandt	W. A.	d
Dec.	10	1953	22169	Brandt	W. E., etc.	d
Feb.	10	1958	25371	Braniff	Dennis J.	d
		1890	1996	Brannan	Anthony	m
		1890	1996	Brannan	Gertrude	m
		1890	1996	Brannan	James	m
		1890	1996	Brannan	Joseph	m
		1890	1996	Brannan	Margaret	m
		1890	1996	Brannan	Peter	m
July	15	1929	10339	Brannum	Murinda	d
Jan.	11	1955	22977	Branscomb	John	d
		1926	9430	Bransen	Dorthea	d
Oct.	7	1912	5413	Bransford	Zerrel W.	d
June	13	1942	14982	Branstadt	Anne Marshall, etc.	d
Aug.	21	1933	11670	Branstetter	Cecil C.	d
Dec.	8	1929	10429	Branstetter	H. Estilla, etc.	d
Feb.	7	1921	7673	Brant	Jacob	d
		[1919-1920]	7258	Braren	Alfred V.	d
Dec.	9	1953	22166	Braren	Emilie C., etc.	d
Apr.	4	1952	21032	Brashear	Arthur C.	d
Aug.	3	1948	18561	Brasher	Almarene, etc.	d
Oct.	28	1939	13770	Brasna	Irma	m
May	5	1943	15412	Brassell	James F.	d
July	5	1944	16064	Brassill	Jessie L.	d
Dec.	28	1950	20075	Braudrick	Huge	d
Feb.	11	1939	13571	Brauer	Mary Helene, etc.	d
		[1908-1911]	4894	Braun	Fredrick	d

Month	Day	Year	File No.	Surname	Given Name	Type
Jan.	9	1951	20146	Braun	Henry F.	d
Jan.	9	1951	20145	Braun	John J.	d
		[1908-1911]	4895	Braun	Margaret	d
July	7	1950	19802	Braun	Theodore	ins
Aug.	29	1953	21979	Brauntigam	Edith, etc.	d
Mar.	9	1927	9558	Brause	Otto	d
May	2	1947	17776	Brautigam	Bruno	d
		1906	4125	Bravo	Innocento	d
Nov.	10	1934	12096	Bravo	Isolerna, etc.	d
Oct.	13	1944	16211	Bravo	Peter, etc.	d
Oct.	21	1954	22767	Bray	Charles A.	d
Sept.	13	1953	22000	Bray	Frank	d
		1877	875	Bray	Horrel	d
		1871	502	Bray	Mary	d
		1892	2234	Bray	Mary	d
Apr.	6	1953	21750	Bray	William C., etc.	d
Jan.	13	1947	17563	Brayton	Blanch M.	d
Feb.	30	1933	11523	Brazil	John T., etc.	d
Oct.	19	1907	4348	Brazil	Manuel G.	d
July	29	1956	24079	Brazil	Mary, etc.	d
May	23	1917	6470	Brazil	Thomas	d
Mar.	20	1956	23876	Breazeale	Jedediah R.	d
Mar.	21	1956	23804	Breazeale	Melsena	inc
		1908	4433	Brechwoldt	Julius	d
Aug.	7	1953	21996	Bredahl	C. Albert	d
July	11	1945	16606	Breem	Hugh	d
		1898	2947	Breen	Catherine	d
July	10	1941	14543	Breen	Hyman, etc.	d
Sept.	14	1952	21294	Breen	Mamie Josephine	d
May	13	1955	23237	Breiner	Martin, etc.	d
Jan.	4	1951	20125	Breitenbach	Charles J., etc.	d
Apr.	11	1951	20329	Breitenbach	Eva	d
		[1919-1920]	7364	Breitenbach	Louis	d
		1892	2161	Breitlauch	William	d
		1906	4149	Bremer	Elmira	m
		1906	4149	Bremer	Jeannette	m
July	18	1933	11667	Bremsen	Eleanor	m
Mar.	7	1918	6661	Brenard	John	d
May	18	1943	15439	Brenard	Maria J.	d
Dec.	2	1947	18111	Brenard	Sarah Ann, etc.	d
June	5	1933	11628	Brendel	Joseph	d
May	4	1928	9963	Brendlin	Charles A., etc.	d

Month	Day	Year	File No.	Surname	Given Name	Type
		1935	12334	Brenendle	Anna	d
Dec.	28	1958	26113	Brennan	Anthony Mark	d
Oct.	17	1932	11411	Brennan	Michael	d
Oct.		1923	8472	Brennan	Philip	d
Oct.	4	1949	19296	Brenner	Leonard	d
Aug.	19	1944	16130	Brent	Ernest L.	d
Aug.	22	1958	25878	Brenton	James G., etc.	con
Oct.	8	1940	14233	Bresciani	Frank	m
Oct.	8	1940	14233	Bresciani	Louis	m
Oct.	8	1940	14233	Bresciani	William	m
Dec.	10	1925	9137	Bresnan	Timothy, etc.	d
Nov.	31	1941	14692	Bress/Bracsialle, etc.	Meli Francis	d
Apr.	6	1931	10932	Brett	George A.	d
		[1908-1911]	4782	Brettgin	Richard H.	d
		1924	8715	Breuelt	William	d
Feb.	25	1952	20876	Brewer	David E.	d
Dec.	9	1930	10807	Brewer	Harry, Jr.	d
		1921	7756	Brewer	Julius A.	d
July	23	1950	19771	Brewer	Ollie	d
June	19	1950	19712	Brewer	Wanda May	m
June	23	1950	19719	Brewster	Elmo, etc.	d
Jan.	17	1953	22240	Brezzo	Agostino, etc.	d
Apr.	15	1941	14482	Brezzo	Cristoforo	d
May	19	1927	9608	Brians	Benjamin P.	d
Dec.	9	1955	23640	Brians	Hattie	d
		1887	1687	Brians	William	d
July	22	1952	21262	Brians	William	d
Aug.	7	1957	24938	Briar	Nadine H.	d
		1893	2319	Brickwell	John	d
		[1908-1911]	4537	Bridge	Gertrude A.	d
		[1908-1911]	4532	Bridge	William E.	d
June	1	1943	15455	Bridgeford	Rebecca B.	d
Mar.	5	1946	17050	Bridgeford	Ellen	d
Feb.	28	1948	18189	Bridgman	Johnn C., etc.	d
Aug.	1	1927	9688	Briesch	Paul	d
Oct.	30	1942	15109	Briesh	Mary	d
Nov.		1914	5836	Brietenbach	Johanna, etc.	d
Nov.	31	1958	26047	Brietz	Adam aka	d
		1903	3695	Briggs	Amanda	d
Feb.	3	1956	23773	Briggs	Beulah P.	d
		1879	1030	Briggs	C. A.	d
		1879	991	Briggs	Edwin	d

Month	Day	Year	File No.	Surname	Given Name	Type
		1902	3415	Briggs	Elizabeth	d
Apr.	17	1933	11563	Briggs	Ellen	d
		1900	3328	Briggs	Frank	d
Aug.	14	1956	24159	Briggs	Frank Earl, etc.	d
Aug.	15	1940	14109	Briggs	Gareth W., etc.	d
		[1919-1920]	7191	Briggs	Hiram etc	d
Apr.	2	1937	12953	Briggs	J. E.	d
Oct.	6	1948	18667	Briggs	Jennie	d
		1905	4024	Briggs	Jerome	d
Dec.	10	1957	25205	Briggs	Louisa M.	d
Nov.	17	1952	21461	Briggs	Louise Meyer	d
		1925	9003	Briggs	Martha J.	d
May	29	1949	19038	Briggs	Minnie	d
May	24	1922	7993	Briggs	Nellie Parry	d
		1883	1295	Briggs	Phebe Adeline	d
		[1919-1920]	7211	Briggs	Sarah L.	d
Feb.	21	1927	9506	Brigham	George H.	d
Jan.	31	1957	25244	Brigham	Richard Douglas	d
		1868	384	Bright	S. B.	d
Mar.	7	1940	13951	Brignole	Rose	d
Feb.	6	1929	10202	Brijandi	John	d
June	6	1952	21175	Brim	J. N.	d
		1887	1699	Brink	Alzada Matilda	d
		1867	347	Brink	Edward	d
		1906	4044	Brink	Edward	d
Apr.	3	1953	21744	Brinkerhoff	Clara D.	d
Oct.	13	1953	22109	Brinkerhoff	John Hornsby, etc.	d
Dec.	30	1954	22897	Brinkman	Edith E.	d
June	5	1937	13021	Brinkman	Ruth O.	inc
July	2	1942	14964	Brinkman	Ruth O.	d
Mar.	10	1922	7954	Briones	Emma	d
Feb.	26	1951	20178	Briones	Mus. J. C., etc.	d
Apr.	8	1948	18270	Britner	Anita R.	d
Dec.	11	1951	20796	Britner	Madlyn, etc.	d
		[1908-1911]	4796	Brittain	Clarence	m
		[1908-1911]	4796	Brittain	George	m
Feb.	21	1943	15242	Brittain	Harvey	d
Nov.	21	1949	19328	Brittain	Julia M.	d
Sept.	7	1940	14139	Brittain	Leonard, etc.	d
Apr.	27	1929	10261	Brittain	Lester	d
		1920	7512	Brittain	Mary Jane	d
Oct.	24	1924	8759	Brittain	Norris	d

Month	Day	Year	File No.	Surname	Given Name	Type
Mar.	31	1938	13234	Brittain	Samuel A.	d
		1926	9425	Brittain	Walter P.	d
Aug.	20	1951	20552	Britton	Leland M.	d
		1884	1424	Britton	M. A.	d
Oct.	3	1940	14222	Brocca	Ben	d
Dec.	6	1938	13451	Brock	C. A.	d
Jan.	10	1944	15755	Brock	Frank M.	d
		1923	8357	Brockelman	William H.	d
Apr.	25	1935	12242	Brodersen	John	d
Apr.	23	1954	22484	Brodersen	Lella P.	inc
Aug.	6	1954	22679	Brodish	Walter B.	d
Aug.	21	1958	25867	Brogan	Agnes	inc
		1908	4468	Brogden	Joseph B.	d
May	21	1950	19642	Broica	William	mp
		1868	387	Brokaw	Brogan	d
Sept.	17	1953	22062	Brondeno	Bernardina	d
Aug.	28	1933	11676	Bronsert	Louis	d
Nov.	29	1928	10102	Bronsert	Maria	d
Feb.	26	1937	12872	Bronsert	William	d
Nov.	10	1950	20038	Bronson	Hollie	d
Dec.	15	1945	16885	Bronstein	Harry	d
Jan.	16	1946	16939	Bronstein	Harry, etc.	d
Apr.	4	1957	24642	Bronstein	Newton	d
July	3	1950	19796	Brooke	Amy	inc
Dec.	18	1958	26160	Brooker	Vivian H., etc.	d
Oct.	14	1928	10063	Brookover	Ruth	d
Nov.	31	1947	18071	Brooks	Albert Ross	inc
Mar.	19 ?	1954	22353	Brooks	Alfred James	d
Aug.	22	1951	20562	Brooks	Arthur M.	inc
Nov.	5	1951	20712	Brooks	Arthur M., etc.	d
June	11	1949	19076	Brooks	Charles W.	inc
Feb.	9	1950	19448	Brooks	Charles W.	d
		1893	2355	Brooks	E. L.	d
		1884	1411	Brooks	Earnest K.	m
Jan.	30	1946	17540	Brooks	Elizabeth	d
Mar.	3	1930	10569	Brooks	Elmont	d
		1884	1411	Brooks	Frederick A.	m
		1860	93	Brooks	Henry	m
		1858	93	Brooks	James	d
May	15	1948	18346	Brooks	James	d
May	1	1930	10590	Brooks	Jane Elizabeth	d
Mar.	15	1956	23794	Brooks	Karl	d

Month	Day	Year	File No.	Surname	Given Name	Type
May	12	1955	23229	Brooks	Lena	d
Aug.	1	1949	19200	Brooks	Lena H.	d
Nov.	17	1933	11744	Brooks	Marcia, etc.	d
Dec.	6	1936	12796	Brooks	Margaret	d
		1860	93	Brooks	Thomas	m
		1882	1272	Brooks	Thomas J.	d
		1895	2495	Brooks	William	d
		1925	9002	Broomhall	Fannie, etc.	d
Oct.	4	1937	13135	Broosllooni	illegible	d
		[1908-1911]	4892	Brooton	John	d
Mar.	12	1956	23855	Brost	Clara	d
Nov.	21	1949	19382	Brotherton	Margaret E. C., etc.	inc
Sept.	10	1935	12400	Brotts	Mary Laura	d
July	12	1944	16077	Broussal	Hippolyte	d
Dec.	3	1954	22899	Broussard	Melvin K.	m
June	7	1957	24779	Brovelli	Angelo, etc.	d
May	21	1919	7089	Brovelli	Atilio	m
		1919	7089	Brovelli	Ernestina	m
May	21	1919	7089	Brovelli	Frank	m
May	21	1919	7089	Brovelli	Lena	m
		[1918-1919]	6859	Brovelli	Stepan	d
June	19	1953	21898	Brovero	Mario	d
Feb.	7	1944	15824	Brown	A. C.	d
		1888	1751	Brown	Ada E.	m
		1924	8816	Brown	Adelaide E.	d
		[1908-1911]	5019	Brown	Albert	d
		1901	3399	Brown	Anastasia	d
June	8	1950	19745	Brown	Anna M.	d
Apr.	6	1951	20259	Brown	Annie D., etc.	d
June	12	1937	13031	Brown	Antonio	d
Dec.	9	1929	10487	Brown	Beatrice	m
Dec.	9	1935	12457	Brown	Benjamin Cole	d
May	14	1947	17747	Brown	Benjamin F., etc.	d
Mar.	4	1953	21677	Brown	Bertha M.	d
Apr.	15	1953	21771	Brown	Bertha, etc.	d
Aug.	18	1939	13760	Brown	Betty Rose	m
Apr.	22	1957	24610	Brown	C. Alice	d
		1870	435	Brown	C. H.	m
Aug.	1	1938	13393	Brown	Cara L.	d
Jan.	20	1954	22302	Brown	Carl E.	d
		1892	2176	Brown	Carrie	m
Dec.		1928	10132	Brown	Carrie	inc

Month	Day	Year	File No.	Surname	Given Name	Type
Apr.	6	1951	20321	Brown	Carrie C., etc.	d
		[1919-1920]	7192	Brown	Catherine	ins
Jan.	15	1947	17572	Brown	Celestine	d
		1884	1399	Brown	Charles	d
June	21	1937	13040	Brown	Charles A.	d
Nov.	5	1952	21434	Brown	Charles A.	d
Nov.	12	1920	7572	Brown	Charles B.	d
Sept.	22	1948	18640	Brown	Charles F.	d
Feb.	9	1943	15266	Brown	Charles Howell	d
Feb.	2	1956	23766	Brown	Chester B., etc.	d
Mar.	13	1956	23863	Brown	Chester B., etc.	d
June	23	1929	10317	Brown	Claude De Voe	d
		1902	3518	Brown	Daniel	d
		1875	780	Brown	Daniel et al	m
Mar.	4	1946	17120	Brown	Daniel, etc.	d
Apr.	6	1946	17124	Brown	Daniel, etc.	d
June	13	1955	23316	Brown	Daryla Gaye	m
Sept.	20	1957	24967	Brown	Edgar	m
Aug.	9	1940	14098	Brown	Edgar A., etc.	d
		1888	1751	Brown	Edith	m
		1896	2642	Brown	Edward S.	d
		1901	3385	Brown	Edwin M.	inc
Dec.	29	1933	11777	Brown	Eleanor, etc.	m
		1921	7784	Brown	Eliza Jane	d
Apr.	9	1948	18331	Brown	Ella L.	d
Sept.	14	1942	15052	Brown	Emily	d
June	3	1941	14539	Brown	Emily, etc.	d
July	16	1947	17893	Brown	Emma C.	d
Jan.	14	1941	14348	Brown	Esther E.	d
Nov.	21	1932	11417	Brown	F. M.	d
Apr.	6	1946	17125	Brown	Florence Bell, etc.	d
Apr.	27	1937	12973	Brown	Florence V.	d
		1893	2365	Brown	Frances E.	d
June	20	1956	24065	Brown	Frank B.	d
		1936	12707	Brown	Frank C.	d
Jan.	17	1947	17573	Brown	Frank J.	d
July		1923	8383	Brown	Frank Walter	d
July	25	1947	17866	Brown	Fred W.	d
		1888	1751	Brown	Genevive	m
		1902	3576	Brown	George C.	d
		1905	3978	Brown	George M.	d
Dec.	17	1948	18784	Brown	George Raymond, etc.	d

Month	Day	Year	File No.	Surname	Given Name	Type
Feb.	17	1918	6648	Brown	George W.	d
June	9	1945	16605	Brown	Gordon de Barde	d
June	21	1940	14040	Brown	Harriet	d
Nov.	21	1950	20059	Brown	Harry	d
		1903	3675	Brown	Harry O.	m
Sept.	5	1926	9353	Brown	Harry W., etc.	d
		1890	2034	Brown	Henry R.	d
Feb.	6	1944	16402	Brown	Ida	d
Nov.	8	1944	16242	Brown	J. H.	d
Jan.	6	1915	5930	Brown	James F.	d
		1904	3880	Brown	John A.	d
		1888	1751	Brown	John McAllen, Jr.	m
Aug.		1926	9342	Brown	John. etc.	d
		1863	235	Brown	Joseph H.	d
Jan.	28	1917	6632	Brown	Kingston	m
June	28	1956	24019	Brown	Laura Maud, etc.	d
Feb.	15	1944	16418	Brown	Lewis T.	d
Mar.	10	1954	22387	Brown	Lillian A.	d
June	16	1952	21192	Brown	Lillian E., etc.	d
Dec.	3	1952	21493	Brown	Lillian Thomas	d
Jan.	18	1946	16942	Brown	Louis	d
June	25	1954	22546	Brown	Louis T.	d
		1890	1956	Brown	Louisa A.	d
		1870	435	Brown	M. B.	m
July	29	1956	24080	Brown	Madeline	d
		1928	10123	Brown	Manuel S.	d
Apr.	6	1946	17126	Brown	Maraetta	d
Apr.	4	1946	17121	Brown	Martha	d
Oct.	22	1933	11722	Brown	Martha Jane	m
Apr.	24	1953	21805	Brown	Mary	d
		1918	6647	Brown	Mary E.	d
Feb.	10	1935	12155	Brown	Mary E.	d
Mar.	14	1952	20979	Brown	Mary E.	inc
July	25	1954	22617	Brown	Mary E.	d
Nov.	12	1937	13164	Brown	Mary W.	d
Nov.	7	1954	22793	Brown	Minnie	d
Feb.	5	1952	20900	Brown	Minnie C.	d
Sept.	10	1932	11356	Brown	Minnie Ricmesto	d
Dec.	4	1956	24368	Brown	Myrtle E.	d
Apr.	19	1916	6180	Brown	Nancy	d
May	4	1948	18373	Brown	Nellie K., etc.	d
June		1919	7112	Brown	Nora R.	d

Month	Day	Year	File No.	Surname	Given Name	Type
		1870	435	Brown	O.	m
		1870	435	Brown	O.	m
		1898	2934	Brown	Olivia M.	d
Nov.	14	1934	12098	Brown	R. H., etc.	d
May	14	1955	23173	Brown	Ralph H.	d
		1900	3213	Brown	Richard	d
Sept.	13	1931	11030	Brown	Richard	d
Jan.	20	1956	23741	Brown	Robert	d
Jan.	27	1957	25239	Brown	Robert Earl	d
Nov.	16	1951	20741	Brown	Rollo B., etc.	d
Nov.	23	1953	22140	Brown	Roy C.	d
Mar.	23	1943	15316	Brown	Ruth	d
		1862	208	Brown	S.	d
		1902	3546	Brown	Samuel	d
		1864	239	Brown	Samuel C.	d
Aug.	6	1938	13395	Brown	Samuel, Jr.	m
		1925	8900	Brown	Susan M.	d
		1870	435	Brown	T. L.	m
Oct.	29	1947	18028	Brown	Thomas Peat ?	d
Jan.	16	1920	7614	Brown	Vinnie	d
		1896	2613	Brown	Viola (Viola Brunnell)	inc
Aug.	2	1948	18554	Brown	W. H.	d
		1898	2982	Brown	Walter T.	d
		1872	567	Brown	Warren F. (no papers)	d
June		1903	3808	Brown	William	d
Sept.		1925	9024	Brown	William	d
Mar.	5	1946	17052	Brown	William Robert	d
		1885	1449	Brown	William S.	d
Jan.	16	1920	7614	Brown	Wilma	d
		1906	4184	Brown	Wilson	d
Apr.	26	1946	17104	Brown	Ella Taft	d
Feb.	11	1938	13215	Brown	Kate	d
		[1908-1911]	4882	Browne	Mary F.	d
May		1924	8612	Brownell	Dickson, etc.	d
Jan.	19	1957	24464	Brownell	Volney H., etc.	d
Nov.	13	1950	20045	Browning	Robert J.	d
June	19	1956	24062	Brownlee	Royce Q.	m
Jan.	12	1943	15223	Brownscombe	Jessie M., etc.	d
Jan.	12	1943	15224	Brownscombe	Thomas F., etc.	d
Feb.	20	1945	16366	Bruccialani	Olympia	d
Oct.	28	1951	20646	Bruce	Ethel	d
Sept.	12	1946	17397	Bruce	Etta H., etc.	d

Month	Day	Year	File No.	Surname	Given Name	Type
Mar.	11	1947	17694	Bruce	J. J.	d
Aug.	14	1957	24948	Bruce	Jennie Lavinia	inc
Feb.	13	1935	12194	Bruce	W. L.	d
Nov.	29	1957	25111	Brucker	August	d
Dec.	5	1944	16304	Brucker	Mollie Yeates, etc.	d
Apr.	1	1932	11245	Bruggemann	Christian Frederick, etc.	d
		1886	1580	Bruggy	Mary	d
Mar.	4	1947	17679	Bruhn	Peter	d
Oct.	5	1925	9074	Bruhn	Peter N.	d
		1874	706	Brumfield	Presilla Grace Anna	m
		1924	8865	Brumfield	Summer	d
Nov.	20	1924	8782	Brumfield	Summers	inc
Feb.	1	1932	11210	Brumie	John	d
Nov.	16	1946	17442	Brumner	Bertha	d
Dec.	1	1932	11429	Brumsen	Charles	d
Apr.	15	1957	24593	Bruna	Jo Ann R.	m
June	14	1957	24796	Brundiga	Arthur Lloyd	d
Sept.	20	1946	17408	Brundige	Amanda , etc.	d
Aug.	3	1953	21926	Brundin	Ida M.	d
Aug.	23	1943	15522	Brune	Frank H.	d
Dec.	22	1933	11796	Brune	Mary E.	d
		1857	33	Bruner	Christian	d
		1854	30	Bruner	Jacob	d
		1870	451	Bruner	John	d
May		1926	9273	Bruner	John	d
		[1908-1911]	4675	Bruner	Philip	d
		[1908-1911]	4770	Bruner	Rosella	d
Dec.	6	1946	17516	Brunette	Mabel Anna	inc
Jan.	15	1954	22286	Brunetti	Adelaide	d
Dec.		1907	4362	Bruning	Bertha	d
		1882	1240	Bruning	Caroline	ins
		1890	1942	Bruning	Henry William	d
		1872	520	Brunk	Hezekiah	d
Oct.	5	1954	22790	Brunk	Paul H.	d
Dec.	22	1946	17493	Brunner	Dora	d
		1903	3766	Brunner	Herman	d
Oct.	3	1928	10083	Brunner	Herman	inc
Sept.		1922	8119	Bruns	George, etc.	d
June	11	1948	18446	Brunsgaard	Kristian	d
Dec.	24	1922	8197	Brunson	A. H.	d
Dec.	29	1946	17501	Brunson	Frank	d
		1921	7866	Brunstad	Irving	m

Month	Day	Year	File No.	Surname	Given Name	Type
		1921	7866	Brunstad	Paul	m
Oct.	20	1921	7866	Brunstad	Ralph	m
Feb.	2	1921	7662	Brunstael	James K.	d
Jan.	6	1950	19443	Brunt	Emma A.	d
Dec.	17	1945	16890	Brunt	Emma, etc.	d
Nov.	14	1958	26081	Brunt	Ernest R.	d
Feb.	2	1915	5950	Brusa	Josephine	d
May	13	1943	15380	Brusa	Marie	d
		[1908-1911]	4928	Brusa	Paola	d
		1879	1037	Brush	D. C.	d
Nov.	10	1944	16264	Brush	George Everton	d
Nov.	13	1944	16263	Brush	Helen	d
Mar.	24	1947	17658	Brush	Henry A., etc.	d
		[1918-1919]	7036	Brush	J. H., etc.	d
July	9	1945	16636	Brush	Joseph M., etc.	d
May	12	1932	11295	Brush	Julia A.	d
Aug.	31	1956	24137	Brush	Lena A.	d
Feb.	19	1945	16427	Brush	Lucy	d
Jan.	19	1950	20110	Brush	Lucy	d
Dec.	15	1912	5419	Brush	Oren H.	d
		[1918-1919]	6966	Brush	Samuel	d
Mar.	26	1946	17029	Brush	Wm. L.	d
June	5	1931	10989	Brusighini	Bergamo, etc.	m
June	5	1931	10989	Brusighini	Fiorenzo	m
June	5	1931	10989	Brusighini	Irlanda	m
June	5	1931	10989	Brusighini	Italo	m
Jan.	28	1927	9793	Bruteiller	Adele	d
		[1919-1920]	7212	Brutsch	Charles	d
		1898	3096½	Bruyne	Gustof de	d
		1882	1238	Bryan	Annie	m
May	4	1945	16558	Bryan	Elizabeth	d
Aug.	3	1953	21989	Bryan	Elizabeth	d
		[1908-1911]	5022	Bryan	Elizabeth	inc
		1882	1238	Bryan	Fred J.	m
Feb.	7	1915	5948	Bryan	Frederick J.	inc
		1882	1238	Bryan	John Leo	m
		1882	1238	Bryan	Joseph	m
		1882	1238	Bryan	Katy	m
		1882	1238	Bryan	Mary	m
		1882	1238	Bryan	Rosa	m
		1881	1147	Bryan	Thomas J.	inc
		1882	1237	Bryan	Thomas J.	d

Month	Day	Year	File No.	Surname	Given Name	Type
Aug.	5	1938	13394	Bryan	William F., etc.	d
		1882	1238	Bryan	Willie	m
		1887	1655	Bryant	Abner	d
		[1922-1923]	8241	Bryant	Allen	d
		1881	1169	Bryant	Ann A.	m
Nov.	5	1958	26061	Bryant	Anna Pearl	d
Jan.		1921	7907	Bryant	Bettie	d
Nov.	29	1913	5646	Bryant	Daniel S.	d
May	26	1952	21087	Bryant	Elizabeth M.	d
		1881	1169	Bryant	John E.	m
		1879	1020	Bryant	Robert L.	d
Nov.		1922	8180	Bryant	Susan E.	inc
		[1908-1911]	4806	Bryant	Susan H.	d
		1881	1169	Bryant	Thomas P.	m
Apr.	4	1931	10931	Bryant	W. H.	d
Mar.	14	1931	10872	Bryant	W. H., etc.	inc
May	29	1949	19037	Bryer	Arthur F. W.	d
		1894	2433	Bryne	M.	d
Dec.	17	1942	15149	Bryson	D. H., etc.	d
July	30	1924	8694	Buans	Enoch	d
Jan.	15	1938	13508	Bucckioni	Virgilio/Vic/Vick Good	d
Jan.	9	1931	10833	Buchan	Catherine E., etc.	d
July	20	1952	21206	Buchanan	Claudia W.	d
May	23	1941	14526	Buchanan	Jean	m
Dec.	5	1958	26128	Buchanan	Lulu F.	d
Nov.	4	1942	15134	Buchanan	Nigel B.	d
Mar.	6	1953	21681	Buchanan	R. H.	d
Nov.	30	1931	11121	Bucher	Eugenia	d
Sept.	21	1933	11693	Bucher	Eugenia	d
Dec.	21	1947	18101	Bucher	Letia B.	d
Jan.	8	1939	13862	Buchignani	Agnese	d
Dec.	8	1939	13861	Buchignani	Angelo	d
Dec.		1925	9125	Buchignani	Furirna	m
		[1919-1920]	7407	Buchignani	George A.	d
		1919	7131	Buchignani	Guseppe	d
		1925	9125	Buchignani	Meri	m
		[1919-1920]	7490	Buchignani	N.	d
		1925	9125	Buchignani	Renato	m
		[1918-1919]	7084	Buchignani	Rizieri	d
Dec.		1925	9125	Buchignani	Rizzieri	m
July	17	1946	17259	Buchignani	Victor	d
Aug.	8	1958	25836	Buchignani	Zeffiro	d

Month	Day	Year	File No.	Surname	Given Name	Type
Mar.	9	1953	21684	Buck	Clifton	m
Nov.	3	1943	15662	Buck	Henrietta	d
June	29	1931	10979	Buck	Mary	d
Mar.	9	1953	21684	Buck	Mary	m
Mar.	9	1953	21684	Buck	Steven Lundbeck	m
Mar.	9	1953	21684	Buck	Stuart	m
Mar.	9	1953	21684	Buck	Virginia	m
Dec.	24	1943	15735	Buck	Henrietta	d
Mar.	14	1939	13574	Buckett	John	d
Sept.	24	1951	20566	Buckingham	Joseph D.	d
		[1908-1911]	4952	Buckland	Elaine V.	m
Sept.	23	1946	17365	Buckle	Mary	d
Aug.	24	1934	12030	Buckner	Charles O.	d
Jan.	9	1918	6640	Buckner	Horace	d
Nov.	9	1920	7568	Buckner	Zachariah E.	inc
Jan.	5	1921	7633	Buckner	Zachariah E.	d
		1898	2983	Buckner	Zerah L.	d
Mar.	7	1927	9554	Bucrhead	John L.	d
July	8	1932	11332	Budd	Agnes L.	d
Nov.	15	1945	16760	Budd	Albert W.	d
Apr.	6	1933	11578	Budd	Edward W.	d
May	25	1944	15945	Budermann	Frank A.	d
Feb.	3	1913	5668	Budie	John Smith	d
		[1918-1919]	7017	Budinger	William M.	d
Oct.	19	1912	5397	Buesing	Frank W.	d
July	11	1957	24867	Buetikofer	Robert	d
Mar.	21	1955	23126	Buffham	Mattie	d
July	8	1947	17883	Buffhaus	James B.	d
Feb.	7	1940	13924	Buffi	Emilio	d
		1906	4049	Buffum	Caroline	d
May	30	1957	24701	Buford	Hayden T.	d
Feb.	3	1930	10545	Bugbee	Clarence, etc.	d
Mar.	3	1930	10568	Buger	Hyman	d
		1857	206	Bugg	B. V.	m
		1857	206	Bugg	S.	m
		1857	206	Bugg	Ulrica S. D.	m
Jan.	28	1945	16906	Bugua	Dante	d
Sept.	28	1953	22033	Buhl	Jens Jorgen Hanson	d
Oct.	21	1945	16731	Buhl	Maebelle H.	d
Sept.	12	1930	10728	Buhlman	Emil A.	d
July	20	1958	25720	Buhrman	Leo	d
Dec.	9	1955	23646	Buhrman	Minnie S., etc.	d

Month	Day	Year	File No.	Surname	Given Name	Type
Oct.	8	1948	18671	Bulatti	Regina, etc.	d
Mar.	10	1936	12547	Bulba	Frank J.	d
Oct.	6	1942	15100	Buletti	Angelo	d
July	25	1948	18475	Buletti	Angelo	d
May	8	1944	15967	Buletti	August, etc.	d
July	9	1934	11994	Buletti	Emilia	d
Apr.	11	1958	25543	Buletti	Gennie	con
May		1925	8949	Buletti	Giovanni, etc.	d
Oct.	6	1942	15100	Buletti	Mario, etc.	d
Nov.	28	1950	20074	Bull	Dickylee, Rodman	m
Apr.	29	1930	10588	Bull	Henry R.	d
June	13	1938	13349	Bulla	John	ins
Nov.	28	1920	7531	Bullard	Adelia	d
Dec.	5	1958	26127	Bullard	Ernie William, etc.	d
Dec.	4	1958	26123	Bullard	Valentina	d
Mar.	13	1931	10912	Bulleri/Balleri	Alemanco/Alaneno	d
Sept.	18	1924	8733	Bullis	Frederich E.	d
Jan.	31	1929	10506	Bullock	Caroline V.	d
Oct.	3	1940	14224	Bullock	Richard	d
Dec.	16	1920	7576	Bullotti	Louis	d
Aug.	30	1934	12012	Bulotti	Abele	d
Feb.	6	1939	13563	Bulotti	Beatrice	d
Sept.	27	1948	18599	Bulotti	Elia, etc.	d
Dec.	6	1915	6145	Bulotti	Frank	d
May	21	1943	15441	Bulotti	Fred	d
Apr.	24	1913	5514	Bulotti	James J.	d
		1918	6687	Bulotti	Vergilio, etc.	d
Oct.	18	1913	5623	Bulsing	Agnes	m
Sept.	18	1913	5623	Bulsing	Edward	m
Oct.	18	1913	5623	Bulsing	Fred	m
June	17	1955	23245	Bumbaugh	Lydia M.	d
Aug.	9	1949	19203	Bumpus	Joe	inc
Jan.	24	1947	17595	Bunce	Burnett L., etc.	d
June	23	1950	19770	Bunce	Howard G., etc.	d
Feb.	24	1947	17596	Bunce	Mary A.	d
Apr.	23	1956	23886	Bunch	George Roy	d
Jan.	4	1946	16911	Bunday	William K.	d
June	1	1936	12655	Bundesen	Anna M. M.	d
Aug.	14	1919	7168	Bundesen	Charles	d
		1925	9132	Bundesen	German T.	inc
Nov.	4	1955	23574	Bundesen	Herman	d
Jan.	18	1947	17579	Bundesen	Karl	d

Month	Day	Year	File No.	Surname	Given Name	Type
Oct.	21	1945	16729	Bundesen	Katherine C.	d
		1925	9107	Bundesen	Martin, etc.	d
June	1	1949	19108	Bundesen	Sylvia E., etc.	d
Feb.	15	1956	23792	Bundesen	William	d
Oct.	19	1956	24285	Bundesin	Christian, etc.	d
June	17	1957	24742	Bundisen	Martin, etc.	d
Feb.	10	1934	11821	Bundschu	Philip S.	m
Sept.	19	1947	18010	Bundschu	Sadie Towle, etc.	d
Dec.	29	1933	11800	Bundschu	Towle	m
July	28	1938	13365	Bundschu	Walter Barbour, etc.	d
June	12	1930	10599	Buner	August	d
Jan.	17	1936	12834	Bungton	Charles J.	d
		1907	4383	Bunn	Frances E.	d
Feb.	20	1951	20223	Bunt	Nancy L. et al	d
Dec.	4	1929	10454	Bunyan	Agnes B.	d
Jan.	28	1943	15738	Bunyan	Hume, etc.	d
June	29	1925	8971	Bunz	Charles	d
Nov.	24	1941	14687	Buonaguidi	Guiseppe	jt
Mar.	29	1940	13945	Buoncristiani	Attilio	d
June	28	1936	12841	Buosncrestiam	Maris	m
June	19	1948	18394	Buratti	Enrico	d
June	22	1943	15485	Buratti	Mamie B., etc.	d
		1873	616	Burbank	Caleb	ins
Aug.	5	1918	6801	Burbank	David B., etc.	d
Sept.	30	1934	12036	Burbank	E. A.	ins
May	15	1926	9254	Burbank	Luther	d
Sept.	26	1950	19892	Burcar	John S.	d
Nov.		1904	3859	Burch	George W.	d
Apr.	14	1928	9935	Burch	Lulu	d
		1902	3418	Burchard	John L.	d
		1901	3346	Burchard	Louisa Ann	d
Oct.	22	1950	19534	Burchard	M. Mildred, etc.	d
Apr.	2	1948	18316	Burcher	Carol Lynn	m
Apr.	22	1949	19029	Burcker	May	d
Jan.	22	1958	25317	Burdell	Irma A.	d
Aug.	13	1950	19815	Burdell	James B., Jr., etc.	d
		1902	3488	Burdell	James Black, Jr.	m
		1898	2899	Burdell	Sila	d
Sept.	21	1930	10713	Burdick	Chester William	m
Sept.	21	1930	10713	Burdick	Orville Sidney	m
July	5	1925	8975	Burdick	Winnifred E.	inc
June	21	1948	18399	Bureker	Leo	d

Month	Day	Year	File No.	Surname	Given Name	Type
Jan.	5	1941	14733	Burg	Betty	d
		1893	2358	Burg	Ferdinand	inc
May	4	1932	11268	Burganne	Roy Stewart	d
Jan.	30	1955	23685	Burgans	Charles M.	d
Oct.	20	1934	12056	Burgard	Charles F.	d
		1865	298	Burger	Abraham	d
Oct.	28	1958	26041	Burger	Albert	d
		1902	3412	Burger	Calvin H.	d
Oct.	3	1927	9731	Burger	Christian F.	m
		1902	3408	Burger	Elmer Ross	m
Sept.	12	1927	9698	Burger	Fillmore	d
Nov.	3	1927	9731	Burger	Hattie	m
Oct.	3	1927	9731	Burger	Henrietta	m
Nov.	3	1927	9731	Burger	Henry	m
		1902	3408	Burger	Lillian	m
Sept.	4	1913	5615	Burgess	Caroline M.	d
Aug.	21	1945	16659	Burgess	David J.	d
May	4	1938	13264	Burgess	Fannie Alberta	d
Mar.	18	1940	13963	Burgess	George W.	d
		[1922-1923]	8253	Burgess	James F.	d
		[1908-1911]	4577	Burgess	Mary Jane	d
Jan.	6	1948	18159	Burgess	Maud E.	d
		1877	858	Burgess	S. G.	d
		[1919-1920]	7185	Burgess	S. G.	d
July	6	1934	11988	Burghard	Mary F.	d
Aug.	15	1940	14148	Burghart	Gustas F., etc.	d
Mar.	27	1950	19535	Burgtorf	Emma C.	d
Mar.	26	1929	10260	Burk	A. J.	d
		1870	459	Burk	Margaret	m
Sept.	5	1924	8744	Burkbart	Joseph	d
		1917	6609	Burke	Andrew J., etc	d
Apr.	24	1953	21803	Burke	Arthur E.	d
		1882	1245	Burke	Ellen	d
Dec.	9	1935	12486	Burke	Helen	d
Mar.	15	1940	13961	Burke	Holmes C., etc.	d
Mar.	25	1945	16435	Burke	John	d
Nov.	25	1946	17452	Burke	John D.	d
Oct.	24	1948	18645	Burke	Marie E., etc.	d
Apr.	21	1930	10583	Burke	Marsena Ann, etc.	d
Jan.	13	1935	12492	Burke	Martha A. Shriver	d
May	20	1931	10971	Burke	Sarah Irene, etc.	d
		1889	1822	Burke	Thomas	d

Month	Day	Year	File No.	Surname	Given Name	Type
Jan.	31	1917	6634	Burke	Thomas	d
		[1908-1911]	4985	Burke	Thomas	inc
		[1908-1911]	4523	Burke/Burk	Kate	d
Oct.	20	1940	14190	Burkett	Annabell	d
Sept.	29	1928	10045	Burkett	Serina Augusta	d
Apr.	3	1941	14461	Burkhardt	George F.	d
Aug.	12	1954	22691	Burkhead	G. L.	d
Dec.	15	1930	10731	Burkholder	Cecil	d
Sept.	3	1957	24996	Burki	Robert C., etc.	d
Dec.	2	1907	4377	Burleson	Alice Maud	d
Aug.	12	1954	22694	Burley	Roy C.	d
Feb.	20	1936	12529	Burling	Alabama	d
		1922	8227	Burmeister	Charles Louis	g
		1922	8088	Burmeister	Henry L.	d
Apr.	8	1948	18269	Burmeister	Otto	d
Nov.	27	1942	15119	Burmenter	Ernester	d
Mar.	13	1930	10573	Burmester	August Frederick	d
Dec.	15	1958	26151	Burmester	C. F. D., etc.	d
Mar.	19	1913	5681	Burmester	Diederich	d
Aug.	4	1952	21282	Burmester	Henry D.	d
		1857	87	Burnes	William K. (insane)	d
June	17	1946	17205	Burness	David R.	d
		1898	2881	Burnett	Annie D.	d
Oct.	14	1958	25998	Burnett	Leslie W.	d
		1886	1589	Burnett	Matt	d
June	18	1934	11955	Burnett	R. O., etc.	d
Oct.	29	1957	25110	Burnett	Stella W., etc.	d
		1870	438	Burnett	William	d
Mar.		1914	5733	Burnett	William	d
July	6	1944	16065	Burnetti	G.	d
		[1908-1911]	4742	Burney	Emily	d
Mar.	8	1927	9556	Burnham	A. E.	d
June	13	1933	11637	Burnham	Cerdenia E., etc.	d
		1896	2673	Burnham	John C.	d
Dec.		1926	9472	Burnham	Kirmess Franklin	m
Jan.		1926	9472	Burnham	Stewart Charles	m
Apr.	16	1957	24671	Burnley	Betty	d
Apr.	10	1953	21689	Burns	Allison Rudolph	m
May	17	1943	15434	Burns	Annie, etc.	d
		1889	1891	Burns	Elizabeth	d
		1906	4247	Burns	Elizabeth Frances	m
		1900	3312	Burns	Eugene F.	d

Month	Day	Year	File No.	Surname	Given Name	Type
Oct.	16	1941	14641	Burns	George	d
		1894	2460	Burns	J. A., Dr.	d
		1886	1599	Burns	James	d
		1900	3325	Burns	James	d
		1876	843½	Burns	James W.	m
Nov.	15	1939	13842	Burns	Jennie V.	d
Oct.	13	1950	19979	Burns	John Francis, etc.	d
		1902	3441	Burns	Joseph	m
		[1919-1920]	7291	Burns	Louis A.	d
		1907	4247	Burns	Mary Gertrude	m
		1906	4042	Burns	Owen	d
Mar.	11	1918	6683	Burns	Peter	d
Oct.	1	1913	5631	Burns	Peter, Jr.	inc
Feb.	20	1917	6422	Burns	Robert W.	inc
Feb.		1917	6431	Burns	Robert W.	d
Mar.	15	1928	9911	Burns	Thomas	d
		[1908-1911]	5004	Burns	Thomas H.	d
Apr.	30	1929	10267	Burns	Thomas R.	d
Apr.	10	1953	21689	Burns	Thomas Thanuel	m
May	2	1941	14502	Burns	William P.	d
Nov.	21	1955	23604	Burr	Carolyn Fairbanks	m
Nov.	21	1955	23604	Burr	Diane Marion	m
June		1922	8079	Burr	Isabel D.	d
May	3	1947	17777	Burrell	Agnes	d
Feb.	30	1941	14368	Burrell	Delbert	m
June	12	1946	17247	Burrell	Delbert Franklin	d
		1889	1869	Burright	Warren	d
Feb.	3	1939	13557	Burright	Warren	d
Feb.	8	1937	12883	Burris	Blanche E.	d
		1903	3730	Burris	David	d
Nov.	3	1931	11124	Burris	Jesse	d
Apr.	24	1943	15327	Burris	John	d
Feb.	9	1921	7674	Burris	Julia Ann	d
Feb.	8	1937	12884	Burris	Laura M.	d
June	9	1958	25681	Burris	Lillian Fisk, etc.	d
		1888	1768	Burris	William	d
		1854	28	Burris	William (no papers)	m
Aug.	17	1954	22646	Burris	Frank M., etc.	d
Nov.	22	1925	9094	Burrough	Alfred	d
Jan.	21	1914	5919	Burrough	James	d
May	16	1958	25633	Burrough	Mary G.	d
Aug.	25	1944	16097	Burrough	Robert S.	d

Month	Day	Year	File No.	Surname	Given Name	Type
July	1	1937	13065	Burrough	Thomas M.	d
Mar.	8	1955	23105	Burroughs	Charles	d
June	5	1916	6255	Burroughs	Eva W.	d
Jan.	17	1947	17576	Burrows	Mabel	ei
Mar.	11	1958	25453	Burrows	Mabel	d
July-Nov.		1914	5814	Burrows	R. R.	d
Jan.	16	1932	11476	Burrows	Robert W., etc.	d
		1900	3219	Burrus	George W.	d
		1870	461	Burrus	J. A.	m
		1870	461	Burrus	M. C.	m
Jan.	19	1951	20162	Burry	John F.	d
Oct.	24	1958	26031	Bursio	Peter	d
Apr.	24	1941	14490	Burson	Charles Franklin	d
		[1908-1911]	4948	Burt	Lewis S.	d
Apr.	31	1927	9583	Burt	Taylor E.	d
Feb.	28	1955	23010	Burtch	Charles	d
		1898	2828	Burtch	Priscilla	d
July	13	1951	20486	Burtner	Jesse Herman	d
Aug.	11	1944	16120	Burtoli	Jacqueline Rose	m
		1886	1573	Burton	Caroline	d
July	15	1948	18518	Burton	George	d
Dec.	30	1955	23617	Burton	Lena Pearl	d
July	15	1948	18517	Burton	Martha Jane	d
		1882	1206	Burton	Noah	d
July	22	1938	13357	Burton	Theodore G. J.	ins
Feb.	17	1946	17649	Busaman	Herman, etc.	d
		1887	1685	Busch	Daniel (adoption)	m
		1887	1685	Busch	Emma (adoption)	m
Aug.		1919	7139	Busch	Julia Agnes	d
Jan.	31	1952	21547	Busch	Adolph	d
June	28	1945	16589	Bush	Alvira P.	d
Mar.	8	1926	9194	Bush	Eli	d
Nov.	26	1948	18700	Bush	Helen T.	d
Aug.	20	1951	20550	Bush	John K.	d
Mar.	14	1949	18948	Bush	Margaret	d
June		1922	8073	Bush	Mary A. P.	d
Sept.	4	1932	11354	Bush	William H.	d
		1895	2515	Bush	William P.	d
		1902	3529	Bushnell	Amasa	d
Feb.	27	1956	23758	Bushnell	Emma H., etc.	d
Mar.	21	1957	24547	Bushnell	Will B., etc.	d
June	23	1944	16050	Busman	Jennie	d

Month	Day	Year	File No.	Surname	Given Name	Type
Feb.	25	1928	9855	Buson	Emma Burbank	d
Aug.	25	1950	19891	Buss	Janet Lynn	m
Sept.	25	1950	19891	Buss	Josephine Ann	m
July	22	1926	9322	Busse	Wm,. etc.	d
Oct.	15	1958	26000	Busselle	John	m
Oct.	15	1958	25999	Busselle	Susan	m
Apr.	2	1957	24636	Bussey	Lewis M., etc.	d
June	27	1958	25738	Bussiere	Joseph J.	d
June	2	1931	10987	Bussing	Alice	inc
Apr.	18	1935	12231	Bussing	J. O.	d
Oct.	28	1953	22084	Bussman	Eva Dale, etc.	d
Dec.	2	1935	12478	Bussman	Mildred	d
Feb.	1	1951	20191	Bussman	Peter W., etc.	d
Apr.	15	1927	9561	Bustard	Emma M.	d
June	27	1926	9290	Bustard	Thomas E., etc.	d
July	1	1944	16063	Butcher	Alice Lorraine	d
		1900	3147	Butcher	Charles W.	m
Dec.	28	1945	16841	Butcher	Frank H.	d
Feb.	3	1949	18882	Butcher	Inez M., etc.	d
		1898	2874	Butcher	Isabel	d
Nov.	22	1946	17492	Butcher	M., etc.	d
Jan.	9	1912	5448	Butcher	Marilla	inc
June	13	1916	6258	Butcher	Marilla	d
		[1908-1911]	5115	Butcher	Marilla	inc
		1900	3318	Butcher	Squire	d
		[1908-1911]	4529	Butcher	William	d
Sept.	5	1927	9691	Butellatti	Luigi	d
Sept.	12	1947	17943	Buten	Horace James, etc.	d
Oct.	28	1956	24239	Buten	Nellie	d
Apr.	22	1941	14488	Buterns	George	d
Apr.	28	1932	11262	Butin	Ella	d
May	10	1957	24729	Butin	J. Roy	d
		1897	2703	Butin	James M.	d
July	29	1954	22620	Butin	Nellie	inc
June	15	1946	17255	Butini	Arnolfo, etc.	d
		1928	9984	Butler	Bernard	m
May	28	1928	9984	Butler	Burnett	m
June	27	1944	16003	Butler	Edith A.	d
Feb.	22	1953	21598	Butler	Frank	d
Aug.	26	1951	20508	Butler	Georgiana	inc
		1876	801	Butler	James	d
Aug.	1	1944	16111	Butler	James Edwin, etc.	d

Month	Day	Year	File No.	Surname	Given Name	Type
		1895	2540	Butler	James H.	d
Mar.	18	1955	23120	Butler	Kate E., etc.	d
May	24	1945	16544	Butler	Margaret	d
		[1908-1911]	4525	Butler	Mary	d
June	28	1928	9984	Butler	Nanne	m
Apr.	20	1918	6698	Butler	Neal W.	d
Mar.	14	1929	10237	Butler	Oresmus G.	d
		[1908-1911]	4982	Butler	Peter	d
		1904	3832	Butler	Philip	d
Mar.	14	1952	20980	Butler	Rose E.	d
		1905	3937	Butler	Thomas B.	d
Feb.	28	1957	24490	Butler	William	d
		1897	2813	Butler	William M.	d
		1928	10106	Butola	Camilla Angela	d
		1928	10105	Butola	David, John, etc.	d
Apr.	10	1953	21759	Butterfield	Elmer P.	d
Jan.	3	1928	10137	Butterfield	Frank	d
Dec.	15	1948	18781	Butterman	Fred R.	d
		1854	31	Butters	Thomas	d
June	24	1957	24756	Buttitta	Enes, etc.	d
		1921	7886	Buttner	Annie Lorna	m
Sept.	1	1921	7837	Buttner	Ernestine Pauline	d
		1921	7905	Buttner	Joseph	d
		1921	7887	Buttner	Joseph Ernest	m
Dec.		1921	7887	Buttner	Percy August	m
Dec.	29	1948	18758	Button	Horace H., etc.	d
		1880	1099	Button	Joseph	d
		1901	3358	Button	Melissa Betsy	d
Feb.	1	1924	8559	Button	Samuel E., etc.	d
Apr.	9	1951	20267	Buttrum	Bertha, etc.	d
		1903	3764	Butts	Bell O.	d
June	16	1933	11642	Butts	Darrell	m
Jan.	30	1955	23690	Butts	Helen M.	inc
June	24	1943	15448	Butts	John William	d
June	16	1933	11642	Butts	Lorraine	m
July	12	1917	6528	Butts	Margaret C.	d
		1903	3651	Butts	Nell	m
Oct.	2	1953	22091	Butts	Rena E.	d
Nov.	28	1916	6272	Butts	Thomas J.	d
June	12	1958	25695	Butts	Thomas Virgil, etc.	d
Aug.	26	1931	11019	Butts	Warren	d
		1898	2861	Buxton	Sarah Jewell	d

Month	Day	Year	File No.	Surname	Given Name	Type
Apr.	25	1915	5971	Buybee	Percy G.	m
Aug.	4	1944	16115	Buzalich	Glenn	m
Aug.	4	1944	16115	Buzalich	Verna	m
		[1919-1920]	7317	Buzzetti	Emiel	m
		[1918-1919]	7081	Buzzetti	Peter Theodore	d
Nov.	31	1949	19338	Buzzine	Albert, etc.	d
Sept.	28	1913	5608	Buzzini	Joseph	ins
Apr.	3	1934	11910	Bybee	Joel T.	d
Oct.	4	1921	7860	Byce	Emma	d
Apr.	23	1934	11899	Byce	Lily Caroline	d
		1921	7760	Byce	Malcolm L.	d
Mar.	25	1955	23134	Byce	Wilbur Elwood, etc.	d
		1865	292	Byers	James	d
Jan.	13	1932	11475	Byington	Horace Daliner, Jr.	m
		1907	4277	Byington	Horace W.	d
Oct.	7	1952	21387	Byman	Anna E.	d
May	20	1946	17177	Byman	Harvey	d
May	13	1957	24732	Byrd	Arthur H.	d
		1850	10	Byrd	John	d
Nov.	21	1945	16824	Byrn	Dora K.	d
		1893	2295	Byrn	George M.	m
Sept.	19	1943	15569	Byrn	George M.	d
Jan.	20	1944	16338	Byrne	Edward F.	d
		1883	1309	Byrne	James	d
Oct.	28	1942	15093	Byrne	Patrick	d
July	9	1942	15007	Byron	Chester A.	d
		[1918-1919]	6903	Byron	James Hugh	d
Nov.	5	1956	24314	Byron	Mabel Ella	d
Aug.	18	1942	15012	Byron	Margaret A.	m

Month	Day	Year	File No.	Surname	Given Name	Type
Apr.	28	1931	10894	Cabanat	Elodie	d
Jan.	30	1933	11729	Cabanot	Bernard	d
		1905	4013	Cabaup	Marianna	d
Feb.	8	1924	8568	Cabral	John	d
July	26	1950	19775	Cabrol	Marie	d
Mar.	19	1954	22354	Cabrol	Sylvain	d
Mar.	27	1924	8584	Cacci	Angelo	g
Mar.	27	1924	8584	Cacci	Nello	g
Apr.	18	1927	9566	Caccia	Joseph P.	d
		1924	8651	Caccia	Paola	d
Mar.	8	1929	10207	Cacho	Casmo	d
Nov.	25	1951	20694	Cadan	George R.	inc
Oct.	9	1953	22106	Cadan	George R.	d
Nov.	13	1951	20734	Cadan	Lulu M. L.	inc
Dec.	1	1958	26117	Cadd	A. R.	d
Dec.	12	1934	12124	Caddick	Martha	d
June	20	1948	18420	Cademartan	Harold	d
June	21	1937	13038	Cademartori	James	d
Sept.	3	1937	13116	Cader	David W.	d
		1926	9208	Cader	Israel Charles	d
July	27	1952	21224	Cadorin	Ettore	d
Feb.	22	1941	14358	Cadra	Lucia, etc.	inc
Nov.	25	1942	15164	Cadra	Lucia, etc.	d
Sept.	30	1952	21311	Cadsul	Victor	d
Jan.	31	1943	15743	Cadwalader	Mary	d
		[1908-1909]	4405	Cadwell	A.	d
May	16	1924	8636	Cadwell	Adeline E.	d
June	1	1916	6242	Cadwell	Harriet M.	d
Jan.	10	1933	11497	Cady	Emma E., etc.	d
May	12	1944	15987	Caelho	Constantino M., etc.	d
Sept.	30	1950	19900	Caffaney	Edward J.	d
May	3	1934	11911	Caffese	Giambatista, etc.	d
		1903	3622	Cagwin	C. N.	d
May	8	1929	10274	Cahill	Evaline T., etc.	d
Aug.	12	1954	22692	Cahill	Jessie C., etc.	d
Sept.	19	1951	20615	Cahill	Sumner E., etc.	d
		1897	2869	Cain	James A.	d
Jan.	17	1937	13193	Cain	Joseph P.	d
		1926	9278	Cain	Millie Matilda, etc.	d
Nov.	30	1953	22156	Cain	Ralph T.	d
Apr.	14	1927	9601	Cain	Raymond	m
Dec.	22	1931	11115	Cain	Robert	d

Month	Day	Year	File No.		Surname	Given Name	Type
Sept.	22	1947	18012		Caine	Priscilla Patricia	d
		1922	8178		Cairns	Aubrey	inc
July	5	1929	10331		Cake	E. D.	d
		1893	2375		Calanchini	Achille	d
Mar.	3	1921	7668		Calanchini	Elvezio	d
Mar.	20	1948	18249		Calaway	Stephen J.	d
		1888	1801		Calder	Alexander	d
		1891	2088		Calderwood	Belle Neil	d
Mar.		1925	8893		Calderwood	Henry Edward, etc.	d
		1917	6497		Calderwood	Sophia	d
Aug.	25	1955	23385		Caldwell	Clara Lydia, etc.	d
		1922	7948		Caldwell	Elizabeth	d
		1887	1694 1/2		Caldwell	F. M.	d
Apr.	26	1928	9954		Caldwell	Francis W.	g
Oct.	9	1944	16202		Caldwell	Francis Wendell	d
Oct.	19	1945	16203		Caldwell	Francis Wendell	d
Sept.	1	1953	22040		Caldwell	Genevieve I.	d
		1864	250		Caldwell	John G.	m
July	5	1952	21239		Caldwell	John W., etc.	d
	2	1922	8029		Caldwell	Joseph H.	d
May	14	1944	15929		Caldwell	Kathleen June	m
		1889	1875		Caldwell	L. A. (alias Addie L.)	d
Dec.	17	1944	16272		Caldwell	Margaret, etc.	d
May	25	1944	15946		Caldwell	Mary D.	d
Sept.	25	1955	23385		Caldwell	R. A., Mrs., etc.	d
		1918	6852		Caldwell	Richard O.	m
May	26	1928	9954		Caldwell	Robert L.	g
		1864	250		Caldwell	Samel T.	m
Jan.		1918	6908		Caldwell	Samuel T.	d
		[1917-1918]	6630		Caldwell	Samuel T.	inc
Oct.	16	1915	6094		Caldwell	William	d
		1887	1679		Caldwell	Joseph Robert	d
Sept.	30	1954	22720		Calegari	Joseph A.	d
Sept.	30	1954	22719		Calegari	Maria	d
Aug.	16	1954	22642		Calfas	Augustine J.	d
June	26	1952	21221		Calfas	James	d
Feb.	15	1944	15840		Calguhoun	Robert	d
Mar.	11	1914	5737		Calhoun	John Edgar	d
Oct.	3	1939	13798		Calhoun	Mary Margaret	m
Oct.	3	1939	13798		Calhoun	Sara Lee	m
Feb.	27	1923	8259		Calhoun	Sarah	d
Jan.	9	1939	13527		Calhoun	William Harold	d

Month	Day	Year	File No.		Surname	Given Name	Type
Oct.	3	1939	13798		Calhoun	William Harold, Jr.	m
May	8	1953	21827		Caligeros	Gus	d
July	3	1958	25755		Caligeros	Jennie, etc.	d
Oct.	30	1952	21393		Calipolis	Peter J.	d
July	16	1956	24100		Calkins	Edith B., etc.	d
Jan.	20	1955	23670		Calkins	Leonard J., etc.	d
Mar.	9	1956	23847		Call	George Carlos, etc.	d
		1907	4260		Call	George W.	d
Apr.	20	1933	11566		Call	Kathryn S.	d
Feb.	17	1934	11829		Call	Mercedes L.	d
Jan.	22	1945	16374		Callahan	Agnes B., etc.	d
Dec.	3	1941	14695		Callahan	Charles, etc.	d
Sept.	8	1933	11660		Callahan	Lamenoc	d
		1917	6415		Callahan	Minnie A.	d
May	20	1951	20348		Callan	Charles W.	d
Dec.	14	1955	23586		Callan	Winona	d
Oct.	27	1948	18646		Callari	Rosa, etc.	d
		1901	3370		Callaway	David	d
		1901	3387		Callaway	David	d
Aug.	9	1921	7809		Callaway	David	d
		1924	8752		Calletti	Alfredo, etc.	d
Nov.	1	1940	14256		Calli	Domenico	d
Dec.	14	1949	19368		Callori	Antonio Geovanni, etc	d
Feb.	18	1932	11231		Callsen	Nes	d
June	9	1936	12670		Calson	Hjalmar	d
Mar.	13	1957	24590		Calson	Josephine	d
Sept.	18	1947	18002		Calson	Violet M.	d
		1907	4322		Caltron	William C.	d
Dec.	4	1951	20786		Calvert	Nancy	m
Jan.	12	1929	10482		Calvi	Dante	m
Nov.	25	1929	10473		Calvi	Luigi	d
May		1919	7066		Cama	Angeline	m
Apr.		1919	7066		Cama	John	m
Apr.		1919	7066		Cama	Josephine	m
Jan.	7	1952	20836		Camara	Edith Grace	d
		1911	5146		Camarda	Giovanni	d
Apr.	18	1941	14440		Camarri	Salvatore, etc.	d
June	2	1931	10983		Camatta	Annie Claire	d
Aug.	20	1957	24968		Cameron	Donald Marsh, etc.	d
Feb.	19	1942	14780		Cameron	Edwin J., etc.	d
		1904	3739		Cameron	Gordon	d
Oct.	23	1952	21414		Cameron	Harriet L., etc.	d

Month	Day	Year	File No.		Surname	Given Name	Type
Feb.	10	1939	13569		Cameron	Helen R.	d
		1878	957		Cameron	Mary E.	m
		1894	2395		Cameron	Russell L.	m
		1904	3738		Cameron	Sarah Jane	d
		1854	34		Cameron	Thos. P.	d
		1878	957		Cameron	I. P.	m
Feb.	13	1957	24533		Camfield	Albert Henry	inc
Oct.	23	1957	25032		Camfield	Albert Henry	d
Oct.	4	1956	24194		Camirand	Albert Joseph	d
Mar.	9	1942	14849		Camm	Catherine V.	inc
June	11	1942	14937		Camm	Catherine V.	d
Feb.	26	1945	16380		Camm	Pearle G.	d
June	19	1957	24816		Camotta	Joseph J.	d
July	27	1932	11322		Camozzi	Charles	m
Feb.	21	1955	22993		Camozzi	Charles V., etc.	d
		1955	22993		Camozzi	Chas., etc.	d
Aug.	31	1931	11041		Camozzi	Giuditta	d
		1930	10593		Camozzi	Pietro	d
Oct.	24	1952	21420		Camozzi	Tony	d
Apr.	17	1953	21699		Camp	Charles	d
Sept.	14	1953	22003		Camp	Claire J.	d
Jan.	23	1943	15729		Camp	Clarence M.	d
		1897	2852		Campa	Giovanni	d
June	25	1956	24014		Campagno	Anthon J.	d
Jan.	28	1956	24422		Campan	Eugenie Vida	d
		[1908-1909]	4410		Campan	Louise H.	d
Dec.	12	1952	21513		Campana	Joe	d
Nov.	21	1928	10072		Campana	Rosalia, etc.	d
Dec.	5	1955	23630		Campbell	Alice J.	d
Apr.	24	1955	23131		Campbell	Anna C.	d
Dec.	1	1949	19396		Campbell	Arthur Lockhart, etc.	d
Sept.		1923	8435		Campbell	Charles	d
Dec.	23	1936	12814		Campbell	Daisy	d
		1922	8033		Campbell	Daniel G.	d
Sept.	23	1940	14189		Campbell	Donald, etc.	d
Sept.	25	1913	5604		Campbell	Doris Bowth	m
		1901	3324		Campbell	Eliza A.	d
June	18	1946	17260		Campbell	Florence G.	d
Apr.	27	1940	14013		Campbell	Francis Alexander, etc	d
		1889	1881		Campbell	George	d
		1921	7734		Campbell	George	d
Mar.	7	1933	11534		Campbell	George R.	d

Month	Day	Year	File No.	Surname	Given Name	Type
		1867	358	Campbell	George S.	m
		1865	281	Campbell	Harry (Hugh Gamble)	ins
Jan.	9	1948	18164	Campbell	J. Otto	d
June	30	1940	14016	Campbell	James A.	d
Oct.	10	1951	20660	Campbell	John R., etc.	d
May	12	1935	12267	Campbell	John Tyler	d
		1898	2918	Campbell	Joseph	d
		1887	1674	Campbell	Joseph H.	d
Feb.	18	1955	23065	Campbell	Leverett	d
		1905	3990	Campbell	Lucy M.	d
		[1909-1911]	4733	Campbell	Margaret Jane	d
Nov.		1915	6096	Campbell	Martha E.	d
June	31	1947	17819	Campbell	Mary E.	d
Sept.		1920	7517	Campbell	Mary J.	d
Dec.		1926	9413	Campbell	Mary J.	d
May	21	1926	9260	Campbell	Nicholas B.	d
		1863	237	Campbell	Peter	d
Dec.	15	1946	17480	Campbell	Rita Julia	d
Sept.	4	1953	22051	Campbell	Robert A., etc.	d
Mar.	21	1931	10887	Campbell	Ross	d
		1921	7694	Campbell	Sarah E.	d
May	26	1955	23199	Campbell	Vernon O.	d
Apr.	7	1924	8629	Campbell	W. A.	d
Jan.	21	1915	5945	Campbell	W. P.	d
May	10	1957	24727	Campi	Lorenzo	d
May	11	1938	13287	Campi	Lorenzo, etc.	d
Dec.	25	1942	15165	Campiani	Peter	d
Sept.	10	1937	13121	Campigli	A. E.	d
Feb.	9	1931	10831	Campigli	Charles	d
		1911	5142	Campini	Emil	d
July	31	1921	7773	Campini	Theresa/Teresa	d
		1919	7111	Campion	Thomas	d
		1878	951	Camron	J. M.	d
Dec.	30	1945	16849	Canabbis	F., etc.	d
Mar.	26	1946	17028	Canafox	David J.	m
Apr.	2	1919	7046	Canapa	David	d
		1918	6837	Canapa	David	inc
Oct.	11	1918	6829	Canapa	Silvio	d
Apr.	7	1919	7053	Canavan	Thomas	d
July	16	1953	21950	Canby	Alexandra	d
Oct.	20	1955	23494	Canby	Lillian S.	d
July	16	1953	21949	Canby	Voldemar	d

Month	Day	Year	File No.		Surname	Given Name	Type
		1921	7763		Canciamilla	Salvatore	d
Apr.	13	1925	8906		Canefa	Ben etc	d
Feb.	16	1956	23797		Canel	John, etc.	d
Feb.		1917	6426		Canepa	Angela	d
Jan.	9	1922	7919		Canepa	Ben	inc
May	6	1958	25600		Canepa	Giuseppe	d
		1890	1963		Canepa	John	d
Feb.		1926	9207		Canepa	Rosina	m
Feb.	26	1931	10848		Caners	George Washington, e	d
Dec.	14	1955	23587		Canessa	Darley	d
May	26	1937	12971		Canessa	Domenico	d
		1919	7093		Canessa	Gianbatista, etc.	d
Dec.	10	1928	10142		Canessa	Richard	d
Feb.	28	1941	14366		Canevari	Francesca	d
Mar.	24	1950	19532		Canevari	Francesco	d
Apr.	18	1935	12232		Canevari	John	d
Jan.	9	1932	11471		Canevascini	L. J., etc.	d
May	18	1937	13002		Canevascini	Margaret	d
Dec.	1	1937	13179		Canevascini	Samuel L.	d
Sept.	18	1924	8736		Canevasini	Samuel J. et al	d
		[1909-1911]	4938		Canfield	Matilda	d
May		1922	8021		Canfield	Rosa	d
		1893	2306		Canfield	William D.	d
Dec.	15	1952	21516		Canha	John Gonsalves	d
Jan.	16	1933	11506		Canier	Orlando S., etc.	d
Dec.	8	1949	19405		Caniff	Robert Townsend	inc
June	5	1948	18429		Canning	Edwin E.	d
June	5	1948	18439		Canning	Edwin E.	d
June	12	1935	12356		Canning	Mary	d
Apr.	10	1957	24657		Cannon	Earl	inc
		1903	3585		Cannon	Ida J.	d
Nov.	5	1927	9762		Cannon	J. H.	d
Mar.	20	1929	10251		Cannon	Jerome B., etc.	d
Dec.	24	1920	7589		Cannon	John P.	d
		1929	10375		Cannon	Joseph Layfutte, etc.	d
June	3	1940	14056		Cannon	L. L., etc.	d
Nov.	8	1940	14268		Cannon	Louis	d
		1876	836		Cannon	Mary A.	d
July	3	1958	25754		Cannon	Meada Alice, etc.	d
June	20	1952	21211		Cannon	Nettie U.	inc
Apr.	8	1955	23166		Cannon	Nettie U.	d
		1884	1386		Cannon	Zora Eleanor (adoptio	m

Month	Day	Year	File No.		Surname	Given Name	Type
Jan.	24	1953	22254		Canobbio	Lena	d
Oct.	7	1955	23522		Canobbio	Serfino	d
June	4	1934	11946		Canora	Peter, etc.	d
Mar.	12	1948	18280		Canova	Clotilde, etc.	d
Mar.	15	1957	24538		Canovi	Federico	d
		1912	5320		Canstner	Henry	d
May	8	1950	19676		Canta	Clemente, etc.	d
Aug.	29	1948	18545		Cantaloube	Francisco	d
Feb.	27	1950	19483		Cantaloube	Hortense	d
		[1917-1918]	6664		Cantel	Eugene	d
Oct.	25	1932	11369		Cantel	Mary Isabel	inc
Oct.	3	1932	11401		Cantel	Mary Isabel	d
		1912	5290		Cantillon	Richard	d
Jan.	8	1915	6152		Cantor	Gussie	d
Sept.	7	1954	22737		Cantrall	Gertrude May, etc.	d
		1878	963		Cantrell	C. H.	d
		1877	893		Cantrell	R. J.	d
Nov.	27	1949	19334		Cantu	Clemente, etc.	d
Nov.	19	1957	25154		Cantwell	Amanda, etc.	d
June	9	1953	21886		Canty	Martin J., etc.	d
June	19	1931	11007		Capanacci	Ida	d
Feb.	10	1953	21637		Capbarat/Capbaret	Marie Lassalle	d
Nov.	11	1946	17435		Capbaret	Marie Lassalle, etc.	inc
Oct.	24	1929	10416		Capek	Anna	d
		1900	3221		Capel	Susan F.	d
Nov.	2	1956	24247		Capell	Ray C.	d
July	6	1932	11328		Capella	James C.	d
		1906	4098		Capezzoli	Carlo	d
Jan.	11	1957	24445		Caponotti	Giuseppe	d
June	18	1957	24814		Cappelli	Onorato, etc.	d
Jan.	15	1941	14741		Cappoletti	Giovanni	d
Apr.	10	1944	15918		Capponi	Marco, etc.	d
July	17	1949	19133		Capri	Maria	d
Jan.		1923	8257		Capri	Rosie	inc
Feb.	5	1923	8299		Capucetti	Frank	d
Aug.	4	1950	19852		Capucetti	Frank C.	d
June	19	1942	14987		Capucetti	L. Antonio, etc.	d
Mar.	4	1927	9528		Caraccis	Ralph	d
		1927	9522		Caracciso	Albert & Josephine	m
Sept.	11	1942	15045		Caranzi	Peter, etc.	d
Nov.	4	1940	14229		Carara	Domenico	d
Jan.	8	1930	10803		Carasali	Carlo, etc.	d

Month	Day	Year	File No.		Surname	Given Name	Type
Oct.	10	1929	10402		Caratti	Antonio	d
		1891	2251		Carberry	Patrick	d
Jan.	27	1951	20820		Card	Florence H.	d
		1878	946		Carder	D. D.	d
June	10	1949	19126		Cardinale	Enrice	d
Mar.	28	1936	12566		Cardoza	Anna	d
May	25	1919	7067		Cardoza	Antone, etc.	d
Dec.	12	1938	13505		Cardoza	Clara Ida	inc
June	5	1933	11603		Cardoza	Jose Silveria aka Joe a	d
		1904	3875		Cardoza	Joseph S.	d
Nov.	17	1958	26078		Cardoza	William	d
Feb.	13	1951	20211		Cardwell	Ennis Scott, etc.	d
Mar.	5	1943	15299		Carelli	Frances	d
Jan.	21	1928	10152		Carelli	Pietro	d
Jan.		1922	8238		Carenini	Joseph	d
Dec.	14	1927	9775		Carenini	Maria Maddalena	d
Nov.	25	1957	25165		Carey	Cora Mary	d
Nov.	15	1935	12440		Carey	John	d
Mar.	20	1933	11545		Carey	Mattie A.	d
		[1909-1911]	4867		Carey	Catherine	inc
Sept.	4	1934	12040		Carfu	Alma M.	m
June	7	1943	15466		Cargeli	Charles W.	d
		1905	4018		Cargile	John B.	d
Apr.	19	1943	15388		Cargile	May, etc.	d
Jan.	28	1927	9519		Cari	Anselmo	d
Dec.	8	1952	21504		Cari	Berenice	d
		1901	3456		Carica	J. W.	inc
Mar.	8	1916	6191		Carico	John Hill	m
Nov.	17	1914	5881		Carico	John Nathan	d
		1901	3329		Carithers	David N.	d
July	2	1923	8375		Carithers	Mary Ellen	d
Sept.	4	1931	11046		Carithers	W. K., etc.	d
Dec.	17	1928	10150		Carkhuff	Norman W.	d
June	4	1943	15462		Carlene	Minnie Arndt	d
Nov.	12	1954	22856		Carli	Adolph, etc.	d
June	31	1949	19106		Carli	Giuditta, etc.	d
Apr.	25	1953	21722		Carli	John	d
Jan.	20	1956	23737		Carlier	Eva Florence, etc.	d
Apr.	13	1942	14895		Carline	Minnie A. Newman	inc
Jan.	25	1933	11723		Carlisle	Joseph	d
Oct.	17	1934	12052		Carliton	Henrietta C.	d
July	15	1955	23370		Carlo	Antonietti, etc.	d

Month	Day	Year	File No.	Surname	Given Name	Type
Dec.	25	1941	14717	Carlsen	John Arendt, etc.	d
Nov.	29	1940	14291	Carlson	Anna	d
July	11	1918	6788	Carlson	Anton F.	d
Jan.	31	1931	11181	Carlson	August O.	d
Oct.	27	1939	13794	Carlson	Axel E., etc.	d
Nov.	9	1940	14269	Carlson	Bror Axel	d
Feb.	18	1931	10883	Carlson	Carl J.	d
		1909	4701	Carlson	Carl Ludwig	d
Mar.	9	1951	20266	Carlson	Carl R., etc.	d
June	12	1916	6238	Carlson	Charles	d
		1900	3174	Carlson	Charles E.	d
Sept.	24	1948	18595	Carlson	Charles Victor, etc.	d
July	6	1956	24088	Carlson	Edith May	inc
Feb.		1924	8871	Carlson	Frieda M., etc.	d
July	11	1952	21246	Carlson	Frieda, etc.	d
		[1908-1909]	4536	Carlson	George	d
July	12	1948	18509	Carlson	John A.	d
May	9	1935	12298	Carlson	John E.	d
Apr.	17	1919	6996	Carlson	John L.	d
Dec.		1914	5907	Carlson	Katherine C.	d
Jan.		1923	8491	Carlson	Louis	d
Sept.	31	1956	24189	Carlson	Louis H.	d
Jan.	12	1923	8244	Carlson	Louisa	d
Mar.	12	1945	16467	Carlson	Maria	d
Feb.	3	1950	19490	Carlson	Nellie O.	d
Jan.	4	1926	9159	Carlson	Olga	d
		1919	7151	Carlson	Virgil	m
July	12	1957	24870	Carmack	Captolia	d
Dec.	18	1952	21522	Carmagnola	Theresa, etc.	d
July	14	1953	21941	Carmarino	Giuseppe	d
Jan.	17	1926	9469	Carmassi	Luigi	d
Oct.	23	1948	18691	Carmel	Raymond Dean	m
		1899	3008	Carmer	Frank F.	d
		1926	9469	Carmessi	Luigi	d
		1884	1842	Carmichael	Archibald	d
		1899	3002	Carmichael	Colen	d
Dec.	12	1950	20102	Carmichael	Della May, etc.	d
Nov.	19	1953	22182	Carmichael	George T.	d
Nov.	11	1937	13141	Carmichael	Grant	d
		1901	3254	Carmichael	Henry E.	d
		1903	3684	Carmichael	Leona	m
Mar.	19	1946	17082	Carmickle	Juanita Elizabeth	d

Month	Day	Year	File No.		Surname	Given Name	Type
July	16	1943	15514		Carmody	Fred L., etc.	d
May	18	1938	13322		Carmody	Isabel, etc.	d
Feb.	14	1944	15838		Carmody	James H.	d
May	24	1938	13330		Carmotta	Gloria	m
May	24	1938	13330		Carmotta	James	m
May	24	1938	13330		Carmotta	Joseph	m
May	24	1938	13330		Carmotta	Marie	m
Aug.	6	1956	24145		Carnahan	Dorothy, etc.	d
Aug.	6	1956	24145		Carnahan	Myrtle E., etc.	d
June	16	1958	25631		Carnazola	Giuseppe	d
Apr.	10	1930	10571		Carnegie	David	d
Nov.	15	1945	16810		Carnegie	Elizabeth	d
Nov.	13	1953	22175		Carney	Dennis	d
		1901	3417		Carney	Hugh	d
Sept.	31	1945	16704		Carney	John J.	d
Apr.	17	1934	11894		Carney	John M.	d
		1875	758		Carney	Thomas	d
Nov.	11	1956	24267		Carolan	Catherine	d
Oct.	27	1940	14193		Carothers	Jimmie, etc.	m
Sept.	4	1953	22045		Carouso	Victor H.	d
May	6	1946	17191		Carp	Tom	d
July	12	1957	24876		Carp	Tom	d
Mar.	1	1938	13258		Carpella	Virginia	d
Apr.	24	1914	5754		Carpenter	Abbie M.	d
		1897	2728		Carpenter	Alice M.	d
Aug.	12	1929	10337		Carpenter	Chriss	d
Oct.	15	1945	16763		Carpenter	Edith Gwen	d
Nov.	7	1958	26064		Carpenter	Flora M.	d
Oct.	3	1958	25980		Carpenter	Flora May	d
		[1908-1909]	4639		Carpenter	Harold Francis	m
Dec.	30	1929	10480		Carpenter	Jay W.	d
Feb.	2	1913	5460		Carpenter	Jerome Richmond	d
May	10	1955	23227		Carpenter	Kathleen A.	d
		1888	1721		Carpenter	L. F.	d
		[1908-1909]	4639		Carpenter	LaFayette Eugene	m
		1920	7347		Carpenter	Leslie Wilbur	d
		[1908-1909]	4639		Carpenter	Leslie Wilbur	m
Apr.	22	1957	24682		Carpenter	Lulu E., etc.	d
July	10	1958	25770		Carpenter	Margaret	inc
Oct.	23	1954	22770		Carpenter	Wilbert A.	d
		[1908-1909]	4639		Carpenter	William Garrot	m
		1862	220		Carper	John	d

Month	Day	Year	File No.		Surname	Given Name	Type
		1896	2669		Carr	Alice P.	d
		1911	5164		Carr	Annie	d
Oct.	11	1954	22804		Carr	Blanche G.	d
Nov.	14	1949	19315		Carr	Charles Carl/Charles C	d
Aug.	23	1923	8416		Carr	Charles Fremont, etc.	d
Sept.	19	1951	20616		Carr	George Merton	d
Oct.	15	1958	26003		Carr	Georgia P.	d
		1896	2643		Carr	Hannah L.	d
Mar.	2	1956	23830		Carr	Joel L.	d
May	9	1950	19684		Carr	Lesslie E., etc.	d
		[1908-1909]	4636		Carr	Mark	d
		1926	9235		Carr	Thomas M., etc.	d
July	21	1940	14073		Carr	W. L., etc.	d
Feb.	14	1917	6420		Carr	William	inc
Oct.	5	1945	16769		Carr	William Call, etc.	d
Feb.	25	1949	18861		Carrall	Charles Harold, Jr., etc	d
June	15	1954	22590		Carreira	J. S.	d
Jan.	9	1956	23711		Carrey	Emely	d
		1892	2279		Carrie	Joseph A.	d
Sept.	26	1929	10390		Carrier	E. Estelle	d
Dec.	29	1954	22895		Carrigan	John	d
Mar.	17	1947	17647		Carrigan	Joyce Marguerite	m
		1899	3023		Carriger	C. C.	d
		1905	4003		Carriger	Levice/Levisa	d
		1891	2164		Carriger	Mary A.	d
		1904	3849		Carriger	Mary A.	d
		1885	1482		Carriger	Nicholas	d
		1853	25		Carriger	Solomon	ins
		1891	2245		Carriger	William W.	d
		1891	2246		Carriger	William W.	d
		1874	704		Carrillo	Amelia C.	m
		1874	704		Carrillo	Catherine A.	m
Mar.	1	1949	18874		Carrillo	Elizabeth	d
		1874	704		Carrillo	Frank J.	m
		1874	704		Carrillo	Frederick A.	m
		1874	688		Carrillo	Guadalupe	d
June	16	1958	25636		Carrillo	Hazel O.	d
Apr.	12	1937	12959		Carrillo	Jennie	d
		1901	3462		Carrillo	Julio	d
Jan.	3	1925	9130		Carrillo	L. E., etc.	d
Dec.	7	1943	15713		Carrillo	L. E., etc.	d
		1874	704		Carrillo	Louisa A.	m

Month	Day	Year	File No.	Surname	Given Name	Type
		1906	4131	Carrillo	Manuel	d
		1851	11	Carrillo	Maria Ignacio Lopez	d
		1874	704	Carrillo	Mary F.	m
		1879	1008	Carrillo	Mary F.	d
Jan.	5	1934	11816	Carrington	Charles Daniel	m
Feb.	27	1920	7305	Carrington	Charles N.	d
June	17	1933	11617	Carrington	Clara	d
Jan.	5	1934	11816	Carrington	Doris Jean	m
		1934	11816	Carrington	Frances Lambert	m
Jan.	5	1934	11816	Carrington	Joyce Arlene	m
Mar.	19	1958	25475	Carroll	Dennis A.	d
Nov.	29	1958	26042	Carroll	Elinor J.	d
Apr.	17	1921	7707	Carroll	Evelyn Marie	m
July	14	1954	22636	Carroll	Helen D., etc.	d
		1868	400	Carroll	James	d
Mar.	17	1921	7707	Carroll	James Carvey	m
Jan.	18	1952	20860	Carroll	James P., etc.	d
Sept.	27	1957	24982	Carroll	John P.	d
Mar.	17	1921	7707	Carroll	John Patrick	m
Apr.	15	1957	24667	Carroll	Mae C.	d
Aug.	30	1956	24135	Carroll	Marie A.	d
		1900	3216	Carroll	Michael	d
Oct.		1917	6536	Carroll	Patrick	inc
Nov.		1919	7214	Carroll	Patrick	d
Jan.	10	1950	19452	Carroll	William, etc.	d
		1922	7921	Carry	Ann	d
Mar.		1921	7704	Carsi	Agostino	m
		1924	8691	Carsin	Katherine	d
Dec.	20	1954	22928	Carson	Catherine M.	d
		1882	1222	Carson	Dorothy	d
		1897	2878	Carson	Dorothy or (Dorothe C	d
		1903	3584	Carson	Jennie Blanch	m
		1903	3584	Carson	Mabel Alma	m
Nov.	1	1932	11430	Carstens	Christ M., etc.	d
Sept.	14	1916	6263	Carstensen	C. A., etc.	d
Feb.	10	1939	13568	Carstensen	Caroline	d
Nov.	1	1932	11430	Carstensen	Christ M.	d
Feb.		1944	15798	Carstensen	Hannah	d
		1897	2737	Carstensen	Samuel	d
Dec.	15	1938	13482	Carstensen	William E.	d
Feb.	8	1957	24520	Carsteraen	Charles R., etc.	d
July	23	1955	23336	Cartasso	Peter G., etc.	d

Month	Day	Year	File No.	Surname	Given Name	Type
		1865	307	Carter	W. F.	d
		1871	482	Carter	A. J.	m
		1879	1027	Carter	Andrew J.	m
		1874	707	Carter	David	d
Aug.	23	1954	22709	Carter	Dora B.	d
		1890	1916	Carter	Elmer	m
Sept.	24	1936	12736	Carter	Frances	d
Oct.	31	1939	13772	Carter	Frances	d
		1861	193	Carter	H. F.	d
July	18	1956	24055	Carter	Harvey H.	d
July	18	1957	24886	Carter	Harvey H.	d
		1906	4183	Carter	J. M.	d
		1898	2974	Carter	John or John A.	d
		1867	356	Carter	Joseph	d
		1890	1972	Carter	Josiah W.	d
Nov.	16	1956	24336	Carter	Kenneth T.	d
		1905	4093	Carter	L. V.	d
		[1914-1915]	5936	Carter	Lou	d
Oct.	27	1950	19947	Carter	Loyal Benton, Jr.	m
		1871	482	Carter	M. L.	m
		1871	482	Carter	M. V.	m
		1879	1023	Carter	Mary E.	d
		1896	2667	Carter	Matilda A.	d
July	29	1943	15533	Carter	Mellie, etc.	ins
		1921	7839	Carter	Robert Lindsay	d
Aug.	2	1949	19202	Carter	William A., Sr., etc.	d
Sept.	29	1944	16145	Carubbi	John	d
		1912	5336	Carvalho	Alfred	m
Feb.	26	1938	13231	Carvallo	Joaquin P.	d
		1889	1824	Carver	Dora C.	m
		1888	1753	Carver	H. E.	d
		1889	1824	Carver	Rolla E.	m
		1922	8217	Carvey	Walter	m
		1893	2354	Carvey	Kate	inc
Feb.	6	1945	16403	Carviglia	Joseph	d
Sept.	27	1926	9369	Cary	Anne E.	d
		1889	1840	Cary	Bartley	d
		1894	2399	Cary	Permelia	d
Aug.	20	1951	20500	Casanova	Angelo	d
Feb.	3	1936	12539	Casarotti	Americo	d
		1917	6507	Casarotti	Charles F.	d
May	9	1952	21115	Casarotti	Charles, etc.	d

Month	Day	Year	File No.	Surname	Given Name	Type
Apr.	2	1953	21741	Casarotti	Clara	d
Dec.	20	1939	13814	Casarotti	Filippo, etc.	d
		1918	6894	Casarotti	Henry	d
		1898	2916	Casassa	Andrea	d
Sept.	31	1930	10697	Cascia	Antonio	d
		1902	3544	Case	A. B.	d
July	12	1943	15473	Case	Edwin Lockwood, etc.	d
June	7	1923	8351	Case	Fannie L.	d
Mar.	18	1953	21654	Case	Frank H.	d
Sept.	4	1921	7821	Case	George, etc.	inc
		1852	19	Case	H. T.	d
		1903	3700	Case	Jeremiah	d
Jan.		1903	3700	Case	Jerry	d
Jan.	13	1915	5937	Case	Philinda	d
Mar.	11	1949	18945	Case	Robert Ransome	d
Mar.	4	1949	18995	Case	Robert Ransome, etc.	d
		1926	9420	Case	Sarah J.	d
May	15	1947	17749	Casebeer	Johnnie R.	d
Aug.	31	1921	7801	Casella	Steve	d
Apr.	24	1943	15324	Caselli	Peter, etc.	d
		1891	2052	Caseras	George	d
		1894	2448	Caseres	C. F.	d
Aug.		1912	5360	Caseres	Frank	inc
Aug.		1912	5355	Caseres	Julius	d
Mar.	26	1949	18862	Casey	Albert, etc.	d
		1894	2450	Casey	David E.	m
		1894	2450	Casey	Elbert H.	m
Jan.	11	1952	20844	Casey	Grace E.	d
June	13	1958	25701	Casey	Helen E.	d
		1895	2524	Casey	Jeremiah	d
		1903	3700	Casey	Jeremiah	d
May	11	1951	20393	Casey	John	d
Jan.	19	1955	23669	Casey	John	d
July	28	1957	24835	Casey	Lloyd D.	d
July	13	1958	25700	Casey	Mary F.	d
Mar.	28	1958	25429	Casey	Richard D.	d
		1919	7169	Casey	Robert McHenry	m
		1870	442	Cash	Job	d
		1919	7155	Cash	Mary Ellen	d
		1874	668	Cashdollar	Algia	m
Mar.	29	1932	11241	Casini	Elsie D.	d
Nov.	7	1940	14232	Casini	Georgia	d

Month	Day	Year	File No.		Surname	Given Name	Type
Aug.	26	1942	14997		Casini	John B.	d
Feb.	13	1948	18220		Casini	Minnie	d
Feb.	13	1948	18223		Casini	Minnie	d
Apr.	23	1956	23879		Casini	Mollie	d
Apr.	4	1952	21035		Casini	Neibo	d
Jan.	2	1935	12479		Casini	Pasquale	d
July	24	1952	21266		Casini	Paul	d
Aug.	7	1940	14137		Casper	Fannie J.	d
Sept.	29	1957	24989		Casperson	Bertha A.	inc
Aug.	26	1935	12367		Casperson	James	d
July	27	1953	21973		Cass	Evelyn, etc.	d
		1921	7878		Cassani	Angelo	d
		[1909-1911]	4719		Cassani	Charles	d
Oct.	19	1944	16180		Cassani	Frank Angelo	d
Mar.	10	1941	14394		Cassani	Teresa	inc
Mar.	2	1954	22368		Cassasa	Louise, etc.	d
Oct.	30	1953	22087		Cassato	Joseph, etc.	d
July	27	1953	21972		Cassato	Rose, etc.	d
Dec.	25	1932	11452		Cassiday	Helen C.	d
Apr.	1	1935	12244		Cassiday	Sara Francis	d
Sept.	18	1932	11366		Cassiday	Sarah F. (insane)	g
Jan.	24	1952	21534		Cassidy	Edward J.	d
June	22	1937	13045		Cassidy	John P.	d
		1912	5264		Cassin	Elizabeth M.	d
July	27	1932	11321		Cassin	John M., etc.	d
Mar.	11	1955	23111		Cassina	F., etc.	d
Jan.	3	1955	23018		Cassity	J. L., etc.	d
Apr.	27	1924	8618		Cassluri	Stephan	d
Nov.	25	1929	10446		Cassrotti	Mario H.	d
Oct.	24	1954	22772		Castagnasso	Henry, etc.	inc
Oct.	27	1946	17416		Castagnetti	George	d
Oct.	27	1946	17417		Castagnetti	William	d
Apr.	4	1958	25520		Castagnetto	Louis	con
Mar.	6	1942	14843		Castagnetto	Rosa, etc.	d
July	24	1949	19144		Castaing	Marcien, etc.	d
Apr.	18	1955	23122		Castegnasso	Henry, etc.	d
		1873	627		Castens	Sophia et al	m
Apr.	31	1942	14881		Caster	George	d
Mar.	7	1944	15879		Castiglioni	Desolina	d
		1918	6811		Castiglioni	Pio	d
Aug.	8	1923	8431		Castiglioni	Pio	d
Apr.	1	1958	25510		Castino	Giacinto	d

Month	Day	Year	File No.		Surname	Given Name	Type
		1901	3354		Castle	Rufus A.	d
Dec.	20	1956	24339		Castor	Arthur U., etc.	d
Dec.	20	1956	24340		Castor	Mary B., etc.	d
Oct.	7	1958	25984		Castro	Edna Gertrude	d
		1918	6887		Casucci	Angelo	d
Feb.	22	1920	7621		Catalani	Martin	inc
May	4	1933	11576		Catania	John	d
Nov.	7	1958	26066		Catarina	Adrian A.	d
Sept.	3	1934	11987		Catea	Robert Taylor, etc.	d
May	27	1943	15402		Catelani	Daniele	d
Feb.	24	1933	11517		Catelani	L.	d
June	20	1932	11302		Catelani	Ottavio	d
Sept.	25	1935	12391		Catelli	G.	d
Aug.	6	1956	24147		Catelli	Jennie, etc.	d
Oct.	3	1940	14221		Catelli	Maris	d
Sept.	28	1929	10394		Catenassi	John, etc.	d
Sept.	10	1940	14141		Catenassi	Madaline	d
Apr.	1	1943	15358		Cathcart	Ernest C.	d
Dec.	18	1951	20806		Cathcart	Florence May	d
Sept.	21	1933	11694		Cathers	Mary A.	d
Sept.	2	1947	17981		Cathers	Thomas	d
		1867	344		Cathey	George	m
		1867	344		Cathey	James	m
		1867	344		Cathey	John	m
		1867	344		Cathey	Paralee	m
July	26	1944	16055		Catilli	Vittoria	inc
Oct.	24	1943	15610		Catin	Edgar H.	d
Dec.	18	1936	12757		Catlin	Anna	inc
Nov.	12	1958	26074		Caton	Olga S.	inc
Sept.	24	1936	12714		Cattabriga	Biagis	d
		1944	15759		Cattalini	Albert	d
Nov.	27	1957	25170		Cattalini	Gary Albert	m
Dec.	13	1957	25217		Cattalini	Gary Albert	m
Dec.	27	1957	25170		Cattalini	Juli Ann	m
Jan.	13	1957	25217		Cattalini	Juli Ann	m
Nov.	27	1957	25170		Cattalini	Kathryn Ann	m
Dec.	13	1957	25217		Cattalini	Kathryn Ann	m
May	28	1917	6494		Cattano	Joseph Rodriquez	d
May	17	1949	19086		Caubet	Peter	d
Feb.	14	1935	12157		Caudelot	Firmin	d
Dec.	3	1928	10104		Caufield	Thomas A.	d
		1911	5166		Caughey	Alexander	d

Month	Day	Year	File No.	Surname	Given Name	Type
Nov.	18	1934	12054	Caughey	Millie M.	d
Jan.	11	1912	5451	Caughey	Osburn	d
Aug.	18	1923	8395	Caughey	Rebecca M.	d
		1904	3731	Caughey	William	d
Nov.	26	1957	25167	Caulfield	Edward N.	d
		1920	7373	Caulfield	James Henry, etc.	d
Mar.	16	1954	22393	Caulfield	John J.	d
Aug.	27	1956	24130	Caulfield	William Patrick, Sr.	d
Mar.	26	1937	12901	Cavagnaro	Charles	d
Apr.	8	1937	12958	Cavagnaro	Charles R., Jr.	m
Apr.	8	1937	12958	Cavagnaro	Joseph	m
Apr.	8	1937	12958	Cavagnaro	Raymond	m
		1899	3071	Cavalli	Carlo	d
		1916	6337	Cavalli	Fortunato	d
Dec.	13	1925	9113	Cavalli	Hilda	m
		1893	2361	Cavalli	Patrico	d
		[1909-1911]	4859	Cavallo	Sebastiano	d
Apr.	12	1948	18336	Cavallo	Teresa	d
Dec.	4	1945	18765	Cavallo	Vencenzo	d
Mar.	27	1948	18257	Cavallo	Vensinzo	d
June	14	1943	15430	Cavanagh	Harriet, etc.	inc
Oct.	4	1943	15585	Cavanagh	Harriet, etc.	d
Dec.	8	1950	20097	Cavanagh	John	d
Apr.	23	1954	22410	Cavanagh	John Edmond	inc
Apr.	9	1954	22445	Cavanagh	John Edwin	d
June	14	1940	14069	Cavanagh	Margaret Ellen	d
Nov.	8	1943	15633	Cavanagh	Mary Jane	d
Feb.	20	1932	11201	Cavanaugh	Mary S.	d
Aug.	8	1940	14096	Cavangh	Margaret Ellen, etc.	d
Sept.	24	1922	8124	Cavelli	Joseph	d
		1926	9383	Cavelli	Peter	g
June	12	1942	14944	Cavert	Roy Johnson, etc.	ins
Jan.	17	1957	25224	Cavevori	Emil	d
Dec.	21	1954	22935	Caviglia	George	inc
Dec.	5	1955	23624	Caviglia	George, etc.	d
Sept.	15	1950	19928	Caxon	George	d
July	20	1931	11009	Cayla	Raymond M., Jr.	d
July	20	1931	11009	Cayla	Shirley May	d
Oct.	16	1948	18678	Cazaux	Louis	d
Jan.	16	1956	23728	Cazaux	Martha, etc.	d
Jan.	19	1942	14777	Cazon	Julius	d
		1858	133	Cecil	John F.	d

Month	Day	Year	File No.		Surname	Given Name	Type
Dec.	2	1932	11463		Celasco	Pietro	d
June	13	1958	25703		Celeri	Dane Allen, etc.	m
July	28	1948	18487		Celeri	Venanzio, etc.	d
Mar.	15	1957	24537		Cella	Caterina, etc.	d
Sept.	27	1940	14192		Cella	Celestine	d
Apr.	5	1954	22434		Cella	Colombo	d
Mar.	17	1945	16421		Cella	Dominick	d
Aug.	24	1954	22710		Cella	Giovanni, etc.	d
Apr.	14	1950	19562		Cencio	Inez B.	d
Jan.	10	1949	18821		Cenquini	Pio, etc.	d
June	6	1944	16019		Cerano	Elsie, etc.	d
Nov.	22	1940	14287		Cereghini	Frances	d
Dec.	6	1940	14259		Cereghini	Mary, etc.	d
		1891	2258		Cereghino	Antonio D.	m
		1891	2258		Cereghino	Attillio	m
		1891	2258		Cereghino	Frederick	m
Dec.	29	1929	10478		Cereghino	Giavanni	d
		1891	2190		Cereghino	Joseph	d
		1891	2258		Cereghino	Joseph	m
Sept.	4	1951	20582		Cereghino	Joseph, etc.	d
Mar.	2	1937	12908		Cereghino	Maria	inc
		1891	2258		Cereghino	Verna M.	m
Oct.	29	1926	9393		Cereghiso	Benedetto, etc.	d
Jan.		1926	9473		Ceresa	Emil	d
May	28	1923	8314		Ceresa	Frank N.	d
Feb.	23	1947	17591		Ceresa	Henry J.	d
May	14	1949	19079		Cerialle	Albert	d
		1907	4398		Cerighino	Attillio	d
Nov.	16	1948	18735		Cerighino	Kattie	d
Apr.	10	1940	14175		Cerini	A., etc.	d
July		1926	9321		Cerini	Angio	d
Sept.		1919	7167		Cerini	Guiseppe	d
Apr.	20	1956	23877		Cerini	John M.	d
July	22	1949	19181		Cerino	Ameris F., etc.	d
Jan.	31	1954	22956		Cerisier	Jane T.	d
Jan.	20	1951	20813		Cerni	Jack	d
Aug.	18	1944	16088		Cerruti	Domenico	d
Apr.	23	1954	22487		Cerutti	Antonio	d
Oct.	22	1954	22820		Cesana	Angelina	inc
		1903	3670		Cesari	Cesare	d
May	12	1945	16568		Chadwick	May Josephine, etc.	d
May	21	1947	17753		Chain	William	d

Month	Day	Year	File No.	Surname	Given Name	Type
		1905	3932	Chalfant	John E.	d
Mar.	26	1951	20290	Chambaud	Angelina	d
June		1923	8332	Chamberlain	Corinthia A., etc.	d
		1891	2178	Chamberlain	David	d
Jan.	24	1931	11177	Chamberlain	J. R.	d
		[1909-1911]	5011	Chamberlain	Martha A.	d
Nov.	12	1954	22860	Chamberlin	Florence Sherwood, et	d
Jan.	13	1946	17525	Chamberlin	George L., etc.	d
		1920	7350	Chambers	Alice Askew	d
Nov.	6	1915	6104	Chambers	Emery J.	d
July	6	1930	10651	Chambers	Herbert William Roy	m
Dec.	26	1912	5440	Chambers	Joseph A.	d
May	15	1952	21059	Chambers	Laura E.	d
		1897	2904	Chambers	Letita	d
		1898	2917	Chambers	Letitia (Mrs J. B.)	d
July	6	1930	10651	Chambers	Russell C.	m
Apr.	25	1957	24612	Chambers	Serva, etc.	d
Nov.	25	1955	23553	Chamley/Chanley	Jack J., etc.	d
		1894	2442	Champion	John	d
Sept.	4	1951	20581	Champion	Mary Frances, etc.	d
Feb.	21	1950	19467	Champion	Milton Keen, etc.	d
Oct.	2	1950	19952	Champion	Minnie A.	d
		1891	2244	Champlin	Charles C.	d
Feb.		1923	8515	Champlin	Maude E.	d
May	29	1957	24760	Chan	Harry	d
Apr.	28	1946	17108	Chance	Gertrude Segesmar	d
July	10	1953	21933	Chance	Kathleen L., etc.	d
Oct.	7	1949	19304	Chance	William	d
Feb.	27	1954	22309	Chancelet	Elisa Emma, etc.	inc
Jan.	18	1957	24465	Chancelet	Eliza Emma	d
Aug.	21	1954	22653	Chancelet	Yves Marie, etc.	d
		1901	3406	Chandler	Bethia	d
May	10	1916	6210	Chandler	Elle Nuessler	d
Sept.	6	1944	16159	Chandler	Gladys, etc.	d
June	12	1931	11000	Chandler	Horace L.	d
Sept.	18	1930	10684	Chandler	Horace L., etc.	d
July	18	1930	10683	Chandler	Horace Leslie	m
Aug.	11	1958	25843	Chandler	Larry L.	m
		1891	2257	Chandler	Noah	inc
Nov.	1	1917	6574	Chandler	R. O., etc.	d
June	5	1958	25672	Chaney	Bessie	d
Dec.	27	1953	22200	Chaney	Henry F.	d

Month	Day	Year	File No.	Surname	Given Name	Type
Oct.	15	1952	21338	Chapel	Elsie M.	d
Feb.	26	1952	20943	Chapin	Alvin. A.	d
Sept.	14	1950	19870	Chapin	Frances Wilma	d
		1891	2044	Chapman	Charles L.	m
		1884	1419	Chapman	Elliott	m
		1886	1565	Chapman	James	d
		1891	2044	Chapman	Maria	m
		1884	1419	Chapman	Mary S.	m
Mar.		1923	8272	Chapman	Maud E.	inc
May	15	1950	19699	Chapman	Palestine May, etc.	d
		1884	1419	Chapman	Phoebe	m
		1882	1226	Chapman	Thomas M.	d
Oct.	10	1952	21395	Chapman	Viola	d
Apr.	9	1946	17132	Chappel	Nellie B.	d
Nov.	9	1950	20036	Chappell	Almira, etc.	ins
Mar.	13	1951	20272	Chappell	Almira, etc.	d
June	15	1954	22592	Chappell	Gene	m
Nov.	26	1950	20011	Chappell	Jacob H.	d
July	17	1951	20491	Chappell	John Jacob	m
May	21	1958	25564	Chappell	Ray E., etc.	d
Oct.	8	1952	21392	Charles	A. H., etc.	d
Feb.	2	1953	21620	Charles	Anna	d
June	30	1940	14018	Charles	Betty	m
Feb.	15	1916	6175	Charles	Elbert R.	inc
Feb.		1918	6916	Charles	Elbert R.	d
July	30	1955	23348	Charles	Erma Lucille	d
Mar.	1	1929	10225	Charles	Frederick Natlu	d
		1881	1145	Charles	George A.	d
		1888	1729	Charles	Leon L.	m
Aug.	20	1943	15536	Charles	Leonard Francis	m
Aug.	29	1952	21270	Charles	Mabel	d
		1901	3416	Charles	Martin Luther	d
Oct.	27	1957	25047	Charles	Mary Addie Call	d
Oct.	25	1947	18019	Charles	Mary Agnes	d
		1888	1729	Charles	Nellie G.	m
Mar.	16	1937	12927	Charles	Oscar Nelson, etc.	d
June	8	1931	10997	Charmley	Maud G., etc.	d
May	14	1956	23988	Chase	Arthur G., etc.	d
Sept.	9	1937	13090	Chase	C. F.	d
Mar.	4	1955	23101	Chase	Christine	inc
Feb.		1924	8573	Chase	Marie S.	d
		1911	5153	Chase	Ross L.	m

Month	Day	Year	File No.	Surname	Given Name	Type
Jan.	4	1952	20829	Chauvet	Henry J.	d
Sept.	24	1951	20629	Cheda	Agello, etc.	d
		1887	1684	Cheda	Candida	d
Mar.	6	1934	11852	Cheda	Elizabeth	inc
Apr.	28	1934	11903	Cheda	Elizabeth	d
Nov.	10	1932	11407	Cheda	Pietro, etc.	d
Oct.	10	1950	19964	Cheesebrough	Frederick, etc.	d
Jan.	28	1956	24420	Cheesman	Kathlyn I.	d
Apr.	4	1949	18898	Cheleni	Casimiro	d
Mar.	26	1958	25421	Chelini	Americo, etc.	d
Jan.	21	1949	18854	Chelini	Casimiro	d
Apr.	9	1916	6192	Chelini	Giuseppe	d
		1920	7428	Chen	Isaac	d
Feb.	20	1939	13580	Cheney	Allan H.	d
		1884	1843	Cheney	E. H.	d
June	7	1938	13341	Cheney	Edmund H., etc.	d
Nov.	9	1922	8160	Cheney	Tammy Amplias	d
Oct.	16	1926	9412	Chenoweth	Mary S.	d
		1916	6324	Chenoweth	Myrtle Ethel	m
Apr.	31	1950	19600	Chenoweth	Robert J.	inc
June	9	1944	16027	Chenoweth	Robert N.	d
Jan.		1916	6324	Chenoweth	Verna Sonoma	m
June	10	1915	6016	Chenowith	Charles J.	m
Nov.	21	1957	25096	Chenowith	Hardin T.	d
		[1909-1911]	4965	Chepekis	George	inc
		[1909-1911]	4973	Chepekis	George	d
		1919	7233	Cherry	Frank Eugene	d
Jan.	24	1953	21605	Cherry	Perry F.	d
Apr.	5	1949	18999	Chesmet	Letitia, etc.	d
Jan.	16	1950	20108	Chesney	Andrew P., etc.	d
Apr.	1	1958	25508	Chesney	Roman P.	d
Mar.	10	1950	19557	Chesse	Alexander L.	d
Feb.	29	1957	24498	Chester	Arthur J.	d
Feb.		1946	16922	Chester	David Stewart, etc.	d
Oct.	28	1951	20645	Chester	Mary Agnes, etc.	d
Apr.	18	1927	9565	Chestnut	Robert	d
Jan.	22	1945	16368	Chetwood	James Monroe	d
Jan.	8	1945	16920	Chetwood	Lydia	inc
Feb.		1919	7296	Chevalier	Adolphe J.	d
Aug.	6	1931	11025	Cheyney	Oria I.	d
June	21	1951	20406	Chiapello	Lorenzo	d
Nov.	23	1954	22884	Chiapello	Teresa	d

Month	Day	Year	File No.	Surname	Given Name	Type
Apr.	25	1950	19649	Chickencoff	John G.	d
Aug.	22	1958	25874	Chilbers	Mary, etc.	d
		1911	5203	Childres	Nathan B.	d
		1896	2679	Childs	George W.	d
		[1908-1909]	4411	Chinn	Lewis F.	d
Mar.	26	1938	13277	Chinnock	H. A.	d
May	29	1932	11266	Chiodi	Erede	d
Mar.	26	1935	12209	Chiodo	Mary E.	d
Nov.	21	1958	26024	Chiotti	Felipa	inc
		1925	8919	Chiotti	Giuseppe	d
June	13	1931	11001	Chiotti	Peter	g
Nov.	30	1935	12420	Chiotti	Peter	d
Apr.	2	1953	21742	Chirich	Steve, etc.	d
Dec.	10	1920	7609	Chisholm	Douglas	m
Dec.	10	1920	7609	Chisholm	Frances Elizabeth	m
		1904	3879	Chisholm	John	d
Dec.	23	1920	7587	Chisholm	William C.	d
June	26	1953	21863	Chisholm	William F., etc.	d
Sept.	15	1958	25924	Chittick	James G., etc.	d
		1898	2981	Chitwood	James M.	d
		1900	3124	Chitwood	John F.	d
		1891	2174	Choate	Rhoda	d
		1919	7196	Chopard	Mary A.	d
Aug.	24	1936	12689	Choquette	Wallace Steven	m
June	10	1957	24784	Chouteau	Augusta	d
		1911	5117	Chow	Young	d
Apr.	26	1957	24615	Choy	Sun Yet	d
Nov.	12	1957	25134	Chrestofferson	May Kelly, etc.	d
		1865	276	Christ	G. W.	d
Mar.	15	1946	17074	Christen	Fannie	d
May	20	1951	20346	Christensen	Bodil	d
Sept.	12	1940	14142	Christensen	C. J.	ins
May	30	1928	9959	Christensen	Charles R. E.	d
Apr.	17	1919	6997	Christensen	Chris K.	d
Sept.	26	1947	17973	Christensen	Christian	d
Apr.	10	1940	14174	Christensen	Christian Jens	d
Aug.	16	1958	25787	Christensen	Florence	d
Feb.	20	1948	18247	Christensen	James Peter, etc.	d
Nov.	26	1929	10448	Christensen	Jens Martin	d
May	9	1952	21113	Christensen	Karen K., etc.	d
May	4	1954	22516	Christensen	Karen K., etc.	m
Dec.	28	1958	26114	Christensen	Margaret, etc.	d

Month	Day	Year	File No.	Surname	Given Name	Type
Sept.		1918	6816	Christensen	Marie, etc.	d
Dec.	25	1952	21481	Christensen	Niels	d
Dec.	18	1953	22245	Christensen	Paul L., etc.	d
Jan.	19	1930	10817	Christensen	Peter Theodore	d
Jan.	17	1927	9779	Christensen	Theresa A.	d
July	23	1942	14992	Christenson	Annie Carmichael	d
Jan.	18	1950	19462	Christenson	Jens R., etc.	d
Mar.	10	1953	21647	Christian	Annie E.	d
Aug.	14	1925	9035	Christian	Charles G.	d
Aug.	13	1932	11336	Christian	Claude J., etc.	d
		1922	8050	Christian	Demetrius	d
June	23	1949	19096	Christian	Emma L.	d
Feb.	8	1959	26192	Christian	Harry H.	con
July	25	1934	11980	Christian	Louis J.	d
		1902	3551	Christian	Edward	d
Dec.	9	1920	7604	Christiansen	Carl	d
Feb.	25	1958	25420	Christiansen	Carl	d
May	1	1944	15951	Christiansen	Christian	d
Jan.	11	1952	20847	Christiansen	Christian P.	d
May	19	1952	21126	Christiansen	Ernest, etc.	d
May	24	1938	13331	Christiansen	Isabella	d
June	28	1938	13333	Christiansen	Isabella	d
		1875	753	Christiansen	Tellef (Rosas)	d
Nov.	3	1942	15096	Christianson	Charles	d
		1917	6478	Christie	Alfred J.	d
May	29	1957	24700	Christie	Elsie M., etc.	d
		1884	1420	Christie	Georgie	m
May	21	1937	13005	Christie	Grace E,	d
		1884	1420	Christie	John	m
		1884	1420	Christie	Mollie	m
Jan.	23	1938	13514	Christie	Myrtle A.	d
		1882	1229	Christlich	Fred	d
May	9	1950	19678	Christman	Lars P.	d
Oct.	14	1937	13123	Christoffer	Emma	d
		1926	9185	Christopher	Martin	d
Sept.	19	1951	20614	Christophersen	Mathilde, etc.	d
		1919	7278	Christopherson	Ole	d
		[1908-1909]	4448	Chritwood	Barbara	d
Feb.	25	1958	25416	Church	Blanche	inc
Feb.	20	1954	22301	Church	Charles Whitney	d
Feb.	23	1928	9850	Church	Cynthia J.	d
Oct.	4	1932	11403	Church	Dorothy	m

Month	Day	Year	File No.	Surname	Given Name	Type
		1901	3365	Church	Edith	m
May	31	1951	20419	Church	Elias P.	jt
June	24	1954	22566	Church	Elizabeth	inc
July	17	1954	22598	Church	Elizabeth, etc.	d
		1900	3152	Church	Frank Hail	d
Dec.	21	1950	20060	Church	Gerald, etc.	m
		1902	3506	Church	J. F.	d
May	31	1951	20419	Church	Mabel A.	jt
		1900	3199	Church	Samuel H.	d
Oct.	14	1954	22809	Church	William T.	d
July	29	1956	24022	Churchill	Abbie, etc.	d
Nov.	22	1943	15687	Churchill	Barbara May	m
Dec.	22	1943	15687	Churchill	Beverly Jane	m
Oct.	14	1932	11388	Churchill	Emma A.	d
Aug.	28	1937	13050	Churchill	H. B.	d
Aug.	31	1945	16674	Churchill	Harold L.	d
Dec.	3	1943	15711	Churchill	J. W.	d
Dec.	22	1943	15687	Churchill	Vernon Martin, Jr.	m
May	12	1915	5995	Churchman	Araminta R.	d
May		1921	7770	Churchman	Charley E.	d
May	24	1921	7769	Churchman	Eliza Ann	d
		1874	721	Churchman	John	m
May		1930	10600	Churchman	John	d
Mar.	26	1937	12870	Churchman	Leonard Edgar	m
		1874	722	Churchman	Maggie	m
July	21	1935	12309	Churchman	Susan	d
		1873	659	Churchman	William	d
		1874	720	Churchman	William	m
Nov.	19	1930	10737	Churchman	William	d
May	21	1941	14446	Ciampi	Guido	d
Oct.	3	1949	19290	Ciampi	Sirio	ins
Jan.	13	1942	14768	Cicola	Emilio	d
Sept.	20	1949	19231	Cicucci	Amelia	d
Dec.	23	1932	11450	Cincera	Attilio	d
Sept.	16	1955	23438	Cinquini	Cosimo, etc.	d
Sept.	19	1950	19934	Cinquini	Domenico	d
Sept.	7	1948	18610	Cinquini	Peter	d
Aug.	6	1948	18569	Cinquini	Valentina	inc
		1920	7444	Cipolla	Andrea	d
Jan.		1925	9119	Ciucci	Donald Calvin	m
Feb.	9	1928	9827	Ciucci	Fillippo A.	d
Aug.	12	1922	8053	Ciucci	Settimo	d

Month	Day	Year	File No.	Surname	Given Name	Type
		1906	4207	Claasun	Jens P.	d
		1886	1567	Clanton	Samuel T.	inc
		1901	3287	Clanton	Thomas D.	d
		1859	153	Clapper	Edward	d
June	11	1958	25690	Clapponi	Brandizio	d
		1926	9226	Clark	Alfred C., etc.	d
		1879	1032	Clark	Alice	d
		1896	2659	Clark	Almer	d
		1905	3944	Clark	Almer	d
		1872	522	Clark	Andrew	d
		1882	1205	Clark	Ann J.	d
		1901	3487	Clark	Anna	d
Dec.	1	1941	14727	Clark	Anna P.	d
July	16	1943	15517	Clark	Annie	d
Jan.		1912	5386	Clark	Augusta	d
June	28	1933	11652	Clark	Beatrice Lillian	m
June	24	1937	13007	Clark	Bert Thomas	d
		1884	1407	Clark	Charles	d
		1888	1714	Clark	Charles	d
		1913	5616	Clark	Charles L.	m
		1869	422	Clark	Charley P.	m
Apr.	23	1937	12941	Clark	Charlotte	d
May	27	1934	11937	Clark	Charlotte P.	d
Dec.	15	1913	5637	Clark	Cordelia A.	d
		1901	3320	Clark	David	d
May		1918	6717	Clark	David F., etc.	d
Jan.	15	1927	9807	Clark	David F., etc.	d
		1898	2923	Clark	David S. F.	m
Sept.	20	1898	2925	Clark	David S. F.	m
Feb.	21	1957	24472	Clark	Dora C.	d
Sept.	9	1915	6033	Clark	Douglas	m
		1907	4242	Clark	Edgar B.	inc
Sept.	14	1913	5601	Clark	Edgar B.	d
May	8	1956	23977	Clark	Edna O.	d
		1901	3486	Clark	Edward	d
Apr.		1926	9226	Clark	Edward C., etc.	d
		1892	2274	Clark	Eliza Jane	d
June	13	1945	16609	Clark	Elizabeth C.	d
Nov.	24	1941	14585	Clark	Emelie L.`	d
		1875	735	Clark	Estella	m
		1886	1555	Clark	Estelle	m
		1869	422	Clark	Florence B.	m

Month	Day	Year	File No.	Surname	Given Name	Type
Oct.	8	1913	5616	Clark	Frances Pauline	m
Mar.	18	1914	5710	Clark	Francis U.	d
Sept.	6	1945	16685	Clark	Frank Adelbert, etc.	d
Mar.	27	1932	11239	Clark	Frank S.	d
July	9	1915	6033	Clark	Franklin	m
		1898	2935	Clark	Fred S.	d
Apr.	28	1947	17716	Clark	Fred W., etc.	d
		1886	1555	Clark	Frederick	m
		1875	735	Clark	Frederick W.	m
Feb.	10	1941	14390	Clark	Gemma E., etc.	d
		1920	7388	Clark	George	d
		1897	2736	Clark	George F.	d
Oct.	30	1914	5781	Clark	George Grossenor	d
		1902	3521	Clark	George W.	d
		1875	735	Clark	Gertrude L.	m
		1886	1555	Clark	Gertrude L.	m
Nov.	6	1944	16247	Clark	Harry A.	d
		1883	1365	Clark	Howard	inc
		1884	1443	Clark	Howard	d
Oct.	7	1948	18666	Clark	Irene H.	d
		1873	643	Clark	James	d
		1893	2340	Clark	James	d
		1904	3777	Clark	James	d
May	10	1915	6014	Clark	James Emmet	m
		1897	2802	Clark	James L.	d
June	28	1933	11652	Clark	James Leland	m
		1875	735	Clark	James M.	m
		1886	1554	Clark	James P.	d
Jan.	12	1942	14763	Clark	James W.	d
Jan.	12	1942	14723	Clark	James W., etc.	d
Dec.	25	1930	10784	Clark	John, etc.	d
		1898	2923	Clark	Lettie A.	m
Sept.	20	1898	2925	Clark	Lettie Ann	m
Apr.	17	1940	14001	Clark	Lillian	d
		1900	3175	Clark	Lucinda M.	d
		1869	422	Clark	M. Alice	m
		1896	2680	Clark	Marcia P.	d
		1905	3969	Clark	Margaret Boyd	d
		1875	735	Clark	Margaret E.	m
July	9	1926	12672	Clark	Marie	d
		1903	3664	Clark	Martha	d
Apr.	31	1944	15903	Clark	Mary	d

Month	Day	Year	File No.	Surname	Given Name	Type
		1887	1630	Clark	Maud E.	m
Oct.	25	1945	16789	Clark	May	d
June	25	1932	11319	Clark	May Dexter	d
Mar.	12	1942	14855	Clark	Mead	d
June	29	1936	12652	Clark	Merle H.	inc
June	9	1915	6033	Clark	Milton Douglas	m
Sept.	28	1946	17370	Clark	Milton F.	d
Oct.	25	1950	19945	Clark	Minnie F.	d
		1886	1583	Clark	Moses E.	d
		1912	5337	Clark	Nevada K.	d
July	14	1944	16036	Clark	R. D., etc.	d
Mar.	18	1946	17079	Clark	Robert	d
June	10	1915	6014	Clark	Robert Edwin	m
Sept.	22	1952	21301	Clark	Roy	d
May	19	1949	19025	Clark	Samuel	d
		1860	160	Clark	Samuel G.	d
		1904	3860	Clark	Stephen Douglas	d
		1898	2908	Clark	Stephen J.	d
May	12	1915	5993	Clark	Stover P.	d
Apr.	9	1957	24656	Clark	Walter A.	d
July	16	1947	17892	Clark	Walter Byron, etc.	d
Feb.	1	1944	15813	Clark	Walter L.	d
		1857	37	Clark	William T.	d
		1857	89	Clark	William T.	m
Apr.	21	1929	10253	Clark	Winfred P.	d
		1897	2754	Clark	Wm. S.	d
Jan.	31	1947	18078	Clark	W. L.	d
July	19	1956	24111	Clarke	Carolann Marie	m
Jan.	25	1952	20878	Clarke	Ina F.	d
Oct.	25	1945	16790	Clarke	James, etc.	d
		1887	1647	Clarke	Jeremiah	inc
		1906	4114	Clarkson	George A.	d
		1901	3259	Clary	Abigail E.	m
		1902	3532	Clary	Dennis	inc
		1903	3532	Clary	Dennis G.	inc
		1901	3259	Clary	Ida Monica	m
Dec.	22	1930	10781	Clary	John F., etc.	d
		1901	3259	Clary	Mary K.	m
		1901	3259	Clary	Paul D.	m
		1901	3259	Clary	Thomas P.	m
		1929	10325	Clasen	Emil	d
Aug.	22	1932	11348	Claus	Richard B.	d

Month	Day	Year	File No.		Surname	Given Name	Type
Oct.	28	1951	20640		Claus	William Henry Emil, e	d
June	10	1926	9277		Clausen	August A.	d
Apr.	17	1933	11562		Clausen	Augusta	d
Nov.	1	1949	19344		Clausen	Augusta	d
		[1909-1911]	4853		Clausen	Hansine	d
		[1909-1911]	4852		Clausen	John	d
Mar.	21	1952	21000		Clausen	Josephine	d
Feb.	4	1927	9527		Clausen	Leo, Frederick, Henry,	m
Jan.	30	1954	22951		Clausen	Ove P.	d
May	5	1944	15954		Clausen	Richard, etc.	d
		1889	1856		Clawson	Alanson	d
		1919	7146		Clawson	Anna	d
Jan.		1907	4347		Clawson	Charles	d
Apr.	11	1955	23168		Clawson	Charles Henry, etc.	d
Mar.	18	1957	24600		Clawson	Cora	d
		1926	9171		Clawson	Edwin Wesley	d
May	29	1935	12286		Clawson	Mary Jane	d
June	28	1951	20412		Clawson	Walter P.	d
		1926	9171		Clawson	William Ellsworth	d
		1864	240		Clay	Jonathan (no papers)	d
Sept.	11	1951	20538		Clayberg	Claude	d
May		1921	7755		Claypool	Jerry W.	d
		1859	154		Clayton	Henry C.	d
		1903	3645		Clayton	John S. A.	d
Dec.	16	1951	20739		Cleary	Edward M., Sr., etc.	d
Aug.	12	1918	6806		Cleary	George	d
		1901	3476		Cleaveland	Bertha	d
		1903	3694		Cleaveland	Harry James	m
Nov.	18	1957	25151		Cleaveland	Robert F., etc.	d
		1903	3694		Cleaveland	Robert Fuller	m
		1895	2514		Cleavland	Ezra	d
Feb.	25	1956	23747		Clegg	Ann	m
Feb.	25	1956	23747		Clegg	Kay	m
May	25	1953	21862		Clegg	Mary Frances, etc.	d
Oct.	28	1947	18067		Clegg	Towne	d
Jan.	25	1956	23747		Clegg	William Ashley	m
Nov.	28	1943	15652		Cleland	Hannah, etc.	d
Mar.	25	1952	21011		Clemens	John	d
Sept.	25	1951	20632		Clement	George	d
Dec.	22	1938	13488		Clement	Hattie M.	d
Dec.	5	1958	26129		Clements	Ethel J.	d
		1885	1496		Clemmensen	Carl J.	d

Month	Day	Year	File No.	Surname	Given Name	Type
		1887	1673	Clemons	Abigail W.	d
Feb.	16	1932	11197	Clendenin	Laura, etc.	d
Nov.	6	1953	22163	Clennell	Sydney H.	d
Feb.	19	1933	11511	Clerici	Antonio, etc.	d
May	10	1956	23981	Clerici	August, etc.	d
Apr.	1	1952	21020	Cleve	Axel	d
Sept.	22	1958	25877	Cleve	Janette	d
Nov.	8	1944	16250	Cleveland	Beulah Lee	d
		1901	3422	Cleveland	Ellen	d
Jan.	31	1953	22258	Cleveland	George H.	d
		1901	3421	Cleveland	Rebecca	d
Aug.	30	1946	17319	Clevenger	Delbert	mp
Aug.	30	1946	17320	Clevenger	Harry	mp
		1917	6513	Clewe	Marie	d
Dec.	3	1937	13182	Clewe	William F.	d
Aug.	29	1952	21274	Clewell	Eugene Crile	d
June	24	1952	21215	Clifford	Kathryn, etc.	d
Jan.	20	1936	12530	Cline	Agnes Nollis	d
Sept.	13	1928	10060	Cline	Hannah A.	d
Jan.	2	1926	9158	Cline	John W.	d
		1934	11818	Cline	Mary Francis, etc.	d
Mar.	11	1941	14395	Cline	Ransom M.	d
May	20	1942	14905	Clinkingbeard	Ray	d
Aug.	17	1940	14111	Clinton	James A.	d
Nov.	7	1941	14509	Clippenger	Lester	d
Apr.	30	1951	20302	Clippinger	John	d
Jan.	13	1940	14305	Clippinger	John, etc.	inc
		1925	9098	Clippinger	Sarah L., etc.	d
Feb.	20	1958	25303	Close	James	inc
May		1939	13606	Close	Leonard A.	d
Dec.	16	1934	12099	Close	Zunis Cass, etc.	d
		1926	9397	Clough	Delia, etc.	d
June	13	1955	23315	Clough	Julian	d
		1934	11835	Clough	Lucie A.	d
Nov.	26	1921	7854	Clough	Manley E./M. E.	d
June	15	1937	13032	Clough	Mary A.	d
June	10	1958	25687	Cloutman	Manfred	d
May	26	1950	19653	Cloutman	Nellie, etc.	d
		1876	842	Clover	Milton	d
June	10	1947	17844	Clozier	John, etc.	d
		[1909-1911]	5021	Cluk	S. P.	m
May	28	1948	18364	Cluner	Henry A.	d

Month	Day	Year	File No.		Surname	Given Name	Type
Feb.	24	1958	25319		Clute	Archie D.	inc
Jan.	27	1945	16902		Clute	Mary H.	d
		1870	457		Clyman	Mary	d
Mar.	11	1947	17689		Cnopius	Anna B., etc.	d
Nov.	19	1920	7585		Cnopius	Annagene Gertrude	g
		1939	13584		Cnopius	Birdie M., etc.	d
		[1908-1909]	4599		Cnopius	Carrie B.	d
		1920	7332		Cnopius	Carrie Gladys	d
June	21	1957	24749		Cnopius	Eugene B.	d
Nov.	19	1920	7585		Cnopius	Gladys Marion	g
Apr.	25	1915	5969		Cnopius	John	d
Oct.	21	1942	15087		Cnopius	Lewis C., etc.	d
May	30	1954	22508		Coates	Edward, etc.	d
Mar.	10	1925	8903		Coatney	Georgia Ann	d
Jan.	16	1929	10494		Coatney	Stephen J.	d
Dec.	26	1948	18750		Coats	William B., etc.	d
June	24	1946	17265		Cobb	Antoinette M.	d
		1874	683		Cobb	Charles	d
July	24	1946	17265		Cobb	Omar O.	d
Sept.		1918	6815		Cobb	Omar R.	d
Feb.	1	1946	16983		Cobban	Georgia	d
Dec.	7	1945	16863		Cobban	M. W.	d
		1904	3724		Coburn	Elizabeth L.	d
		1899	3079		Coburn	George	m
Aug.	14	1926	9338		Coburn	James A.	d
		1904	3733		Coburn	Joseph	m
		1904	3733		Coburn	Mabel	m
		1899	3079		Coburn	Walter	m
Aug.	25	1957	24908		Cochet	Frank	d
May	30	1943	15406		Cochran	Ina A.	d
Apr.	27	1928	9918		Cochrane	Charlotte Miller	d
July	26	1952	21222		Cochrane	Helen Gates, etc.	d
Oct.	11	1914	5787		Cochrane	Herbert M.	m
Dec.	26	1928	10127		Cochrane	John Gates	d
Mar.	15	1943	15277		Cochrane	Martha Luella	m
Apr.	13	1940	13958		Cochrane	Thalia N.	d
Apr.	28	1952	21016		Cochrane	U. W., etc.	d
		1859	145		Cock	John	d
		1883	1312		Cocke	William E.	d
		1879	1024		Cocke	W. T.	d
		1906	4208		Cockerell	Robert E.	d
		1857	38		Cockerill	Harrison	d

Month	Day	Year	File No.		Surname	Given Name	Type
		1853	35		Cockerill	James A.	d
Feb.	7	1958	25367		Cockett	Bret H., Jr., etc.	d
		1886	1592		Cockrell	Didamia	d
		1922	8195		Cockrill	Lurellie L.	d
		1884	1410		Codding	G. R.	d
Mar.	9	1934	11887		Codding	George C.	d
July	16	1956	24099		Codiroli	Angelina	d
		1894	2417		Cody	Mary	d
		1874	685		Coe	Callie	d
		1873	630		Coe	Frank H.	d
		1906	4176		Coelho	Joas Joaquin/John Kin	d
		[1909-1911]	4987		Coen	James	d
June		1918	6746		Coenhour	Clyde	m
		1862	218		Cofer	Elliott	d
Sept.		1924	8726		Coffey	Carlton Timothy	m
		1883	1327		Coffin	Mary Emeline (adoptic	m
		1897	2906		Coffman	Anna M. (nee Wilson)	d
Apr.	4	1944	15910		Coffman	Charles	d
Mar.	25	1955	23083		Coffman	Georgia Marion	d
		1898	2957		Coffman	Henry W.	m
		1912	5277		Coffman	Henry W.	d
May	13	1943	15427		Coffman	James Trisler, etc.	d
		1898	2957		Coffman	Mary G.	m
Mar.	19	1914	5748		Coffman	N. B.	d
Mar.	20	1942	14828		Cogla	Julius	d
Jan.		1921	7893		Cogley	Eugene H.	d
		1922	8015		Cogley	Irma Irene	m
		1922	8015		Cogley	Lottie Viola	m
Sept.	4	1931	11069		Cogo	Giovanni Battista	d
Oct.	14	1949	19260		Cohen	Alex	d
June	9	1942	14974		Cohen	Clara B., etc.	d
Feb.		1924	8861		Cohen	David	m
		1879	1055		Cohen	I. L.	d
Mar.	4	1914	5691		Cohen	Maxwell T.	m
		1879	1054		Cohen	Nettie	m
		1879	1054		Cohen	Rossa	m
Oct.	14	1931	11077		Cohen	Sam, etc.	d
Apr.	23	1951	20292		Cohen	Sarah	d
		1924	8861		Cohen	Wilfred	m
Mar.	14	1924	8603		Coisson	Henry	d
Sept.		1922	8134		Coke	Sarah E.	d
Feb.	3	1941	14372		Coker	Susan L.	d

Month	Day	Year	File No.	Surname	Given Name	Type
Feb.	3	1941	14372	Coker	Wiley R.	d
Mar.	10	1924	8598	Colabella	Carlo	d
Mar.	29	1945	16499	Colabella	Nick	d
Oct.	9	1927	9695	Colabella	Solvatore, Nicola, Giu	m
Mar.	5	1934	11850	Colahella	Angelina	d
May	7	1957	24718	Colbroth	Cora L., etc.	d
		1906	4187	Colbroth	Harriet L.	d
Feb.	18	1938	13223	Colbroth	Lucy B.	d
Mar.	25	1938	13251	Colbroth	Mary Josephine	d
Feb.		1915	5947	Colburn	Marietta Arvilla	d
		1922	8024	Colburn	Orlin F.	d
Nov.	31	1952	21433	Cole	Addie E.	inc
June	6	1947	17836	Cole	Charles B., etc.	d
May	27	1954	22498	Cole	Donel C.	d
Sept.	30	1928	10046	Cole	Elizabeth C.	d
June	10	1949	19124	Cole	Emily	d
Sept.	3	1946	17377	Cole	Estella, etc.	d
Nov.	18	1944	16226	Cole	George H.	d
Apr.	9	1951	20324	Cole	Harriet	d
		1919	7235	Cole	Jane E.	d
		1899	2995	Cole	John	d
June	16	1952	21193	Cole	John R., etc.	d
Sept.	30	1951	20512	Cole	John Sterling, Jr.	inc
Apr.	20	1947	17700	Cole	Julius	d
June	17	1947	17802	Cole	Kenneth T.	d
Apr.	27	1954	22497	Cole	Martha L.	d
Jan.	17	1955	22985	Cole	Mary D.	d
Dec.	8	1935	12455	Cole	Milo	d
Sept.	5	1957	24997	Cole	Roy H., etc.	d
Jan.	20	1953	21592	Cole	S. W., etc.	d
Oct.	6	1952	21386	Cole	Vincent L.	d
Aug.	26	1925	8992	Cole	Waldo J., etc.	d
Apr.	29	1924	8623	Cole	Willard & Hugh K.	m
July		1940	14088	Cole	Willard C., etc.	d
July	27	1918	6756	Cole	Charles Barry	d
		1887	1645	Cole	J. W.	d
Mar.	31	1942	14803	Colebrook	Horace William	d
		1885	1505	Coleman	Ambrose	d
		1920	7394	Coleman	Annie M.	d
June	29	1950	19729	Coleman	Con	d
		1912	5232	Coleman	George E.	d
Mar.	30	1935	12174	Coleman	H. J.	d

Month	Day	Year	File No.	Surname	Given Name	Type
May	17	1946	17149	Coleman	Harold P.	m
Apr.	17	1946	17149	Coleman	Linzy W., Jr.	m
		1905	3923	Coleman	Mary	d
Sept.	7	1937	13119	Colerane	Clarinda Harrison	d
May	23	1953	21800	Colgan	Annie E.	d
		[1908-1909]	4413	Colgan	Charles L.	d
		1873	592	Colgan	E. P.	d
Feb.	19	1951	20221	Colgan	George Washington, e	d
Aug.	27	1948	18539	Colgan	Wesley, Jr.	m
		1919	7153	Colguhouer	Hugh	d
Mar.	24	1956	23812	Coli	Narciss, etc.	d
		1869	418	Collect	Louis	d
Feb.	9	1950	19510	Colleran	Edwin H.	d
Nov.	5	1935	12454	Collett	Augusta Cecile	d
Apr.	20	1931	10920	Collett	Frederick William, etc	d
		1871	472	Collier	Ira	d
		1872	549	Collier	Shedrick F.	d
		1882	1221	Collier	Susan	d
May	12	1950	19692	Collier	W. L.	d
Aug.	20	1942	15015	Collier	William, etc.	d
May	17	1942	14901	Collier	William, Sr.	d
Nov.		1921	7868	Colling	Anthony J.	inc
Nov.	29	1924	8764	Collings	Charles M.	inc
Dec.	24	1944	16287	Collings	Eliza J.	d
May	1	1951	20372	Collings	Walter	inc
Mar.	2	1956	23827	Collings	Walter	d
Mar.	5	1947	17681	Collins	Billie	inc
Sept.	18	1923	8440	Collins	Carrie E.	d
Feb.	13	1919	6994	Collins	Charlotte	d
Mar.	12	1953	21691	Collins	Earle J., etc.	d
Apr.	13	1956	23924	Collins	Edward K.	inc
Apr.	16	1948	18284	Collins	Eva May	d
Feb.	15	1913	5679	Collins	George	d
Feb.	19	1924	8575	Collins	J. J.	d
June	12	1958	25696	Collins	James Robert	d
		1904	3737	Collins	James W.	d
July	25	1918	6774	Collins	John Barney	d
July	16	1924	8683	Collins	John F.	d
Oct.	24	1935	12418	Collins	Joseph H.	d
		1867	338	Collins	Lafayette	d
Sept.	5	1958	25896	Collins	Mae E.	d
May	13	1930	10622	Collins	Marion R.	m

Month	Day	Year	File No.	Surname	Given Name	Type
		1907	4226	Collins	Mary B.	d
Apr.	24	1913	5501	Collins	Mary R.	d
		1883	1302	Collins	Mathew	d
Nov.	28	1920	7552	Collins	Patrick James	d
May	6	1946	17190	Collins	Samuel	d
		1904	3874	Collins	Stephen	d
May	5	1949	19055	Collins	Velia C.	d
Apr.	14	1935	12227	Collins	William A.	d
Aug.	15	1958	25786	Collins	William Armstrong, et	d
Mar.	1	1938	13237	Collins	William E.	d
		1923	8490	Collins	William P.	d
June	26	1930	10635	Collins	William, etc.	d
		1874	669	Colmar	Illegible	d
Sept.	17	1957	25024	Colognato	Frank, etc.	d
June	24	1930	10633	Colombani	Olinto	d
Mar.	19	1951	20222	Colombani	Primo	d
Feb.	27	1953	21610	Colombano	Eligio, etc.	d
Jan.	13	1947	17564	Colombano	Ruth Marie	d
Nov.	22	1932	11447	Colombini	I.	ins
Nov.	30	1912	5387	Colombo	Catherine	m
May	29	1957	24699	Colombo	Charles H., etc.	d
		1912	5219	Colombo	Clemente	d
		1912	5387	Colombo	Fannie	m
Dec.	30	1951	20778	Colombo	John Edward, etc.	d
June	24	1944	16001	Colombo	Mary Louise	ins
Aug.	30	1912	5387	Colombo	Oliver	m
Aug.	30	1912	5387	Colombo	Romilo	m
Feb.	4	1924	8531	Colosio	Joseph L.	d
June	16	1929	10284	Colson	Charles	d
June	26	1936	12646	Coltrin	William Wallace	d
Mar.	21	1950	19528	Colusci	John, etc.	d
		1905	3928	Colwell	Albert G.	d
		1898	2942	Colwell	Alice	d
		1891	2046	Colwell	Caroline E.	d
		1907	4309	Colwell	Charles Edward	d
		1893	2287	Colwell	Edwin B.	d
July	26	1937	13048	Comalli	Americo	d
Sept.	14	1947	17950	Comalli	Angelo, etc.	d
Mar.	23	1942	14862	Coman	Mary McMeans	d
Oct.	13	1944	16165	Comazzi	Lucia	d
Aug.	29	1943	15534	Combs	Ethel B.	d
Oct.	10	1958	25995	Combs	May C., etc.	d

Month	Day	Year	File No.		Surname	Given Name	Type
Feb.	11	1951	20152		Combs	Monroe C.	d
		1890	1929		Comerford	Richard	d
Aug.	2	1948	18556		Comolini	Lawrence B., etc.	d
July	25	1948	18480		Comolini	Lawrence, etc.	ins
June	24	1952	21138		Comozzi	James	d
		1903	3680		Compton	Sarah L.	d
Dec.	5	1950	20086		Compton	William Dan	d
Feb.	18	1939	13866		Comstock	Addie Lena	d
Dec.	24	1950	20065		Comstock	Charles W.	d
May	23	1930	10631		Comstock	Hattie L.	d
Mar.	28	1944	15855		Comstock	Hubert G.	d
		1920	7624		Comstock	John A.	d
July	17	1940	14071		Comstock	Nellie Hurd, etc.	d
		1884	1444		Comstock	Philena C.	d
Jan.	14	1932	11194		Comstock	W. G.	d
Dec.	3	1931	11125		Comstock	William E.	d
Oct.	1	1952	21373		Comyns	Alice H., etc.	d
Apr.	29	1929	10263		Conan	Florence I.	d
		[1909-1911]	4998		Conan	Samuel M.	d
Jan.	10	1941	14339		Conant	Alice E.	d
		1929	10360		Conch	William N.	d
May	21	1952	21074		Condiff	Teddy W.	m
June	26	1950	19728		Condit	Henry V., etc.	d
Mar.	21	1952	21001		Condit	John C.	d
Feb.	30	1948	18182		Condon	Eugenia Marie, etc.	m
Feb.	30	1948	18182		Condon	Grace Elizabeth, etc.	m
Jan.	30	1948	18182		Condon	Lawrence Dana, etc.	m
Apr.	10	1953	21761		Conklin	Arnie A.	d
Sept.	14	1931	11052		Conklin	Elmer E.	d
Nov.	19	1931	11111		Conlan	Amelia	d
Nov.	25	1957	25166		Conley	Archie M.	d
Jan.	20	1954	22299		Conley	John J.	d
June	19	1945	16575		Conley	Robert M.	d
		1903	3698		Conn	William John	d
		1897	2806		Connell	Charles H.	d
Nov.	14	1927	9741		Connell	John	d
Feb.	24	1956	23811		Connell	Vigil S., etc.	d
Dec.	27	1957	25172		Connelly	Michael D.	d
		1877	913		Connelly	Patrick	d
		[1908-1909]	4641		Conner	Elizabeth H.	d
Jan.	31	1934	12142		Conner	Judith E.	d
Nov.	15	1953	22116		Conner	Albert B.	d

Month	Day	Year	File No.	Surname	Given Name	Type
		1912	5345	Conner	Homer Frederick	m
		1918	6889	Conners	Alexander Franklin	d
Oct.	13	1950	19978	Conners	Alice	inc
		1918	6888	Conners	Emma E.	d
		1919	7118	Conners	Frederick P., etc.	d
Jan.	6	1948	18158	Conners	G.W., etc.	d
		1904	3898	Conners	George	d
Feb.	29	1952	20886	Conners	George W., etc.	d
June		1925	8941	Conners	Hebert Thompson	m
Apr.	27	1925	8941	Conners	Jeanette Belle	m
Feb.	29	1952	20887	Conners	Lenna Belle	d
		1897	2727	Conniff	Bridget C.	d
		1894	2398	Conniff	Bridgett	ins
		[1909-1911]	4840	Conniff	James H.	d
		1903	3646	Conniff	John A.	d
Oct.	17	1916	6265	Conniff	Michael, etc.	d
		1898	2945	Conniff	Patrick	d
		1904	3897	Conniff	Susan	d
June	22	1943	15486	Conniff	T. E.	d
July	22	1946	17305	Conniff	W. F.	d
Jan.		1922	8220	Connihan	Sarah, etc.	d
Apr.	23	1954	22407	Connolly	Alice E.	d
Jan.	13	1932	11474	Connolly	Annie A.	d
		1900	3188	Connolly	Arthur H.	m
		1886	1533	Connolly	Arthur Henry	m
		1912	5300	Connolly	B. J.	d
Jan.	3	1950	19442	Connolly	Catherine E.	d
		1929	10326	Connolly	Charles L.	d
		1900	3188	Connolly	Clarence	m
July	1	1950	19735	Connolly	Cornelius	inc
Apr.	20	1954	22469	Connolly	Cornelius	d
		[1909-1911]	4956	Connolly	Ellen	d
		1881	1151	Connolly	Frances	m
		1920	7368	Connolly	Frank J.	d
Jan.	31	1935	12506	Connolly	Helen M.	d
Sept.		1920	7476	Connolly	John D.	d
		1900	3188	Connolly	Leo V.	m
		1887	1701	Connolly	Michael W.	d
		1900	3188	Connolly	Paul A.	m
		1901	3433	Connolly	Rose L.	d
		1881	1151	Connolly	Thisore	m
		1881	1151	Connolly	Thomas	m

Month	Day	Year	File No.	Surname	Given Name	Type
		1901	3473	Connors	Jennie	d
Oct.	15	1942	15053	Conolly	Louisa A., etc.	d
		1873	609	Conrad	Simon	d
Mar.	19	1945	16424	Conran	Charles Lawrence	d
May		1939	13627	Conti	Edward H.	d
Sept.	26	1939	13769	Controwith	Hattie M.	d
		1891	2240	Converse	Allen A.	d
		1923	8466	Converse	Clara, etc.	inc
June	20	1955	23259	Converse	Hilda	d
June	6	1947	17835	Converse	Lucy J.	d
Nov.	31	1947	18072	Convrse	Charles L.	d
June	23	1924	8665	Conway	Edward P.	d
Feb.	9	1941	14385	Conway	Ella G.	d
June	5	1952	21166	Conway	Frank	d
July	8	1948	18501	Conway	Jim M.	d
June	18	1927	9604	Conway	John T.	d
Aug.	25	1939	13738	Conway	Mary E.	d
June	9	1946	17194	Conway	Mary, etc.	d
Mar.	11	1920	7314	Conway	S. D.	d
May	18	1956	23997	Conway	William V., etc.	d
		1887	1696	Conwell	Caroline	d
		1884	1414	Conzelman	Gottlieb	d
		1904	3787	Coods	Johanna F.	d
		[1908-1909]	4603	Cook	Abiah H.	d
		1897	2765	Cook	Ann M.	d
July	10	1958	25765	Cook	Anna Kabra Morris	d
		1907	4313	Cook	B. L.	d
Dec.	20	1954	22930	Cook	Basha P.	d
Apr.	19	1955	23184	Cook	Charles C., Mrs., etc.	d
June	6	1952	21168	Cook	Charles, etc.	d
Apr.	11	1921	7733	Cook	Christian F. A.	d
		1870	464	Cook	D. P.	d
		1890	1977	Cook	David W.	d
May	24	1956	24012	Cook	Earl Harry, etc.	d
		1917	6462	Cook	Eliza	inc
		1926	9192	Cook	Eliza	d
Sept.	8	1958	25907	Cook	Elsie M.	d
		1858	125	Cook	F. L.	m
		1887	1642	Cook	Fisher	inc
June	2	1943	15456	Cook	Frederick B., etc.	d
June	12	1924	8677	Cook	George Julius	m
		1874	687	Cook	George M.	d

Month	Day	Year	File No.	Surname	Given Name	Type
		1887	1606	Cook	Gilbert	d
May	6	1949	19063	Cook	Harry H.	d
Apr.	11	1949	19009	Cook	Harry H., etc.	d
		[1909-1911]	4937	Cook	Hazel	m
Apr.	19	1955	23184	Cook	Ione J., etc.	d
Apr.	26	1917	6436	Cook	Isaac F., etc.	d
Oct.	1	1943	15625	Cook	Isaac N., etc.	d
		1902	3516	Cook	Israel	inc
		1902	3561	Cook	Israel	d
		1858	125	Cook	James W.	m
Dec.	10	1939	13806	Cook	Jefferson D.	d
Aug.	28	1913	5550	Cook	John	d
		1929	10370	Cook	John	d
Nov.	1	1949	19342	Cook	Louise M., etc.	d
Apr.	1	1955	23150	Cook	Lourinda W., etc.	inc
		1858	125	Cook	Lurinda E.	m
		1884	1413	Cook	Martha	d
		1904	3829	Cook	Mary J.	d
June	6	1944	16026	Cook	Mary L.	d
July	11	1928	9972	Cook	Mineva S.	inc
Apr.	30	1948	18309	Cook	Rafella	d
Apr.	15	1947	17748	Cook	Rafella, etc.	inc
Dec.	27	1937	13171	Cook	Raymond E.	d
Apr.	31	1942	14879	Cook	Rebecca	d
Nov.	1	1949	19343	Cook	Richard	d
Mar.	14	1956	23864	Cook	Ross Homer	d
		1911	5068	Cook	Shelley E.	d
		1863	234	Cook	Thomas A.	d
Mar.	10	1921	7702	Cook	Thomas G.	d
May	24	1956	24011	Cook	Wilda	d
Nov.	16	1948	18737	Cook	William E.	d
		1858	125	Cook	Mary A.	m
Aug.	30	1953	21981	Cooke	Edith, etc.	d
		1857	39	Cooke	M. E.	d
	26	1926	9212	Cooke	Minnie F.	d
Sept.	24	1947	18018	Cooley	Charles H.	d
		1899	3043	Cooley	Chas. H.	d
		1917	6534	Cooley	Edward A.	d
		1901	3261	Cooley	Hannah A.	d
Sept.	13	1948	18626	Cooley	Hazel H., etc.	d
Nov.	20	1925	9093	Cooley	James F., etc.	d
June	13	1932	11314	Cooley	John S.	d

Month	Day	Year	File No.	Surname	Given Name	Type
Aug.	26	1950	19836	Cooley	Mary A.	d
May	28	1950	19655	Cooley	Mary A., etc.	inc
Mar.	17	1937	12932	Cooley	Walter H.	d
		1883	1329	Coolidge	Nellie	m
Jan.	11	1944	16317	Coombs	Emma Barton	d
Dec.	16	1948	18739	Coombs	Inathe L., etc.	d
Sept.	3	1929	10396	Coombs	Susie Vanhalia	d
Jan.	1	1936	12821	Coombs	W. B.	d
		1919	7116	Coomes	A. M.	d
		1896	2629	Coon	Arthur	m
Sept.	23	1934	12009	Coon	Clara J.	d
		1896	2629	Coon	Frederick	m
May	30	1945	16502	Coon	Hannah A.	d
		1868	396	Coon	Hugh	m
Sept.	4	1940	13992	Coon	J. T., etc.	d
May	17	1933	11589	Coon	Jack Mervyn	d
		1896	2629	Coon	Josephine	m
		1907	4267	Coon	Lydia A.	d
Sept.	8	1940	13991	Coon	Parmenus	d
		1894	2391	Coon	R. W.	d
Mar.	12	1956	23854	Coon	Robert S., etc.	d
Dec.	10	1952	21443	Coon	Vernie Raymond, Jr.	d
		1896	2629	Coon	William	m
Mar.	18	1958	25473	Cooney	George F., etc.	d
Dec.	4	1928	10138	Cooney	James	d
Dec.	23	1953	22191	Cooney	James Patrick, etc.	d
Sept.	19	1926	9340	Cooney	John	d
Apr.	26	1958	25496	Cooney	Margaret, etc.	d
Apr.	24	1943	15325	Coons	Mary	d
Aug.	12	1912	5377	Cooper	Alma B.	g
May	26	1950	19726	Cooper	Annie E.	d
		1901	3461	Cooper	Benjamin	d
Feb.	23	1958	26174	Cooper	Benjamin S.	d
		1906	4177	Cooper	Delitha	d
		1902	3501	Cooper	Della Wallison	d
June	4	1958	25667	Cooper	Earl R.	d
Apr.	8	1958	25530	Cooper	Ella V.	inc
Aug.	13	1956	24156	Cooper	Esther, etc.	inc
Dec.	14	1956	24398	Cooper	Esther, etc.	d
May	19	1948	18353	Cooper	F. Marian, etc.	d
July	23	1958	25724	Cooper	Frank E.	d
Aug.	12	1912	5377	Cooper	George C.	g

Month	Day	Year	File No.	Surname	Given Name	Type
Apr.	31	1921	7725	Cooper	Henry Wallace, Jr.	m
July	2	1958	25753	Cooper	Iva Mae	d
		1856	36	Cooper	James	d
		1907	4268	Cooper	John	d
		1871	491	Cooper	John A.	d
May	3	1955	23214	Cooper	John B. R.	d
Oct.	24	1925	9042	Cooper	John David	d
		1905	3947	Cooper	John R.	d
Oct.	20	1958	26017	Cooper	Leslie F., etc.	d
May	17	1936	12617	Cooper	May N.	d
Nov.	16	1936	12752	Cooper	Orilla K.	d
July	5	1941	14506	Cooper	Peggy	m
		1899	2998	Cooper	Roda	d
		[1917-1918]	6658	Cooper	Thomas G.	d
		1912	5343	Cooper	William Elmer	d
		1886	1584	Cooper	William W.	d
		1884	1394	Cooper	Wm. McK.	d
June	24	1946	17221	Cooper	Janet	d
		1904	3876	Cootes	William F.	inc
Jan.	17	1921	7885	Cope	Fred J.	d
		1858	128	Cope	Herman	d
		1890	2139	Cope	Lois L.	d
July	18	1947	17890	Copenhauer	David D., etc.	d
Mar.	8	1929	10170	Coppage	Elizabeth A.	d
		1916	6314	Coppin	Albert	d
Dec.	18	1956	24406	Coppo	Bartolomeo	d
Mar.	11	1958	25449	Coppo	Louis Philip, etc.	d
May	16	1957	24740	Coppo	Maggiorina	d
		1944	15745	Copsey	Raymond	inc
Dec.	7	1951	20788	Copsey	Raymond	d
		1905	3912	Coralet	Jean	d
		[1909-1911]	4723	Corbaley	Arthur	m
		[1909-1911]	4712	Corbaley	Walter B.	d
		1866	316	Corban	M. A. K., Jr.	m
Apr.	18	1938	13270	Corbelli	Isola	d
		1920	7460	Corbet	Annah M.	d
May	17	1913	5509	Corbett	John H.	d
Sept.	22	1958	25879	Corbett	Marvin E.	d
Feb.	4	1958	25359	Corbett	Orpha	con
Aug.	12	1958	25848	Corbett	Orpha E.	d
Dec.	7	1956	24378	Corbey	John Francis, etc.	d
		1926	9465	Corbin	David W.	d

Month	Day	Year	File No.		Surname	Given Name	Type
Apr.	5	1935	12260		Corbin	Ellen C.	d
Apr.	4	1935	12257		Corbin	Ellen Clarinda	d
		1933	11644		Corbin	Frances B.	ins
Dec.	3	1934	12114		Corbin	Francis B., etc.	d
		1900	3173		Corbin	Geo. Benjamin	m
		1906	4205		Corda	Carlo	d
Oct.	15	1957	25086		Corda	Henry, etc.	d
		[1908-1909]	4426		Corda	John Doe	d
Mar.	4	1943	15296		Cordano	Antone	d
Dec.	27	1938	13520		Cordans	Mary	d
Mar.	18	1927	9542		Cordelloo	Harry	d
Apr.	8	1949	19007		Corder	Mary Alice	d
Mar.	21	1952	20941		Cordero	Joseph, etc.	d
		1906	4188		Cordi	Rodolfa	d
Mar.	24	1925	8890		Cordingley	Robert	d
		1919	7277		Cordingly	Ray	d
		[1917-1918]	6619		Cordoza	Antoine	d
Aug.		1927	9667		Cordoza	Julia C.	d
Feb.	3	1958	25348		Core	Addie E.	d
		1879	999		Corey	C.. R.	d
		1881	1148		Corey	Malinda	d
Mar.	4	1920	7340		Corfu	Charles etc.	d
Sept.	1	1950	19908		Corfu	Elvizia M., etc.	d
Sept.	4	1934	12039		Corfu	John E.	m
Nov.	26	1938	13469		Coriano	Kathrine, etc.	d
Dec.	18	1951	20809		Corick	Joseph	d
Jan.	10	1955	22966		Corino	Louis	d
Aug.	29	1949	19196		Corino	Teresa	d
June	17	1935	12305		Corippo	Benjamin H.	d
Dec.	1	1931	11152		Corippo	Peter, etc.	d
Nov.	29	1945	16795		Corkett	C. B., etc.	d
Jan.	16	1957	24460		Corkill	James J.	d
June	19	1919	7086		Corliss	Albert	d
June	15	1933	11639		Corliss	Albert James	d
Feb.	14	1927	9502		Corliss	Frank Wesley	d
Oct.	18	1927	9567		Corliss	J. Marina & Albert Jar	m
		1922	8001		Corliss	J. Roy	m
Apr.	5	1921	7730		Corliss	Joseph L. Ray	d
		1901	3300		Cornelison	Joseph	d
Aug.	18	1939	13727		Cornelius	Ella W.	d
Oct.	22	1931	11087		Cornelius	George	d
		1866	308		Cornelius	J. C. A.	d

Month	Day	Year	File No.		Surname	Given Name	Type
Mar.	24	1956	23813		Cornelius	James	d
Jan.	1	1944	16298		Cornelius	Kittie L.	d
Apr.	28	1952	21015		Cornelsen	John Louie	d
Sept.	20	1935	12413		Cornett	E. W.	d
		[1909-1911]	4865		Cornihan	Elinor, etc.	m
Aug.	22	1958	25872		Cornilsen	Henry S., etc.	d
		1917	6597		Cornwall	Frank, etc.	d
		1929	10374		Cornwell	Clara Ann	m
Dec.	18	1958	26159		Cornwell	John J.	d
		1919	7166		Corrick	Adam L.	d
Nov.	8	1957	25131		Corrick	Bessie B.	d
		1895	2575		Corrick	Louisa	inc
		1891	2231		Corrick	Louisa A.	inc
Nov.	10	1949	19362		Corrighan	Kristin	m
		1920	7335		Corry	Fanny Constance	d
July	26	1925	8990		Corry	Frederick J., etc.	d
June	1	1931	10930		Corsi	Ferdinand etc	d
July	16	1951	20487		Cortage	James Charles	d
Dec.	8	1953	22217		Cortain	Mike	d
Dec.	8	1953	22217		Cortan	Michael E.	d
Apr.	8	1914	5764		Corvi	Giovanni	d
June	25	1952	21216		Corville	John	d
July	15	1951	20441		Corville	William	d
June	28	1925	8943		Cory	Joaquin	d
Oct.	3	1950	19956		Coskery	Ruth M.	d
Dec.	8	1938	13497		Coskett	Clarence C., etc.	d
		[1909-1911]	4875		Costa	Adelaide	d
Sept.	7	1928	10053		Costa	Antone, etc.	d
		1917	6388		Costa	Giacomo	d
		1905	3938		Costa	James	inc
Jan.	19	1958	26169		Costa	Joseph V.	d
Dec.	19	1934	12082		Costa	Misa Emma, etc.	d
		[1909-1911]	5032		Costello	Bridget M.	d
		1889	1860		Costello	Thomas	d
Jan.		1919	7282		Costentino	Bolla	d
Jan.	28	1947	18109		Coster	Rilla L.	d
Jan.	7	1936	12520		Costes	Parthen	inc
Mar.	15	1936	12552		Costes	Parthen	d
May	2	1952	21099		Costigan	Lydia, etc.	d
		1871	506		Coston	Addie	m
Mar.	17	1944	15887		Cotta	Celia	inc
Apr.	17	1944	15888		Cotta	Modesta	inc

Month	Day	Year	File No.		Surname	Given Name	Type
Feb.	30	1945	16385		Cotta	Modesta	d
		1900	3166		Cottini	Peter	d
June	24	1954	22545		Cottini	Enrico	d
May	25	1930	10610		Cottle	Jethro Walden	d
		1901	3384		Cottle	Thomas J.	d
June	26	1932	11285		Couch	Ida G.	d
Jan.	1	1913	5666		Coughian	Martha E.	d
Feb.	19	1916	6179		Coughian	Wiley	d
Oct.	22	1954	22819		Coughlin	Edward L., etc.	d
Oct.	3	1951	20651		Coughlin	Mary	d
May	16	1953	21774		Coughlin	Mary C.	inc
July	15	1954	22638		Coughlin	Mary C., etc.	d
		1879	987		Coul	John B.	d
Dec.	15	1949	19370		Coul	John, etc.	d
Jan.	20	1950	19465		Coulier	Justen	d
Sept.	10	1943	15555		Coulier	Marie	d
		1911	5097		Coulson	Lucinda M. (guardians	inc
		1924	8793		Coulter	Alice R.	inc
Sept.	9	1928	10015		Coulter	Charles	d
Jan.	5	1939	13856		Coulter	Minnie	d
Nov.	13	1957	25140		Coulter	Nellie J., etc., et al	d
June	27	1929	10321		Coulter	W. S., etc.	d
Apr.	28	1932	11265		Coultu	Alice R.	d
		1895	2557		Councilman	Almeda J.	d
Mar.	2	1923	8271		Counihan	James M.	m
Apr.	6	1930	10548		Counihan	John	d
Mar.	2	1923	8271		Counihan	Michael E.	m
Oct.	13	1937	13122		Couran	George, etc.	d
Mar.	6	1946	16992		Couran	W. Martin	d
May	18	1941	14484		Couran	William	d
Apr.	22	1946	17089		Couran	William Martin	d
Feb.	14	1947	17568		Courounistis	Platon A., etc.	d
		1891	2196		Courtney	Patrick	d
Mar.		1921	7693		Courtois	John	d
Apr.	13	1954	22457		Courtright	Idonia	d
Nov.	13	1955	23532		Couso	Bruna, etc.	d
Mar.	7	1913	5465		Coustoll	Julie Eulali Vesque	d
		1926	9480		Coutts	Jane, etc.	d
		1926	9264		Coutts	William B., etc.	d
		[1908-1909]	4526		Coventry	John	d
July	10	1939	13721		Covert	George W.	d
Oct.	31	1956	24192		Covey	Annie M., etc.	d

Month	Day	Year	File No.	Surname	Given Name	Type
Mar.	1	1942	15174	Covey	Daniel	d
		1872	546	Covey	George	m
Aug.	27	1945	16667	Covey	Hattie G.	d
Oct.	16	1950	19981	Covey	J. W.	d
		1872	546	Covey	Mary	m
		1921	7820	Covey	Sarah Ann	d
		[1908-1909]	4684	Covey	Uriah	d
June	19	1946	17261	Covey	William, etc.	d
	4	1929	10328	Covey	Zahn Dwight	d
June	18	1937	13033	Covington	Dorothy	m
July	13	1956	24096	Cowan	Edward	d
Jan.	27	1949	19428	Cowan	James M., etc.	d
July	28	1934	11984	Cowan	Laura R.	d
Sept.	4	1949	19243	Cowan	Samuel W.	d
Feb.	17	1939	13535	Cowan	William F.	d
Mar.	5	1914	5731	Coward	Tom	d
May	4	1948	18376	Cowden	Robert P.	d
June	11	1948	18386	Cowden	Robert P.	d
Jan.	6	1956	23702	Cowell	Arthur E.	d
		1903	3598	Cowen	Philip	d
Sept.	7	1954	22735	Cowger	Ella W.	inc
Jan.	20	1955	22992	Cowger	Ella W., etc.	d
Aug.	18	1928	9976	Cowgill	C. C.	d
Apr.	1	1946	17118	Cowle	Herbert	d
		1863	225	Cowles	N. C.	d
Sept.	25	1953	22026	Cowling	Arthur D.	d
Apr.	14	1952	21054	Cowls	Charles	d
Aug.	24	1954	22713	Cowls	Charles	d
		[1908-1909]	4424	Cowperthwait	Dorcas	d
Sept.	1	1954	22724	Cox	Alice M.	d
Oct.		1919	7201	Cox	Asbury M.	d
Nov.		1922	8159	Cox	Bertha M.	d
Feb.	16	1951	20217	Cox	David E.	d
Dec.	20	1951	20811	Cox	Francis M.	d
Mar.	6	1951	20261	Cox	Francis, etc.	d
		1919	7275	Cox	Frederick P.	m
		1874	710	Cox	George W.	m
		[1909-1911]	4908	Cox	Harry J.	d
		1901	3373	Cox	Henrietta A.	m
		1859	147	Cox	Henry F.	m
		1924	8638	Cox	Henry Tolliver, etc.	d
		1892	2281	Cox	Jesse C.	d

Month	Day	Year	File No.	Surname	Given Name	Type
		1901	3373	Cox	Jesse I.	m
		1860	171	Cox	John T.	d
		1859	147	Cox	John W.	m
Nov.	22	1914	5885	Cox	Loleta	d
		1896	2622	Cox	Maggie A.	d
		1912	5278	Cox	Matilda M.	d
	19	1923	8308	Cox	Melvyn R.	m
July	27	1946	17276	Cox	Miriam C.	ins
July	25	1946	17311	Cox	Miriam S.	d
		1919	7275	Cox	Phyllis	m
		1877	898	Cox	Richard	d
July	14	1958	25783	Cox	Solomon Bradley, Sr.	d
May	15	1956	23991	Cox	Violet A. E., etc.	d
July	13	1953	21890	Coy	Helen H.	d
		1920	7442	Coylay	Erma Irene	g
		1920	7442	Coylay	Lottie Viola	g
Oct.	10	1951	20658	Coyle	John J.	d
Apr.	1	1928	9864	Cozad	Daniel Webster	d
Mar.	1	1928	9863	Cozad	Samantha Jane	d
		1897	2893	Cozzens	Abbie	d
		1919	7219	Cozzens	Davenport	d
		[1908-1909]	4610	Cozzens	Davenport	d
Apr.	2	1934	11907	Crabtree	Albert Franklin, etc.	d
May	24	1956	23950	Crabtree	Fred	d
		1859	148	Crabtree	Mary J.	m
Mar.	13	1946	17070	Craft	William	inc
May	3	1957	24713	Cragin	Laura Emily, etc.	d
		1918	6709	Craig	A. J.	d
Oct.	29	1958	25958	Craig	Alice May, etc.	d
		1895	2603	Craig	Daniel H.	d
		1914	5897	Craig	David N.	d
Feb.	8	1924	8565	Craig	Dorothy Margaret	g
June	11	1951	20433	Craig	Francis Alexander, etc	d
		1907	4232	Craig	James	inc
Feb.	24	1936	12532	Craig	John P.	d
Feb.	8	1924	8565	Craig	Leslie Marion	g
		1922	8147	Craig	Mary E.	d
		1891	2075	Craig	Oliver W.	d
Mar.	28	1944	15858	Craig	Robert Carl	d
		1904	3861	Craig	Sophia T.	inc
		1905	4045	Craig	Sophia T.	d
Jan.	6	1915	6125	Crain	Melba, et al	m

Month	Day	Year	File No.		Surname	Given Name	Type
Dec.	6	1915	6125		Crain	Myron, et al	m
		1891	2105		Cramer	Abraham (Mendocino	d
Sept.	25	1935	12382		Cramer	Annie	ins
July	17	1946	17300		Cramer	Annie	d
Oct.	3	1957	25058		Cramer	Annie	con
July	3	1950	19794		Cramer	Arthur I.	d
June	22	1945	16580		Cramer	C. W.	d
Feb.	1	1938	13235		Cramer	Cornelius	d
Jan.	26	1952	21537		Cramer	Erwin Louis	d
Nov.	30	1952	21430		Cramer	Fanny L.	d
June	24	1952	21214		Cramer	Gertrude	d
July	17	1947	17855		Cramer	Henry D., etc.	d
Nov.	13	1956	24325		Cramer	James	d
Oct.	30	1952	21430		Cramer	John F.	d
Feb.	29	1923	8261		Cramer	Judson L.	d
July		1926	9306		Cramer	Lillian	d
Nov.	28	1920	7530		Crandall	Moses H.	d
Jan.	30	1946	17503		Crane	Adaline P.	d
		[1909-1911]	4802		Crane	Charles C.	d
		1920	7362		Crane	Edith G.	m
Jan.	27	1942	15169		Crane	Elizabeth M.	d
		1920	7362		Crane	Harold F.	m
		1893	2345		Crane	Jane E.	d
Dec.		1913	5635		Crane	Joel (termination)	blank
Apr.	6	1928	9927		Crane	John D.	d
Mar.	28	1952	20949		Crane	Laurence E., etc.	d
		1919	7276		Crane	M. J., Mrs.	d
Oct.	21	1922	8145		Crane	Mary S.	d
May	14	1945	16570		Crane	May Jane, etc.	d
		1919	7242		Crane	Nancy J.	d
Aug.	9	1913	5567		Crane	Nelson L.	d
Feb.	27	1936	12535		Crane	Oliver L.	d
Oct.	18	1953	22063		Crane	Richard Lincoln, etc.	d
		1900	3230		Crane	Robert	d
May	10	1943	15420		Crane	Robert Lee	d
		1920	7362		Crane	Roy W.	m
Feb.	7	1919	6935		Crane	Susanna C., etc.	d
Mar.	5	1940	13880		Crane	Wade H., etc.	d
Feb.		1917	6411		Crane	William C.	inc
Apr.	19	1917	6466		Crane	William Cary, etc.	d
Apr.	16	1948	18348		Craner	Frank W., etc.	d
		1887	1692		Crannell	Patrick	d

Month	Day	Year	File No.		Surname	Given Name	Type
May	27	1938	13303		Cranshaw	Martha Washington	m
Nov.	4	1957	25124		Craven	Donald, etc.	d
Jan.	22	1945	16896		Crawder	Bertha L.	inc
		1946	16917		Crawder	Bertha L.	d
Dec.	17	1914	5900		Crawford	B. F.	d
Jan.	27	1934	12141		Crawford	Charles Leonidas, etc.	d
Jan.	24	1949	19423		Crawford	E. H.	d
Apr.	12	1944	15923		Crawford	Edwin Henry	d
		[1909-1911]	4903		Crawford	Frances E.	d
May	14	1951	20397		Crawford	Harry L.	d
Oct.	9	1925	9076		Crawford	Maggie M., etc.	d
Apr.	26	1917	6432		Crawford	R. F.	d
June	14	1928	9997		Crawford	Richard Francis	m
July	26	1943	15529		Crawford	Richard Francis	d
Feb.	18	1955	23063		Crawford	Seth B.	d
Jan.	30	1914	5925		Crawford	Jesse B.	d
Oct.	29	1938	13418		Crawley	James J., etc.	d
Nov.	26	1948	18698		Crawley	Peter	d
May	23	1917	6469		Crayne	Daniel	d
Aug.	18	1918	6792		Crayne	Rebecca	d
Apr.	8	1958	25533		Creaser	Ida	inc
Oct.	18	1958	25937		Creaser	Ida	d
Feb.	29	1953	21617		Creger	Charles	d
		1939	13600		Creger	Sylvia E.	d
Oct.		1917	6568		Cregin	Charles C.	d
		[1909-1911]	4784		Creighton	Byrrel J.	m
Nov.		1942	15105		Crepazzi/Crivelli	Clementina, etc.	d
Nov.	17	1930	10734		Crept	Tracy Richard, etc.	d
July	15	1944	16082		Crescenzo	Louis Joseph, etc.	d
Jan.	10	1937	13187		Crespa	Martha	d
Apr.	12	1948	18339		Crespo	Ricardo	d
May	29	1945	16500		Cressenzo	Jennie	d
June	10	1949	19125		Cretser	C. F.	d
Nov.	29	1948	18707		Crevelli	Antone	d
Feb.	16	1931	10878		Crichfield	Charles A.	d
Aug.	15	1932	11364		Crichfield	Charles A.	d
June	3	1934	11944		Crider	Armilda, etc.	d
Nov.	18	1946	17443		Crigler	Della B.	d
		1908	4402		Crigler	Thomas M.	d
May	25	1955	23198		Crinella	Anna	d
June	29	1927	9619		Crinella	Frank	d
Oct.	1	1906	4168		Crippen	C. P.	d

Month	Day	Year	File No.		Surname	Given Name	Type
Aug.	21	1924	8714		Crippen	Harriet	d
		1889	1905		Crippen	Perry	d
Oct.	4	1949	19301		Crippen	Virdie E.	d
Sept.	12	1950	19923		Crippen	Walter A.	d
		1864	252		Crisp	John B.	m
		1860	161		Crisp	John W.	d
		1864	161		Crisp	Maggie E.	m
		1864	252		Crisp	Sarah J.	m
		1860	175		Crisp	Wm. H.	m
July	25	1946	17312		Criss	Gradyn Anna	m
June	21	1948	18468		Crist	E. L.	d
		1877	872		Crist	Rosa A.	ins
		1891	2095		Crist	William	d
		1901	3314		Crist	William H.	d
Nov.	26	1954	22828		Cristiani	Steve, etc.	d
Nov.	4	1932	11433		Critchlow	John, etc.	d
Apr.	13	1956	23925		Crocker	Belva E.	d
Feb.	25	1958	25419		Crocker	Harry, etc.	d
July	23	1953	21967		Crocker	Roy L.	d
		1922	8196		Crockett	Fred P.	d
		1860	167		Crockett	Jeremiah T.	d
Apr.	29	1915	5949		Croman	Annie	d
July	25	1939	13681		Croman	Eliza	inc
Dec.	20	1943	15725		Croman	Eliza S.	d
Nov.	28	1920	7582		Cromwell	F. A. (in re: Lippitt)	t
Oct.	25	1925	9065		Cromwell	Frank A.	d
Oct.	23	1945	16723		Cromwell	Sallie E., etc.	d
May	16	1918	6744		Cronare ?	Edward	d
Aug.	14	1950	19868		Crone	Edwin	d
		1918	6814		Cronin	Hannah	inc
		1920	7389		Cronin	Hannah	d
		1925	9004		Cronin	Hugh	d
June	24	1957	24754		Cronin	John F.	inc
		1918	6809		Cronin	Patrick	d
Jan.	12	1941	14738		Cronk	Sadie C.	d
Oct.	13	1949	19256		Cronkite	Burt E., Jr.	d
Nov.	1	1954	22841		Cronkite	Lee Ann	m
Nov.	1	1954	22841		Cronkite	Nancy Jo	m
July	3	1913	5520		Cronley	Nancy A.	d
Sept.	10	1954	22746		Crook	Frank W.	d
		1860	174		Crook	J. J.	ins
June	14	1943	15428		Crook	Merett D.	d

Month	Day	Year	File No.		Surname	Given Name	Type
		1894	2418		Crooker	John S.	d
May		1914	5768		Crooker	Martha	inc
		1917	6401		Crooker	Martha	d
July	14	1953	21942		Crosariol	Giuseppe	d
July	14	1953	21943		Crosariol	Giuseppe	d
		1922	8016		Crosbie	Alice	ins
Jan.		1923	8256		Crosbie	Alice	d
Aug.	28	1953	21975		Crosby	Ida B.	d
		1906	4122		Crose	Mary	d
Aug.	27	1956	24183		Crosetti	Giacomo, etc.	d
Aug.	14	1950	19817		Crosier	Florence S., etc.	d
		1916	6316		Crosland	Elizabeth	d
Jan.	2	1936	12508		Cross	Edith	d
		1907	4237		Cross	Francis Marion	d
May	1	1939	13657		Crosta	Anselmo	d
May	31	1951	20418		Crothers	Homer L.	inc
Dec.	19	1955	23666		Crothers	Homer L.	d
Apr.	3	1953	21748		Crottogini	Battista Giovanni	d
June	25	1929	10345		Crotts	Annie G.	d
June	25	1929	10345		Crotts	Annie G.	d
Apr.	4	1927	9587		Crotts	H. R.	d
Nov.	17	1927	9746		Crotts	Irene, Alice & Harvey	m
June	13	1927	9651		Crotts	Sarah	d
	11	1919	7186		Crow	Emma Jane	g
		1885	1492		Crow	William W.	m
Jan.	12	1923	8246		Crow	Jim	d
Feb.	26	1941	14414		Crowder	James William, etc.	d
Jan.	15	1936	12833		Crowder	Mary	d
Aug.	29	1947	17917		Crowe	Marrion	d
Feb.		1944	15773		Crowe	Robert F.	m
Apr.	14	1952	21054		Crowell	Charles	d
Aug.	24	1954	22713		Crowell	Charles	d
		1907	4239		Crowell	Roy Victor	m
Mar.	27	1951	20240		Crowell	Sena	d
July	10	1958	25771		Crowley	Mary	inc
May	19	1946	17157		Crowley	Thomas J.	d
Mar.	29	1927	9684		Crowley	William M.	d
Apr.	13	1948	18343		Crowninshield	Danial A., etc.	inc
July	19	1945	16616		Crownover	Fred Jennings	d
Nov.	27	1945	16793		Crownover	Glenda Jean	m
		1924	8795		Crozier	Priscilla B.	d
Sept.	31	1949	19241		Crozier	Robert John, etc.	d

Month	Day	Year	File No.	Surname	Given Name	Type
Feb.	11	1936	12548	Cruickshanks	Nancy Adeline	d
July	18	1945	16613	Crul	Sidney P., etc.	d
Mar.	24	1958	25489	Crumboker	Hazel J.	d
Apr.	13	1936	12584	Crume	Nancy Rosanna	d
Jan.	25	1937	12860	Crume	Wallace W.	d
July	20	1947	17857	Crump	Emma O.	d
Nov.	30	1951	20705	Crutchfield	William H.	d
Feb.	18	1952	20929	Crutchoff	John Waldorf	d
June	17	1931	10946	Cruttenden/Crittenden	James A.	d
		1914	5912	Cruzon	John A.	d
Nov.	6	1938	13450	Cryst	Margaret	d
		1911	5188	Crystal	Kate E.	d
June	26	1953	21864	Cuadro	Bernard	d
Mar.	4	1954	22326	Cucchi	Ben	d
Sept.	6	1929	10400	Cufer	Frank	d
		1919	7250	Cuicello	J. G., etc.	d
June	26	1952	21142	Cuicello	Susie E. Turner, etc.	d
Sept.	3	1953	22044	Cullen	John	d
Oct.	4	1950	19957	Cullen	Lloyd Gale, etc.	d
		1872	563	Culligan	James	d
		[1908-1909]	4671	Culligan	James	d
Aug.	25	1957	24907	Culp	Ben	d
Oct.	28	1945	16742	Culton	Charles W., etc.	d
Mar.	3	1942	14838	Culton	Clara E.	d
		1901	3500	Culver	Charles Francis	d
Dec.	22	1954	22923	Culver	Corwin M.	d
		1903	3707	Culver	Lewis C.	d
Nov.	28	1954	22834	Culver	Magee E.	d
		1935	12334	Cummings	Anna	d
Nov.	10	1955	23582	Cummings	Caroline T., etc.	d
June	17	1955	23242	Cummings	Charles R., etc.	d
Aug.	21	1947	17905	Cummings	E. J.	d
Sept.	10	1938	13347	Cummings	Eva	d
Aug.	10	1938	13346	Cummings	Frank	d
Aug.	12	1918	6789	Cummings	Fred M.	d
		1917	6587	Cummings	H. K.	d
Mar.	14	1930	10522	Cummings	Isabel J.	d
Nov.	5	1951	20713	Cummings	Joseph Martin	d
		1915	6051	Cummings	Joseph S.	d
May	5	1941	14504	Cummings	Lawrena I.	d
Dec.	26	1935	12475	Cummings	Lawrence B.	d
		1888	1728	Cummings	Leander	d

Month	Day	Year	File No.	Surname	Given Name	Type
Feb.	24	1928	10155	Cummings	Mary A.	d
Mar.	24	1955	23076	Cummings	Mary M.	d
Feb.	11	1927	9490	Cummings	Matilda	d
		1902	3504	Cummings	Michael	d
May	24	1936	12596	Cummings	Michael Edward	d
Apr.	21	1914	5751	Cummings	Susan A.	d
		[1908-1909]	4662	Cummings	Waller B.	d
		1891	2063	Cummings	William	d
		1872	562	Cummings	William	d
		1911	5192	Cummings	William F.	d
May	5	1941	14504	Cummings	Winifred L.	d
		1919	7162	Cummins	C. Howe	d
Apr.	26	1957	24692	Cummins	Clara C.	inc
		1921	7738	Cummins	George A. M.	d
		[1917-1918]	6692	Cummins	Jhilson P.	d
Apr.	12	1957	24663	Cummins	William C.	d
May	25	1958	25577	Cumpston	Debra E.	m
		[1908-1909]	4699	Cundiff	Alpha Bernice (mothei	m
		[1908-1909]	4699	Cundiff	Jesse Donald (mother	m
July	12	1945	16643	Cundiff	Christopher, etc.	d
Nov.	7	1938	13477	Cuneo	Aldo	m
Dec.	19	1956	24408	Cuneo	Anne Carmel, etc.	d
Dec.	8	1930	10802	Cuneo	Antonio	d
		1922	8109	Cuneo	Antonio	d
Feb.	2	1923	8267	Cuneo	Antonio	m
June	31	1938	13335	Cuneo	Carmela	ins
Nov.	7	1938	13477	Cuneo	Delio	m
Feb.	2	1923	8267	Cuneo	Dina	m
Feb.	2	1923	8267	Cuneo	Ernesto	m
Feb.	2	1923	8267	Cuneo	Florido	m
Oct.	10	1955	23526	Cuneo	Frank, etc.	d
Dec.	26	1937	13154	Cuneo	Gerolamo, etc.	d
Sept.	12	1948	18577	Cuneo	Joseph	d
Nov.	7	1938	13477	Cuneo	Lino	m
Feb.	22	1950	20115	Cuneo	Mary	d
July	15	1955	23372	Cuneo	Mary Philomena, etc.	d
Nov.	8	1954	22851	Cuneo	Emilia	d
Sept.	31	1944	16107	Cunha	Carl C.	d
Mar.	19	1929	10249	Cunha	John Rose	d
Aug.	29	1949	19195	Cunha	Joseph	d
Aug.	4	1937	13082	Cunha	Joseph Ferrcira	m
July	18	1954	22603	Cunha	Joseph, etc.	d

Month	Day	Year	File No.		Surname	Given Name	Type
Feb.	7	1930	10515		Cunha	Mabel Rose	d
May	18	1949	19010		Cunha	Manuel F., etc.	d
Sept.	4	1937	13082		Cunha	Mary Lorainne	m
Aug.	22	1958	25873		Cunio	Clementina, etc.	d
July	8	1939	13668		Cunio/Cuneo	Sabino, etc.	d
		1901	3284		Cunningham	Andrew	d
Oct.	30	1947	18031		Cunningham	Andrew	d
		1891	2218		Cunningham	F. Z.	d
May	9	1958	25609		Cunningham	Gilbert R.	d
Mar.	28	1947	17667		Cunningham	Grace L.	d
Nov.	13	1943	15676		Cunningham	Isaac Burns	d
		1901	3497		Cunningham	Jacob	m
		1890	1985		Cunningham	John	d
		1926	9180		Cunningham	Lucille	m
		1924	8634		Cunningham	Lucy	inc
Sept.		1925	9038		Cunningham	Lucy A.	d
		1920	7339		Cunningham	Mary Catharine	d
		1897	2716		Cunningham	Robert	d
		1925	8887		Cunningham	Robert	d
		1869	421		Cunningham	Robert A.	d
		1901	3497		Cunningham	Winifred L.	m
		1902	3543		Cunningham	Winifred L.	m
		1901	3313		Cunningham	Zina H.	d
July	11	1951	20434		Cunninghame	Mabel	d
Oct.	6	1927	9733		Cunninghame	Stephen A.	d
Aug.	11	1947	17940		Cunninghame	William Mc G.	d
Oct.	3	1953	22092		Cupp	Alice Charlene	m
Jan.	31	1948	18807		Cuppoletti	Attilis	d
Nov.	16	1950	19982		Curfman	Carl	d
Apr.	26	1958	25495		Curles	Harvey	d
July	21	1957	24818		Curless	George G.	d
June	22	1937	13006		Curran	Helen	ins
June	23	1944	15999		Curran	Horace E., etc.	d
Sept.	7	1943	15551		Curran	Pearl M.	d
May		1922	8042		Curricen	Daniel	inc
July	2	1952	21233		Currie	James R., etc.	d
Apr.	10	1951	20327		Currie	Louise C.	d
Feb.	26	1923	8290		Currier	Daniel G.	d
		1905	3961		Currier	Susan C.	d
		1900	3144		Currier	William	d
		1899	3016		Currier	William H.	d
July	17	1927	9653		Curry	James	inc

Month	Day	Year	File No.		Surname	Given Name	Type
June	17	1927	9654		Curry	James	Inc
		1894	2410		Curry	John	d
Mar.	16	1922	7927		Curry	Juliette, etc.	d
Nov.	25	1928	10076		Curry	Louise C,. etc.	d
Aug.	6	1956	24145		Curry	Myrtle E., etc.	d
May	1	1919	7076		Curry	Patrick	d
Dec.	5	1940	14302		Curt/Coit	Frances	d
Jan.	20	1940	14313		Curt/Coit	Manuel J.	d
Feb.	31	1939	13551		Curti	Vincenzo	d
		1923	8467		Curtis	Austin James	d
Jan.	24	1952	20871		Curtis	Caryl Masten	d
May		1918	6725		Curtis	Catherine	d
Oct.	9	1946	17432		Curtis	Ed, etc.	d
		1894	2474		Curtis	Galena C.	d
Nov.	17	1957	25090		Curtis	George Richard	d
Nov.	27	1957	25174		Curtis	Harry, etc.	d
		1898	2978		Curtis	James H.	d
Nov.	31	1932	11427		Curtis	John H.	d
Dec.	12	1956	24390		Curtis	John Melvon, etc.	d
		1891	2120		Curtis	Richard H.	d
		1920	7453		Curtis	Walter V.	d
June	8	1943	15468		Curtiss	George C.	d
July	8	1943	15469		Curtiss	Sarah J.	d
Nov.	10	1920	7569		Curto	Domino	m
Nov.	10	1920	7569		Curto	Eppi Del	m
Nov.	10	1920	7569		Curto	Rina Del	m
Jan.	16	1942	14773		Cushing	Frederick W.	d
Aug.	4	1913	5585		Cushman	Hazel	m
Aug.	4	1913	5584		Cushman	Loretta E.	m
May	2	1950	19666		Cussins	Dorothy A.	d
May	27	1956	23955		Custer	Mary A.	d
Apr.	21	1943	15390		Custis	Fannie M.	d
Oct.	7	1955	23480		Cuthill	James Sinclair	d
Jan.	21	1941	14357		Cuthill	Mary	d
Dec.	18	1950	20109		Cuthill	William Hayward, etc.	d
Sept.	27	1946	17369		Cutten	Agnes	d
Oct.	21	1948	18635		Cutter	Alfred Reed, etc.	d
Sept.	14	1954	22757		Cutter	Cedric E.	d
Apr.	19	1940	13938		Cutter	Charles S.	d
		1871	510		Cutter	Joseph S.	d
June	27	1932	11320		Cutter	Maria Vallejo, etc.	d
Oct.	24	1952	21361		Cutter	Henry P.	d

Month	Day	Year	File No.		Surname	Given Name	Type
Sept.	17	1923	8460		Cutting	David C.	d
May	12	1943	15426		Cutts	Lloyd	m
Dec.	25	1958	26108		Cutts	Marie	d
Mar.	21	1932	11257		Cuvreau	Daisy	d
Feb.	28	1946	16971		Cyrus	Ethel C./Mrs. Edward	d

Month	Day	Year	File No.	Surname	Given Name	Type
May	4	1952	22515	Dabner	Cynthia	m
		1883	1296	Dabner	Frank	m
		1882	1216	Dabner	John	d
		1923	8479	Dabner	Lucinda W.	d
		1883	1296	Dabner	Manuel	m
		[1898-1899]	2890	Dabner	Mary	d
		[1908-1909]	4618	Dabney	Columbus W.	d
Feb.	31	1950	19485	Dabney	Harland F., etc.	d
		1888	1767	Dabney	Martha C.	d
May	29	1958	25586	Daddi	Albina	d
		1913	5580	Daddi	Ferdinand	d
July	11	1935	12676	Daddi	Ferdinand	d
Dec.	8	1954	22801	Daddi	John	d
Nov.	28	1924	8718	Daddi	Virginia	d
July	29	1953	21873	Dado	Arnold W.	d
Mar.	26	1923	8258	Dado	Attilio A., etc.	d
June	27	1935	12653	Dado	Carolina	d
Sept.	7	1923	8451	Dado	Loretta E.	g
Mar.	3	1932	11214	Dado	Paldina O.	d
Sept.	8	1923	8430	Dado	Paul, etc.	d
Aug.		1923	8415	Dado	Silvia J.	inc
	13	1925	8905	Dado	Silvio J.	d
Sept.	7	1923	8451	Dado	Vernon E.	g
Apr.	28	1954	22408	DaFonseca	Maoel J.	d
Apr.	28	1954	22408	DaFonseca/da Fonseca	Manuel Joaquim/Manc	d
Aug.	24	1933	11649	Daggett	Jennie N.	d
		[1871-1872]	511	Daggett	Margaret	ins
		1872	542	Daggett	Margaret	d
Feb.	29	1946	16975	Dagnello	Bonte, etc.	d
June	18	1957	24813	Dagnello	Carlo, etc.	d
Feb.	5	1940	13881	Dagnello	Girolamo	d
June	18	1957	24812	Dagnello	Vittoria	d
Oct.	18	1925	9036	Dagnin	Francis H.	d
Oct.	22	1958	26027	Dahl	Charles William	m
Oct.	23	1940	14157	Dahl	Frank H.	d
Nov.	15	1956	24270	Dahl	George Russell, etc.	d
Nov.	22	1958	26027	Dahl	Joanne Charlene	m
Dec.	24	1940	14246	Dahlgren	Fritz E., etc.	d
		1906	4041	Dahlman	Alba F.	m
		1906	4041	Dahlman	Eugene C.	m
		1906	4041	Dahlman	Eunice F.	m
		1881	1135	Dahlman	Fred S.	m

Month	Day	Year	File No.	Surname	Given Name	Type
		1906	4041	Dahlman	Gladys M.	m
		1881	1135	Dahlman	Henry	m
		1881	1135	Dahlman	Martha	m
		1906	4041	Dahlman	Meriam K.	m
		1906	4041	Dahlman	Wadsworth H.	m
		1906	4041	Dahlman	Wilma G.	m
Mar.	21	1921	7709	Dahlmann	Frederich, etc.	d
May	27	1951	20365	Dahlmann	Henry	d
Aug.	15	1949	19215	Dahlmann	Retta I.	d
July	24	1949	19142	Dahlmann	Retta Irene. etc.	d
Feb.	19	1937	12864	Dailey	Joseph C.	d
Sept.	11	1958	25914	Dains	Valchor Valson	inc
May	15	1918	6741	Daitoku	Kaguhiyo	m
	15	1918	6741	Daitoku	Kiyoko	m
May	15	1918	6740	Daitoku	Nakago	d
	15	1918	6741	Daitoku	Teruko	m
Jan.	26	1927	9516	Dajas	Louis	d
Sept.	26	1945	16664	Dake	Amelia R.	d
Mar.	5	1946	17051	Dake	Forrest C.	d
May	6	1948	18324	Dake	Forrest C., etc.	d
	2	1924	8646	Dakin	Walter R.	d
		1913	5490	Dakin	William Henry	d
		1911	5202	Dakin	Zephaniah	d
		1890	1918	Dakin	Zepheniah	d
Mar.	24	1941	14411	Dal Paggetto	Madelina	d
	29	1921	7818	Dal Poggetto	Charles	d
June	10	1941	14430	Dal Poggetto	Dena	m
Apr.	15	1934	11827	Dal Poggetto	Emilio, etc.	d
July	10	1941	14430	Dal Poggetto	Ilene	m
Mar.	4	1935	12148	Dal Poggetto	Maria	d
Aug.	21	1940	14076	Dal Poggetto	Newton F.	d
June	10	1952	21182	Dale	Anna L., etc.	d
Sept.	31	1953	21985	Dale	Annas H.	d
Aug.	16	1956	24101	Dale	Harvey	d
Dec.	3	1934	12069	Dale	Martha Ellen, etc.	d
Feb.	16	1939	13531	Dalessi	Charly	d
		1858	107	Dallingham	John R.	d
May	28	1952	21088	Dalloca	Frances L.	d
		1914	5829	Dalluege	Ernst	d
May		1923	8319	Dalpino	Albert	m
Apr.		1923	8319	Dalpino	Samuel	m
Nov.	22	1941	14685	Dalto	Guiseppe	d

Month	Day	Year	File No.	Surname	Given Name	Type
		1914	5722	Dalton	James	d
		1920	7617	Dalton	James	d
Dec.	26	1923	8482	Dalton	Libertina N.	g
		1923	8512	Dalton	Libertina N.	d
		[1881-1882]	1155	Dalton	William H.	d
		[1908-1909]	4606	Daly	James	d
		1904	3772	Daly	John	d
		1911	5105	Daly	Matilda	d
Oct.	18	1958	25938	Daly	Thelma M.	d
Jan.	16	1940	14307	D'Ambragi	Giovanni, etc.	d
Aug.	20	1948	18588	D'Ambrogi	Della, etc.	d
Aug.	22	1939	13707	Dambroski	John	d
Sept.	8	1952	21289	Damgaard	Soren	d
		1906	4151	Damico	Luigi	d
June	5	1935	12662	Damm	Stephen	d
June	20	1955	23256	Damon	Florence B.	d
Sept.	26	1952	21367	Damostene	Manuel D.	d
		1892	2198	Dana	Alfred H.	m
		1893	2334	Dana	Alfred H.	m
		1893	2333	Dana	Alfred W.	d
		1892	2198	Dana	Charles B.	m
		1893	2334	Dana	Charles B.	m
		1892	2198	Dana	E. Mabel	m
		1893	2334	Dana	E. Mabel	m
		1892	2198	Dana	Frank	m
		1893	2334	Dana	Frank	m
Feb.	13	1958	25378	Dana	George Frederick, etc.	d
		1892	2198	Dana	Harold B.	m
		1893	2334	Dana	Harold B.	m
		1892	2198	Dana	John A.	m
		1893	2334	Dana	John A.	m
		1892	2198	Dana	Ruth	m
		1893	2334	Dana	Ruth	m
		1892	2198	Dana	William	m
		1893	2334	Dana	William	m
Feb.	8	1939	13567	Danati	Elisa, etc.	d
		[1894-1895]	2396	Dancer	W. H.	d
Sept.	6	1946	17332	Dand--?	Werner	d
Aug.		1916	6246	Dane	Albert	d
Oct.	3	1940	14130	Daneri	Attilio, etc.	d
Feb.	15	1943	15233	Daneri	Henry F.	d
July	7	1944	16068	Danhausen	R. F.	d

Month	Day	Year	File No.	Surname	Given Name	Type
Apr.	16	1954	22459	Daniel	Adolf, etc.	d
Aug.	6	1927	9642	Daniel	Julia E.	d
Apr.		1924	8578	Danieli	Charles	d
Mar.	3	1950	19547	Danieli	Charles R.	d
Nov.	25	1946	17453	Danieli	Mary	d
June	22	1950	19716	Danielli	Crespino	d
Sept.		1914	5857	Daniels	Christina L.	d
		1920	7408	Daniels	Edward John	d
Jan.	10	1956	24382	Daniels	Gerhard F.	d
		[1889-1890]	1855	Daniels	Henry	d
Nov.	28	1945	16842	Daniels	James T.	d
May	3	1949	19049	Daniels	Joe	d
Jan.	23	1954	22939	Daniels	John Fran	d
Feb.	28	1914	5874	Daniels	Lucile B.	m
Jan.	27	1930	10823	Daniels	Mary L.	d
		1904	3804	Daniels	Newell	d
June	1	1935	12631	Daniels	Rex	m
		[1876-1877]	820	Daniels	Seneca	d
		[1909-1911]	4657	Daniels	William E.	d
		[1908-1909]	4547	Daniels	Frederick V./Frederick	d
Feb.	21	1927	9544	Danielsen	Martin	d
July	25	1934	11981	Danielsen	Martin	inc
May	11	1939	13640	Danielson	Martin	d
July	19	1940	14000	Danielson	Peter Magnus	d
Dec.	29	1945	16843	Danker	Herbert	d
Jan.	29	1945	16844	Danker	Herbert	d
Feb.	4	1946	16990	Dankinh	Harry	d
Apr.	4	1953	21678	Dannemark	George H., etc.	d
		[1904-1905]	3831	Dannhausen	Clemens	d
		1913	5548	Dannhausen	Deidrick	m
		1913	5548	Dannhausen	Grant Carl	m
		1913	5548	Dannhausen	Herbert	m
		1913	5485	Dannhausen	Meta	d
		1913	5548	Dannhausen	Meta	m
		1913	5548	Dannhausen	Rudolph	m
		1913	5506	Dannhausen	William	d
		1913	5548	Dannhausen	William	m
Apr.	21	1956	23806	Danzel	Leah Cora	d
		1858	157	Dapkins	Samuel	d
Aug.		1924	8710	Darala/Davis	Annie	d
Jan.	15	1939	13841	Darby	Augusta L.	d
Mar.	27	1950	19536	Darby	Floyd D., etc.	mp

Month	Day	Year	File No.	Surname	Given Name	Type
Jan.	11	1950	20100	Darby	Floyd D., etc.	d
		[1900-1903]	3452	Darby	Floyd Donald	m
		[1900-1903]	3452	Darby	Jasper Basil	m
		[1900-1903]	3451	Darby	Josephine	d
Jan.	15	1946	16938	DaRider	Albert, etc.	d
June		1917	6447	Darling	E. C.	d
Apr.	11	1952	21049	Darnell	John Merritt	d
July	2	1924	8667	DaRosa	Jose F.	d
July	2	1941	14570	Darrah	Frank Marion, etc.	d
Nov.	28	1945	16840	Darrong	Anna	inc
Feb.	14	1927	9496	Darst	Margaret E.	inc
July	1	1927	9638	Darst	Margaret E.	d
		[1890-1892]	1948	Darwin	Andrew M.	d
June	18	1951	20400	Darwood	Frankie B., etc.	d
Oct.	18	1951	20612	Dashiell	Thomas J.	d
Jan.	4	1956	23696	Dashwander	Robert J.	d
Sept.	6	1957	24998	daSilveria	Jose Maria, etc.	d
		1918	6832	D'Aubrogi	Cecil	d
Aug.	18	1955	22988	Dauenhauer	Donald Lee	m
Jan.	9	1954	22909	Dauenhauer	Florian M., etc.	d
Jan.	10	1955	22967	Dauenhauer	Leo E., etc.	d
		1955	22988	Dauenhauer	Leo Robert	m
Nov.	13	1915	6128	Daugaard	Asge Emil	d
Jan.	13	1915	6128	Daugard	Fred, etc.	d
June	10	1952	21184	Daugherty	Barbara Lynn	m
Apr.	8	1933	11584	Daugherty	Frank Willis, etc.	d
Oct.	2	1954	22673	Daugherty	Jane Ellen	m
July	10	1952	21184	Daugherty	Jerry Arthur	m
Apr.	6	1954	22437	Daugherty	Joseph A., etc.	d
July	10	1952	21184	Daugherty	Margaret	m
June	10	1952	21184	Daugherty	Michael Jon	m
June	10	1952	21184	Daugherty	Wanda Jean	m
Nov.	4	1915	6122	Daughney	John J.	d
Sept.	16	1908	4543	Dauguet	F.	d
		1908	4545	Dauguet	T.	d
May	6	1957	24715	Daus	Maude E.	inc
Sept.		1920	7492	Dauuhausen	Meta, Jr.	d
		1923	8298	Davala/Davis	Manuel	d
Apr.	13	1940	13930	Davaz	Anna, etc.	d
June	23	1938	13325	Davaz	Thomas	d
July	5	1925	8974	Davidson	Addie McDowell	d
		1911	5204	Davidson	Alexander T.	d

Month	Day	Year	File No.	Surname	Given Name	Type
		[1906-1907]	4201	Davidson	Amanda K.	d
Sept.	7	1951	20530	Davidson	Amelia W., etc.	d
		[1886-1887]	1568	Davidson	Anna M.	d
Apr.	3	1944	15866	Davidson	Annie	d
Apr.	12	1943	15379	Davidson	Frank T.	d
Feb.	4	1958	25354	Davidson	Harold C./Chris D.	d
Aug.	23	1949	19182	Davidson	Harold G., etc.	d
		[1884-1885]	1445	Davidson	Jacob E.	d
		1916	6281	Davidson	James	inc
Oct.	11	1916	6317	Davidson	James	d
		1905	4001	Davidson	Smith E.	inc
		1906	4102	Davidson	Smith E.	d
Feb.	2	1942	14804	Davidson	W. J.	d
May	21	1948	18398	Davies	Bertha Benjamin	d
Sept.	25	1922	8125	Davies	Ivan J.	inc
	4	1926	9160	Davies	Morgan T.	d
July	28	1950	19781	Davini	Allessandro	d
Mar.	3	1931	10897	Davini	Carlo	inc
Aug.	24	1955	23340	Davini	Hugo Joseph	d
July	7	1946	17288	Davini	Joseph, etc.	d
Nov.	23	1945	16787	Davini	Vincent	d
		1906	4062	Davis	Alys Marie	m
June	24	1945	16549	Davis	Anna M. W.	inc
July	17	1948	18462	Davis	Anna M. W.	d
June	19	1941	14553	Davis	Arthur F.	d
		[1897-1898]	2788	Davis	Calvin P.	inc
		1906	4082	Davis	Calvin P.	d
Mar.	15	1949	18955	Davis	Charles N.	d
Oct.	16	1955	23437	Davis	Cheryl Kay	m
July	13	1958	25622	Davis	Conell, et al	m
Oct.	13	1927	9721	Davis	Daisy C. alias	d
Dec.	7	1944	16308	Davis	Dora M.	d
		1926	9179	Davis	Douglas, etc.	d
		[1909-1911]	4755	Davis	E. A.	d
		[1900-1903]	3575	Davis	Edward W.	d
		1874	677	Davis	Edwin	m
June	17	1957	24743	Davis	Eleanor Levy	m
		1923	8372	Davis	Elizabeth	d
		1874	677	Davis	Ella	m
		1911	5073	Davis	Ezekiel W.	d
Apr.	16	1945	16479	Davis	Flora J.	d
Sept.	6	1930	10648	Davis	Frances M.	d

Month	Day	Year	File No.	Surname	Given Name	Type
May	17	1958	25560	Davis	Frances M.	d
Nov.	18	1948	18680	Davis	Frank E.	d
Mar.	8	1946	16994	Davis	Frank N.	d
		1896	2600	Davis	Gary V.	d
		1883	1298	Davis	George B. (adoption)	m
Apr.	2	1952	21025	Davis	George J. O.	d
July	1	1952	21232	Davis	George Norman, etc.	d
Feb.	26	1944	16339	Davis	Hazel I./Mrs. James T.	d
		1874	677	Davis	Henry	m
Apr.	3	1951	20306	Davis	Henry A.	d
Aug.	21	1937	13072	Davis	Henry D.	d
		[1906-1907]	4169	Davis	Henry Smith	d
Mar.	26	1952	20944	Davis	Homer G., Jr.	m
July	1	1948	18495	Davis	Howard L.	d
		1904	3802	Davis	Hugh H.	d
Feb.	2	1943	15257	Davis	Illie Josiah	d
		[1907-1908]	4240	Davis	J. E.	d
		1913	5463	Davis	J. M.	inc
May		1921	7737	Davis	John C.	d
Apr.	11	1934	11822	Davis	John L.	d
Dec.	11	1930	10469	Davis	John Valentine	d
		[1899-1900]	3036	Davis	Joseph W.	d
May	4	1949	19054	Davis	Josephine	d
		[1890-1892]	1941	Davis	Josias	d
Apr.	25	1955	23137	Davis	Josie M.	d
Aug.	8	1956	24153	Davis	Kathleen, etc.	d
Oct.	21	1956	24221	Davis	Kathleen, etc.	d
		[1896-1897]	2696	Davis	L. T.	d
		[1899-1900]	3048	Davis	Lizzie B.	d
Jan.	11	1943	15219	Davis	Louise M., etc.	d
July	19	1949	19178	Davis	Luella	d
Mar.		1921	7641	Davis	Manuel	d
Jan.	12	1944	16321	Davis	Manuel J., etc.	d
Sept.	31	1952	21276	Davis	Margaret	ins
June	11	1957	24866	Davis	Margaret/Margaret Pis	d
Sept.	13	1957	25017	Davis	Marion E.	d
		[1899-1900]	3026	Davis	Martha A.	d
Dec.	26	1929	10389	Davis	Marvin Bryan	d
		[1907-1908]	4248	Davis	Mary E.	inc
Aug.	28	1921	7772	Davis	Mary E.	d
Sept.	16	1949	19216	Davis	Mary E.	d
Apr.	27	1918	6703	Davis	Mary E. Ore	d

Month	Day	Year	File No.	Surname	Given Name	Type
		1913	5577	Davis	Mary Elizabeth	d
Mar.	3	1924	8794	Davis	Mary Florence	d
Nov.	3	1915	6120	Davis	Mary Francis	d
Oct.	19	1945	16779	Davis	Mary H.	d
May	10	1918	6715	Davis	Mary Laverne	m
Feb.	2	1931	10857	Davis	Mary Laverne	d
Sept.	21	1953	21964	Davis	Michael	d
Feb.	14	1934	12126	Davis	Millie	d
		[1909-1911]	4848	Davis	Milo S.	d
June	12	1944	15925	Davis	Nan M., etc.	d
Mar.	8	1914	5910	Davis	Nancy	inc
Apr.	5	1915	5976	Davis	Nancy	d
Oct.	16	1955	23437	Davis	Nancy Francine	m
Mar.	18	1949	18906	Davis	Patricia	m
Apr.	7	1933	11581	Davis	Pearl Elizabeth	d
		1913	5676	Davis	Perry H.	d
Aug.	16	1957	24960	Davis	Robert Earl, etc.	d
Nov.	17	1925	9090	Davis	Robert Irving	m
May	26	1957	24698	Davis	Robert L.	d
Apr.	21	1935	12560	Davis	Sarah Ann	d
Apr.	15	1917	6443	Davis	Tabitha J.	d
		1918	7015	Davis	William	d
		1904	3641	Davis	William Boyd	m
Nov.	25	1950	20008	Davis	William James, etc.	d
		1873	603	Davis	William K.	d
Oct.	24	1935	12716	Davis	William P.	inc
June	10	1954	22525	Davis	Wilson Buford, Jr.	m
		1876	804	Davis	James S.	d
Mar.	28	1949	18869	Davis	Tom (aka Dades, Atha	d
		[1892-1893]	2210	Davison	John	d
Sept.	17	1946	17346	Davison	Margaret	d
Apr.	22	1957	24611	Davisson	Dora Zella, etc.	d
		1855	40	Davisson	Jesse	d
Nov.	24	1953	22078	Davitto	Bernard	d
Sept.	18	1939	13759	Davoy	Ella M.	d
Dec.	18	1942	15150	Daw	Jesse W.	d
June	28	1952	21147	Dawes	Roger Curtis	m
June	28	1952	21147	Dawes	Walter Jack	m
Sept.	13	1954	22633	Daws	Annie E.	d
July	13	1949	19128	Dawson	James W., etc.	d
		[1892-1893]	2211	Dawson	Louisa	d
Feb.	23	1958	26176	Dawson	Margaret D.	d

Month	Day	Year	File No.	Surname	Given Name	Type
		1911	5227	Dawson	Rebecca	d
Dec.	26	1951	20766	Dawson	William	d
		[1917-1918]	6694	Dawson	William J. G.	d
Jan.	3	1950	19435	Day	Bernice, etc.	d
Oct.	24	1945	16733	Day	Dana W., etc.	d
		[1897-1898]	2751	Day	David	d
		[1873-1874]	658	Day	Elias	d
Sept.	25	1928	10005	Day	Elizabeth	d
Oct.	30	1952	21370	Day	Elizabeth	d
		[1907-1908]	4481	Day	George W.	d
Oct.	2	1951	20650	Day	Harriet M., etc.	d
Sept.	27	1944	16191	Day	Henry L.	d
		[1906-1907]	4189	Day	Henry Wayne	d
Jan.	13	1953	21570	Day	James F.	d
		[1899-1900]	2966	Day	Joseph W.	d
June	25	1931	10974	Day	Louis Franklin	d
		1895	2525	Day	Louis T.	d
		[1909-1911]	4722	Day	Louisa	inc
July	7	1919	7018	Day	Louisa	inc
Apr.	2	1934	11908	Day	Louisa	d
Sept.		1927	9701	Day	Mary E.	d
Jan.	11	1942	15188	Day	Oscar F.	d
Nov.	12	1951	20668	Day	Pete, etc.	d
Sept.	4	1951	20583	Day	Robert L.	d
		[1889-1890]	1889	Day	Susan B.	d
Aug.	13	1949	19214	Day	William George	m
Mar.	25	1953	21663	Dayhuff	Anna, etc.	d
Jan.	17	1958	25291	Dayley	Carrie E.	d
		1888	1776	Days	Mary	d
Jan.	4	1945	16860	Dayton	Anna	d
Dec.	19	1958	26164	Dayton	Gertie	inc
Dec.	20	1952	21468	Dayton	Wilmer W.	inc
Oct.	17	1958	26012	Dayton	Wilmer, etc.	d
		[1906-1907]	4164	Dayton/Datin)	John J.	ins
Dec.	4	1935	12823	Daywalt	Fannie H.	d
Nov.	28	1941	14689	Daywalt	Helen M.	d
Nov.	24	1916	6331	Dazet	Louis	d
Jan.		1924	8807	De Aguier	Maria Fernandes	m
Oct.	21	1923	8462	De Alberts	Adolph	inc
		[1907-1908]	4450	De Amaral	Mary Jane Francisco	inc
Mar.		1924	8807	De Aquiar	Maria Fernandes	m
		1912	5447	De Bernadi	James	d

Month	Day	Year	File No.	Surname	Given Name	Type
May	10	1948	18382	De Bernardi	Evaristi, etc.	d
Nov.	1	1945	16800	De Bernardi	Mary C., etc.	d
Jan.		1924	8540	De Bernardi	Peter C., etc.	d
		[1900-1903]	3304	De Bolt	John H.	d
Oct.	7	1941	14670	De Bolt	Perry F., etc.	d
Jan.		1922	8213	De Carli	May	d
June	5	1946	17232	De Carli	Battista	d
Feb.	13	1953	21578	De Castle	Diane Kinyon	m
May	21	1952	21076	De Chesne	Bertha	d
Sept.	21	1951	20560	De Co	Henrietta A.	d
		[1906-1907]	4174	De Costa	Manuel F.	d
		1912	5379	De Ferree	Louise	d
June	21	1915	6002	De Fitch	Josefa C.	d
Aug.	26	1949	19186	De Foreest	Fred I.	d
Apr.	20	1953	21711	De Freez	Richard, Jr.	m
Feb.	26	1953	21665	De Geus	Leonard	d
Dec.	21	1946	18102	De Giorgi	Elvezio, etc.	d
Apr.	22	1954	22478	De Giorgi	Ersilia	d
Apr.	6	1940	13920	De Giorgi	S.	d
Jan.	23	1953	22248	De Grood	Sylvia	d
Jan.	31	1953	22259	De Grood	Sylvia	d
May	3	1924	8593	De Gueer	Frank, Jr,. etc.	d
Jan.	21	1947	17587	De Gueer	Maria Jose,. etc.	d
Apr.	20	1948	18355	De John	Nicholas, etc.	d
July	16	1953	21951	De Journel	Catherine Margaret Ty	inc
May	12	1955	23233	De Journel	Catherine T., etc.	d
Mar.	15	1915	6131	De Lano	Viola F.	inc
Nov.	8	1947	17898	De Lashmutt	Margaret A.	d
July	8	1947	17897	De Lashmutt	W. J., etc.	d
Nov.	23	1945	16786	De Laurenetis	Dante A., etc.	d
Dec.	3	1943	15639	De Long	Alice	d
Mar.	15	1939	13578	De Martin	Maringa, etc.	d
June	6	1949	19064	De Martini	Angiolina, etc.	d
June		1947	17783	De Martini	Francescan	d
June	22	1925	8964	De Martini	Frank	d
Jan.	18	1946	16940	De Martini	Fredalino, etc.	d
		[1900-1903]	3503	De Martini	Joseph	d
June	24	1942	14909	De Martini	Mansueto, etc.	d
Oct.	1	1943	15583	De Martini	Rosa, etc.	d
Sept.	4	1945	16707	De Martinis	Frank	ins
May	6	1952	21101	De Mattei	Jack, etc.	d
Oct.	16	1938	13433	De Moss	W. L.	d

Month	Day	Year	File No.	Surname	Given Name	Type
Mar.	9	1938	13242	De Rose	Mary	d
Jan.	29	1920	7592	De Rose	William	inc
Dec.	2	1935	12822	De Smit	Annabelle	d
Jan.	6	1946	17513	De Souza	Grace Marie	inc
Nov.	12	1917	6531	De St. Denis	Edward Benjamin	d
		1925	9040	De Turk	Anna J.	d
		[1896-1897]	2621	De Turk	Isaac	d
Oct.	11	1948	18673	De Turk	William S.	d
Mar.	12	1954	22388	De Vilbiss	Leonard John	d
Mar.	25	1945	16375	De Voto	Alice Bisseil, etc.	inc
Nov.	10	1941	14703	De Vries	Elizabeth	d
Apr.	9	1945	16512	De Wells	Mary A., etc.	d
Feb.	29	1951	20824	De Witt	Walter O.	d
Oct.	10	1944	16205	Deala	Annie H.	d
Oct.	17	1951	20609	Dean	Annabelle	d
Nov.	7	1952	21390	Dean	Charles Porter, etc.	d
July	22	1949	19180	Dean	Ethel, etc.	d
		1925	9085	Dean	Frank W.	d
Dec.	16	1944	16219	Dean	James E.	d
Feb.	30	1953	21619	Dean	Jessie	d
Mar.	18	1958	25474	Dean	John Joseph, etc.	d
Oct.	22	1944	16183	Dean	Lucille H. (Albini), etc	d
Sept.	8	1958	25906	Dean	Walter Edwin	d
Nov.	31	1939	13829	Dean	Leslie C.	d
Mar.	16	1937	12894	Deane	La Verne	d
Mar.	17	1944	15784	Deane	Sarah Agnes, etc.	d
Dec.	9	1943	15672	Dearborn	Sharba Kathleen	m
Mar.	21	1958	25407	Dearduff	Howard W., etc.	d
Mar.	29	1924	8557	Dearing	Raymond York	d
		1914	5750	DeBernadi	Giovanni	d
		[1893-1894]	2366	DeBernardi	Maria	d
		1924	8546	DeBernardi	Peter	d
		[1899-1900]	2971	DeBernardi	Pietro	m
Dec.	17	1929	10382	DeBernardi	Rose Blanche	d
Sept.	23	1950	19887	Debney	Charles F.	d
		[1899-1900]	3096½	DeBruyne	Gustaf	d
Oct.		1922	8133	Decanini	Edward	m
July	20	1955	23325	DeCarli	Elmira M.	d
		1900	3136	DeCarly	J. B.	d
Dec.	7	1958	26063	DeCarly	James A., etc.	d
Feb.	10	1941	14387	Decatur	Alfred E., etc.	d
Feb.	10	1941	14388	Decatur	Millie A., etc.	d

Month	Day	Year	File No.	Surname	Given Name	Type
		[1898-1899]	2907	Dechenne	Frances	d
Aug.	11	1942	14978	Deckelman	Ella	d
Mar.		1921	7661	Decker	George	inc
		1922	7996	Decker	George	d
		[1903-1904]	3699	Decker	Hannah	d
		1887	1639	Decker	Henry	d
		1862	215	Decker	James	d
		[1907-1908]	4438	Decker	Margaret A.	d
Apr.	27	1916	6222	Decker	Mary	d
Oct.	1	1957	25054	Decker	T. E., etc.	d
Jan.	23	1952	21533	Decker	William M.	d
		1922	8048	Decknini	John	d
May	10	1918	6730	DeClercq	Arthur R., etc.	d
Sept.	15	1930	10730	Dedwith	Agnes M.	d
July	5	1957	24853	Dedwith	Thomas V., etc.	d
June	13	1938	13295	Deeds	William M.	d
		[1890-1892]	1978	Deems	Carrie Mabel	m
Oct.	18	1957	25029	Deeney	William	d
Feb.	13	1958	25381	Deeths	Henry	d
		1920	7468	Deffenbaugh	Willim H.	d
Feb.	21	1946	16949	Defner	L. G., etc.	d
		[1864-1866]	266	Defrees	Elizabeth	d
Aug.	24	1956	24123	Degen	Andrew	d
Dec.	29	1933	11777	DeGens	Eleanor, etc.	m
Mar.	9	1932	11249	Deghi	Antonio	d
Apr.	4	1929	10198	Deghi	Battista	d
Mar.	3	1948	18200	Degiorgis	Ernesto	d
		[1909-1911]	5020	DeGueer/Geer	Frank, Sr.	d
Jan.	7	1923	8517	DeHay	Armand J., etc.	d
Apr.	17	1931	10914	DeHay	Emile B., etc.	d
Nov.	15	1945	16813	Dehay	Marie L.	d
Apr.	2	1952	21028	Dehay	Paul L.	d
		[1907-1908]	4264	Dehay	Theodore J.	d
		1912	5235	Dehtlefsen	Elizabeth	d
June	24	1935	12311	Deini	Andrea	d
Sept.	11	1935	12706	Deini	Frank	d
July	11	1935	12705	Deini	Josephine	d
		1935	12317	Deini	Leonardo	d
Jan.	20	1942	15151	Dekleva	Joseph, etc.	d
June	6	1952	21173	Del Buono	Hugo	d
June	27	1953	21868	Del Carlo	Alberto	d
June	15	1929	10244	Del Carlo	Angelo, etc.	m

Month	Day	Year	File No.	Surname	Given Name	Type
Jan.	15	1927	9777	Del Carlo	Domenico	d
Nov.	26	1928	10025	Del Carlo	Felicia, etc.	d
June	30	1931	10928	Del Carlo	Mary	d
Sept.	5	1944	16157	Del Curto	Agostino	d
Jan.	23	1950	19469	Del Curto	Calesto, etc.	d
Jan.	14	1938	13457	Del Curto	Dominic	d
June	21	1951	20402	Del Curto	Sabina	d
Aug.	1	1951	20422	Del Giudici	Benedetto, etc.	d
June	28	1945	16591	Del Prete	Fernando, etc.	d
Feb.	8	1947	18124	Del Prete	Francis Joseph, etc.	d
Nov.	14	1949	19365	Del Prete	Margharita, etc.	d
Dec.	27	1951	20772	Del Prete	Peter E.	inc
Apr.	27	1949	18986	Del Tredici	Gilbert	d
		1911	5059	Delafield	Emily P.	d
June	4	1935	12324	Delagnes	Caroline	d
July	17	1932	11254	Delagnes	G. P.	d
		1894	2385	Delahanty	May	m
Apr.	13	1915	5957	Delameter	Mary J.	d
Apr.	21	1951	20287	Delaney	Clara M.	d
		[1884-1885]	1432	Delaney	James	d
May	24	1956	23949	DeLaurentis	Luigi	d
Jan.	12	1957	25210	DelCarlo	Josephine	d
Feb.	6	1958	25363	DelCarlo	Josephine	d
Oct.	12	1958	25916	DelCarlo	Letizia	d
		1920	7569	DelCurto	Rina, Eppi & Domino	m
		[1893-1894]	2341	Delehanty	James	d
June	25	1943	15450	Delesky	Martha, etc.	d
Mar.	8	1935	12546	Delessio	Edmond	m
July	22	1956	24074	DelFava	Neri	d
Feb.	14	1943	15225	Delfino	Carlo	d
Jan.	11	1957	24453	Delfino	Frank, Jr.	m
Jan.	11	1957	24453	Delfino	Gary	m
Feb.	11	1957	24453	Delfino	Michael	m
June	30	1934	11941	Deling	Mary Ann	d
		1920	7338	Delk	Ada J.	d
Aug.	4	1927	9689	Delk	Nellie, etc.	d
Dec.	30	1930	10751	Dell Aca	Peter	d
Oct.	1	1954	22725	Dell Armi	Fortunato Pasquale, etc	d
July	28	1957	24836	Della Maggiora	Filomena	d
Apr.	1	1938	13257	Della Maggiora	Giovannina	d
May	5	1953	21825	Della Maggiora	Peter, etc.	d
Oct.	1	1946	17420	Dellasso	U., etc.	d

Month	Day	Year	File No.	Surname	Given Name	Type
Dec.	15	1958	26148	DeLong	Albert, etc.	d
Jan.	12	1927	9495	DeLong	D. H. aka Doris H.	d
June	3	1955	23292	DelPonte	Alfonso S.	inc
		1923	8288	Delucchi	Angela	d
June	30	1946	17115	Delucchi	Giovanni, etc.	d
Sept.	22	1956	24176	Delucchi	Madalena	d
		1864	247	Delzell	Isaac A.	d
Sept.	31	1937	13114	Demaria	Frank	d
Nov.	14	1931	11053	DeMartin	Amelia V.	blank
Mar.	1	1946	17036	DeMartini	Emilia, etc.	d
		[1909-1911]	4714	DeMartini	Eveline	m
		1926	9402	DeMartini	John	d
May		1947	17787	Demartini	Maria, etc.	d
Oct.	9	1958	25987	DeMartini	Marie/William, Mrs., e	d
Jan.	11	1926	9403	DeMartini	Paul	d
		[1906-1907]	4186	Demartini	Albert	d
Dec.	13	1933	11760	DeMattei	Mary, etc.	ins
Feb.	13	1956	23724	DeMent	John Simpson, etc.	d
Nov.	3	1940	14220	Dement	Katherine	d
Apr.	4	1957	24646	Demeo	Nicholas, etc.	d
		1888	1808	Demetz	Anna	m
		1888	1808	Demetz	Edward	m
		1895	2543	DeMetz	Edward	m
		1888	1808	Demetz	Louisa	m
Dec.	8	1927	9769	Demmer	Esther	inc
Mar.	15	1946	17007	Demmick	Frank E.	d
Mar.		1918	7013	Dempey	Susan Leele	d
Mar.	9	1959	26195	Dempsey	John P.	d
Jan.	22	1958	26172	Dempsey	Mary G.	d
Dec.	28	1953	22202	Dempsey	Peter Francis, etc.	d
Mar.	20	1950	19576	Dempsey	Vivian V.	d
Dec.	15	1953	22232	Dempsey	Alice M., etc.	d
June	15	1948	18457	Demude	W. S., etc.	d
Apr.	28	1958	25500	Denham	Charlotte, etc.	d
Sept.	30	1930	10668	Denham	Drury	d
Nov.	10	1950	20040	Denhard	Harry W.	d
		[1917-1918]	6638	Denison	Henry C.	d
May	22	1949	19032	Denison	Robert Clayton	m
May	22	1949	19032	Denison	William Henry	m
Nov.	7	1940	14265	Denker	Carl	d
Nov.	7	1940	14265	Denker	Carl	d
Nov.	22	1950	19938	Denman	Catherine D.	d

Month	Day	Year	File No.	Surname	Given Name	Type
Aug.	12	1950	19867	Denman	Charlotte E.	d
		[1894-1895]	2490	Denman	Ezekiel	d
Mar.	17	1955	23061	Denman	Grant H.	d
		1917	6567	Denman	Isabell	d
		1895	2511	Denman	James W.	d
		1895	2513	Denman	Martin P.	d
		1895	2512	Denman	Mary A.	d
July	29	1947	17901	Denman	Nellie L.	d
May	15	1953	21842	Dennes	Edward F.	d
		[1892-1893]	2241	Denning	Julia A.	d
Apr.	22	1947	17757	Dennis	Billy Milvisi	m
		1892	2225	Dennis	Nelson	d
May	5	1939	13667	Dennis	William Ritchie	d
May	15	1953	21773	Dennison	Carl E.	d
Dec.	3	1935	12769	Dennison	Ethel S.	d
Dec.	31	1944	16239	Dennison	James Hartley, etc.	d
Nov.	9	1951	20730	Denny	Agnes Duhun, etc.	d
Aug.	20	1958	25865	Denny	Arthur	d
Nov.	15	1946	17441	Denny	Charles	d
July	10	1936	12523	Denny	Emma A.	d
Jan.	9	1953	21560	Denny	Minnie B.	d
Oct.	19	1915	6074	Densmore	Charles	d
Apr.	3	1942	14841	Densmore	George F.	d
		1925	8974	Denson	Addie E.	d
		1913	5671	Dent	William	d
May	9	1952	21108	Dente	Jessie M.	d
July	11	1957	24869	Denton	Alfred	d
Jan.	11	1956	24386	Denton	Ruth	d
Oct.	26	1952	21368	Denun	Agnes Drury	d
Aug.	2	1940	14091	Depires	Achille	d
June	2	1944	16012	Deppen	Louise	inc
Feb.	29	1930	10824	Deprey	Lida J.	d
Dec.	16	1922	8163	DeRanieri	Casere	ins
Mar.	1	1919	7203	Deranieri	Cesere	g
		[1896-1897]	2692	Derby	A. B.	d
May	25	1953	21861	Derby	Bertha M.	d
		[1904-1905]	3848	Derby	Harriet M.	d
		[1909-1911]	4900	DeRose	Antone	d
Dec.	5	1934	12119	Derrick	Columbus A.	d
June	10	1938	13348	Derrick	Elizabeth, etc.	d
June	11	1957	24787	DeShields	Harry E., etc.	d
May	4	1956	23972	DeSousa	Charlyn	m

Month	Day	Year	File No.	Surname	Given Name	Type
June	4	1956	23972	DeSousa	Christopher	m
May	4	1956	23972	DeSousa	David	m
July	22	1956	24069	DeSousa	Joe	d
May	4	1956	23972	DeSousa	John	m
May	4	1956	23972	DeSousa	Paul	m
June	2	1928	9922	Destruel	Jean	d
Mar.		1921	7833	Deter	Vinton Daily	m
Apr.	6	1947	17623	Detjen	Eva	d
Oct.	10	1944	16206	Detjins	Fred H.	d
May	22	1953	21856	Dettman	Carol Louise	m
May	22	1953	21855	Dettman	Dorothy Marie	m
May	22	1953	21855	Dettman	Janice Irene	m
May	22	1953	21856	Dettman	Jerry Lynn	m
		1905	3959	Devens	Edward T.	d
Mar.	23	1951	20171	Dever	Amey, etc.	d
		[1909-1911]	4823	Deveraux	Carrie M.	d
		[1917-1918]	6681	Deveraux	Richard E., etc	d
		1906	4056	Devereaux	E. W.	d
Dec.	16	1953	22237	Devine	James Patrick	d
Feb.	18	1937	13127	Devine	James Patrick, etc.	inc
July	10	1944	16073	Devinsenzi	Lawrence, Sr., etc.	d
		[1909-1911]	4870	Devoto	Arthur	m
		1925	9010	Devoto	David	d
		[1909-1911]	4870	Devoto	Hazel	m
		1925	9028	Devoto	Melvin H. & Robert C.	m
Mar.	21	1929	10184	Dewey	David P.	d
Oct.	19	1938	13379	Dewey	Flora L.	d
July	8	1952	21242	Dewey	Frank A., etc.	d
Jan.	9	1953	21561	Dewey	Harriet E.	d
Apr.	15	1953	21772	Dewey	Margaret	d
Nov.	10	1939	13837	Dewey	Rachel B.	d
June	28	1948	18418	Dewey	Rosaline M.	d
June	19	1946	17156	Dewey	William Carlton, etc.	d
		1907	4231	Dewey	William H.	d
Jan.	30	1957	25242	DeWitt	Harry L.	d
Aug.	8	1927	9694	Di Bez	Charles, etc.	d
Jan.	16	1952	21519	Di Fiore	Mary	d
Sept.	7	1917	6505	Dianda	Domenico	d
		1920	7415	Dianda	Ensuia/Zaria	d
		[1889-1890]	1892	Dianda	G. R.	d
Oct.	1	1958	25966	Dias	George M., etc.	d
		1878	907	Dias	H. L.	d

Month	Day	Year	File No.	Surname	Given Name	Type
		[1884-1885]	1446	Dias	Isaac L.	d
		[1886-1887]	1549	Dias	Rosa L.	d
Oct.	10	1949	19251	Diaz	Henry R., etc.	d
Jan.	18	1939	13867	Dibble	Charles Roland, etc.	d
Dec.	24	1914	5872	Dibble	Jennie	inc
		1920	7499	Dibble	Jennie	d
Sept.	20	1948	18589	Dicello	Angelo	d
June	10	1950	19752	Dicello	Angelo	d
Feb.	30	1950	19484	Dicenzo	Biago, etc.	d
Oct.	28	1934	12011	Dicicco	Rosa	d
Aug.	19	1945	16656	Dick	Anthony Summer	m
July	19	1945	16656	Dick	Gordon Pietre	m
July	19	1945	16656	Dick	Marc Andre	m
Apr.	28	1927	9551	Dick	Richard	d
Oct.	12	1941	14603	Dicke	Ruth	m
May	24	1943	15445	Dickelman	Ella May, etc.	d
July	21	1957	24823	Dickey	Claude D.	d
Dec.	6	1944	16306	Dickey	George Washington	d
Mar.	17	1958	25392	Dickey	James W.	d
Nov.	27	1925	9100	Dickey	Mabel	ins
July	12	1958	25616	Dickey	Reva Estel	m
Aug.	20	1923	8398	Dickey	W. J.	d
Jan.		1926	9434	Dickie	Joseph	d
Jan.	28	1950	20071	Dickinson	George Donald, etc.	d
		[1909-1911]	4826	Dickinson	John H.	d
Apr.	22	1947	17756	Dickinson	Merton J.	d
May	29	1947	17772	Dickinson	Merton J.	d
Dec.	17	1958	26157	Dickinson	Philomena	con
May	30	1952	22505	Dickson	Annie L., etc.	d
		1859	155	Dickson	Charles H.	m
Nov.	28	1915	6115	Dickson	David S.	d
Jan.	13	1935	12404	Dickson	David S.	d
Dec.	16	1948	18736	Dickson	Ethel G.	d
Mar.	25	1935	12207	Dickson	Frank M., etc.	d
Dec.	17	1935	12755	Dickson	Joan	m
May	27	1939	13622	Dickson	John Mc Caul	d
		[1883-1884]	1369	Dickson	Joshua Bates	m
Nov.	6	1942	15101	Dickson	Lucille	d
		1859	155	Dickson	Margaret	m
Apr.		1925	8924	Dickson	Myrtle A.	d
		1905	4031	Dickson	Olive W.	d
		1859	151	Dickson	Richard	d

Month	Day	Year	File No.	Surname	Given Name	Type
July	1	1915	6026	Dickson	Sarah Francis	d
Sept.	30	1948	18602	Diebold	Anna	d
		[1890-1892]	2003	Diebold	David	d
May	11	1925	8957	Diebold	George	d
Dec.	26	1954	22827	Diedisch	Frank	d
		1874	667	Diedrick	John R.	d
Apr.	25	1952	21013	Dielkus	Harriet L.	d
May	29	1950	19597	Diemer	Raymond Ligouria	d
Sept.	18	1916	6296	Dierssen	Johannes Ludwig, etc.	d
June	9	1935	12671	Dierx	Mari	d
May	7	1951	20384	Dietle	Leopold Arthur	d
Nov.	28	1955	23558	Dietlein	Robert	d
		[1900-1903]	3483	Dietrich	Gottlieb	d
Aug.	22	1948	18528	Dietrich	Mary E., etc.	d
May	22	1955	23189	Dignan	Allie, etc.	d
June	8	1944	15916	Dignan	Mary B.	d
		1913	5594	Dilenarda	P.	d
		1913	5647	Dill	Robert Henry	d
Apr.	21	1939	13583	Dillan	William	d
May	29	1947	17771	Dillard	Lottie	d
Aug.	25	1950	19832	Dillon	Earl W.	d
		[1906-1907]	4182	Dillon	George	d
Mar.	16	1931	10876	Dillon	Martha J.	d
Jan.	7	1943	15211	Dillon	Myrtle Charles	d
Mar.	26	1949	18982	Dillsbough	Sandra Catherine	m
		1917	6601	Dimmick	George Washington	d
June	10	1957	24731	Dimmick	Hattie Rose, etc.	d
Sept.	26	1958	25882	Dimmick	L. B., etc.	d
Oct.	29	1944	16195	Dimmitt	Jesse L.	d
		1913	5592	Dineen	Daniel W.	d
Nov.	7	1942	15140	Dineen	Elizabeth	d
Oct.	24	1948	18642	Dinelli	Emilio	d
Jan.	18	1946	16941	Dinelli	Robert O.	d
May	25	1935	12240	Dingman	Richard L.	d
Jan.	26	1949	18864	Dingwall	Lewis A.	d
Jan.	14	1934	12125	Dinic	Joseph	d
June	26	1925	8970	Dinsmore	Ava L.	ins
Dec.	24	1934	12031	Dinucci	Adalina, etc.	d
May	7	1935	12608	Dinucci	Albert A.	d
Dec.	5	1930	10801	Dinucci	Angelo	d
May	23	1943	15397	Dinucci	Ercelia, etc.	d
Sept.	14	1942	15051	Dinucci	Ernestine	d

Month	Day	Year	File No.	Surname	Given Name	Type
Oct.	19	1932	11346	Dinucci	Felice, etc.	d
Sept.	5	1950	19909	Dinucci	Fred A., etc.	d
Apr.	17	1942	14820	Dinucci	Guisto, etc.	d
Dec.	12	1935	12828	Dinucci	Isabella	d
		1913	5559	Dinucci	Madalena	d
June	17	1939	13673	Dinucci	Pellegrino	d
July	19	1937	12964	Dinucci	Vincenza	d
		1880	1113	Dinwiddi	Laura J.	d
June	11	1923	8358	Dinwiddie	J. H.	d
		1904	3771	Dinwiddie	J. L.	d
		1904	3769	Dinwiddie	William G.	d
Aug.	11	1958	25844	Diperno	Grazia	d
Apr.	2	1957	24634	DiPiero	Francesco	d
Feb.	27	1941	14720	Dipper	Louis	d
		1922	8141	Diricco	Fred	ins
Feb.	11	1955	23044	Diringer	Benjamin	d
May	30	1956	23960	Dissmeyer	Walter F.	d
May	1	1947	17773	Dittinson	Minna, etc.	d
Jan.	24	1928	10074	Dittman	Phillip, Frederick, Mar	m
Nov.	14	1948	18675	Dittman	William, etc.	d
Apr.	9	1926	9248	Dittmann	Chas. A.	d
Mar.	15	1954	22344	Dix	Laura E., etc.	d
Feb.	3	1956	23774	Dixon	Alice Haigh, etc.	d
Mar.	17	1952	20987	Dixon	Annas Gertrude, etc.	d
Jan.	21	1951	20816	Dixon	Bessie R.	d
		1905	3935	Dixon	Charles	m
Apr.	23	1948	18300	Dixon	Charles P.	d
		1904	3789	Dixon	Dixon	d
Sept.	29	1949	19236	Dixon	Ernesto Niel, etc.	d
July	10	1954	22579	Dixon	Ethel I., etc.	d
		[1900-1903]	3584	Dixon	George Harold	m
Apr.	1	1958	25513	Dixon	Helen B.	d
Dec.	30	1956	24300	Dixon	Howard L.	d
		[1907-1908]	4478	Dixon	J. F.	d
Nov.	19	1930	10739	Dixon	James	d
		1906	4124	Dixon	John	d
		[1900-1903]	3584	Dixon	Leona	m
Nov.	9	1939	13835	Dixon	Louise G.	d
Apr.	14	1956	23789	Dixon	Stephen Willard, etc.	m
		[1900-1903]	3584	Dixon	Walter Chinch	m
		1912	5348	Dixon	William	d
		[1900-1903]	3584	Dixon	Winona	m

Month	Day	Year	File No.	Surname	Given Name	Type
Aug.	25	1941	14559	Dizner	Stephen	d
Apr.	7	1932	11467	Dobbie	James R.	d
May	16	1952	21123	Dobbs	Logan L., etc.	d
Aug.	5	1958	25830	Docherty	John	d
Jan.	2	1953	21551	Docherty	Myrna Ewing	d
Sept.	22	1958	25874	Dockar	Grace, etc.	d
Aug.	15	1946	17254	Dockham	John N.	d
Apr.	1	1935	12212	Doclling	John R., etc.	d
Aug.	6	1915	6064	Doda	John B.	d
July	15	1946	17252	Dodd	Frank	d
Apr.	7	1955	23103	Dodd	Frank S., etc.	d
Oct.	10	1951	20659	Dodd	Gaye	d
July	1	1957	24844	Dodd	Wallace L.	d
Apr.	12	1946	17067	Dodge	Alice C.	d
Oct.	15	1957	25088	Dodge	Beverly J.	m
Feb.	22	1922	8226	Dodge	David	d
Nov.	15	1957	25088	Dodge	Earl L.	m
		[1907-1908]	4286	Dodge	Ernest J.	d
Oct.	15	1957	25088	Dodge	George O.	m
		[1870-1871]	467	Dodge	I. H. H.	d
		1866	317	Dodge	Simon B.	d
		[1882-1883]	1260	Dodge	Susan G.	d
Nov.	28	1920	7532	Dodge	Thomas H.	ins
		[1870-1871]	449	Dodge	William R.	d
Jan.	13	1953	21575	Dodrill	Forest	d
		[1906-1907]	4199	Dods	McRae	d
Aug.	16	1948	18583	Dodson	Daniel Melvin	d
Jan.	4	1925	9105	Dodson	Lucile	m
Feb.	22	1935	12469	Doelling	Mary	d
Aug.	10	1948	18524	Doelling	Minnie M.	d
		1921	7637	Doescher	Charles	d
Aug.	12	1933	11635	Doescher	Cora E.	d
May	20	1935	12593	Dogali	George Paul (aka Gior;	m
Feb.	14	1935	12405	Dogali	Julia	d
Feb.	16	1931	10875	Dogliani	Angelina	d
Jan.	9	1956	23707	Doherty	Edward H.	d
Mar.	15	1949	18953	Doherty	Edward Hugh, etc.	mp
Apr.	23	1943	15287	Dohn	Mabel B.	d
Sept.	15	1952	21339	Dohn	Mabel, etc.	d
		1918	6821	Doitline	John	d
		[1883-1884]	1323	Dolan	Annie	d
		[1883-1884]	1324	Dolan	Annie	m

Month	Day	Year	File No.	Surname	Given Name	Type
		[1883-1884]	1324	Dolan	Charles	m
July	20	1950	19766	Dolan	Delphin J.	inc
Oct.	3	1952	21379	Dolan	James R., etc.	d
		[1883-1884]	1324	Dolan	Katie	m
		[1883-1884]	1324	Dolan	Maggie A.	m
		[1883-1884]	1324	Dolan	Martha R.	m
July		1920	7437	Dolan	Delphin Delmar	m
Apr.	9	1954	22444	Dolcini	Emilio M., etc.	d
Apr.	12	1957	24661	Dolcini	Isolina	d
May	22	1954	22482	Dolcini	M.	d
Oct.	3	1932	11353	Dolcini	Michail, etc.	d
Sept.	20	1957	24966	Dole	Edward J., etc.	d
Oct.	16	1957	25022	Dole	Lodia M.	inc
June	11	1956	24038	Dolfini	Annie Acquistapace, e	d
Feb.	20	1929	10498	Dollar	Sam	d
Apr.	30	1948	18312	Dollar	William B.	d
		1869	409	Dollinger	Xavier	d
May	26	1955	23200	Dolzadell	Constant	d
Mar.	13	1957	24534	Domane	Mary F.	d
Jan.	9	1935	12375	Domenichelli	Peniegio	d
		1906	4109	Domeniconi	Joseph	d
July		1919	7078	Domeniconi	Joseph	d
		1916	6334	Domenzet	Joseph	d
		1884	1382	Domine	Frederick	d
Apr.	10	1942	14892	Domitelli	Dorothy, etc.	m
Sept.	29	1957	24987	Domitilli	Angelina	d
May	30	1957	24702	Domitilli	John	d
Nov.	6	1950	20028	Donaghy	Cecilia, etc.	d
Dec.	12	1952	21447	Donaghy	John, etc.	d
July	20	1945	16640	Donahue	Ella	d
June	2	1931	10986	Donahue	Emmett I.	d
May	11	1938	13290	Donahue	James M.	d
Aug.	7	1915	6032	Donahue	John W.	d
May	12	1950	19626	Donahue	Joseph D.	d
Sept.	14	1951	20601	Donahue	Thomas Michael	d
Jan.	14	1933	11787	Donald	John T.	d
Apr.	8	1958	25534	Donald	Mary La Vern	inc
		[1875-1876]	749	Donaldson	John	d
June	9	1956	23979	Donati	Claire, etc.	d
Jan.	23	1955	23677	Donati	Ermalinda Sartori, etc.	d
Sept.	30	1937	13076	Donati	Vincenza	d
Dec.	24	1953	22079	Donegan	Isabel F., etc.	d

Month	Day	Year	File No.	Surname	Given Name	Type
Aug.	25	1950	19833	Donegan	William	d
		1912	5318	Donelley	Ellen	inc
July	25	1917	6472	Donenzet	Luella Elizabeth	m
		1867	351	Donigan	Rosa	m
Sept.	13	1951	20599	Doninelli	Victor	d
Dec.	30	1943	15654	Donley	William A., etc.	d
		1918	6802	Donnelly	Ann, etc.	d
		[1886-1887]	1591	Donnelly	Ellen	d
		[1887-1888]	1646	Donnelly	Peter	d
		1874	673	Donner	George	d
July		1922	8075	Donner	Giselle	d
		1911	5181	Donner	Margaret	d
Mar.	20	1950	19575	Donner	Paul Edward	m
Aug.	5	1931	10994	Donohue	Emmett Rockwell	m
Sept.	5	1931	10995	Donohue	James Lockwood	m
June	5	1931	10993	Donohue	Joan	m
	23	1921	7714	Donovan	Aileen Dorothy	m
Sept.	23	1943	15520	Donovan	Buthite	m
Nov.	21	1927	9726	Donovan	C. C.	d
Sept.	23	1943	15520	Donovan	Daniel	m
Feb.	13	1944	15767	Donovan	Evelyn G.	d
Apr.	9	1945	16408	Donovan	Frank M.	d
June	18	1927	9605	Donovan	Frank N.	d
		1921	7714	Donovan	Geraldine Isabelle	m
Oct.	4	1943	15628	Donovan	Graham Oliver	m
Feb.	27	1941	14363	Donovan	John	d
Mar.		1919	7208	Donovan	Laura M.	d
Mar.	23	1921	7714	Donovan	Mary Elva	m
Jan.	17	1948	18788	Donovan	May L.	d
July	23	1943	15520	Donovan	Robert	m
Aug.	22	1929	10363	Donovan	Susie D.	d
		1897	2743	Donovan	William	d
Feb.	22	1940	13902	Dont	John G.	d
		[1906-1907]	4153	Dont	Joseph	d
Dec.	10	1932	11406	Dont	Joseph	d
Dec.	2	1946	17466	Dont	P. A.	d
July	1	1945	16607	Dont	Rose	d
May	9	1945	16514	Dooley	Frank A.	d
		1921	7852	Dooley	J. F.	d
		[1899-1900]	3059	Dooley	Neil	d
Nov.	7	1949	19311	Dooley	Patrick, etc.	d
Oct.	10	1946	17393	Doran	George L.	d

Month	Day	Year	File No.	Surname	Given Name	Type
		[1897-1898]	2745	Doran	William M.	d
Jan.	14	1955	22976	Doran	Robert E.	d
Mar.	7	1931	11157	Doras	Leicester	d
June	26	1943	15451	Dorati	Elizabeth M.	d
Aug.	15	1958	25786	Dorian	Walter Richard, etc.	d
Sept.	15	1938	13351	Dorig	Emil	d
July	21	1943	15483	Dorkham	John Nugent, etc.	d
		[1907-1908]	4459	Dormann	John	d
Dec.	3	1946	17509	Dormetta	Annella, etc.	Inc
Feb.	24	1947	17598	Dormetta	Annetta, etc.	inc
Dec.	3	1946	17508	Dormetta	Modesto, etc.	inc
Mar.	24	1947	17598	Dormetta	Modesto, etc.	d
Apr.	23	1957	24687	Dorn	Albina Elizabeth	d
Dec.	12	1958	26140	Dorn	Charles A.	d
Sept.	21	1956	24174	Dorn	Ernst Richard	d
Apr.	9	1957	24654	Dorn	Richard Ernst	d
		1913	5522	Dorons	Vernon	d
Sept.	22	1927	9707	Dorous	Martha Jane	d
Nov.	21	1942	15089	Dorrah	Enid	m
Dec.	6	1957	25193	Dorsett	William A.	d
June	3	1915	5988	Dortmund	Marie Therese	d
		1914	5790	Dorward	Andrew	ins
		1914	5841	Dorward	Andrew	d
		1914	5840	Dorward	Annie	d
Jan.	24	1927	9813	Dorward	J. C., etc.	d
Aug.	27	1925	9025	Doss	Albert B.	d
June	13	1957	24791	Doss	Alvin, etc.	d
		1911	5211	Doss	Calvin H. et al	m
May	23	1943	15398	Doss	Cora	d
		[1903-1904]	3652	Doss	Ester Ann	d
Oct.	21	1956	24219	Doss	H. R., etc.	d
Apr.	25	1927	9545	Doss	Hazel Amand	d
June	11	1932	11250	Doss	Joel A.	d
		[1909-1911]	4857	Doss	John R.	d
Apr.	15	1943	15278	Doss	Josephine I.	d
		[1909-1911]	5002	Doss	Melvin G.	m
Nov.	17	1942	15148	Doss	Oliver R.	d
		1924	8707	Doss	Willetta M.	m
		1906	4113	Dotta	Leopoldo	d
Oct.	9	1919	7129	Dotta	Lepold R.	d
		1911	5179	Dotta	Maria	d
Sept.	16	1944	16169	Dotts	Easley	d

Month	Day	Year	File No.	Surname	Given Name	Type
Jan.	6	1956	23699	Doty	Archie A., etc.	d
Aug.	22	1957	24899	Doty	Irving N., etc.	d
Dec.	9	1956	24321	Doty	John A.	d
Oct.	7	1950	19914	Doty	Louise G., etc.	d
July	4	1943	15463	Doty	R. O,	d
Feb.	5	1958	25361	Doty	Walter M., etc.	d
Dec.	21	1931	11085	Doty	William J.	d
Apr.	3	1952	21031	Dougherty	Arabella, etc.	d
		1886	1546	Dougherty	Ellen	d
Mar.	3	1952	20960	Dougherty	Florence Margaret	d
Jan.	20	1940	14314	Dougherty	Helen L.	d
Apr.	29	1949	18989	Dougherty	Michael Patrick, etc.	d
		1916	6341	Dougherty	Samuel K.	d
Mar.	23	1951	20170	Dougherty	William N., etc.	d
Dec.	16	1948	18740	Doughney	Katherine	d
Mar.	11	1941	14393	Doughty	C. E.	d
Apr.	9	1937	12920	Douglas	Alexander S., etc.	d
Apr.	3	1953	21745	Douglas	Andrew	d
Jan.	27	1925	9120	Douglas	Dand	d
Mar.	16	1950	19519	Douglas	David John	d
Oct.	27	1948	18648	Douglas	David William, etc.	d
		1924	8735	Douglas	Elausion	m
		[1909-1911]	4943	Douglas	George W.	d
Sept.	8	1952	21324	Douglas	Harold V.	d
		[1889-1890]	1908	Douglas	John	d
Dec.	12	1946	17476	Douglas	Mary	d
		1888	1804	Douglas	Robert	d
		[1909-1911]	4667	Douglas	Robert, Sr.	d
July	29	1944	16060	Douglas	Mary	inc
July	23	1944	16049	Douglass	Annie (aka Douglas, N	d
		1909	4626	Douglass	Annie Irene	d
		1909	4640	Douglass	Flora B.	m
		1909	4640	Douglass	Frank A.	m
		1909	4651	Douglass	George V.	d
		1918	6941	Douglass	John C.	d
Mar.	14	1957	24592	Dove	Violet Elizabeth, etc.	d
Apr.	13	1925	8907	Dovey	Mary E.	d
		1870	448	Dovey	Stephen	d
June	19	1939	13674	Dovins	Carlo	d
Mar.	12	1916	6170	Dow	Eliza Veeder	d
July	18	1949	19175	Dow	George W., etc.	d
Sept.	15	1952	21359	Dow	William M.	d

Month	Day	Year	File No.	Surname	Given Name	Type
		1912	5396	Dowd	Frank E.	d
		[1908-1909]	4557	Dowd	James	d
May		1920	7344	Dowd	Mary Jane	d
June	2	1930	10643	Dowd	Sarah	d
Nov.	6	1942	15138	Dowdall	Agnes	d
Oct.	20	1946	17407	Dowdall	John N., etc.	d
Jan.	27	1946	17538	Dowdall	Richard J.	d
Dec.	4	1957	25123	Dowdy	Eoline B.	d
May	28	1946	17225	Dowell	Frank M.	d
June	27	1927	9617	Dowell	Nina A.	d
Aug.	18	1932	11343	Dowling	Catherine	d
July	3	1916	6225	Downes	Ernest	d
July	2	1939	13686	Downey	Alice	d
Apr.	19	1958	25476	Downey	George, etc.	d
		[1896-1897]	2645	Downey	John W.	d
Jan.	18	1935	12838	Downey	Robert	inc
Mar.	17	1937	12895	Downey	Wallace M.	d
		[1875-1876]	784	Downing	J. C.	d
		1918	6765	Downing	Samuel etc	d
		1922	8118	Downs	Bernice Ruth et al	m
Aug.		1922	8118	Downs	Dorothy	m
		[1909-1911]	4726	Downs	George H.	d
Mar.	4	1957	24568	Downs	Hilda Claire, etc.	d
		1922	8118	Downs	Richard Punington	m
		1922	8118	Downs	Vernon Legro	m
		1921	7832	Downs	Vernon, etc.	d
June	20	1930	10579	Dows	Josephine	d
Mar.	17	1931	10881	Dows	Louise	d
		1912	5240	Dows	Samuel	d
		1927	9672	Doyle	Catherine Frances	inc
Nov.	10	1927	9736	Doyle	Catherine Frances	d
Aug.	12	1948	18578	Doyle	Frank P., etc.	d
		1913	5614	Doyle	Howard J.	d
		1871	495	Doyle	James	d
		[1876-1877]	840	Doyle	James	d
		[1900-1903]	3198	Doyle	John Charles	m
June	1	1934	11966	Doyle	Joseph	d
Oct.	1	1916	6301	Doyle	Manville	d
		1926	9223	Doyle	Mary E.	d
Apr.	27	1944	15901	Doyle	Michael	d
June	4	1949	19056	Doyle	Nellie J.	inc
June	7	1957	24780	Doyle	Nellie Jane	d

Month	Day	Year	File No.	Surname	Given Name	Type
Jan.	10	1944	15765	Doyle	Polly O'Meara	d
Dec.	15	1952	21514	Doyle	Rose	d
July	21	1932	11318	Doyle	Sally Lou	m
June	11	1954	22528	Doyle	Theodore H., etc.	d
May	4	1951	20380	Doyle	Thomas	d
		[1900-1903]	3198	Doyle	Winifred	m
July	18	1928	10000	Doyton	Julia R.	d
		1916	6437	Dozet	Martha	m
		1874	716	Dozier	A. W.	d
		1875	726	Dozier	Roland	d
		[1904-1905]	3887	Drago	Nelson	d
Apr.	19	1957	24680	Drake	Aimee, etc.	d
		1906	4047	Drake	Ben F.	m
Feb.	17	1929	10179	Drake	Emma, etc.	d
Oct.	22	1942	15057	Drake	Floyd G.	d
Sept.	29	1950	19899	Drake	Frederick Sneath, etc.	d
Feb.	9	1931	10867	Drake	Harry, etc.	inc
Jan.	27	1938	13470	Drake	Harry, etc.	d
		1906	4047	Drake	Henry D.	m
		1906	4047	Drake	Louis G.	m
		1905	4033	Drake	Richard S.	d
		[1895-1896]	2581	Draper	Elizabeth	d
		1895	2545½	Draper	Elizabeth	d
May	24	1948	18409	Draper	John, etc.	d
		1868	395	Draper	Rueben	d
		[1882-1883]	1250	Drees	August H.	d
		[1890-1892]	2013	Drees	C. P. A.	m
		[1890-1892]	2013	Drees	Carson F.	m
		[1889-1890]	1865	Drees	Diederich C.	d
Feb.	28	1931	11147	Drees	E E., etc.	d
		[1883-1884]	1348	Drees	E. E.	m
		1924	8627	Drees	Emma L.	d
		[1907-1908]	4355	Drees	Grace E.	m
		[1907-1908]	4342	Drees	Gustave August	d
		[1883-1884]	1348	Drees	H. A.	m
		[1889-1890]	1871	Drees	H. A.	m
		1918	6923	Drees	Herman A. (aka H. A.,	d
		[1883-1884]	1348	Drees	J. E.	m
		1888	1817	Drees	Johanna H. L.	d
		[1890-1892]	2013	Drees	John R. A.	m
Aug.	29	1955	23399	Drees	Lucy, etc.	d
		[1907-1908]	4355	Drees	Sybil V.	m

Month	Day	Year	File No.	Surname	Given Name	Type
		[1889-1890]	1871	Drees	W. E.	m
		[1883-1884]	1348	Drees	Wm. E.	m
Nov.	25	1933	11700	Drees/Dreas	Johanna E., etc.	d
June	24	1955	23270	Dresbach	Sarah Elizabeth, etc.	d
June	14	1955	23319	Dresbach	Walter W.	m
June	14	1955	23319	Dresbach	William III	m
Apr.	16	1933	11543	Dresel	Carl	d
		1892	2149	Dresel	Julius	d
June	16	1944	16040	Dresel	Rosie	d
Oct.	5	1945	16748	Dresel	Gustas	d
		[1869-1870]	419	Dressel	Emil	d
Dec.	25	1957	25104	Dressen	Albert Peter	d
Oct.		1916	6300	Dresser	Augustus W.	d
		1895	2538	Dresser	Levi	d
		[1899-1900]	3009	Dresser	Peter I.	d
		[1878-1879]	965	Drever	David	d
Sept.	1	1939	13747	Drever	David	d
		[1898-1899]	2846	Drew	Frank S.	d
Jan.	1	1937	12907	Drewes	Juliane	d
June	11	1933	11587	Drewes	William	d
Dec.	3	1947	18075	Drews	Frank F.	d
July	1	1953	21876	Dreyfus	Herbert	d
Feb.	20	1928	9842	Dries	Emil E.	inc
Aug.	29	1952	21271	Dringenberg	Henry, etc.	d
		[1883-1884]	1346	Driscoll	Cornelius	d
		1895	2546	Driscoll	Jane E.	d
		1912	5429	Driscoll	John	d
		1883	1322	Driscoll	Lemuel R.	d
July		1921	7753	Driver	Edward	d
Mar.	15	1940	13962	Drolett	Francis	d
		[1893-1894]	2352	Drosbach	Andrew	d
Apr.	27	1918	6714	Drosbach	Fredericka	d
		1920	7438	Drouillard	Joseph W.	d
Jan.	28	1949	19388	Drucks	Otto	inc
Apr.	27	1950	19587	Drucks	Otto	d
		[1889-1890]	1914	Drummond	John H.	d
May	10	1935	12265	Drummond	Lucy Elizabeth Campb	d
Aug.	26	1951	20457	Drummond	Powys	d
Dec.	17	1958	26158	Drury	Myrtle Angie, etc.	inc
Dec.		1923	8498	Dryden	Amande E.	g
		[1907-1908]	4365	Dryden	Elizabeth C.	d
Oct.	18	1939	13787	Dryden	Hiram E., etc.	d

Month	Day	Year	File No.	Surname	Given Name	Type
		1914	5847	Dryden	R. H.	d
		[1906-1907]	4204	Dryden	William R.	d
Jan.	31	1935	12847	Dryden	William R.	d
Mar.	14	1944	15820	Du Bois	Leon	d
Mar.	22	1954	22305	Du Commun	Elizabeth L., etc.	d
Feb.	17	1941	14708	Du Vander	David H.	d
Nov.	26	1915	6080	Duane	C. M./Cora M.	d
Feb.	30	1956	23762	Duane	E. A.	inc
July	24	1957	24828	Duane	Edward A., etc.	d
Apr.	24	1928	9853	Duart/Dowatt/Dwarte	Domingo	d
Aug.	1	1955	23402	Duarte	Marie	d
Apr.		1926	9243	DuBois	Coral W., etc.	d
		1926	9244	DuBois	Nathan Asbury, etc.	d
Aug.	8	1942	14971	Ducey	Ellen et al	d
June	8	1942	14971	Ducey	P. J.	d
May	6	1931	10934	Duckart	Max E., etc.	d
		1916	6224	Ducker	Andrew	d
		1922	8019	Ducker	Daisy, etc.	d
Nov.		1920	7551	Ducker	Henretta	d
		1895	2555	Ducker	Sarah	inc
		1899	2964	Ducker	Sarah	inc
		1900	3141	Ducker	Sarah	d
		[1900-1903]	3146	Ducker	Sarah	d
		1885	1491	Ducker	William	d
Mar.	18	1958	25470	Duckhorn	Anna	d
Dec.	5	1958	26130	Duckhorn	Katherine, etc.	d
Mar.	16	1948	18236	Duckworth	Augusta, etc.	d
Mar.	7	1941	14425	Ducourno	Philibert	inc
Aug.	12	1929	10354	Ducret	Anna	d
		[1906-1907]	4197	Dudley	Henry	d
Oct.	15	1945	16764	Dudley	Ruth F.	d
		1924	8697	Dudley	William S., etc.	d
Sept.	26	1952	21366	Dudson	Lily	d
June	10	1928	9874	Duer	Annie	d
Apr.	29	1957	24622	Duer	Mabel E.	inc
Jan.	5	1949	19401	Duer	Marcus	d
Sept.	21	1944	16090	Duerson	Alden E.	d
Jan.	3	1958	25256	Duerson	Cleveland, etc.	d
Aug.	28	1934	11983	Duerson	George W., etc.	d
Mar.	21	1957	24469	Duerson	Hadie W.	d
Jan.	9	1958	25275	Duerson	Harriet A.	d
Dec.	28	1958	26040	Duerson	Harriet A., etc.	d

Month	Day	Year	File No.	Surname	Given Name	Type
		[1894-1895]	2465	Duerson	John H.	d
May	8	1925	8925	Duerson	Joseph B.	d
		[1904-1905]	3843	Duerson	Lorinda A.	d
May	8	1925	8926	Duerson	Lucy E.	d
Nov.	27	1945	16838	Duerson	William H., etc.	d
July	14	1947	17851	Duesolieker	Joseph Fred, etc.	d
Oct.	17	1926	9283	Duff	John J.	d
June	12	1946	17249	Duffield	Andrew J.	inc
Feb.	9	1953	21633	Duffin	Katerena	inc
		[1897-1898]	2812	Duffy	Thomas	d
		1911	5074	Duffy	Thomas	d
Feb.	31	1937	12866	Dufke	Herman	d
Feb.	15	1954	22289	Dufranc	Louise Collin, etc.	d
Apr.	13	1951	20277	Dugan	Frank E.	d
July	16	1935	12683	Dugan	Nelson L.	d
Nov.	25	1939	13818	Dugan	William E., etc.	d
Aug.	23	1957	24902	Dugon	Melanie	d
		1904	3820	Duhring	Dorothea	d
		[1889-1890]	1884	Duhring	Frederick	d
July	8	1952	21242	Duine	Frank A., etc.	d
Apr.	16	1957	24670	Dukes	Kate C., etc.	d
		[1871-1872]	513	Dumars	William	d
		1922	8085	Dumford	William T.	d
Feb.	21	1941	14591	Dumont	Jean Baptiste, etc.	d
Dec.	22	1949	19384	Dunaway	W. C.	d
Dec.	13	1939	13839	Dunbar	Charles	d
Feb.	20	1958	25304	Dunbar	Edith	inc
		1923	8453	Dunbar	John	d
Feb.	25	1932	11420	Dunbar	John J., etc.	d
June	28	1942	14917	Dunbar	Mabel Peterson	inc
Nov.	22	1950	20062	Dunbar	Mary J.	d
Jan.	3	1943	15705	Dunbar	Ulris S. J.	d
		1883	1301	Dunbar	William F.	d
June	3	1950	19742	Duncan	Alvin B.	d
July	25	1929	10295	Duncan	Charles Albert	d
Jan.	9	1955	23647	Duncan	Dora	inc
Oct.	15	1939	13785	Duncan	Edith Cernon	d
June	16	1934	11923	Duncan	Frank	d
Aug.	7	1939	13715	Duncan	Georgie Alberta	inc
		1903	3590	Duncan	J. H.	d
Feb.	21	1939	13539	Duncan	Jane A.	d
Apr.	28	1938	13253	Duncan	Marion, etc.	d

Month	Day	Year	File No.	Surname	Given Name	Type
Apr.	4	1958	25522	Duncan	Ruby, etc.	d
July	17	1929	10341	Duncan	T. J., etc.	d
June	10	1946	17240	Duncan	William James	d
Feb.	6	1931	10830	Dundon	Annie Frances, etc.	d
Mar.		1916	6397	Dundon	Mary	inc
Mar.	26	1929	10503	Dunford	Anna M.	d
		[1907-1908]	4274	Dunham	Azariah	d
Oct.		1926	9389	Dunham	Azariat	d
Oct.	26	1927	9757	Dunham	Phyllis J.	m
		1922	8097	Dunkel	Edward P.	d
		1889	1831	Dunkin	Samuel	d
June	24	1933	11594	Dunlap	Chrissia O., etc.	d
Aug.	22	1958	25802	Dunlap	Paul E., etc.	d
		[1882-1883]	1259	Dunn	Caleb L.	d
Sept.	6	1923	8429	Dunn	Delia A.	d
Apr.	28	1947	17717	Dunn	Edwin M.	d
		1922	8111	Dunn	Emily	d
		1923	8325	Dunn	Fannie	d
Aug.		1918	6761	Dunn	George E.	d
Mar.	22	1952	20865	Dunn	Harry J., etc.	d
		1874	691	Dunn	John	d
Oct.	9	1939	13801	Dunn	Moses C.	d
		1912	5268	Dunn	Philip H., etc.	d
		[1899-1900]	3030	Dunn	Thomas M.	d
Oct.	14	1957	25083	Dunnahoe	Barbara Grace	m
		1877	870	Dunne	John	d
		1919	7143	Dunning	Benjamin	d
		1922	7986	Dunton	Fannie A.	d
June	1	1940	13980	Dunton	George	d
Nov.	25	1949	19330	Dunton	George Raymond	inc
Jan.	14	1933	11788	Dunucci	Adolph	d
		[1871-1872]	498	Dupont	J. B.	d
Feb.	6	1941	14327	Dupont	Hilda Susanna	d
		[1909-1911]	4792	Durand	Joseph B.	d
Apr.	16	1947	17750	Durand	William Sherwood, etc	d
June	12	1950	19693	Durands	Domenic, etc.	d
Mar.	13	1951	20276	Durango	John	d
Nov.	9	1933	11684	Durant	Kate, etc.	d
June	21	1930	10584	Durant	Mary Ellen	d
Oct.	9	1925	9077	Durant	William	d
		[1876-1877]	844	Durban	A.	d
Sept.	17	1948	18631	Durbin	James Reece, etc.	d

Month	Day	Year	File No.	Surname	Given Name	Type
June	2	1948	18426	Durbin	Joe Berthune, etc.	d
Sept.	2	1953	22042	Durfee	Edwin	d
May	13	1951	20334	Durham	Genora P.	d
Apr.	31	1952	21018	Durham	Genora P.	d
Nov.	15	1951	20670	Durham	Hattie G.	d
Mar.	4	1949	18932	Durker	George W., etc.	d
Jan.	5	1939	13524	Durphy	Dora Roos	d
Dec.	24	1950	20063	Durrett	Fred	d
		[1900-1903]	3351	Durst	Fredolini	inc
		1900	3369	Durst	Fredolini	d
Jan.	26	1928	10128	Dusek	Russell R.	d
Feb.	24	1939	13573	Dutcher	Emily, etc.	d
Sept.		1914	5853	Dutel	Jean	d
Apr.	26	1957	24695	Dutra	Antone	d
June	2	1952	21163	Dutro	Mabel Edna	d
May	6	1950	19675	Dutton	David A.	m
		[1897-1898]	2770	Dutton	Emily	d
Jan.	20	1947	17583	Dutton	George W., etc.	d
Jan.	17	1947	17578	Dutton	Harriet E.	d
Sept.	18	1944	16084	Dutton	Harriet E., etc.	d
May	9	1951	20390	Dutton	Nathan, etc.	d
Oct.	13	1949	19257	Dutton	Phoebe	inc
		1898	2828	Dutton	Priscilla	d
Mar.	3	1930	10544	Dutton	William Reed	d
July	18	1954	22602	Dutton	Pheobe	d
		[1900-1903]	3234	Duval	Frankie	d
May		1926	9258	DuVander	George Ferdinand	d
Feb.	21	1958	25308	DuVander	Mabel W., etc.	d
		1926	9263	DuVander	Rae M.	d
Feb.	25	1937	13153	Duzan	Lucille	d
Oct.	20	1948	18587	Dwald	C. H.	d
Dec.	28	1955	23560	Dwyer	J., etc.	d
Nov.	24	1945	16831	Dwyer	John	d
Nov.	6	1945	16805	Dwyer	P. J.	d
Nov.	21	1952	21412	Dyche	Johnny Melvin	m
Feb.	23	1947	18145	Dye	Anna M.	d
Jan.	6	1948	18767	Dye	Anna M.	d
June	29	1948	18425	Dye	Fred	d
Oct.	4	1943	15586	Dye	Joseph Z.	d
Sept.	2	1945	16679	Dyer	Amelia Jarvie/Mrs. Ge	d
		1879	1029	Dyer	Claborn	d
		[1882-1883]	1239	Dyer	Delia Ann	d

Month	Day	Year	File No.	Surname	Given Name	Type
July	26	1948	18483	Dyer	George P.	d
Aug.	1	1954	22622	Dyer	Julia E.	d
Jan.	7	1949	18816	Dyer	Marie Lynt, etc.	d
May	28	1953	21810	Dyer	Neal D.	d
Nov.	28	1943	15652	Dyle	Hannah, etc.	d
Sept.	11	1956	24202	Dysart	James P.	d
Mar.	23	1955	23075	Dysart	Mary Katheryne	m
Dec.	15	1955	23590	Dysart	Mary Katheryne	m
June	19	1956	24057	Dyslin	May	inc

Month	Day	Year	File No.	Surname	Given Name	Type
		1935	12358	Eachus	Clifford & Floyd	m
June	14	1952	20983	Eachus	Edgar P.	d
Nov.	28	1943	15618	Eades	George H.	d
Mar.	3	1939	13555	Eagler	Mary E.	d
Sept.	29	1946	17280	Earhart	W. H., etc.	d
Dec.	29	1954	22837	Earle	E. Clinton	d
Sept.	16	1944	16069	Earley	Ellen S., etc.	d
Feb.	27	1941	14721	Earley	Raymond Carl, etc.	d
Oct.	16	1953	22060	Early	Harriet	d
Feb.	28	1951	20641	Early	J. F.	d
Aug.	23	1940	14121	Early	J. Warren	d
Mar.	14	1941	14347	Early	William H., etc.	d
Apr.	12	1953	21690	Earnshaw	William C., etc.	d
		1869	414	Easley	A. M.	m
		1869	414	Easley	Sarah F.	m
		1869	414	Easley	Wm. P.	m
May	25	1958	25490	Eason	Louise, etc.	d
Feb.	5	1955	23627	Easson	Flossie	d
Mar.	24	1958	25323	Easson	Melville	inc
		[1909-1910]	4809	East	Sarah	ins
		[1909-1910]	4819	East	Sarah	d
Aug.	12	1933	11501	East	Thomas J., etc.	d
Dec.	6	1946	17384	Easter	Emma Belle	d
Oct.	27	1945	16666	Eastman	Frank	d
		1903	3636	Eastman	Lucretia M.	d
		[1900-1903]	3302	Eastman	Mary	d
Sept.	13	1928	10019	Eaton	Henry	d
Mar.	25	1957	24482	Eaton	Ola K.	d
Feb.	24	1915	6135	Eberl	George	d
		[1909-1910]	4777	Eberlein	Roy West	m
		[1909-1910]	4777	Eberlein	William Paul	m
June	23	1954	22409	Eberstadt	Edward N., etc.	d
Nov.	8	1955	23578	Eby	Edward	d
June		1915	5935	Eby	Helen	m
Feb.	28	1927	9790	Echert	Madeline	d
Jan.	10	1944	16256	Ecker	Charles	d
Mar.	11	1951	20797	Eckert	Albert P.	d
Jan.	21	1932	11416	Eckert	Edward C.	d
Dec.	25	1948	18695	Eckert	Ethel	d
Nov.	25	1948	18694	Eckert	Frederick W., etc.	d
Feb.	12	1943	15674	Eckert	Joseph Louis	d
Sept.	23	1938	13360	Eckert	Julius M.	d

Month	Day	Year	File No.	Surname	Given Name	Type
Jan.	14	1950	20048	Eckhardt	Anna L.	d
Dec.	7	1953	22102	Eckland	Frank Philip	d
Mar.	14	1929	10462	Ecklind	Robert Kenneth	g
June	12	1935	12268	Eckman	Jennie aka Susan Jane	d
June	21	1937	13037	Eckman	John	d
Dec.	1	1935	12450	Eckman	Percy I.	d
June	9	1950	19683	Eckman	William Henry, etc.	inc
Sept.	27	1950	19780	Eckman	William Henry, etc.	d
		[1918-1922]	7618	Eckstein	Cassius W.	d
May	27	1942	14836	Eckstein	Oscar	d
		[1907-1909]	4647	Eckstrom	Harry R.	d
Dec.	20	1935	12412	Eddelbuttall	Maude	d
Sept.	30	1948	18551	Eddy	Annie L., etc.	d
		1858	101	Eddy	D. K.	d
		[1903-1907]	3951	Edelmann	Johan Jacob	d
Sept.	7	1943	15464	Eden	Martin	d
Apr.	10	1956	23918	Edenburn	Chester F., etc.	d
July	3	1951	20378	Edgar	Oscar	d
Aug.	28	1958	25811	Edge	Chester W.	d
		[1918-1922]	6961	Edgerton	Henry	d
Feb.	22	1947	18142	Edgerton	Henry, etc.	d
Sept.	14	1941	14516	Edgerton	William F.	d
Oct.	25	1950	19942	Edison	Anna	d
June	9	1928	9929	Edison	Minnie Ida	d
May	30	1948	18311	Edles	John	d
Nov.	16	1952	21345	Edlund	Teodor, etc.	d
Aug.	13	1948	18515	Edman	Agnes E.	d
May	14	1941	14432	Edman	William, etc.	d
July	8	1958	25606	Edmed	Alice Maud	inc
June	14	1953	21696	Edmed	Chas. P.	d
Jan.	15	1950	20107	Edmed	Emma J.	d
		[1892-1894]	2207	Edminster	Mary L.	d
Jan.	5	1929	10371	Edmunds	J. S.	d
		1859	142	Edmunson	Emily H.	m
		1859	142	Edmunson	Hugh R.	m
		1859	143	Edmunson	John C.	m
		1859	140	Edmunson	Richard P.	m
		[1858-1859]	105	Edmunson	Rufus	d
		1859	141	Edmunson	Thomas J.	m
		1859	142	Edmunson	William F.	m
Dec.	5	1915	6103	Edsall	Juana B.	d
		[1888-1890]	1780	Edsall	Juana B.	ins

Month	Day	Year	File No.	Surname	Given Name	Type
Aug.	2	1939	13662	Edstrom	Frank	d
Apr.	16	1948	18285	Edwards	Richard Gary	m
July	21	1940	14077	Edwards	Angela Mabel	jt
Mar.	19	1956	24409	Edwards	Arthur Eden	d
Dec.	14	1946	17477	Edwards	Basel, etc.	d
		1896	2610	Edwards	Benjamin	m
		1896	2610	Edwards	Bessie H.	m
Mar.	28	1958	25333	Edwards	Clarence A., Jr.	d
Jan.	5	1917	6592	Edwards	Clinton E.	m
		[1903-1907]	4050	Edwards	Edward	d
Jan.	5	1943	15629	Edwards	Eleanor Dolores	m
May	18	1957	24602	Edwards	Florence R.	inc
		1896	2610	Edwards	Frank G.	m
		1872	544	Edwards	George	m
Oct.	24	1949	19141	Edwards	Grant H.. etc.	d
Aug.	16	1927	9703	Edwards	H. S.	d
July	18	1949	19016	Edwards	Hazel Swift	d
Nov.	6	1946	17383	Edwards	Isla Edwina	d
Oct.	28	1932	11290	Edwards	James R., etc.	d
		1912	5365	Edwards	John	d
Mar.	15	1928	9879	Edwards	John	d
July	27	1912	5363	Edwards	John	d
Mar.	18	1930	10760	Edwards	John, Jr.	d
		1872	544	Edwards	Joseph	m
		1896	2610	Edwards	Joseph L.	m
July	21	1940	14077	Edwards	June Catherine	d
May	8	1958	25607	Edwards	Kenneth Paul	d
		1896	2610	Edwards	Leland S.	m
Oct.	31	1945	16675	Edwards	Lillie	d
		1896	2610	Edwards	Lulu A.	m
		[1898-1899]	2948	Edwards	Martha Ann	d
		1872	544	Edwards	Mary	m
		1896	2610	Edwards	Mary	m
		1917	6445	Edwards	Sarah	d
July	22	1953	21903	Edwards	Serena C., etc.	d
Dec.	6	1950	19959	Edwards	Sussanne Estelle, etc.	d
		1872	559	Edwards	Thomas	d
		1868	398	Edwards	Uriah	d
		1872	545	Edwards	Uriah, Jr.	d
		[1918-1922]	7245	Edwards	William H.	d
Jan.	11	1946	16926	Egan	Charles	d
Oct.	3	1941	14628	Egan	Daniel F.	d

Month	Day	Year	File No.	Surname	Given Name	Type
Jan.	11	1946	16929	Egan	Daniel F.	d
Jan.	11	1946	16925	Egan	Nellie	d
Jan.	11	1946	16927	Egan	Raymond O.	d
Jan.	11	1946	16924	Egan	Samuel	d
Feb.	14	1949	19314	Egesty	Clovis	d
Feb.	14	1946	17529	Egesty	Mary, etc.	d
		1900	3193	Eggers	H. F.	d
Sept.	8	1958	25835	Egholm	Lorentz M., etc.	d
July	20	1948	18397	Egholm	Sadie A.	d
		1888	1741	Ehlers	John Hardwick	d
Aug.	21	1926	9344	Ehlri	Anna	d
Sept.	30	1946	17317	Ehmann	George E.	d
Apr.	7	1955	23028	Eichhorn	William H., etc.	d
		1924	8583	Eichman	Ludwig	d
Oct.	12	1932	11192	Eichman	Minnie	d
Mar.	19	1938	13434	Eichmeyer	Henry	d
Feb.	22	1922	8225	Eick	Annie	d
Oct.	5	1944	16154	Eickhorn	Johanna, Mrs.	d
Mar.	21	1950	19526	Eickmeyer	George R.	d
July	13	1953	21939	Eidswick	Ingvald	d
Mar.	3	1950	19491	Eiferly	Caroline	inc
Dec.	21	1951	20623	Eiferly	Caroline	d
Mar.	23	1928	9852	Eiferly	John	d
Jan.	26	1932	11424	Eifert	Leota Pauline	d
Mar.	28	1946	17032	Einardt	Rene Eugene	m
		1923	8355	Einhorn	Joseph Herman	d
Apr.	21	1950	19578	Eisele	Isabelle G. Kelley, etc.	d
Jan.	10	1948	18728	Eisenbeise	William	d
Nov.	30	1933	11750	Eisermann	E. Franz, etc.	d
		1892	2167	Eisermann	Rudolph	d
July	3	1953	21924	Eisiminger	Eva Gillen, etc.	d
June	31	1930	10539	Eitel	Willis D.	d
Aug.	3	1929	10347	Eiy	Robert Lee, etc.	d
June	25	1930	10787	Ekardt	John	d
Oct.	11	1948	18674	Ekstrom	Herbert E.	d
Jan.	20	1956	24217	Elam	Augustus M., etc.	d
		1875	755	Elder	Charles G.	m
Apr.	2	1925	9126	Elder	Christina	d
Feb.		1907	4263	Elder	Eleanor Louisa	d
July	24	1948	18359	Elder	Fred A.	d
		1875	755	Elder	Helen M.	m
Mar.	26	1923	8312	Elder	James H.	d

Month	Day	Year	File No.	Surname	Given Name	Type
July	4	1933	11682	Elder	James W.	d
		1875	755	Elder	Jessie H.	m
		1875	755	Elder	John M.	m
		1875	755	Elder	Madison L.	m
		1875	755	Elder	Monroe C.	m
		[1888-1890]	1783	Eldred	John J.	d
July	16	1954	22461	Eldridge	Albert	d
Nov.	16	1935	12379	Eldridge	George S.	d
Nov.	11	1929	10351	Eldridge	James L.	d
		[1900-1903]	3628	Eldridge	William	d
Mar.	20	1953	21593	Eldridge	Ada	d
May	14	1950	19630	Elkins	Frank E.	d
Sept.	17	1951	20549	Elkins	John C.	d
Nov.	7	1930	10671	Elledge	Ethel Jane	m
July	17	1930	10657	Elledge	Marie L, etc.	d
Oct.	7	1930	10671	Elledge	Marie Louise	m
Apr.	12	1932	11191	Elledge	Milliard Fillmore, etc.	d
June	3	1943	15459	Elli	Garry	d
Nov.	21	1939	13729	Ellington	David T.	d
Oct.	8	1954	22739	Elliott	Alice F.	d
Oct.	20	1953	21960	Elliott	Annie L.	d
Aug.	11	1947	17742	Elliott	Edward John, etc.	d
Mar.	6	1948	18209	Elliott	Elizabeth	d
Dec.	3	1922	8059	Elliott	Frank E.	d
Sept.	20	1953	21959	Elliott	Henry H., etc.	d
Oct.	23	1955	23457	Elliott	Henry Harrison	d
		1912	5353	Elliott	John	d
		1918	6690	Elliott	Milton	d
Nov.	23	1957	25948	Elliott	Sharon	m
May	22	1955	23188	Elliott	Sweet Mohon, etc.	d
Mar.	6	1958	25436	Elliott	Vera Claire, etc.	d
		[1914-1915]	5828	Elliott	Robert	d
June	10	1957	24730	Ellis	Deborah J.	m
Apr.	4	1944	15819	Ellis	Frank Richard	m
Mar.	3	1943	15457	Ellis	Garry	d
Feb.	23	1953	22253	Ellis	Garry	d
July	10	1957	24730	Ellis	Gerard S.	m
Sept.	26	1954	22658	Ellis	Isabel L.	d
Sept.	26	1954	22658	Ellis	John A.	d
		[1918-1922]	7042	Ellis	John Dixon	d
		[1907-1909]	4670	Ellis	Leander G.	d
		1918	6712	Ellis	Nancy E.	d

Month	Day	Year	File No.	Surname	Given Name	Type
Feb.	5	1949	19159	Ellis	Victoria, etc.	d
Apr.	9	1937	12918	Ellis	William Edwin	d
Jan.	29	1945	16845	Ellison	Rodney	d
May	12	1951	20330	Ellmaker	Mary M.	inc
		1873	602	Ellmore	Samuel O.	d
Sept.	16	1947	17960	Ellsworth	Annie	d
June	11	1943	15273	Ellsworth	Fred D., etc.	d
		[1900-1903]	3327	Ellsworth	LeGrand	d
		[1888-1890]	1879	Ellsworth	Leonard F.	d
		[1888-1890]	1894	Ellsworth	Leonard F.	m
Jan.	13	1953	21576	Ellsworth	Myron Oliver, etc.	d
		1897	2741	Ellsworth	Percy L.	d
		1914	5786	Ellsworthy	Winnie May	m
Feb.		1923	8497	Ellwood	Martha	inc
Dec.	13	1952	21448	Elmer	Martin	d
Sept.	6	1946	17382	Elmers	Fred	d
Mar.	9	1948	18213	Elmore	Joseph	d
June	29	1945	16626	Elmore	Mary Agnes	ei
		1895	2568	Elmore	Mary Jane	d
Sept.		1922	8028	Elmore	Merritt W.	d
July	29	1945	16626	Elmore	Orris C.	ei
July	29	1945	16627	Elmore	Orvis W., etc.	d
Jan.	28	1952	21487	Elonen	Hilja J.	d
Mar.	30	1936	12697	Elphick	Archie Roy	m
May	7	1941	14381	Elphick	Birdie B., etc.	d
		[1918-1922]	7511	Elphick	Elijah	d
Feb.	21	1957	26095	Elphick	Eliza F.	d
Apr.	23	1954	22356	Elphick	Eugene	d
Oct.	25	1925	8967	Elphick	Henry	d
July	20	1956	23940	Elphick	Henry	d
Mar.	5	1945	16351	Elphick	Hester C.	d
Dec.	13	1947	18043	Elphick	James	d
Feb.	5	1945	16351	Elphick	James F.	d
June	10	1935	12488	Elphick	Jeanie R.	d
July	18	1936	12685	Elphick	T. R.	ins
		1913	5509	Elphick	Thomas	d
		[1910-1911]	4995	Elphick	Elijah	inc
		1911	5010	Elphick	Esther A.	m
		[1918-1922]	7038	Elphick	Henry	d
Mar.	14	1918	6642	Elrod	Charles H.	m
June	18	1945	16498	Elsca	Cory Boyle, etc.	d
May	4	1942	14923	Elverts	Charles	d

Month	Day	Year	File No.	Surname	Given Name	Type
Apr.	15	1956	23790	Ely	Flora Dell, etc.	d
		[1903-1907]	4135	Ely	Florence Josephine	d
July	19	1929	10289	Elzi	Alfred Johannis, etc.	d
Jan.	2	1922	8219	Emanuelli	Carlo	d
Nov.	3	1957	25895	Embree	Lester Whitfield	d
Apr.	20	1951	20166	Emenegger	Centennea Mason	inc
Jan.	31	1944	16238	Emerson	Harry E.	d
		[1910-1911]	4926	Emerson	Henry Wilkie	d
Apr.	17	1942	14824	Emerson	Olivia, etc.	d
		[1894-1895]	2406	Emerson	William J.	d
Apr.	1	1949	18923	Emery	Benjamin, etc.	d
Aug.	17	1952	21195	Emery	Fred A.	d
Feb.	24	1948	18798	Emery	Lane O.	d
Nov.	7	1955	23523	Emery	Murray Brooks, etc.	d
Mar.	3	1949	18881	Emery/Evans/Eat	Hard Josph/H./Harold Joseph	d
Jan.	25	1941	14718	Emmerick	Moritz, etc.	d
Apr.	20	1934	12104	Emmons	William Pressley	d
		[1912-1913]	5382	Emory	Benjamin Franklin	d
Oct.	17	1954	22761	Emory	Etta Pearl, etc.	d
June	25	1950	19648	Emory	Ira	d
		1918	6825	Emory	Mary A.	d
Sept.	1	1952	21281	Emperor	Augusta	inc
Jan.	5	1953	21553	Emperor	Augusta J.	d
		[1918-1922]	7596	Endicott	James Bridges, Jr.	d
		1895	2532	Endres	Jacob	inc
June	12	1935	12491	Enemark	Lola L./Lola Belle	d
		[1907-1909]	4332	Engel	Joseph	d
Sept.	22	1952	21263	Engel	Katharina, etc.	inc
Mar.	19	1954	22298	Engel	Katharina, etc.	d
		1894	2401	Engelbert	Charles W.	d
		[1910-1911]	4983	Engelbright	Henry	d
		[1894-1895]	2428	Engelbright	Mary Ann	d
		[1900-1903]	3344	Engelhart	Frederick	d
		[1900-1903]	3431	Engelhart	Mary W.	d
		[1918-1922]	7503	Engelke	Emma	g
Sept.	21	1918	6700	Engelke	Louis	d
		[1903-1907]	3709	Engelke	Louis	d
Sept.	26	1956	24125	Engelke	Louise	d
Oct.	23	1943	15521	Engell	C. A. Hansen	d
July	28	1939	13654	Engels	Leland M.	m
Jan.	14	1957	26080	Enger	Norval	d
May	23	1924	8757	Engilke	Adolph Blaine	d

Month	Day	Year	File No.	Surname	Given Name	Type
May	3	1951	20311	England	Edwin O.	d
June	3	1945	16507	England	Ethel T.	d
Aug.	12	1955	23232	Engle	Blanche Mae	d
June	28	1943	15284	Engle	Frank Benjamin	d
July	2	1935	12251	Englehardt	August George	d
		[1911-1912]	5165	Englehardt	Samuel	d
		1890	1946	Englehart	James	d
Nov.	22	1941	14649	Engleman	Carl	d
Apr.	7	1928	10033	Engler	George	d
		1879	1014	Engler	Mathias	d
Apr.	26	1917	6430	Engler	Matthias, etc.	d
		[1918-1922]	7510	Englin	Charlotte	d
June	3	1915	6012	English	David Barton	d
Jan.	24	1939	13851	English	George	d
Oct.		1915	6046	English	Lanora Emily	d
Feb.	27	1942	14796	English	Thomas Vincent, etc.	d
Jan.	1	1952	21490	Enlow	Ephraim Ellsworth, etc.	d
Oct.	22	1955	23497	Ennis	Frank	d
		1899	3045	Ennis	Frank F.	d
Mar.	10	1953	21688	Ennis	Pauline	d
Sept.	2	1950	19738	Enos	Harry F.	d
		1898	2859	Enos	John S.	d
July	28	1937	13015	Enos	Lydia`	ins
Sept.	17	1915	6043	Enos	Susie T.	d
		[1918-1922]	6860	Enquist	August	d
July	10	1930	10572	Enquist	Hans R.	d
Nov.	8	1954	22797	Ensley	Caroline W.	d
Aug.	21	1955	22995	Ensley	Caroline W., etc.	d
May	6	1957	24572	Entelman	Ida Louise	inc
June	3	1951	20377	Entriken	Carrie Frances, etc.	d
Jan.	26	1931	11016	Entzminger	Lorentz, etc.	d
		1912	5284	Enzenauer	Hanna	d
Nov.	29	1947	18027	Enzenauer	Hannah W.	d
Sept.	31	1947	17922	Enzenauer	Joe	d
Oct.	27	1933	11522	Enzenauer	Valentine	ins
Oct.	19	1947	18008	Ephlin	Nellie	d
Jan.	29	1940	14252	Epidendis	Dominica	d
		[1879-1880]	804	Epperly	Levi O.	ins
		1891	2106	Epperly	Levy O.	m
		1923	8279	Epperson	E. A.	d
Apr.		1947	17643	Epping	Carl H.	inc
July	26	1958	25649	Epple	Ruth E.	con

Month	Day	Year	File No.	Surname	Given Name	Type
Jan.	24	1930	10532	Epson	John	d
June	29	1946	17111	Epstein	Anna	d
Mar.	27	1936	12718	Eraldi	David John (terminate joint t	d
Feb.	12	1938	13375	Eraldi	Enrico	d
Oct.	23	1940	14159	Eraldi	Maria	jt
Apr.	7	1939	13597	Erazmus	Pearl Irene	d
Apr.	7	1945	16405	Erbetta	Guiseppe	d
Apr.	16	1934	12002	Ericksen	Emma, etc.	d
		[1918-1922]	7189	Erickson	Albert	d
June	14	1922	8017	Erickson	Alexander	d
Apr.	15	1944	15782	Erickson	Claus	d
Apr.	24	1950	19584	Erickson	Margaret L.	d
		[1918-1922]	6848	Erickson	Marie	m
		[1903-1907]	3705	Erickson	Swan	d
Sept.	11	1958	25842	Erickson	Walter	d
Jan.	10	1947	18088	Erixon	Alexandere, etc.	d
May	18	1958	25472	Erland	Allen, etc.	d
May	28	1928	9920	Erlandsor	Edward L.	d
Mar.		1917	6614	Ermentrout	Sallie Justen, etc.	d
Feb.	2	1948	18203	Ernest	Tony	d
June	29	1949	18987	Ernst	Anna	d
May	1	1955	23091	Ernst	August M.	d
Apr.	2	1928	9893	Erving	Mary E.	d
Aug.	15	1927	9603	Erwin	Abner	d
Jan.	23	1931	11014	Erwin	Albert O.	d
	20	1955	22991	Erwin	Clara N.	d
		[1899-1900]	3063	Erwin	Elizabeth L.	d
May	22	1937	12939	Erwin	Emma	d
		1923	8562	Erwin	Martha Ann	d
May	26	1924	8739	Esaia	G. B., etc.	d
Nov.	17	1927	9704	Escolle	Joseph	inc
July	19	1929	10290	Escolle	Joseph	inc
Sept.	3	1924	8670	Eshbach	Emma	d
		[1903-1907]	4211	Eshbach/Eschbach	D. M.	d
		[1907-1909]	4548	Eskel	Frances L.	d
Nov.	29	1940	14161	Eskilson	Mary.	d
May	24	1939	13619	Eskin	Lillie Bell	d
July	2	1946	17119	Esmond	Nellie M.	d
		[1886-1888]	1571	Espey	Catherine	d
		[1888-1890]	1859	Espey	David P.	d
		1886	1570	Espey	John	d
July	15	1958	25785	Espindola	Bruce Marten	m

Month	Day	Year	File No.	Surname	Given Name	Type
June	18	1937	13003	Espindola	Lewis S.	inc
Aug.	15	1958	25785	Espindola	Robert Stephen	m
		1908	4434	Espinosa	Damien de Espinosa de los M	d
		1914	5747	Espinosa	Helen	d
		1914	5747	Espinosa	Joaquin	d
Jan.	16	1953	22177	Espinosa	Joseph, etc.	d
		1914	5747	Espinosa	Marie	d
		1865	301	Espy	John	d
Mar.	11	1951	20149	Essiva	Alfred C.	d
Jan.	1	1939	13746	Esterling	Mary E.	d
		[1903-1907]	3669	Estes	Artillus	d
		1862	210	Estes	C. F.	d
		[1918-1922]	6857	Estes	George	d
July	5	1925	9075	Estes	Laurence E.	d
		1916	6375	Estes	Madison E.	d
July	16	1937	13063	Estes	Mary F.	d
		[1918-1922]	6939	Estes	Sarah A.	d
Nov.	15	1945	16761	Etchebest	Elsie/Alice Olive	d
July	9	1945	16637	Etchebest	Jean P., etc.	d
Apr.	9	1946	17059	Etheridge	Edward Martyn, etc.	d
		[1894-1895]	2454	Ethridge	Darius (no. 1)	d
		[1894-1895]	2456	Ethridge	Darius (no. 2)	d
		1895	2602	Ethridge	Darius (no. 3)	d
Oct.	7	1948	18615	Etter	Jnnie E.	d
Sept.	10	1955	23426	Etter	Marie	d
Dec.	15	1925	8980	Eudey	Lois	m
Apr.	2	1951	20246	Eugley	Walter A.	d
July	25	1954	22618	Eurskens	Elizabeth, etc.	d
Jan.	3	1954	22900	Eva	James M., etc.	d
Jan.	18	1955	23601	Eva	James M., etc.	d
Aug.	11	1940	14100	Evahn	Albert E.	d
Feb.	12	1942	14945	Evans	Anna D.	d
Mar.	23	1953	21602	Evans	Arthur B.	d
June	5	1952	20904	Evans	Bessie	m
		1880	1103	Evans	Charles	d
Sept.	27	1941	14533	Evans	Charles O.	d
		1876	811	Evans	Charles W.	m
Jan.	18	1957	24811	Evans	Clara Bell/John D., Mrs., etc	d
		1860	178	Evans	David	d
Jan.	22	1927	9705	Evans	David	d
Nov.	3	1941	14662	Evans	Earl	d
Dec.	11	1922	8136	Evans	Edward R., etc.	d

Month	Day	Year	File No.	Surname	Given Name	Type
		1923	8411	Evans	Ellen M.	d
Jan.	19	1957	24891	Evans	Ernest G.	d
Feb.	20	1942	15152	Evans	Ester M.	d
Apr.	14	1928	10065	Evans	Esther Ann & Lizzie Jane	m
		1923	8260	Evans	Eugene	d
May	3	1944	15907	Evans	Frank L.	d
		[1903-1907]	4172	Evans	George	d
Nov.	2	1953	22090	Evans	George Alan	m
Sept,	2	1954	22727	Evans	George H., etc.	d
Nov.	23	1915	6097	Evans	George Henry	d
Sept.	7	1956	24033	Evans	Jack, etc.	d
Aug.	1	1951	20423	Evans	James Henry, etc.	d
	29	1917	6573	Evans	James M.	d
Feb.	26	1946	16961	Evans	John	d
Feb.	6	1948	18157	Evans	John I., etc.	d
Sept.	3	1951	20467	Evans	John K., etc.	d
		1876	811	Evans	John W.	m
		1885	1463	Evans	John, Rev.	d
June	6	1925	8951	Evans	Josephine Alice Shutter	d
June	5	1931	10902	Evans	L. L., etc.	d
Aug.	3	1955	23213	Evans	Lewis James II	m
Apr.	4	1947	17550	Evans	Louis	d
May	7	1941	14510	Evans	Louis B., etc.	d
		1876	811	Evans	Lucy Jane	m
July	15	1928	9973	Evans	Lyda K.	inc
Sept.	3	1944	15908	Evans	Lyton E.	d
July	6	1952	21178	Evans	Mabel M.	d
May	27	1942	14915	Evans	Martha E.	d
July	3	1947	17724	Evans	Mary	d
Apr.	13	1956	23723	Evans	May C.	d
Jan.	3	1946	17511	Evans	Merle L., etc.	d
Aug.	29	1928	10011	Evans	Myrtle G.	d
Mar.	28	1946	16970	Evans	N. Mark	d
June	1	1953	21740	Evans	Nolan Rufus	d
Jan.	11	1940	13889	Evans	Rose	d
		[1875-1876]	782	Evans	Thomas	d
Sept.	5	1944	15959	Evans	Walter	d
Jan.	19	1954	22874	Evart	Cecilia G.	d
Mar.	12	1949	18829	Evart	Clara M.	d
Feb.	8	1958	26193	Evart	Edwin J., etc.	d
July	2	1958	25752	Evart	Frank R., etc.	d
		[1907-1909]	4500	Eveland	Harmon D.	d

Month	Day	Year	File No.	Surname	Given Name	Type
Dec.	18	1956	24213	Everly	Daisy V.	d
Jan.	15	1945	16762	Everson	Marie	d
Dec.	18	1955	23598	Evert	Carl Gustave, etc.	d
Nov.	18	1952	21349	Every	Mary M.	d
May	3	1937	12955	Ewell	Ida May	d
		[1888-1890]	1759	Ewell	Mary M.	ins
July	19	1953	21897	Ewing	Denver	d
		1910	4842	Ewing	Edward	m
		[1907-1909]	4679	Ewing	Edward E.	m
		1910	4842	Ewing	Florence	m
		1910	4842	Ewing	Hallie	m
		1910	4888	Ewing	Harry	m
		1921	7830	Ewing	Harry L.	d
		[1909-1910]	4750	Ewing	Hattie C.	d
		[1879-1880]	1052	Ewing	Ids A.	m
		[1911-1912]	5279	Ewing	Lillian May	d
Feb.	14	1940	14273	Ewing	Lottie L.	d
Sept.	9	1917	6460	Ewing	Mary Ann	d
June	16	1956	23929	Ewing	Maude M.	d
		1910	4888	Ewing	Myrna	m
Nov.		1917	6488	Ewing	William	d

Month	Day	Year	File No.	Surname	Given Name	Type
Nov.	5	1927	9735	Fab	Charles	d
Mar.	21	1945	16487	Fabbro	Erasmo	d
		[1908-1911]	4763	Faber	Charles F.	d
Mar.	13	1945	16413	Fabrenbrog	John W., etc.	d
Sept.	8	1944	16251	Fabris	Albert Antonio, etc.	d
		1874	681	Face	Solomon	d
Feb.	23	1952	21528	Facendini	Guglielmo, etc.	d
Oct.	3	1931	11067	Facietti	M.	d
Oct.	12	1958	25919	Fadelli	Angelo	d
Dec.	9	1952	21505	Faden	Nellie	d
		1873	651	Fader	Anna H.	m
		1873	651	Fader	Helen M.	m
		1873	651	Fader	Katie A.	m
		1873	651	Fader	Victor V.	m
May	3	1930	10543	Fagan	Emma E.	d
Oct.	29	1932	10543	Fagan	Emma E.	d
		1922	7988	Fagas	Maud Frates, etc.	d
July	25	1934	11960	Fagerstrom	John Petter, etc.	d
		1924	8631	Fagioli	Pietro	d
Feb.	18	1950	19463	Fahle	Karl W., etc.	d
Dec.	15	1957	25148	Fahnensteil	John George	d
Apr.	6	1953	21751	Fahrenholtz	Katheryne G.	d
		[1896-1897]	2655	Fahrion	Harold C.	m
		[1896-1897]	2655	Fahrion	Wallace G.	m
May	11	1956	23983	Failda	Nicholas, etc.	d
July	29	1927	9621	Failla	Giovanni, etc.	d
		1903	3596	Faio	Amelia	m
		1896	2652	Faio	Anton Brown	d
		1903	3596	Faio	Ida	m
		1903	3596	Faio	Maria	m
		1903	3596	Faio	Mariana	m
		1865	294	Fairbairn	Sarah M. E.	d
		[1899-1902]	3449	Fairbanas	J. F.	d
		[1906-1907]	4166	Fairbank	James K.	d
		[1908-1911]	4607	Fairbanks	D. B.	d
Dec.		1918	6873	Fairbanks	Emila Josephine, etc.	d
Mar.	3	1940	13917	Fairbanks	Fred E.	d
		[1886-1887]	1518	Fairbanks	Harriet J.	d
May	9	1950	19679	Fairbanks	James K.	d
May	24	1953	21802	Fairbanks	Joseph N., etc.	d
Oct.	10	1927	9719	Fairbanks	Julius Tracy	d
		[1888-1889]	1779	Fairbanks	Osmond H.	d

Month	Day	Year	File No.	Surname	Given Name	Type
Nov.	27	1924	8789	Fairchild	Elizabeth J.	d
Dec.	30	1926	9395	Fairchild	Fred F., etc.	d
Mar.	31	1928	9861	Fairchild	Thomas, etc.	d
May	14	1914	5744	Fairclo	Mary E.	d
		1916	6188	Fairman	Mary E.	d
		[1919-1921]	7302	Faithful	Edward	d
Mar.	12	1946	17069	Fakhouri	Andrew N.	d
Oct.	9	1942	15105	Falcetti	Clementina, etc.	d
July	7	1958	25759	Falder	Theresa	d
May	2	1958	25594	Fales	Ernest T.	d
June	24	1942	14866	Faletti	Antonio	d
Nov.	5	1948	18715	Faletti	Antonio	d
Nov.	5	1948	18765	Faletti	Antonio	d
Jan.	29	1947	18149	Faletti	Maria	d
Dec.	6	1951	20716	Falk	Axel John, etc.	d
Jan.	26	1936	12782	Falletti	S,	d
Feb.	25	1946	16965	Fallon	James P.	d
		[1895-1896]	2544	Fallon	Mary	d
		1876	797	Falvey	Margaret	d
June	26	1950	19725	Falvey	Mary	d
		1921	7875	Fan	Firmin	d
		1887	1622	Fanning	Ann	d
Dec.	23	1948	18749	Fansini	Paul C.	d
Feb.	6	1959	26188	Fanucchi	Angelo	d
Sept.	25	1926	9320	Fanucchi	Elita	m
Jan.	4	1929	10484	Fara	Martino, etc.	d
June	20	1954	22540	Faraone	Frank	d
		1925	9079	Farell	Freeman F.	d
Apr.	4	1952	20961	Farlander	Arthur W.	d
May	22	1946	17161	Farley	Charles W.	d
		1922	8090	Farley	Dorothy G.	m
Oct.	24	1954	22771	Farley	Mary A.	d
Dec.		1935	12446	Farley	Walter Ray	d
Aug.	7	1957	24937	Farley	William M.	d
		[1903-1906]	3828	Farmer	Charles R.	d
		[1908-1911]	4631	Farmer	Charles Ralph	m
		1885	1504	Farmer	E. T.	d
Oct.	15	1934	12077	Farmer	E. T., etc.	d
Oct.	8	1943	15589	Farmer	Eugene F.	d
		1919	7215	Farmer	Gene Caroline	m
		1919	7106	Farmer	Grace	d
		[1894-1895]	2439	Farmer	Henry T.	d

Month	Day	Year	File No.	Surname	Given Name	Type
Mar.	24	1953	21719	Farmer	Jasmine	d
Mar.	27	1953	21728	Farmer	Judith P.	m
Mar.	17	1953	21698	Farmer	Laloy Darlene, etc.	d
Mar.	27	1953	21728	Farmer	Linda J.	m
		[1912-1913]	5690	Farmer	Lou	d
Apr.	27	1953	21728	Farmer	Louana	m
Oct.	14	1919	7215	Farmer	Mary Virginia	m
Mar.	27	1953	21728	Farmer	Richard G.	m
May	5	1954	22435	Farmer	Richard G.	d
Mar.	27	1953	21728	Farmer	Susan	m
Oct.	6	1946	17331	Farmschlag	Katie	d
Mar.	20	1941	14444	Farni	Enrico	d
May	27	1939	13586	Farnsworth	Laura Mae	d
Apr.	27	1953	21725	Farnsworth	Bertha E.	d
Dec.	10	1935	12487	Farnsworth	Stephen F.	d
		[1924-1927]	9167	Farour	John	d
		1870	444	Farquhar	Nora	m
		1870	444	Farquhar	Winnefried	m
		[1889-1890]	1888	Farrar	Jane	d
		1908	4412	Farrar	Moses C.	d
Mar.	16	1956	23727	Farrar	Newell	d
		[1908-1911]	4830	Farrell	David E.	d
		1907	4336	Farrell	Martin	d
Jan.	4	1956	23697	Farrell	Mary B., etc.	d
Oct.	6	1958	25982	Farrell	Nellie M.	d
Jan.	9	1949	19406	Farrell	Sarah G.	d
Feb.	28	1916	6383	Farrell	William Fitz Maurice, etc.	d
Mar.	15	1942	15229	Farrell	William J., etc.	d
		1954	22600	Farrington	E. O.	d
July	18	1954	22601	Farrington	Mary F.	d
		[1871-1872]	501	Farris	Allen C.	d
July	24	1957	24755	Farris	Lila Winter, etc.	d
		[1912-1914]	5692	Farro	William Edward	m
Oct.	29	1952	21369	Fassas	Harry J.	d
Feb.		1946	16982	Fassio	Al	d
Feb.	30	1934	11845	Fastrup	Peter C., etc.	d
Jan.	16	1957	25220	Fatturini	Giuseppe	d
		[1873-1874]	653	Faucett	Thomas	d
Apr.	1	1952	21023	Faudre	Brice A., etc.	d
		1922	8176	Faught	Armstrong	d
Feb.	28	1949	18867	Faught	Carole	d
Oct.	21	1940	14188	Faught	Emma Gertrude	inc

Month	Day	Year	File No.	Surname	Given Name	Type
		1890	1995	Faught	Jabez	d
Feb.	5	1944	16305	Faught	John, etc.	d
		1890	2040	Faught	Madison	d
July	28	1955	23346	Faught	Nancy	d
May	2	1955	23210	Faught	Willis	d
		1890	2039	Faught	Willis, Jr.	d
		[1908-1911]	4863	Faulconer	Joseph C.	d
Mar.	18	1952	20928	Faulk	James M.	d
Dec.	24	1954	22888	Faulkner	Celesta, etc.	d
		[1908-1911]	5001	Faulkner	Elisabeth R.	d
		1882	1268	Faulkner	James	d
Oct.	27	1928	10077	Faunti	Charles A. Mildred Dorotl	m
Feb.	4	1955	23023	Faure	Frank Charles, etc.	d
Feb.	14	1955	22975	Faure	Mary Elizabeth	d
Dec.	9	1958	26135	Faurie	Christine A., etc.	d
		[1908-1911]	4632	Faust	Flora W.	d
Sept.	20	1923	8461	Faust	R. M.	d
June	3	1938	13260	Favour	Alberta	d
Jan.	18	1926	9167	Favour	John	d
Mar.	4	1954	22379	Fawcett	Wilfred Brick, etc.	d
		[1872-1873]	588	Fay	Bridget T.	m
Mar.	28	1958	25427	Fay	Catherine	d
Dec.	21	1929	10468	Fay	G. E.	d
		[1899-1902]	3244	Fay	Hiram	d
Oct.	6	1948	18665	Fay	James Wrae, etc.	d
		[1912-1914]	5597	Fay	John S.	d
		[1919-1921]	7269	Fay	Thomas	d
		1871	471	Fay	W. J.	d
June	23	1946	17216	Fazio	Joseph	d
July	23	1946	17308	Fazio	Mary, etc.	d
Jan.	20	1957	25231	Fazzio	Angela	d
May	21	1958	25563	Fazzio	Giovanni	d
Oct.	3	1936	12698	Feaney	Maria	d
Dec.	17	1941	14677	Fear	Victor	d
Jan.	15	1956	23656	Fears	Irene B., etc.	d
Apr.	20	1948	18295	Fechter	George	d
July	25	1951	20454	Fechter	John H., etc.	d
Oct.	20	1926	9388	Fect	Rubin J.	d
Nov.	17	1944	16123	Fedderson	Anna	d
May	22	1957	24681	Fedderson	Olive	d
		[1908-1911]	4576	Feedler	James William	m
		1895	2498	Feehan	E. M.	m

Month	Day	Year	File No.	Surname	Given Name	Type
		1895	2498	Feehan	Mary F.	m
		1895	2498	Feehan	N. E./U. E.	m
		1903	3609	Feehan	Edwin M.	d
		[1899-1902]	3404	Feely	Bridget	d
May	4	1956	23969	Feely	Daniel P., etc.	d
Dec.	24	1942	15159	Feely	Francis, etc.	d
		[1908-1911]	4565	Feely	Michael J.	d
		[1924-1927]	9366	Feeny	Mary E.	d
		1924	8602	Fees	Curtis Dalton	m
		1924	8602	Fees	Roy Eugene	m
Mar.	13	1924	8602	Fees	Ruby Isola	m
		1921	7732	Fees	Thomas	g
		[1919-1921]	7268	Fees	Lillie	d
		1874	693	Feese	Joseph	d
Feb.	9	1952	20915	Feesey	John	d
June	27	1930	10527	Fehler	Henry	d
May	1	1950	19665	Fehrmann	Paul F. E., etc.	d
Jan.	6	1945	16861	Feichert	Harry Edward, etc.	d
Sept.	2	1954	22669	Feifer	Lilly Bell, etc.	d
May	26	1943	15352	Feige	Adeline	d
Mar.	18	1952	20925	Feigley	Martin M.	d
Sept.	27	1950	19777	Feinstein	Louis	d
		1921	7722	Felciano	John J., etc.	d
		[1922-1923]	8247	Felder	Joseph	d
Mar.	5	1954	22381	Felder	Theresa	inc
Feb.	19	1914	5845	Feldmeyer	B. W.	d
Mar.	2	1943	15626	Feldmeyer	Clemens A.	d
Dec.	15	1915	6054	Feldmeyer	Gustav A.	d
June	11	1923	8359	Feldmeyer	Iva Wilhelmina	m
Sept.	18	1943	15568	Feldmeyer	Wilhelmina	d
		[1919-1921]	7376	Feldmeyer	William B.	d
		1923	8359	Feldmeyer	William Walter	m
Feb.	8	1942	15215	Feliz	Charles	d
Sept.	20	1927	9631	Feliz	G. C.	d
Oct.	13	1954	22748	Feliz	Ross A., etc.	d
Oct.	25	1954	22823	Fellers	Laura Whitney	inc
Nov.	24	1939	13852	Fellers	Norman Vance	m
June	24	1925	8891	Fellows	Eva	d
July	25	1952	21218	Fellows	Fred	d
Aug.	28	1943	15495	Fels	Frederick W.	d
		1922	8083	Fels	Hermine	blank
Oct.	8	1946	17430	Fels	Wilhelmina	d

Month	Day	Year	File No.	Surname	Given Name	Type
Mar.	4	1943	15297	Fels	Wilhelmina H., etc.	d
Nov.	5	1949	19302	Felsing	Albert H., etc.	d
Dec.	12	1935	12490	Felt	Cecilia	inc
		1911	5177	Feltz	Augusta	d
Dec.	19	1951	20747	Feltz	Carl E. R.	mp
May	18	1950	19708	Feltz	Carl Joseph	d
Dec.	22	1941	14648	Feltz	Cecilia	m
July	26	1941	14531	Feltz	Charles F.	d
Sept.	22	1941	14648	Feltz	Leo J.	m
		1889	1827	Feltz	Louise	m
Aug.	26	1941	14531	Feltz	Pauline W.	d
Oct.	22	1941	14648	Feltz	Regina	m
May	29	1955	23206	Fenaci	Louisa, etc.	d
Oct.	11	1911	5031	Fenili	B.	inc
		[1889-1890]	1893	Fennelly	Mary	d
May	12	1947	17790	Fenner	Edward D., etc.	d
Feb.	28	1957	24489	Fenner	Marie	d
Sept.	12	1945	16717	Fenske	Tina	d
June	22	1954	22475	Fenton	Edward	d
Mar.	22	1949	18974	Fentress	Chester Burt	d
Jan.	7	1955	22965	Ferchen	Frank E., etc.	d
		[1912-1914]	5488	Ferdinand	Antonio	d
Nov.	28	1954	22833	Ferdinand	Ida May	d
		[1919-1921]	7534	Ferdinand	Louisa	d
Jan.	16	1937	13097	Ferdinand	Marie	m
Jan.	15	1931	11166	Ferdinand	Mary	d
		1918	6721	Ferenc	Stephen	d
Aug.	5	1958	25829	Ferencz	Elizabeth, etc.	d
		[1889-1890]	1880	Feretti	Luigi	d
		[1919-1921]	7251	Ferguson	Charles T.	d
Feb.	28	1948	18188	Ferguson	D. M.	d
Aug.	9	1951	20474	Ferguson	Edward J.	d
Nov.	25	1931	11089	Ferguson	Emelia	d
		[1924-1927]	8988	Ferguson	Emmett C.	m
July	5	1944	16016	Ferguson	Emmett Coleman	d
Dec.	17	1924	8805	Ferguson	Ethel	d
Mar.	29	1954	22310	Ferguson	Eugenie W.	d
Apr.		1951	20203	Ferguson	George	d
July	13	1951	20540	Ferguson	Grocer C.	d
Feb.	5	1951	20198	Ferguson	Grover C.	d
		[1893-1894]	2312	Ferguson	Hannah	d
Sept.	20	1956	24114	Ferguson	Harriet M., etc.	inc

Month	Day	Year	File No.	Surname	Given Name	Type
		[1893-1894]	2311	Ferguson	John	d
		[1899-1902]	3405	Ferguson	John F.	d
Oct.	14	1958	25996	Ferguson	Louis Elton	d
May		1923	8356	Ferguson	Mary Ellen	d
Apr.	30	1946	17116	Ferguson	Mary Ellen	d
		[1912-1914]	5645	Ferguson	Naomi E., etc.	d
		1872	534	Ferguson	Peter	d
Oct.	27	1933	11725	Ferguson	Sarah A.	d
		[1924-1927]	8950	Ferguson	Walter H.	d
Sept.	12	1947	17888	Ferguson	William R.	d
		[1919-1921]	7237	Fermi	P. G.	d
		1890	2086	Fernald	Johnson	d
		1894	2377	Fernald	Mary Lillian	d
		[1899-1902]	3303	Fernald	Nathaniel J.	inc
		1894	2377	Fernald	Orlando J.	m
		1924	8681	Fernandez	Elizabeth	d
Aug.	6	1937	13087	Fernandiz	A.	ins
Apr.	12	1945	16524	Ferrando	Battista D.	d
May	28	1930	10613	Ferrando	Gladys M., etc.	d
May	13	1945	16525	Ferrando	Mary	d
		1911	5049	Ferrando	Pietro	d
June	11	1915	5980	Ferrari	Adone	d
		[1894-1895]	2383	Ferrari	Angelica	m
Feb.	21	1949	18851	Ferrari	Carlatta	d
		[1894-1895]	2383	Ferrari	Carlo	m
Apr.	30	1934	12088	Ferrari	Eurico, etc.	d
Feb.	27	1943	15617	Ferrari	Frank	d
Sept.	20	1951	20556	Ferrari	Frank	d
July		1922	8043	Ferrari	Giuseppe	d
Mar.	17	1941	14439	Ferrari	Joseph	d
Jan.	14	1954	22914	Ferrari	Kelly David, etc.	d
May	19	1948	18354	Ferraris	Joe, etc.	d
		[1912-1914]	5379	Ferree de	Louise	d
Jan.	7	1957	24435	Ferreira	Antonio G.	d
June	5	1933	11601	Ferreira	Barbara, etc.	d
May	9	1956	23844	Ferrera	Joseph A., etc.	d
May	12	1949	19010	Ferrera	Manuel C., etc.	d
Aug.	29	1958	25818	Ferrero	Carlo	d
Oct.	21	1956	24175	Ferrero	Corrado, etc.	d
Nov.	26	1936	12781	Ferrero	Frank	d
June	18	1955	23247	Ferrero	Giovanni	d
Oct.	12	1955	23486	Ferrero	Lena	d

Month	Day	Year	File No.	Surname	Given Name	Type
Nov.	5	1954	22849	Ferrero	Louis, etc.	d
July	27	1957	24757	Ferrers	Paulina, etc.	d
Nov.	22	1945	16780	Ferrette	Charles	d
Dec.	28	1955	23556	Ferris	James	d
		[1899-1902]	3311	Ferris	John Milton	d
June		1922	8020	Ferroni	Emelia	d
June	12	1937	12960	Ferroni	Enrico	d
May	5	1935	12261	Ferroni	Norma	d
Mar.	28	1950	19592	Ferry	Mary Annetta	d
Apr.	1	1958	25509	Fessel	Pauline	con
Jan.	2	1931	10827	Fessell	Annie	d
Apr.	12	1957	24582	Fesselmeyer	Walter H., Jr.	d
Oct.	30	1957	25052	Fest	Arthur Ernst, etc.	d
Mar.	24	1943	15328	Fett	Peter	d
	5	1922	8132	Fetters	Emma	d
Jan.	20	1941	14747	Fetzer	Morrison	d
Dec.	14	1933	11762	Feysinger	William Martin, etc.	d
Nov.	13	1928	10090	Fiala	Albertine	d
Dec.	16	1931	11135	Fiala	Theodore R.	d
		[1924-1927]	9342	Fias	John W.	d
		1910	4832	Fichtinger	Otto	d
		1910	4832	Fichtinger	Wenzel	d
		[1888-1889]	1794	Fick	Henry William	m
		[1888-1889]	1794	Fick	Hermine Doreth	m
		[1888-1889]	1743	Fick	John F.	d
		[1888-1889]	1794	Fick	John Frederick	m
		[1908-1911]	4781	Ficken	Catherine/Kittie	d
Feb.	29	1957	24495	Fidiam	James F.	d
June	21	1951	20405	Fiege	Henry	d
July	5	1917	6521	Field	C. E.	d
		[1912-1914]	5654	Field	John	d
June	13	1919	7025	Field	Maria Susan	d
Jan.	27	1925	8996	Field	Samuel B.	d
Nov.	10	1942	15106	Field	William E.	d
		[1877-1878]	908	Field	Effa	m
		1899	2994	Field	Emma	d
		[1877-1878]	881	Field	James	d
		[1874-1875]	713	Field	Thomas A.	d
		[1912-1914]	5607	Fielden	Lewis Anthony	d
		[1902-1903]	3512	Fields	Ethel	m
Apr.	24	1958	25487	Fields	Frank, etc.	d
		[1902-1903]	3512	Fields	Harry	m

Month	Day	Year	File No.	Surname	Given Name	Type
Jan.	6	1956	23704	Fields	John Allen	d
Sept.	9	1945	16690	Fields	Joseph	d
Apr.	10	1952	21045	Fields	Lillian	d
Feb.	16	1934	11870	Figone	Giovanni	m
June	6	1958	25599	Figone	Kate, etc.	d
Feb.	5	1937	12853	Figone	Lena Bjornestad	d
Mar.	16	1934	11870	Figone	Louisa	m
Feb.	16	1934	11870	Figone	Mario	m
Jan.	4	1915	6060	Figone	Silvio	d
Sept.	14	1933	11664	Figoni	Giovanni	d
June	2	1942	14965	Fike	Lucy Rose	d
		[1872-1873]	535	Fike	Stephen S.	m
July	27	1958	25737	Files	Johnny A.	d
Apr.	22	1955	23192	Filhes	Victorine, etc.	d
Sept.	2	1931	10984	Filhol	Joseph	d
Nov.	31	1930	10642	Filippelli	Annucita	d
Jan.	18	1956	24404	Filippi	Edigio	d
Aug.	29	1942	14999	Filippi	Maria	d
Sept.	2	1943	15573	Filippi	Oscar, etc.	d
May	8	1914	5785	Filippini	Achille	d
June	4	1944	15871	Filippini	Anita	d
May	22	1953	21851	Filippini	Celestina, etc.	d
Apr.	2	1914	5727	Filippini	Charles	d
Aug.	30	1915	6047	Filippini	Coralee	d
		1917	6416	Filippini	Emilia	d
Feb.	6	1945	16401	Filippini	Emilio John, etc.	d
		1914	5796	Filippini	Evelyn	m
Nov.	18	1944	16173	Filippini	Geremia, etc.	d
May	8	1914	5796	Filippini	Henry	m
May	8	1914	5796	Filippini	James	m
Aug.	8	1914	5796	Filippini	Joseph	m
Feb.	8	1951	20138	Filippini	Leonardo R., etc.	d
Dec.	2	1956	24246	Filippini	Louis B.	d
Jan.	26	1926	9417	Filippini	Massimo, etc.	d
Mar.	16	1948	18235	Filippini	Ora M.	d
May	8	1914	5796	Filippini	Robert	m
Feb.	16	1958	25290	Filippini	Victoria Russell, etc.	d
Feb.	16	1930	10525	Filkius	Alice M.	ins
Feb.	14	1951	20800	Filley	William P.	d
		1919	7001	Fillippini	Evelyn	g
Feb.	19	1919	7001	Fillippini	Henry	g
Feb.	19	1919	7001	Fillippini	James	g

Month	Day	Year	File No.	Surname	Given Name	Type
	19	1919	7001	Fillippini	Josephine	g
Feb.	19	1919	7001	Fillippini	Robert	g
July	29	1956	24024	Fillmore	Marguerite Mary, etc.	d
Apr.	26	1954	22417	Fillmore	James Everand, Jr., etc.	m
		1935	12361	Filmer	Forrester	d
		[1899-1902]	3423	Filton	John H.	d
June	17	1952	21197	Finali	Mary	d
May	22	1929	10255	Finch	Edward	d
June	6	1933	11530	Finch	Elizabeth E.	d
Jan.	1	1930	10793	Finch	Richard E.	d
Jan.	11	1949	18827	Finch	William Joseph	d
		[1872-1873]	584	Findley	David	m
		[1872-1873]	584	Findley	Elizabeth	m
		[1872-1873]	584	Findley	Harvey	m
		[1872-1873]	584	Findley	Katherine	m
		[1872-1873]	584	Findley	Samuel	m
		1866	327	Fine	Abraham	m
		[1891-1893]	2276	Fine	Abraham	d
Mar.	19	1946	17081	Fine	Edward, etc.	d
		1866	327	Fine	Emeline	m
Jan.	18	1946	16943	Fine	Emily	d
		1866	327	Fine	Emsley	m
June		1915	5999	Fine	Enisley	d
		1846	2	Fine	I. M.	d
		1907	4307	Fine	Joff	d
		1862	217	Fine	John F.	d
Apr.	26	1917	6433	Fine	John Wesley	d
May	18	1953	21845	Fine	Mattie E., etc.	d
		1866	327	Fine	Wm. Petis	m
Jan.	8	1954	22271	Finegan	James J.	d
July		1955	23361	Finegan	James J.	d
Jan.	5	1955	23625	Finigan	Elizabeth A.	d
July	10	1917	6525	Fink	Edward	m
Feb.	14	1958	25385	Fink	Edward C.	d
July	10	1917	6525	Fink	Elsie	m
Oct.	16	1938	13409	Fink	Felix F.	d
		1917	6525	Fink	Helen	m
		1918	6853	Fink	Holdie	d
Aug.	10	1937	13060	Fink	Jennie	ins
July	10	1917	6525	Fink	John	m
Dec.	24	1942	15157	Fink	John	d
		1917	6525	Fink	Lena	m

Month	Day	Year	File No.	Surname	Given Name	Type
May	30	1946	17504	Fink	Magdalena Elizabeth	d
July	10	1917	6525	Fink	Otto	m
		[1924-1927]	9345	Finlaw	Anne Love	d
		[1903-1906]	4023	Finlaw	William	d
May	2	1929	10300	Finley	Andrew J.	d
Apr.	11	1937	12890	Finley	Charles W.	d
Nov.	2	1942	15132	Finley	Ernest L., etc.	d
Jan.	27	1932	11351	Finley	George	m
		1917	6530	Finley	Harrison	d
Oct.		1918	6724	Finley	Henry H.	d
May	16	1934	11924	Finley	J. P.	d
Aug.	21	1948	18467	Finley	James P.	d
Aug.	31	1946	17321	Finley	Joan M.	m
		[1908-1911]	4981	Finley	John	d
		1919	7024	Finley	Leon Grover	d
June	3	1942	14840	Finley	Livonia J.	d
May	2	1937	12954	Finley	Mary J.	d
Apr.	24	1928	9889	Finley	Robert	d
Dec.	27	1932	11351	Finley	Ruth	m
Oct.		1917	6554	Finley	Samuel E.	d
		[1912-1914]	5569	Finley	William A.	d
Aug.	31	1946	17321	Finley	William L.	m
Dec.	18	1953	22067	Finley	Wilson E., etc.	d
Jan.	18	1953	22241	Finn	Ethel May	d
Jan.	17	1950	20050	Finn	Grace E.	d
July	1	1939	13659	Finnegan	John Francis, etc.	d
		1921	7964	Finnell	Albertus	d
Mar.	6	1942	14759	Finnell	Eliza E.	d
June	12	1947	17190	Finner	Edward D., etc.	d
Nov.	22	1948	18686	Finnerty	Edward J.	d
Feb.	20	1958	25301	Finnigan	Rose	inc
		[1912-1914]	5700	Finos	Giovani	d
Mar.	21	1946	17017	Finsterbusch	Gary C.	d
		1924	8628	Fiorelli	Joseph, etc.	d
Feb.	2	1945	16393	Fiori	Attilio	d
Dec.	19	1954	22876	Fiori	Erminia	d
July	15	1951	20440	Fiori	Hazel	d
Feb.	9	1918	6912	Fiori	Henry E.	d
Mar.	2	1956	23829	Fiori	Mary E.	d
Apr.	24	1928	9916	Fiori	O.	d
Sept.	9	1955	23421	Fippins	Benjamin Franklin, etc.	d
Sept.	23	1955	23454	Fippins	Elizabeth	inc

Month	Day	Year	File No.	Surname	Given Name	Type
Oct.	25	1947	17909	Firpo	Evabelle	d
June	21	1952	21075	Firpo	Peter E.	d
		[1922-1923]	8249	Fischer	Lena	d
Dec.	20	1945	16822	Fischer	Louise A.	d
June	22	1926	9173	Fischer	Max	d
Jan.	13	1948	18775	Fischer	William	d
Sept.	2	1944	16243	Fiscus	Fred	d
Mar.	7	1945	16406	Fiscus	George W.	d
		[1877-1878]	906	Fiscus	George W.	d
Feb.	31	1928	9860	Fish	Elizabeth C.	d
		[1919-1921]	7366	Fish	Irene Beauchamp	d
Apr.	21	1957	24608	Fish	Sarah B., etc.	d
Apr.	6	1950	19550	Fishbain	David	d
Oct.	9	1921	7782	Fisher	Antone	d
		1903	3568	Fisher	Augustus L.	d
		[1899-1902]	3245	Fisher	Augustus L.	g
		[1893-1894]	2302	Fisher	Charles C.	d
		[1908-1911]	4979	Fisher	Charles Edward	m
Feb.	5	1931	10829	Fisher	Charles Edward, etc.	d
		[1893-1894]	2360	Fisher	Clare V.	m
Oct.	28	1919	7148	Fisher	Daniel	g
June	23	1945	16542	Fisher	Daniel	d
Feb.	13	1955	22973	Fisher	Dora	d
		1918	6710	Fisher	Dora Wulff	ins
Jan.	24	1945	16889	Fisher	Edmond T.	d
		[1864-1865]	267	Fisher	Edward	d
		[1924-1927]	9068	Fisher	Emile	d
Mar.	10	1942	14762	Fisher	Emily I.	d
Nov.	27	1947	18065	Fisher	Frank J.	d
Jan.	18	1947	18095	Fisher	Frank J., etc.	d
Mar.	24	1955	23077	Fisher	Harry Leslie, etc.	d
		[1906-1907]	4112	Fisher	John J.	d
Jan.	21	1932	11482	Fisher	John T.	d
Jan.	18	1954	22294	Fisher	Marjorie Lois	m
Dec.	25	1930	10786	Fisher	Nellie	ins
Aug.	22	1937	13046	Fisher	Nellie R.	d
Oct.	11	1957	25079	Fisher	Peter P.	d
Feb.	4	1958	25352	Fisher	Ruth Hoyt	d
Oct.	23	1958	25945	Fisher	Serena R.	d
Dec.	4	1931	11153	Fisher	Thomas	d
Sept.	18	1952	21348	Fisiker	George M., etc.	d
		[1874-1875]	711	Fisk	Andrew	d

Month	Day	Year	File No.	Surname	Given Name	Type
July	29	1945	16631	Fisk	Charles G.	d
Sept.	1	1953	22037	Fisk	Emillie K.	d
		[1874-1875]	711	Fisk	Frank	m
July	15	1946	17257	Fisk	Frank L., etc.	d
		[1924-1927]	9681	Fisk	George L.	d
Sept.	17	1951	20608	Fisk	Harry P.	d
		[1912-1914]	5342	Fisk	M. Sarah	d
Jan.	23	1957	24475	Fisk	Sarah B.	inc
		1856	41½	Fitch	Anna	m
		1856	41½	Fitch	Charles	m
		1878	961	Fitch	Clara	d
		1879	986	Fitch	Clara	m
May	18	1950	19638	Fitch	George S.	inc
Mar.	3	1952	20959	Fitch	George S.	d
		1856	41	Fitch	Henry D.	d
		1879	986	Fitch	Herman	m
		1856	41½	Fitch	John B.	m
		1897	2750	Fitch	Joseph	d
		1881	1141	Fitch	Joseph, Jr.	m
Apr.	20	1926	9471	Fitch	M. L.	d
		1879	986	Fitch	Natalia	m
Jan.	6	1936	12795	Fitch	Sarah Jane	d
		1879	986	Fitch	William C.	m
		1886	1516	Fitton	Edward	d
		[1919-1921]	7574	Fitts	Jonathan Perry, etc.	d
June	23	1953	21858	Fitz	Patrick Josephine	d
Mar.	4	1941	14378	Fitzgerald	Daniel H.	d
Aug.	20	1940	14153	Fitzgerald	David	d
Apr.	24	1941	14449	Fitzgerald	David, etc.	d
		1871	474	Fitzgerald	E.	d
		[1887-1888]	1636	Fitzgerald	Enos	d
Apr.	12	1932	11273	Fitzgerald	James G. B., Jr.	m
July	1	1915	6028	Fitzgerald	John A.	d
		[1922-1923]	8278	Fitzgerald	Joseph L.	d
		1911	5317	Fitzgerald	Patrick	d
June	16	1938	13353	Fitzgerold	Daniel H.	d
Oct.	30	1940	14194	Fitzgibbons	Hannah	d
June	4	1945	16560	Fitzolram	Anton	d
		1907	4304	Fitzpatrick	Andrew	d
Mar.	27	1957	24558	Fitzpatrick	Anna Nora	d
Feb.	28	1946	16969	Fitzpatrick	Charles J.	d
		1888	1708	Fitzpatrick	Frank	d

Month	Day	Year	File No.	Surname	Given Name	Type
		[1924-1927]	8817	Fitzpatrick	Frank J.	d
		[1919-1921]	7601	Fitzpatrick	John J.	d
Jan.	28	1931	11179	Fitzpatrick	John K.	d
Nov.	8	1930	10701	Fitzpatrick	Margaret	d
May	23	1934	11931	Fitzpatrick	Peter D.	d
Jan.	25	1938	13468	Fitzpatrick	Thomas	d
June	2	1952	21098	Fitzpatrick	Walter Thomas, Jr.	d
		1903	3527	Fix	Joshua	d
Dec.	22	1952	21526	Flack	Ada Mary, etc.	d
Apr.		1924	8624	Flack	Racilla R.	d
		1916	6172	Flagg	Eldridge Davis	d
July	24	1958	25804	Flaherty	Halina A.	d
May	11	1958	25544	Flaherty	Joseph E.	d
		1916	6200	Flaherty	Joseph Patrick	d
		[1919-1921]	7462	Flaherty	Thomas	d
Apr.	22	1946	17095	Flammang	Peter	d
July	21	1946	17264	Flanagan	Charlotte Ellen, etc.	d
		1916	6273	Flanagan	Leo	d
		1871	478	Flanary	Philip	d
Mar.	20	1914	5846	Flannery	Sheldon J.	d
		1922	8154	Flaugher	Emma Roslyn	d
Mar.	9	1953	21564	Flecken	Ferdinand	d
		1860	173	Fleeman	Wm.	d
		[1874-1875]	712	Flege	Henry	h
		1867	348	Flege	Henry	ins
		[1874-1875]	712	Flege	Mary A.	h
Apr.	1	1940	13946	Fleisner	Lillian	d
Oct.	10	1936	12724	Fleissner	Hugo H.	d
		[1908-1911]	4803	Fleming	Hannah A. I.	d
Apr.	4	1932	11267	Fleming	James D.	d
		1924	8607	Fleming	Thomas R.	d
Dec.	18	1928	10094	Fleming	William Y.	d
May	8	1917	6480	Fleming	Mattie Maud	d
Aug.	23	1953	21905	Flenniken	Major H.	d
		1912	5341	Flesher	Sophia	d
June	3	1925	8873	Fletcher	Albert W.	m
Apr.	8	1930	10551	Fletcher	Clara	d
Mar.	23	1946	17022	Fletcher	George Ellis	m
Mar.	12	1923	8519	Fletcher	James Albert	d
Sept.		1923	8445	Fletcher	John Thomas	d
May	23	1950	19721	Fletcher	Kenneth	d
Oct.	24	1939	13733	Fletcher	Marion A.	d

Month	Day	Year	File No.	Surname	Given Name	Type
Feb.	2	1925	8869	Fletcher	Mary Jane	inc
Apr.	20	1934	11878	Fletcher	Mary Jane	d
		[1908-1911]	4832	Fletcher	Otto	d
Jan.	15	1915	6158	Fletcher	Pauline M.	d
Feb.	20	1929	10499	Fletcher	Sarah Margaret, etc.	d
Feb.	2	1925	8870	Fletcher	William Henry	inc
Jan.	23	1934	12084	Fletcher	William Henry	inc
		[1912-1914]	5467	Fletcher	William R.	d
Dec.	25	1924	8813	Flewelling	W. M.	d
		[1903-1906]	3796	Flier	Tillie	m
May	8	1943	15370	Flinn	Matilda Ann, etc.	d
Jan.	1	1924	8820	Flintjer	Dorothy U.	m
Dec.	1	1924	8820	Flintjer	Emma R.	m
Dec.	1	1924	8820	Flintjer	John D.	m
		[1924-1927]	8803	Flintjer	John D.	d
Feb.	1	1924	8820	Flintjer	Ross H.	m
		1917	6487	Flocchini	Francesca	d
Aug.	26	1942	14995	Flock	William C.	d
Feb.	20	1918	6926	Flockhart	John	d
		[1856-1857]	43	Flogdell	David W.	d
Aug.	7	1957	24936	Flohr	Gertrude E., etc.	d
Apr.	19	1934	11896	Flohr	Marcus	d
		1875	745	Flood	Joseph C.	d
		[1899-1902]	3211	Florence	Jane B.	d
		1919	7231	Florence	L. J.	d
Dec.	31	1958	26051	Florence	Lucy Pells, etc.	d
Jan.	5	1946	16912	Florence	Viecea ? M.	d
May	15	1930	10627	Flosi	Helen (minor)	g
Aug.	15	1930	10627	Flosi	Leo (minor)	g
Feb.	30	1933	11808	Flosi	Silvio	d
Dec.	19	1956	24280	Flournoy	Ethel R.	d
Nov.	24	1958	26035	Floyd	Baird J.	d
July	6	1958	25603	Floyd	Mabel R.	d
		1922	8158	Floyd	Merle J.	m
Aug.	23	1929	10316	Floyd	Merle J.	m
		1922	8158	Floyd	Monroe H.	m
May	23	1929	10316	Floyd	Monroe H.	m
		1922	8157	Floyd	Pearl J.	d
		1922	8158	Floyd	Perle J.	m
Aug.	23	1929	10316	Floyd	Perle J.	m
Sept.	30	1940	14164	Fluegler	Esther L., etc.	d
Sept.	7	1948	18613	Fluke	Sarah Anne Elizabeth, etc.	d

Month	Day	Year	File No.	Surname	Given Name	Type
Oct.	2	1958	25970	Flynn	Anne	d
Jan.	3	1958	25250	Flynn	Arleigh John, etc.	inc
Sept.	20	1940	14154	Flynn	John J.	d
		1869	406	Flynn	Patrick	ins
July	11	1947	17887	Fobes	Charles F.	d
May	15	1948	18345	Focha	Anna M.	d
May	28	1956	23894	Focha	Frank, etc.	d
June	4	1948	18437	Focha	Joseph	d
		[1912-1914]	5437	Focha	Manuel Furtado	d
		1935	12422	Fochetti	Julius W.	d
Dec.	27	1929	10421	Fochetti	Juluis W.	d
Nov.	30	1952	21372	Fockers	Carl Theodore, etc.	d
June	6	1943	15414	Fogerty	Edward Lee, etc.	d
Aug.	16	1946	17349	Fognini	Louis	d
July	10	1946	17290	Fognini	Louis, etc.	inc
Sept.	10	1953	21934	Folden	Lewis Anthony, Jr.	m
Aug.	28	1955	23393	Foley	Barbara	m
Mar.	11	1957	24531	Foley	Bartholomew Emmett	m
Feb.	11	1957	24530	Foley	Joseph A.	d
May	17	1936	12587	Foley	Martin J.	m
Mar.	2	1953	21622	Foley	Mary	d
June	9	1953	21886	Foley	Tomas	d
Oct.		1919	7209	Foley	Victoria, etc.	g
Feb.	11	1957	24531	Foley	William Joseph	m
		[1891-1893]	2145	Folger	Hiram	d
June	4	1949	19053	Folger	Mary Green	d
May	3	1929	10301	Folk	Agnes	d
Mar.	8	1946	17057	Folkers	Bertha Cornelia	d
June	3	1948	18431	Folkers	Ella C.	d
Jan.	16	1933	11505	Fomasi	Pietro	d
Apr.	25	1949	18915	Foncrault	Louis J.	d
Oct.	28	1935	12390	Fonda	Walter Gibbs, etc.	d
Apr.	23	1954	22408	Fonseca	Manuel Joaquin Da, etc.	d
Feb.	27	1951	20183	Fontana	Joseph Dan, etc.	d
Feb.	25	1945	16376	Fontani	Luigi	d
		[1908-1911]	4597	Foote	George H.	m
		[1908-1911]	4597	Foote	Gilbert F.	m
June	26	1948	18415	Foppiano	August	inc
Feb.	4	1950	19439	Foppiano	August	d
July	5	1955	23356	Foppiano	G. B., etc.	d
Apr.	1	1935	12247	Foppiano	John B.	d
		[1924-1927]	8711	Foppiano	Louie, etc.	d

Month	Day	Year	File No.	Surname	Given Name	Type
July	17	1937	13000	Foppiano	Rose	d
Oct.	30	1957	25048	Forbes	Arleigh C.	d
Sept.	25	1952	21363	Forbes	Carol Ann	m
Aug.	17	1945	16650	Forbes	Gertrude	d
Dec.	25	1957	25103	Forbes	Henry	d
Sept.	14	1944	16214	Forcier	Richard A.	d
July	8	1957	24858	Ford	Cora T.	d
May	18	1952	21069	Ford	Donald	m
Sept.	23	1929	10388	Ford	Eugene	m
Apr.	9	1932	11224	Ford	G.	d
May	5	1950	19674	Ford	J. W.	d
Apr.	18	1952	21069	Ford	Kenneth Eugene	m
June	21	1948	18405	Ford	Linwood	d
		[1897-1899]	2855	Ford	Lydia E.	m
Apr.	27	1951	20236	Ford	Margaret E.	d
Nov.	17	1938	13410	Ford	Mary L., etc.	d
Nov.	23	1929	10388	Ford	Mattie Lee	m
Oct.	18	1956	24214	Ford	Ora L.	d
Apr.	18	1952	21069	Ford	Robert Nicholas	m
		[1919-1921]	7374	Ford	Robert W.	d
Apr.	18	1932	11198	Ford	Robert William	d
		[1888-1889]	1763	Fordyce	Grace	m
		[1888-1889]	1763	Fordyce	Mabel	m
Sept.	26	1957	24980	Foreman	Carl	d
		1923	8384	Foreman	Edward Lorin	d
Dec.	18	1955	23539	Foreman	Gypsy L.	d
Jan.	9	1956	23710	Foreman	James E., etc.	d
Aug.	25	1958	25807	Foreman	Lorin	d
Apr.	5	1948	18320	Foreman	Park	d
Apr.	16	1946	17145	Forenti	Ruben, etc.	d
June	4	1951	20425	Fores	Richard B.	m
June	21	1928	9947	Forester	James	d
Feb.	6	1932	11185	Foresti	August	d
Mar.	5	1948	18266	Foresti	E. M., etc.	d
Apr.		1917	6438	Foresti	Frank	d
May		1923	8331	Foresti	Giacominia	d
		[1903-1906]	3980	Foresti	Rafael	d
May	29	1914	5778	Forgett	Lillie Belle	d
Nov.	19	1946	17484	Form	Dora	d
Aug.	8	1940	14022	Forman	Dora	ins
Apr.	20	1939	13538	Forman	William	d
Aug.	12	1955	23364	Forme	Antonio, etc.	d

Month	Day	Year	File No.	Surname	Given Name	Type
		1883	1371	Formschlag	Peter	d
June	7	1944	15878	Formschlage	John, etc.	d
Oct.	12	1934	11972	Formschlog	August, etc.	d
Aug.	19	1957	24894	Fornelli	John	d
May	26	1946	17171	Forni	Dave	d
Nov.	8	1940	14234	Forni	Gigia, etc.	d
Feb.	2	1948	18199	Forni	Natale, etc.	d
Sept.	21	1926	9364	Forrest	Richard Augustin, etc.	d
		[1881-1882]	1143	Forster	Annie	d
Jan.	18	1953	22246	Forster	Fred R., etc.	d
		1907	4230	Forsyth	Caroline	d
Oct.	4	1927	9732	Forsyth	H. M., etc.	d
		1880	1058	Forsyth	Henry M.	m
July	21	1956	24067	Forsyth	Ida N.	d
Mar.	16	1916	6193	Forsyth	John H.	d
Apr.	30	1955	23144	Forsyth	Mary E., etc.	d
Mar.	8	1957	24579	Forsyth	Maude A.	d
June	14	1934	11951	Forsyth	Sarah I.	d
		1922	8188	Forsyth	Raymond	d
Apr.	25	1941	14451	Forsythe	Frederick Allen, etc.	d
Jan.	27	1944	16291	Forsythe	Henry M.	d
Nov.	3	1945	16783	Forsythe	Jess T., etc.	d
Aug.	10	1945	16639	Forsythe	Louise Dehay	d
Jan.	23	1948	18184	Forsythe	M. D.	d
Oct.	25	1939	13768	Forsythe	Nancy C.	d
June	28	1936	12625	Forsythe	William B.	d
		[1864-1865]	254	Forte	James	d
		[1891-1893]	2216	Fortier	Edward	m
		[1891-1893]	2177	Fortier	Marie	d
		1890	1954	Fortier	Peter	d
		[1891-1893]	2216	Fortier	Peter	m
		[1891-1893]	2216	Fortier	Willie	m
Jan.	29	1933	11803	Fortin	Candace A.	d
Jan.	10	1925	9138	Fortin	Timothy R.	ins
May	26	1947	17800	Fortunati	Antonio	d
Jan.	9	1958	26137	Fortunati	John	d
Jan.	12	1946	16932	Fortune	Christina Shand	d
Sept.	13	1952	21335	Fosberg	Edith	d
Sept.	22	1958	25869	Fosen	Harold Alfred, etc.	d
		[1880-1881]	1129	Foster	A. W.	d
Jan.	17	1933	11509	Foster	Adam Simpson	d
June	11	1938	13216	Foster	Anna	d

Month	Day	Year	File No.	Surname	Given Name	Type
Feb.		1916	6404	Foster	Arminda	d
Apr.	18	1952	21068	Foster	Bonnie	d
Nov.	20	1924	8687	Foster	David	d
Sept.	26	1950	19727	Foster	Fannie E., etc.	d
June	28	1951	20413	Foster	J. Walter, etc.	d
		[1912-1914]	5431	Foster	Jacob W.	d
Oct.	25	1947	18062	Foster	Jesse	d
Nov.	19	1951	20683	Foster	John W.	d
July	14	1945	16610	Foster	Leland J., etc.	d
Nov.	26	1954	22825	Foster	Louise Edith	d
Mar.	2	1954	22370	Foster	Manuel L.	d
Feb.	17	1928	10148	Foster	Mary E.	d
Feb.	14	1938	13480	Foster	Mary Emma, etc.	d
Apr.	28	1958	25428	Foster	Paul Leigh	m
Sept.	19	1957	24964	Foster	Paul Llewellyn, etc.	d
		[1919-1921]	7542	Foster	R. A.	d
Apr.	23	1948	18301	Foster	Robert W.	d
Apr.	29	1935	12171	Foster	Stephen D.	d
Apr.	9	1940	13955	Foster	William Anderson Scott, e	d
Sept.	4	1951	20580	Foucrault	E. C.	d
July	5	1949	19057	Fournier	Adrienne	d
Sept.		1917	6538	Foushey	Diantha, etc.	d
Oct.	20	1951	20619	Foutch	Thomas G.	d
Dec.	9	1935	12485	Fouts	Alberta I.	d
		[1912-1914]	5434	Fouts	Clara A.	d
		1907	4216	Fouts	Edward	d
Aug.	19	1957	24895	Fouts	Robert J., etc.	d
July	7	1955	23358	Fowler	Cornelia C.	d
		1874	675	Fowler	Edgar J.	m
Apr.	26	1945	16493	Fowler	Ethel A., etc.	d
June	4	1937	12851	Fowler	Ethel E.	d
		[1888-1889]	1740	Fowler	Henry R.	d
		1958	26149	Fowler	Ida M.	inc
		[1908-1911]	4729	Fowler	John H.	d
Sept.	4	1945	16706	Fowler	Joshua G.	d
July	5	1957	24857	Fowler	Laurie Elizabeth	m
Mar.	28	1937	12870	Fowler	Leonard Edgar	m
Sept.	18	1933	11691	Fowler	Mary J., etc.	d
		1874	686	Fowler	Phoebe	d
		[1856-1857]	42	Fowler	Richard	d
		1881	1175	Fowler	Robert F.	inc
		1868	375	Fowler	S. L.	d

Month	Day	Year	File No.	Surname	Given Name	Type
Dec.	24	1925	8986	Fowler	Sarah A.	d
		[1903-1906]	3732	Fowler	Stephen Cornell	d
		1874	675	Fowler	William W.	m
		[1903-1906]	3950	Fownes	William H.	d
Aug.	2	1956	24084	Fox	Agnes	d
		1890	1965	Fox	Charles	d
Mar.	2	1955	23095	Fox	David Edward	m
Jan.	12	1930	10812	Fox	Dona F.	d
		[1908-1911]	4440	Fox	Elizabeth	m
Dec.	12	1916	6275	Fox	Henry	d
Dec.	26	1948	18753	Fox	John W., etc.	d
		[1903-1906]	3913	Fox	Lola Jessie	d
		[1897-1899]	2940	Fox	Otto	d
Dec.	4	1935	12424	Fox	Theodore W.	d
Feb.	7	1952	20834	Foy	Arthur	d
Feb.	25	1958	25417	Foye	Frederick M.	inc
Aug.	13	1944	16079	Fracchia	Chester, etc.	d
Jan.	22	1946	16953	Fracchia	Giovanna	d
Sept.	6	1940	14183	Fradenburg	James B.	d
Sept.	18	1952	21354	Frahm	John H.	d
		[1903-1906]	3857	Frain	Maria	ins
Sept.		1923	8423	Frain	Marie	d
May	17	1927	9503	Fraine	Fanuin	inc
Aug.	11	1938	13401	Frame	Lavancia A.	d
Dec.	10	1952	21441	Frame	Mary E.	d
		[1908-1911]	4449	Frampton	Charles Ephraim	d
June	28	1956	24018	Frampton	Ruby C.	d
Feb.	1	1957	24508	Frampton	Ruby C.	d
Sept.	11	1941	14602	Francard	Camille Nicholas	d
Feb.	24	1933	11518	Francard	Genevieve	d
May	27	1947	17715	Francard	Leon	d
Mar.		1923	8488	Francard	Louis	d
		1893	2290	France	Frank D.	m
		1893	2290	France	Mabel A.	m
		1893	2290	France	Waldo E.	m
Feb.	23	1925	8864	Franceschi	Alfonso/Alphonso	d
May	18	1929	10248	Franceschi	Bernardo	d
Oct.	4	1954	22783	Franceschi	Clorinda	d
Mar.	17	1936	12554	Franceschi	Raffaela	d
Nov.	6	1942	15137	Franceschini	Mathilda	d
		[1919-1921]	7583	Franceschini	Michael, etc.	d
Oct.	26	1942	15063	Francesconi	Armida	d

Month	Day	Year	File No.	Surname	Given Name	Type
Aug.	26	1942	15062	Francesconi	Raffaello, etc.	d
Jan.	1	1950	20081	Franchetti	James P.	d
Mar.	19	1949	18907	Franchetti	James P., etc.	d
Dec.	4	1953	22213	Franchetti	James Peter	m
Dec.	4	1953	22213	Franchetti	Laura Lynn	m
Mar.	14	1955	23116	Franchetti	Louis J., etc.	d
Feb.	11	1957	24529	Franchetti	Mary, etc.	d
Nov.	19	1951	20680	Franchetti	Myrle J.	d
May	21	1932	11282	Franchini	Bemaneno, etc.	d
July	17	1935	12306	Francis	Charlotte W.	inc
Mar.	10	1943	15272	Francis	James J.	d
Feb.	20	1936	12527	Francis	Charlotte W.	d
Oct.	7	1948	18614	Francisco	Beverly Ann	d
Apr.	18	1936	12555	Francisco	Irvin`	d
		1891	2107	Francisco	Manuel	d
Sept.	18	1957	25028	Franco	Arnold	m
July	28	1932	11288	Franco	Camillo	d
Sept.	19	1953	22015	Franco	Mary, etc.	d
Apr.	4	1917	6458	Frank	Arthur James	m
Apr.	4	1917	6458	Frank	Eugene Wellington	m
Jan.	23	1952	21529	Frank	Florence, etc.	d
Nov.	2	1944	16153	Frank	George	d
		1917	6458	Frank	Lillian	m
Mar.	2	1945	16450	Frank	Louis Burdett	d
Oct.	8	1955	23483	Frank	Margaret	d
Apr.	11	1955	23167	Frank	Martin	d
Oct.		1922	8149	Frank	Raymond	m
May	4	1917	6458	Frank	Thomas	m
Apr.	4	1917	6458	Frank	Wilbur Ervin	m
May	3	1950	19670	Frank	Elsa Tavares, etc.	d
Apr.	4	1917	6458	Frank	William Ellis	m
Jan.	16	1954	22918	Frankel	Daniel	d
Mar.	12	1958	25456	Frankel	Gusta	inc
Sept.	8	1958	25908	Frankhauser	Christian	d
		1864	248	Frankish	Robert	d
Aug.	9	1940	14138	Franklin	D. B., etc.	d
		[1903-1906]	3691	Franklin	Jesse W.	d
Mar.	8	1957	24576	Franklin	Sophia T.	d
July	18	1948	18464	Franquelin	Mayme J.	d
Apr.	21	1941	14486	Fransioli	Diomiro, etc.	d
		[1919-1921]	7232	Fransoli	Florido	d
		[1891-1893]	2152	Franz	Frederick W.	d

Month	Day	Year	File No.	Surname	Given Name	Type
		1907	4320	Franzinelli	Antonio	d
Sept.	26	1948	18531	Frappier	Hannah	d
Oct.	11	1934	11995	Fraser	Colin Monroe	inc
Mar.	23	1946	17496	Fraser	Donald A.	d
Mar.	24	1943	15329	Fraser	John	d
Sept.	27	1958	25886	Fraser	John E.	d
Feb.	5	1949	18904	Frasier	Frank Byron, etc.	d
		[1919-1921]	7328	Frasier	V. L., etc.	d
		1922	8099	Fraters	Mary Gloria	d
Apr.	7	1958	25523	Frates	Albert A.	d
May	22	1917	6493	Frates	Anthony	m
May	28	1917	6494	Frates	Anthony	m
		1915	5955	Frates	Ellen	d
		[1903-1906]	3936	Frates	Frank M.	d
May	22	1917	6493	Frates	Henry	m
May	28	1917	6494	Frates	Henry	m
July	19	1935	12275	Frates	John	d
		1922	7987	Frates	Joseph Fagas, etc.	d
May	22	1917	6493	Frates	Maurice	m
May	28	1917	6494	Frates	Maurice	m
May	19	1949	19024	Frates	William A.	d
June	2	1946	17183	Frati	Alesandro Luigi, etc.	d
Jan.	24	1935	12499	Frati	Andy ?	m
Sept.	15	1952	21248	Frati	Fred	d
May	17	1951	20343	Frati	Joseph, etc.	d
Oct.	25	1944	16096	Frati	Mary, etc.	d
Feb.	24	1935	12499	Frati	Myrtis	m
Dec.	4	1953	22050	Frati	Salvatore	d
Apr.	22	1953	21797	Frati	William S.	d
June	22	1953	21854	Frati	William S.	d
Mar.	11	1940	13890	Fratini	Casimira	d
Feb.	1	1946	16985	Fratis	Joseph, etc.	d
Apr.	29	1937	12950	Fratis	Michael	d
Nov.	12	1940	14270	Fratis	William A.	inc
Mar.	19	1954	22296	Fraumeni	Onofris	d
Aug.	28	1938	13366	Frazee	Charles Carl	m
Aug.	28	1938	13366	Frazee	Donald Eugene	m
		[1919-1921]	7538	Frazee	Isabella I.	d
July	7	1943	15465	Frazee	Linnie Katherine	d
July	26	1940	14012	Frazer	Edwin Charles, etc.	d
Oct.	28	1942	15069	Frazer	Henry De Wit, etc.	d
May	16	1940	13999	Frazer	Louise C., etc.	d

Month	Day	Year	File No.	Surname	Given Name	Type
		[1893-1894]	2344	Frazie	Charles D.	d
		1873	601	Frazier	Addie E.	m
		[1897-1899]	2882	Frazier	James	d
		[1872-1873]	590	Frazier	Julia A.	d
		[1912-1914]	5686	Frazier	Samuel A.	d
		1873	601	Frazier	Wm. J.	m
May	17	1943	15432	Frazier	Silas H.	d
Oct.	15	1928	9998	Frechetti	Lottie	d
		1896	2635	Frederichs	Gerhard	d
Feb.	1	1955	23016	Frederick	Adolph N., etc.	d
July	30	1955	23350	Frederick	Florence M.	d
Mar.	7	1950	19503	Frederick	Frances E.	d
Jan.	10	1949	18820	Frederick	Frank J., etc.	d
		1955	23016	Fredericks	Adolph N., etc.	d
		1916	6276	Fredericks	Francisca, etc.	d
		[1924-1927]	8812	Fredericks	J. C., etc.	d
Nov.	19	1940	14282	Fredericks	Maurice H., etc.	d
Feb.	11	1919	6992	Fredericks	Theodora G.	d
Nov.	20	1952	21410	Fredericks	William Richard, etc.	d
Mar.		1919	7003	Frederickson	F. O.	ins
		[1912-1914]	5697	Frederickson	F. O.	ins
Oct.	24	1947	18061	Frediani	Annunciata	d
Dec.	10	1952	21442	Frediani	Narsico	d
Mar.	29	1940	14292	Frediani	Peter	d
Oct.	19	1951	20684	Frediani	Umberto	d
Jan.	2	1948	18763	Fredrichsen	John, etc.	d
Mar.	18	1944	15846	Fredrick	Andine Theodore, etc.	d
June	6	1952	21167	Fredricks	Georgia C.	d
Sept.	27	1952	21223	Fredricks	Georgia C.	d
Oct.	12	1949	19168	Fredricks	Isabella, etc.	d
Mar.	31	1928	10157	Fredson	Oscar A.	d
Nov.	1	1940	14196	Free	Joseph Allen, etc.	d
		[1895-1896]	2536	Freeborn	Eleanor	d
		1923	8315	Freehill	Thomas	d
		1857	44	Freeland	A. C.	d
		1858	117	Freeland	Albert C.	m
Apr.	11	1952	21050	Freeland	Ethel H.	d
		1858	114	Freeland	Wm.	d
May	2	1949	19048	Freeman	Artie V.	inc
May	24	1953	21804	Freeman	Artie V.	d
Aug.	8	1957	24939	Freeman	Artie V., etc.	d
June	26	1936	12644	Freeman	Belle	d

Month	Day	Year	File No.	Surname	Given Name	Type
Oct.	11	1945	16755	Freeman	Charles J., etc.	d
Oct.	20	1939	13816	Freeman	Daniel W., etc.	d
Nov.	5	1948	18719	Freeman	Edward	d
June	10	1955	23310	Freeman	Estella E.	d
		1890	1997	Freeman	John M.	d
Oct.	20	1945	16726	Freeman	Marie O., etc.	d
Dec.	23	1950	20003	Freeman	Max L., etc.	d
Jan.	30	1927	9794	Freeman	Warren I.	d
May	16	1931	10840	Freeman	Warren W., etc.	d
Jan.	9	1926	9163	Freese	Ahlrich Heinrich	d
June	11	1951	20431	Freese	Walter H.	d
Dec.	10	1930	10769	Fregulia	Giovanni, etc.	d
		[1924-1927]	9335	Frehe	Minnie	d
Mar.		1921	7825	Frei	John	d
Sept.	20	1945	16696	Frei	Louise	d
July	9	1944	16029	Frei	Walter C.	d
June	14	1931	10874	Freitas	Frank A., etc.	d
Dec.	3	1954	22901	Freitas	Joe	d
Aug.	6	1939	13692	Freitas	T. A.	d
Apr.	19	1946	17155	Frellson	Anna P.	d
		[1899-1902]	3191	Frellson	Broder	d
Mar.	20	1929	10216	Frellson	Walter B.	d
Aug.		1954	22635	French	Donelle Shelley	m
June	18	1957	22635	French	Donnelle Shelley, etc.	m
		1874	670	French	Ellen	d
Aug.	5	1940	14094	French	Emily	d
Sept.	20	1948	18586	French	George Washington, etc.	d
Mar.	10	1941	14429	Frengal	Fred	d
Feb.	4	1957	24509	Frengle	George A., etc.	d
Nov.	21	1957	25097	Frengle	Kathryn W.	d
Dec.	16	1931	11107	Frengle	Mary	d
Oct.	16	1947	17998	Frescia	Robert G., etc.	d
Aug.		1914	5837	Frese	Henry	d
Oct.	5	1951	20653	Frese	Pearl M.	d
Nov.	26	1940	14290	Freshette	Omar C.	d
		1911	5273	Freshour	Irene	m
		1911	5273	Freshour	Marie	m
Dec.	15	1949	19369	Frevold	Ben, etc.	d
Jan.	27	1949	19424	Frevold	Thorvald, etc.	d
Feb.	21	1958	25403	Frey	Anthony S.	d
Aug.	5	1955	23413	Frey	Claude C.	d
		1922	8120	Frey	Elizabeth	inc

Month	Day	Year	File No.	Surname	Given Name	Type
		1923	8287	Frey	Elizabeth	d
May	22	1955	23194	Frey	Elsie A.	d
Apr.	16	1928	9937	Frey	Frederick Charles, etc.	d
Sept.	23	1954	22657	Frey	Gurine, etc.	d
Oct.	2	1949	19113	Frey	Henrietta C.	d
June		1921	7742	Frey	Lawrence	d
May	30	1933	11524	Frey	Petrea	d
Nov.	30	1939	13828	Frick	Mary	d
May	12	1953	21832	Frick	Vinsinz	d
Aug.	12	1940	14143	Frideger	Daniel S.	d
		1907	4243	Frideger	Mary	inc
Jan.	18	1946	16940	Fridolino	De Martini, etc.	d
		[1908-1911]	4954	Fried	Friedaricka	d
Nov.	19	1950	19931	Friedlund	August	d
July	14	1947	17850	Friedman	Joseph	d
June	26	1931	10976	Friedman	William, etc.	d
Jan.	7	1951	20789	Friedrichsen	Peter	d
July	12	1932	11293	Friedricks	Wilhelmini	d
		1890	2030	Frietas de	John M./John Marshall	d
Apr.	27	1945	16494	Frieze	Ella V.	d
Nov.		1922	8173	Friis	Hans, etc.	d
Apr.	6	1917	6559	Frisk	Carl Edward	d
Oct.	19	1939	13812	Fritsch	Anna M.	d
		1902	3475	Fritsch	John	d
Apr.	16	1917	6580	Fritsch	John Raymond	d
		[1903-1906]	3984	Fritsch	Mabel Isabel	m
		[1903-1906]	3984	Fritsch	Walter Mecham	m
		[1908-1911]	4352	Fritsch	Walter Mecham	m
Dec.	23	1945	16830	Fritsch	Walter Mecham, etc.	d
Nov.	11	1946	17436	Fritsch	Walter Micham, Jr.	m
		1906	4097	Fritsch	Walter S.	d
Mar.	24	1943	15332	Fritte	Albertina	d
Nov.	26	1942	15117	Fritter	Albertina	d
Dec.	14	1949	19316	Fritz	Frances E., etc.	d
		[1899-1902]	3183	Fritz	Herman	d
Mar.	10	1955	23109	Frizelle	Jennie F.	inc
Apr.	28	1955	23140	Frizelle	Jennie F.	inc
Aug.	9	1955	23420	Frizelle	Jennie, etc.	d
Mar.	11	1955	23110	Frizelle	Seymour R., etc.	d
Nov.	4	1954	22845	Froehlich	A. J., etc.	d
Aug.	22	1941	14582	Frohlking	Wilhelmina H.	d
Feb.	19	1916	6177	Frohlking	William	d

Month	Day	Year	File No.	Surname	Given Name	Type
Jan.	11	1956	24384	Frolich	Frank	d
Jan.	21	1927	9752	Froment	Eugenie C., etc.	d
Nov.	5	1924	8798	Froment	J. A. M.,/James/Antoine, e	d
Apr.	22	1921	7653	Fromenti	Marguerite	m
Aug.	12	1929	10377	Frost	Annie	d
Dec.	3	1958	26052	Frost	Chester C.	d
Nov.	18	1948	18679	Frost	Edward N., etc.	d
		[1868-1869]	381	Frost	Thomas	d
		[1924-1927]	8783	Froth	John T.	d
		[1908-1911]	4487	Frugoli	Ernesto	d
May	20	1951	20351	Frugoli	Ida M., etc.	d
Mar.	12	1929	10236	Frugoli	Joseph B., etc.	d
July	10	1936	12675	Frugoli	Margaret Ann Fox	m
		[1908-1911]	4488	Frugoli	Marianna	d
Mar.	9	1954	22385	Frugoli	Millicent	d
Aug.	10	1936	12675	Frugoli	Robert Edward	m
Feb.	13	1934	11863	Frugoli	Vigilio	d
Apr.	1	1957	24628	Fruiht	Bryce Eupen	m
Apr.	1	1957	24628	Fruiht	Justina	m
Apr.	1	1957	24628	Fruiht	Thomas Bradford	m
		1877	817	Fruits	Jacob	d
July	21	1958	25796	Fruits	John S.	d
		[1868-1869]	376	Fruits	John S.	m
		[1896-1897]	2663	Fruits	Martha A.	d
		[1868-1869]	376	Fruits	Robert F.	m
Feb.	29	1939	13854	Fry	Charles W., deceased	jt
May	29	1950	19595	Fry	Lucy G., etc.	d
Jan.	29	1939	13854	Fry	Lucy G., petitioner	jt
Oct.	3	1955	23512	Frye	Charles	d
		[1924-1927]	9034	Frye	Louis , Jr.	inc
May	18	1926	9170	Fuchs	Charles	d
Sept.	24	1923	8469	Fujita	Eigi	m
Sept.	24	1923	8469	Fujita	Katsumi	m
		1923	8469	Fujita	Michi	m
July	13	1933	11638	Fujita	Michiko, etc.	m
Dec.	24	1923	8469	Fujita	Tomeo	m
Aug.	13	1933	11638	Fujita	Tomoe	m
Dec.	14	1918	6856	Fulkerson	Amanda	inc
Sept.		1922	8100	Fulkerson	Amanda Ellen	d
		[1903-1906]	3720	Fulkerson	Fannie M.	d
		[1887-1888]	1695	Fulkerson	Richard	d
		[1889-1890]	1828	Fulkerson	Richard	m

Month	Day	Year	File No.	Surname	Given Name	Type
		1911	5234	Fulkerson	S. T.	d
June	23	1955	23264	Fulkerson	Theodorus, etc.	d
		[1888-1889]	1784	Fullagar	Alfred	d
		1885	1513	Fullager	William	d
		1907	4244	Fullen	James	d
Nov.	27	1939	13823	Fuller	Alfred Gibbs, etc.	d
Mar.	5	1943	15301	Fuller	Arthur	m
Jan.	2	1941	14732	Fuller	Charles Edward, etc.	d
Apr.	18	1928	9941	Fuller	George B. Jr.	m
Aug.	23	1943	15523	Fuller	Harry B., Jr.	d
Oct.	5	1942	15099	Fuller	Harry Boyd, Jr.	m
Dec.	4	1942	15209	Fuller	Harry K.	d
June	6	1939	13636	Fuller	Jacob Louis, etc.	d
Sept.	26	1928	9955	Fuller	Jennie D.	d
Mar.	25	1937	13106	Fuller	Jesse P.	d
Sept.	30	1941	14624	Fuller	Laura	d
Aug.	4	1942	15032	Fuller	Sarah M.	d
		[1875-1876]	775	Fuller	Thomas	d
Oct.	5	1942	15099	Fuller	William Allen	m
		[1872-1873]	576	Fulligar	Elizabeth	m
		1884	1391	Fulton	David	d
		[1868-1869]	390	Fulton	Richard	d
		[1902-1903]	3534	Fulton	Somers	d
Feb.	27	1948	18187	Funasoli	Rachel	d
Dec.	2	1953	22209	Fundan	Thomas	d
Dec.	1	1942	15171	Fuqua	Minne Jenne	d
Oct.	21	1945	16730	Furbei	George C., etc.	d
July	13	1916	6213	Furber	E. G.	d
Aug.	27	1926	9292	Furber	Elizabeth	ins
		1874	701	Furber	Geoge C.	d
		[1899-1902]	3243	Furber	Mary J.	d
Feb.	14	1950	19516	Furber	Rosa Butler	d
Mar.	30	1956	23760	Furber	William Wallace, etc.	d
Nov.	4	1940	14258	Furgerson	Joseph K.	d
Mar.	18	1955	23067	Furgerson	Nellie S.	d
Sept.	12	1952	21333	Furia	Alfonso	d
Sept.	16	1931	11004	Furia	Elisio, etc.	d
Sept.	12	1952	21334	Furia	Elvira L.	d
Oct.	25	1951	20635	Furletti	Casimiro, etc.	d
May	14	1956	23987	Furlong	Andrew James, etc.	d
Apr.	18	1952	20994	Furlong	Charles A.	d
Oct.	19	1933	11745	Furlong	Edna Marie	m

Month	Day	Year	File No.	Surname	Given Name	Type
Oct.	19	1933	11745	Furlong	Edward James	m
Nov.	19	1933	11745	Furlong	Howard John	m
Oct.	5	1927	9666	Furlong	James	d
Dec.	20	1928	10119	Furlong	Joanna	d
		[1919-1921]	7395	Furlong	John	d
Oct.	19	1933	11745	Furlong	Patricia A.	m
July		1916	6216	Furlong	Patrick	d
July	12	1947	17847	Furlong	Patrick Arden	d
Nov.	19	1933	11745	Furlong	Raymond Henry	m
Oct.	11	1933	11709	Furlong	Sarah	d
		[1912-1914]	5420	Furlong	Thomas	d
Oct.	19	1933	11745	Furlong	Thomas F., Jr.	m
Oct.	19	1933	11745	Furlong	William P.	m
Dec.	9	1933	11757	Furrer	Joseph, etc.	d
Oct.	13	1950	19925	Furrer	Mary	d
Dec.	20	1947	18070	Furster	Joseph	d
Mar.	3	1954	22372	Fuschia	Agnes J.	inc
Nov.	19	1946	17485	Fuson	Charlotte	m
July		1919	7101	Futterer	Louisa	d

Month	Day	Year	File No.	Surname	Given Name	Type
July	9	1942	14974	Gable	Clara, etc.	d
Jan.	14	1927	9776	Gabrielli	Felix	d
Aug.	25	1927	9711	Gabrielli	Marguerite	d
July	17	1940	14112	Gabrielli	Marguerite Giovannoni	d
		1928	9924	Gadaway	Marie Enfield	inc
Sept.	25	1952	21268	Gaddini	Jennie	d
		[1906-1907]	4055	Gaddis	Amanda A.	d
		[1906-1907]	4054	Gaddis	Joseph H., Jr.	d
Sept.	11	1947	17982	Gadie	Jacob J., etc.	d
Dec.	1	1917	6591	Gaffney	Andrew	d
		[1910-1911]	5024	Gaffney	Catherine	d
		1918	6862	Gaffney	Catherine, etc.	d
		[1900-1902]	3234	Gaffney	Francis (aka Frank Duval)	d
Nov.	29	1930	10750	Gaffney	John	d
Oct.		1918	6863	Gaffney	Joseph, etc.	d
Jan.		1921	7884	Gaffney	Marly T.	inc
June	4	1923	8380	Gaffney	Martin Thomas	d
		[1902-1903]	3523	Gaffney	Miles M.	d
Jan.	30	1916	6299	Gaffney	Miles M., etc.	d
May	14	1941	14480	Gafner	Gottlieb, etc.	d
June	20	1927	9632	Gaggia	Berth	d
Apr.	13	1912	5286	Gagliardo	Benedetto et al	m
Mar.	13	1912	5286	Gagliardo	Ella	m
May	13	1912	5286	Gagliardo	George	m
		[1907-1908]	4463	Gagliardo	iroloma	d
Jan.	17	1930	10528	Gahn	John J.	inc
Mar.	20	1931	10885	Gahn	John J.	d
		[1917-1918]	6691	Gaige	Albert E.	d
Feb.	29	1952	20958	Gainer	Elizabeth Ann	m
		[1919-1920]	7528	Gaines	W. C.	d
Nov.	25	1946	17451	Gaines	Walter N.	d
Nov.	19	1954	22873	Gaither	Carol Jane	m
Nov.	19	1954	22873	Gaither	Donald Charles	m
Nov.	19	1954	22873	Gaither	Gerry Sue	m
Nov.	19	1954	22873	Gaither	Nancy Lee	m
Nov.	19	1954	22873	Gaither	Peggy Lorraine	m
Nov.	14	1952	21401	Gaither	William	d
Oct.	16	1934	12000	Galanti	Paris Aristide	d
Jan.	16	1929	10406	Galbraith	Harvey D., etc.	d
Mar.	21	1931	10895	Galbraith	Stella	d
July	19	1957	24890	Galbraith	Walter V.	d
June	5	1930	10616	Gale	Cordelia	d

Month	Day	Year	File No.	Surname	Given Name	Type
Nov.	15	1932	11442	Gale	D. R.	d
		[1899-1900]	2968	Gale	Demus	d
June	15	1916	6233	Gale	Eliza Ann	d
		[1919-1920]	7434	Gale	George L.	d
		[1907-1908]	4319	Gale	L. D.	d
		1924	8792	Gale	Marie Isabelle	m
May	23	1956	23946	Gale	Minnie L.	ins
July	11	1956	23984	Gale	Minnie L.	d
Mar.	10	1953	21686	Gale	Wallace S., etc.	d
Jan.	10	1958	25277	Galeazzi	Mussimo Costante, etc.	d
Dec.	19	1936	12811	Galgani	Catherine	d
Sept.	23	1949	19228	Galgani	Guiseppe	d
Jan.	19	1936	12812	Galgani	Joseph	d
Apr.	12	1956	23922	Galimba	Maximov	m
		1921	7880	Gallagher	Charles H.	d
		[1919-1920]	7283	Gallagher	Conchita Molaben	m
Jan.	29	1937	13198	Gallagher	Elizabeth Norton	d
		[1919-1920]	7283	Gallagher	Eufrancio Molaben	m
Apr.	15	1921	7743	Gallagher	Hugh James	d
		1954	22920	Gallagher	James, etc.	d
		[1900-1902]	3339	Gallagher	John	inc
		[1908-1909]	4552	Gallagher	John	d
Feb.	14	1946	16934	Gallagher	Joseph R., etc.	d
		[1910-1911]	5119	Gallagher	Josephine H.	d
		[1919-1920]	7283	Gallagher	Leonia Molaben	m
		[1897-1898]	2744	Gallagher	Margaret	d
Mar.	2	1945	16449	Gallagher	Margaret	inc
Jan.	2	1949	19398	Gallagher	Margaret	d
Dec.	13	1911	5222	Gallagher	William John	d
Dec.	2	1938	13476	Gallaher	Alexander J.	d
July	2	1954	22559	Gallantinko	Manuel Enos, etc.	d
		1919	7110	Gallard	Nicholas	d
		[1917-1918]	6672	Gallaway	A. J.	d
Sept.	28	1942	15023	Gallaway	Amanda, etc.	d
		[1919-1920]	7381	Gallaway	Laura A.	d
Oct.	27	1942	15120	Gallaway	Nanie E.	d
Nov.	23	1956	24290	Galley	Sadie- Marie Stauffer, etc.	d
Sept.	26	1947	17974	Galli	Giuseppe	d
Oct.	12	1958	25915	Gallman	Jerome W.	d
Aug.	14	1953	22006	Gallo	Bartolomeo, etc.	d
		[1875-1876]	746	Galloway	Allen R.	m
		[1875-1876]	746	Galloway	Amanda A.	m

Month	Day	Year	File No.	Surname	Given Name	Type
		[1875-1876]	746	Galloway	Andrew J.	m
		[1875-1876]	746	Galloway	Elizabeth	m
May	20	1931	10948	Galloway	W.	d
Feb.	11	1937	12868	Galpin	Arthur	d
Dec.	24	1954	22888	Galupe	Celesta I. F., etc.	d
Oct.	29	1957	24990	Galvan	Tony, etc.	d
July	8	1958	25761	Galvanis	Margaritis	d
July	10	1958	25772	Galway	Catherine	inc
		[1894-1895]	2405	Galway	Isabella	d
Dec.	8	1924	8800	Gambetta	G.	d
Feb.	13	1958	25380	Gambetta	Joseph John	d
Feb.	5	1953	21554	Gambetta	Peter	d
Aug.	27	1950	19839	Gambetti	Peter, etc.	ins
Mar.	26	1944	15854	Gambettsa	Peter	d
Dec.	15	1932	11443	Gambini	Alta Cole	d
May	19	1930	10578	Gambini	Celeste	d
Jan.	24	1947	18099	Gambini	Ella C.	d
Aug.	27	1948	18543	Gambini	Larrie, etc.	d
Apr.	23	1957	24686	Gambini	W. Robert	d
June	5	1933	11631	Gamble	Charles E., etc.	d
May	12	1952	21118	Gamble	Fannie L.	d
		1909	4643	Gamble	George A.	ins
May		1918	6747	Gamble	George A.	inc
Dec.	24	1920	7590	Gamble	George A.	d
July	15	1930	10629	Gamble	George A., etc.	d
Mar.	14	1958	25466	Gamble	Grady	d
		[1865-1869]	281	Gamble	Hugh (aka Harry Campbell)	ins
Dec.	24	1958	26101	Gamble	Irene	d
May	15	1942	14950	Gamble	Martha Louise, etc.	d
Apr.	24	1950	19531	Gamboni	Luigi,etc.	d
Aug.	11	1949	19163	Gamboni	Assunta M.	d
		1918	6842	Gambonini	Battista	d
Mar.	8	1945	16460	Gambonini	Janet	m
June	7	1957	24719	Gambonini	Janet, etc.	d
Apr.	2	1955	23092	Gambonini	Maria	d
Nov.	20	1958	26018	Gambonini	Sylvia J.	d
Dec.	3	1913	5652	Gambonini	Valente A.	d
Sept.		1921	7793	Gambonini	Giaconeo	d
Dec.		1915	6136	Gamma	Joseph	d
		1909	4695	Gamsjager	Joseph	inc
		[1910-1911]	5030	Gamsjoger	Joseph	d
		1925	8886	Gandola	Julia	d

Month	Day	Year	File No.	Surname	Given Name	Type
Aug.	1	1950	19846	Gann	Harriet E.	d
Mar.	2	1943	15207	Gannon	Dora Cleveland, etc.	d
		1849	3	Gant	John	d
Oct.	10	1948	18623	Garanatt	Dorothy V.	d
July	12	1940	14102	Garavent	Gertrude, etc.	d
Apr.	17	1916	6196	Garaventa	Giromolo	d
Nov.	8	1956	24319	Garayalde	Ignacio	d
Sept.	24	1956	24226	Garayalde	Marcel M.	d
		1924	8808	Garayalde	Peter	d
		1928	9933	Garbarini	Theresa, etc.	d
Oct.	17	1946	17405	Garber	Constance	d
		1905	3963	Garber	Sophie	d
Aug.	22	1927	9657	Garboluio	Philip	d
		1928	9932	Garborino	Teresa	d
		[1906-1907]	4127	Garborino	Tomaso	d
Feb.	14	1927	9498	Garcar	Joe aka Joe Mayer	d
July	12	1950	19753	Garcia	A. M., etc.	d
July	10	1955	23309	Garcia	Carmen	d
Mar.	12	1958	25457	Garcia	Cerefino Martinez, etc.	d
Dec.	25	1949	19386	Garcia	Jeans	d
May	25	1949	19034	Garcia	Mabel M.	d
		1850	9	Garcian	Frederick	d
June	24	1951	20408	Garcin	John J., etc.	d
July	9	1957	24860	Gard	Albert Buford, etc.	d
Feb.	18	1956	23735	Gard	Arthur L., etc.	d
Mar.	17	1922	8194	Gard	Levi, etc.	d
Mar.	20	1956	23801	Gard	Martha B.	d
Apr.	13	1956	23927	Gard	Mary Elizabeth	m
Apr.	13	1956	23927	Gard	Meull Frederick	m
		1909	4715	Gardella	C. S.	d
		[1910-1911]	5055	Gardella	Catherine	d
Apr.	26	1953	21724	Gardenhire	Walter Edward	d
Mar.	24	1933	11519	Gardiner	Elizabeth Mae, etc.	d
Apr.	18	1935	12165	Gardiner	John A., etc.	inc
	26	1912	5384	Gardiner	Philip W.	d
Sept.	4	1941	14592	Gardner	Archibald Ogilvie, etc.	d
Feb.	18	1934	12131	Gardner	Arthur C., etc.	d
	25	1926	9175	Gardner	David	d
Jan.	18	1938	13222	Gardner	Elizabeth	d
Oct.	9	1957	25074	Gardner	Elizabeth Devine, etc.	inc
Feb.	8	1950	19506	Gardner	Ellen McDonald, etc.	d
Aug.	1	1949	19201	Gardner	Hana, etc.	d

Month	Day	Year	File No.	Surname	Given Name	Type
		[1919-1920]	7295	Gardner	James	d
		[1903-1905]	3563	Gardner	Joel	d
		[1894-1895]	2455	Gardner	John William	d
		1918	6877	Gardner	L. B.	d
Dec.	29	1957	25179	Gardner	Lillian Inez, etc.	d
Aug.	22	1935	12364	Gardner	Mendel	d
		1922	8018	Gardner	Nancy T., etc.	d
		1926	9224	Gardner	Nelson	d
Dec.	17	1943	15683	Gardner	Vannesa	d
Mar.	3	1945	16451	Gardner	Wallia	d
Sept.	14	1956	24160	Gardner	William H.	d
Dec.	20	1943	15697	Gardo	James Ross, etc.	d
Dec.	19	1949	19378	Gareffa	Ethel A.	d
Sept.	20	1931	11034	Gargini	Felice	d
Dec.	2	1955	23620	Gargini	Giuseppe, etc.	d
Aug.	17	1951	20489	Garich	Leo Frank, etc.	d
Mar.	8	1950	19508	Garihan	Bertean William	m
Dec.	13	1955	23653	Garihan	Ellis Herbert	d
Mar.	14	1949	18899	Garitti	Ferino, etc.	d
June	5	1913	5554	Garl	Abraham	d
		[1910-1911]	4837	Garland	Harry	m
Oct.	24	1954	22775	Garland	John	d
		[1910-1911]	4837	Garland	Wm. E.	m
Oct.	19	1952	21351	Garloff	Annita G,	d
May	3	1937	12982	Garloff	Carl H.	d
May	3	1939	13594	Garloff	Jessie, etc.	d
Feb.	4	1940	14228	Garloff	John A., etc.	d
Oct.	7	1957	25065	Garloff	Mamie E.	d
Aug.	20	1928	10024	Garloff	William F.	d
Aug.	7	1925	8899	Garmo	Herman Henry, etc.	d
	7	1924	8773	Garms	Andina, etc.	d
Feb.	4	1947	17620	Garner	Constance Ann	m
Sept.	26	1949	19234	Garner	Ethel May, etc.	d
June	7	1936	12632	Garner	Joseph W.	d
June	9	1953	21887	Garnett	Edna F., etc.	d
Feb.	11	1954	22278	Garnett	Edna F., etc.	d
		1922	7973	Garoni	Giuseppe, etc.	d
Nov.	15	1945	16811	Garrett	Albert Walker	d
Nov.	15	1945	16818	Garrett	Albert Walker, etc.	d
		1885	1453	Garrett	Eliza J.	d
May	24	1946	17168	Garrett	Lydia N.	inc
Aug.		1946	17328	Garrett	Lydia N.	d

Month	Day	Year	File No.	Surname	Given Name	Type
Sept.	6	1948	18566	Garrett	Mary	d
Nov.	4	1947	18079	Garrett	Nancy Lee	d
Sept.	7	1948	18611	Garrett	Wayne S.	d
Feb.	15	1946	17004	Garrison	Amanda	d
Aug.	25	1945	16585	Garrison	Charles, etc.	d
		1919	6967	Garrison	Della May	d
Apr.	18	1957	24599	Garrison	Ida H.	d
		[1919-1920]	7555	Garrison	Mary Jane	d
May	19	1949	19023	Garrison	R. W.	d
May	28	1952	21091	Garrison	Sarah A.	d
Nov.	18	1957	25150	Garrison	William E.	d
Oct.	20	1914	5827	Garrison	William J.	d
Feb.	21	1952	20934	Garsee	Judy Lynne	m
Nov.	31	1912	5372	Garske ?	Carl Ernst	d
July	8	1958	25761	Garufis	Marl	d
Dec.	20	1942	15153	Garzali	William	d
Nov.	13	1957	25141	Garzelli	Anna	d
Mar.	13	1953	21644	Garzoli	Alice E., etc.	d
June	9	1958	25614	Garzoli	Aurelia	d
Aug.	11	1928	9994	Garzoli	Basilio	d
Jan.	19	1937	12863	Garzoli	Enis V. C., etc.	d
Apr.	9	1941	14469	Garzoli	Ennis	m
Apr.	9	1941	14469	Garzoli	Fulvio	m
Feb.	28	1958	25334	Garzoli	Joshua	d
Apr.	9	1941	14469	Garzoli	Valentina	m
Apr.	23	1934	11900	Garzoti	Joseph F., etc.	d
Apr.		1937	12916	Gasiman	Susan	d
		1872	539	Gaskill	Abigail	d
Apr.	11	1942	14816	Gaspar	Edward A.	d
		1916	6259	Gaspar	Joseph	d
Feb.	21	1930	10531	Gaspari	Giulio	d
June	27	1936	12649	Gaspari	Mary	d
Aug.	19	1916	6279	Gasper	Harry	m
Aug.	19	1916	6279	Gasper	Mary	m
Dec.	7	1916	6288	Gasper	Mary	ins
June	15	1944	15984	Gasper	Mary	d
July	24	1943	15447	Gasper/Gasperick	John	d
Jan.	25	1948	18505	Gassamann	Marcel	d
Mar.	24	1947	17659	Gassaway	Sue Frances	d
Dec.	28	1948	18805	Gassmann	Marcel	d
Mar.	11	1936	12571	Gaston	Dora A.	d
		[1880-1881]	1092	Gaston	Dora E.	m

Month	Day	Year	File No.	Surname	Given Name	Type
		1921	7900	Gaston	Ellen	d
		1926	9447	Gaston	George W., etc.	d
		[1889-1890]	1915	Gaston	Hamilton	d
Oct.	15	1932	11389	Gaston	Hattie Winn, etc.	d
		[1903-1905]	3602	Gaston	Hugh	d
		[1880-1881]	1091	Gaston	Martin	d
		1923	8296	Gaston	Mary Ann	d
		1924	8746	Gaston	William H., etc.	d
Dec.	23	1934	12083	Gater	Carrie E.	d
Feb.	7	1939	13565	Gater	Earl C.	d
		[1893-1894]	2315	Gater	James D.	d
Aug.		1923	8382	Gater	James E.	d
Jan.	23	1955	23680	Gates	Caleb F.	d
Sept.	17	1948	18584	Gates	Carvel Elvers	d
Feb.	7	1957	24438	Gates	Donna Stanton	m
		1895	2494	Gates	F. I.	d
June	18	1944	15990	Gates	F. I.	d
Dec.	24	1958	26104	Gates	Franklin Q., etc.	d
Aug.	20	1956	24063	Gates	Grace B., etc.	d
May	5	1917	6459	Gates	Henry H.	d
Mar.	18	1958	25469	Gates	Herbert Wright, etc.	d
June	27	1931	10977	Gates	Horace Delphos, etc.	d
Sept.	6	1947	17986	Gates	Marie F.	d
Apr.	21	1958	25484	Gates	Theodore	d
Jan.	20	1946	17533	Gathergood	Robert R.	d
Nov.	26	1933	11650	Gatlen	Gertrude A.	d
Nov.	24	1928	10075	Gatshell	Beda, etc.	d
Jan.	6	1958	25261	Gatter	Fred N.	d
June	2	1951	20375	Gatto	Angelo Louis	d
Feb.	30	1945	16386	Gatto	Rosa	d
June	5	1936	12663	Gatto	William	d
		[1906-1907]	4185	Gaudenzio	James D. (aka Giacomo D.)	d
Dec.	21	1957	25159	Gauld	William R., etc.	d
		[1860-1865]	179	Gauldin	Benjamin F.	m
		[1860-1865]	179	Gauldin	John V.	m
		[1909-1910]	4795	Gauldin	Josiah	d
		1926	9380	Gauldin	Lodema A.	d
		[1860-1865]	179	Gauldin	Martha A.	m
		[1860-1865]	179	Gauldin	Willis W.	m
Jan.	24	1914	5886	Gauldin ?	Willis W.	d
		1873	628	Gaulia	George	d
		1919	6983	Gautier	Endoxia V.	d

Month	Day	Year	File No.	Surname	Given Name	Type
	26	1925	9067	Gautier	Leonidas	d
Jan.	18	1952	21522	Gava	Teresa Maria, etc.	d
Aug.	13	1955	23313	Gavello	John	d
		1909	4704	Gaver	Andrew P.	d
		[1909-1910]	4745	Gaver	Andrew Poe	m
		[1910-1911]	4910	Gaver	Gideon	d
Mar.	6	1912	5260	Gaver	Susan	d
July	13	1930	10652	Gavin	Ruth	inc
Jan.	12	1956	24391	Gavron	Zigmund W., etc.	d
June	31	1933	11624	Gaye	Albert M.	d
		1915	6030	Gaye	Marcelin	d
Oct.	29	1947	18026	Gaye	Marie	d
Nov.	16	1956	24275	Gayer	Terry B.	d
Aug.	16	1955	23439	Gaylord	Hazel F.	d
July	11	1930	10674	Gaynor	Lucy E.	d
		[1910-1911]	5136	Gearing	Jessie	d
Apr.	24	1958	25488	Geary	Barbara Kay	m
		1887	1683	Geary	Edward B.	d
Oct.	26	1932	11350	Geary	Janet McNab	d
May	9	1952	21116	Geary	W. Finlaw, etc.	d
		[1893-1894]	2348	Gebaneres	Louise M.	m
		[1894-1895]	2453	Gebauer	Charles	d
Feb.	1	1937	12877	Gebelein	Kurigunde	d
		[1888-1889]	1785	Geer	Cyrus V.	d
		1924	8593	Geer	Frank, Jr.	d
May	27	1939	13683	Geer	Joseph, etc.	d
Feb.	21	1947	17587	Geer	Mari	d
Feb.	25	1952	20880	Gehring	August	d
Sept.	20	1947	17965	Gehrke	Julius C.	d
Mar.	10	1939	13570	Geils	George F., Jr.	d
Mar.	19	1947	17654	Geils	Minna	d
Nov.	25	1952	21362	Geisenhofer	Elsie K.	d
Dec.	2	1955	23623	Geisler	Leslie F., etc.	d
		[1910-1911]	5104	Geisselman	Aldolph	m
		[1910-1911]	4864	Geisselmann	Albert B.	m
Aug.	27	1946	16871	Geissen	Mary	d
Aug.	15	1946	17291	Geisser	Louise K.	d
Sept.	29	1958	25889	Gelan	Charles L.	d
July	28	1952	21226	Gelatini	Charles/Carlo	d
Dec.	24	1945	16832	Gelle	William Fred	d
Aug.	13	1956	24156	Geller	Esther, etc.	inc
Dec.	9	1958	24398	Geller	Esther, etc.	d

Month	Day	Year	File No.	Surname	Given Name	Type
May	1	1939	13661	Gellissen	Andrew	d
Dec.	30	1941	14660	Gelpi	Louis, etc.	d
Dec.	12	1949	19397	Geltz	John	d
July	13	1951	20483	Geltz	John C., etc.	d
Sept.	16	1952	21343	Gemetti	Marcus W.	d
		1934	12050	Gemetti	Thomas, etc.	d
July	4	1942	14967	Gemini	Clarence	d
		[1899-1900]	3187	Gemmill	David L.	m
		[1899-1900]	3187	Gemmill	Grace	m
		[1899-1900]	3187	Gemmill	Lillie J.	m
		[1899-1900]	3187	Gemmill	Wm. C.	m
Dec.	31	1942	15127	Gemstra	Antonio	d
Feb.		1935	12476	Genazzi	Clelia	d
		1906	4051	Genazzi	John	inc
		[1919-1920]	7341	Genazzi	John C.	d
		1918	6748	Genazzi	John Frederick	m
Sept.		1918	6818	Genazzi	Mary	d
June	24	1940	14048	Genazzi	Stella	m
	21	1918	6748	Genazzi	Viola Rose	m
Sept.	16	1938	13407	Gendar	Harriet E., etc.	d
Jan.		1923	8495	Gender	Edward F.	d
Jan.	9	1944	16313	Genelly	Angelo, etc.	d
Aug.	12	1955	23367	Genelly	Herbert A.	d
Aug.	17	1947	17856	Genelly	Muriel	m
Dec.	12	1913	5657	Generto	George	d
Dec.	7	1943	15714	Genini	Michele, etc.	d
Feb.	6	1957	24518	Genovesi	Carlo	d
Mar.	29	1934	11839	Genozzi	Elia M., etc.	d
Oct.	24	1954	22773	Genter	Annie Elizabeth, etc.	d
		1921	7724	Gentherodt	William	d
Aug.	9	1949	19208	Gentry	Alpha Harriett	d
Aug.	9	1949	19209	Gentry	Alpha Harriett, etc.	d
Aug.	19	1957	24962	Gentry	Bernice E.	d
Aug.	7	1913	5565	Gentry	Charles	inc
Feb.	2	1914	5688	Gentry	Charles	d
Mar.	24	1958	25410	Gentry	John	d
Aug.	6	1957	24935	Gentry	John W.	inc
June	4	1947	17833	George	B. R.	d
Apr.		1937	12905	George	Clara Blace	inc
Nov.		1925	9092	George	Emma Jane	d
Aug.	28	1958	25810	George	Gratia	d
Jan.	17	1934	12130	George	J. M.	d

Month	Day	Year	File No.	Surname	Given Name	Type
Nov.	12	1944	16212	George	J. W.	d
Apr.		1925	8895	George	James Henry	inc
		[1907-1908]	4326	George	Jason R.	d
Jan.	18	1956	24403	George	Kenneth Doyle	d
		[1905-1906]	3992	George	Lilla E.	inc
Dec.	5	1937	13138	George	May	d
Jan.	16	1953	22236	George	Rollin A.	d
Apr.	20	1956	23942	Georgea	Alex	d
Oct.	29	1944	16193	Georgeson	Constantin	d
Aug.	23	1957	24905	Gerace	John, etc.	d
Mar.	3	1927	9524	Gerald	James Thomas	d
May	23	1954	22486	Gerald	Shiela E.	d
Nov.	24	1948	18682	Gerardini	John, etc.	d
		[1893-1894]	2313	Gerber	August	d
		[1899-1900]	3047	Gerber	Charles	d
Jan.	31	1936	12850	Gerberding	Reuben Hill	d
Dec.	6	1955	23633	Gerbi	Frank, etc.	d
Mar.	17	1948	18292	Gerdes	Gerhard, etc.	d
		[1907-1908]	4471	Gerdsen	Carsten	d
July	10	1928	9971	Gerenza	John	d
		[1894-1895]	2438	Gerger	Anton	d
July	7	1942	15004	Gerhardt	Anna M.	d
Jan.	5	1937	13162	Gerhardt	Chris	d
Mar.	20	1928	9847	Geri	Martin	d
		1919	7040	Gericke	Julia	inc
		[1875-1876]	769	Gerl	Charles	d
		[1893-1894]	2338	Gerl	Janet	d
		1908	4510	Gerlach	Frederick	d
Mar.	12	1945	16468	Gerlfsen	H.	d
Apr.	1	1938	13257	Gerli	Giovannini, etc.	d
Nov.	14	1927	9742	Germain	Rock	d
		1881	1180	German	Charlotte	d
Sept.	12	1928	10058	Germanis	Catherine	d
May	10	1937	12991	Germano	Giuseppe	d
July	21	1949	19139	Germond	Adele H.	d
Nov.	6	1943	15630	Germone	Joseph, etc.	d
Mar.	17	1948	18290	Gerner	Howard Clyde	m
July	18	1937	13004	Gertosio	Guiseppe	d
Apr.	1	1935	12213	Geruke	George	d
Oct.	15	1958	25928	Gervasoni	Charles, etc.	d
Oct.	16	1947	17995	Gesek	Christian	d
Feb.	28	1947	17609	Gesek	Katherine	d

Month	Day	Year	File No.	Surname	Given Name	Type
June	21	1933	11593	Gessler	Dorothea	inc
		1925	9122	Gessler	Hugo	d
Oct.	14	1943	15597	Gestra	Luigi, etc.	d
		1917	6607	Geurkink	B. U.	d
Feb.	9	1925	8877	Geuster	Louise	d
Mar.	16	1941	14743	Geusti	Antone, etc.	d
		1908	4528	Geuzumian	Joseph	d
Sept.	31	1951	20577	Ghidossi	Ottavia	d
Oct.	15	1958	26001	Ghigliazza	Bernardo J.	d
Sept.	15	1929	10281	Ghilaidi	Vittorio	d
Feb.	1	1946	16980	Ghilins	Rosa	d
Apr.	16	1946	17078	Ghilins	Vic M.	d
Aug.	7	1956	24148	Ghiotti	Andrea	d
		1929	10259	Ghiotti	Guiseppe	d
Sept.	13	1946	17340	Ghisletta	Rocco	d
Aug.	3	1956	24141	Ghizzardi	Emilio, etc.	d
Nov.	20	1958	26019	Gholson	Margaret B., etc.	d
Sept.	3	1952	21238	Giacomelli	Bert	inc
Jan.	14	1948	18174	Giacomelli	Gerald E.	m
Apr.	5	1954	22436	Giacomelli	Victor, etc.	d
July	15	1930	10680	Giacometti	Albert William	m
July	15	1930	10680	Giacometti	Anna	m
July	15	1930	10680	Giacometti	Buddy	m
July	15	1930	10680	Giacometti	Gladstone	m
July	15	1930	10680	Giacometti	Gloria	m
July	15	1930	10680	Giacometti	Julia	m
July	15	1930	10680	Giacometti	Victor John	m
Feb.	10	1925	8850	Giacomini	A., etc.	d
Dec.	26	1948	18751	Giacomini	Altavis	d
		[1919-1920]	7393	Giacomini	M.	d
June	3	1948	18430	Giacomini	Maria A., etc.	d
Mar.	13	1933	11504	Giacomini	Mary J., etc.	d
Dec.	16	1955	23661	Giampaolo	Raffael	d
May	1	1940	13981	Gianali	Antonio	d
Oct.	26	1942	15118	Gianali	Roberta Mabel	m
		[1898-1899]	2870	Gianella	Gioconda	d
		1891	2208	Gianella	Lorenzo	d
Nov.	18	1957	25149	Gianelli	Carolina, etc.	d
Mar.	25	1930	10534	Giannecchini	Ida, etc.	d
Apr.	20	1934	11879	Giannecchini	Maria	d
June	17	1958	25708	Giannecchini	Venanzio	d
Dec.	3	1957	25187	Giannini	Lorenzo	d

Month	Day	Year	File No.	Surname	Given Name	Type
May	8	1938	13286	Giannini	Maria	d
Dec.	9	1928	10108	Giannini	Pietro	d
Sept.	10	1958	25911	Gianoli	Beatrice	d
Apr.	27	1938	13232	Gianoli	Eugene	m
Mar.	27	1938	13232	Gianoli	Roberta	m
		[1890-1891]	2015	Gianoni	Peter	d
June	19	1958	25717	Gianotti	Sabina	con
June	19	1958	25716	Gianotti	Severino	d
Apr.	6	1944	15881	Gianouris	Mike, etc.	d
May	26	1912	5315	Gianque	Elizabeth	d
Dec.	25	1952	21479	Gibbe	William Curt	m
Feb.	28	1939	13591	Gibbens	Margaret May Leslie. etc.	d
		1905	3902	Gibbens	Robert Lee	d
		1905	3957	Gibbens	Rose Elliott	m
		[1886-1887]	1560	Gibbons	Edward	d
		1888	1727	Gibbs	Elizabeth A.	d
Aug.	20	1942	15014	Gibbs	Eunice U.	d
Apr.	6	1934	11913	Gibbs	Harriet	d
		[1890-1891]	2018	Gibbs	Henry	d
Mar.	19	1945	16426	Gibbs	Martha	d
		[1903-1905]	3886	Gibbs	Sophronia	inc
		[1905-1906]	4008	Gibbs	Sophronia	d
Feb.	19	1945	16425	Gibbs	William M.	d
Jan.	6	1914	5878	Giberson	John	d
Dec.		1925	9099	Giberson	Katherina L.	d
May	7	1958	25604	Giblin	Arthur	inc
June	10	1946	17242	Giblin	Minnie, etc.	d
		[1900-1902]	3330	Gibney	George	d
Jan.		1924	8826	Giboli	William	d
		[1907-1908]	4432	Gibson	Annie E.	d
Nov.	1	1949	19341	Gibson	Calvert	d
Dec.	8	1924	8825	Gibson	Charles W.	inc
Feb.	18	1924	8827	Gibson	Charles W.	d
Jan.	1	1932	11457	Gibson	Cordelia	d
Sept.	17	1954	22760	Gibson	Dell D.	d
Sept.	20	1933	11645	Gibson	F. H.	d
		1860	158	Gibson	Geo. W.	d
May	6	1941	14520	Gibson	H. F.	d
July	26	1944	16053	Gibson	James W.	d
Dec.	29	1956	24352	Gibson	Jess M.	d
May	25	1955	23197	Gibson	Jessie Marion	inc
		1891	2209	Gibson	John	d

Month	Day	Year	File No.	Surname	Given Name	Type
		[1910-1911]	4878	Gibson	John R.	inc
Aug.	18	1951	20493	Gibson	Mamie	d
Mar.	7	1933	11554	Gibson	Myron Bartlett, etc.	d
May	17	1945	16531	Gibson	Myrtle T.	inc
		[1900-1902]	3260	Gibson	Polly A.	d
		[1910-1911]	4879	Gibson	Samira	inc
Jan.	19	1911	5224	Gibson	Samira	d
Sept.	25	1927	9679	Gibson	Samuel	d
		[1893-1894]	2349	Gibson	Sarah W.	d
Aug.	27	1941	14532	Gickey	Laura B.	d
May	28	1953	21811	Gidall	Mary	d
June	24	1958	25726	Gidall	Zaharia	d
July	25	1940	14081	Gidaris	Angelo	d
		[1907-1908]	4262	Giese	J. Harry	d
Apr.	23	1931	10923	Giese	Josephine	d
		[1906-1907]	4181	Gifford	J. J.	d
Jan.	8	1942	15185	Gigerich	Nellie A.	d
Nov.	28	1917	6541	Giggus	Louis F.	d
July	24	1941	14527	Gilardi	Palma	d
Nov.	4	1946	17467	Gilardi	Richard	m
Nov.	11	1913	5598	Gilardi	Stefano	d
June	2	1944	16014	Gilardi	Virginia	d
June	14	1937	12998	Gilardoni	Attilio	d
Oct.	3	1949	19291	Gilardoni	Ernegler	d
June	6	1949	19114	Gilardoni	John	d
		[1900-1902]	3335	Gilbert	Francis	d
Oct.	8	1943	15588	Gilbert	Henry D.	d
		1875	727	Gilbert	Jacob	d
Oct.	28	1945	16741	Gilbert	James William	inc
Nov.	16	1945	16770	Gilbert	James William	d
Nov.	4	1949	19297	Gilbert	L. O., etc.	d
Jan.	25	1946	17497	Gilbert	Nellie I.	inc
		[1898-1899]	2887	Gilbert	Platt B.	d
		1873	645	Gilbert	S. W.	d
		1909	4690	Gilbertson	Adam G.	m
		1909	4635	Gilbertson	Ida	d
		1909	4690	Gilbertson	Inor G. J.	m
		1909	4690	Gilbertson	Otto G.	m
Oct.	14	1913	5574	Gilbride	Roger	d
		[1910-1911]	4890	Gilder (aka Benninghe	Emma	d
		[1883-1884]	1313	Giles	Lewis R.	d
Nov.	30	1913	5648	Giles	William A.	d

Month	Day	Year	File No.	Surname	Given Name	Type
		1924	8734	Gilfillan	John R., etc	d
		[1876-1878]	856	Gilham	J. B.	d
July	10	1935	12300	Gilkey	Laura Belle	inc
		[1902-1903]	3424	Gill	Ann	d
		1871	504	Gill	Antonette	m
Jan.	4	1930	10510	Gill	Antonette	d
		[1903-1905]	3666	Gill	Charles	m
Aug.	30	1936	12719	Gill	Charles W.	d
		[1903-1905]	3716	Gill	Frederick W.	d
		1870	447	Gill	George	d
Mar.	6	1945	16457	Gill	James	d
		[1907-1908]	4373	Gill	Leon	m
Feb.	5	1953	21625	Gill	Nellie Anita, etc.	d
Sept.	28	1958	25814	Gill	Rosalie	d
		[1894-1895]	2484	Gill	Sarah V.	d
		[1907-1908]	4373	Gill	Warren L.	m
Dec.	27	1939	13821	Gillan	Eda C.	d
Oct.	22	1924	8737	Gillan	Edwin W., etc.	d
		1905	3909	Gillen	Sarah M.	d
		1898	2854	Gillespie	Henry	d
Apr.	12	1956	23851	Gillespie	Norma A.	d
		1935	12443	Gillespie	Thomas B.	d
Oct.	23	1942	15090	Gillet	Elise	d
Oct.	20	1939	13706	Gillet	Pierre	d
Aug.	17	1930	10681	Gillett	Charles	inc
July	13	1932	11315	Gillett	Charles	d
Aug.	22	1930	10690	Gillett	Ida E.	d
July	24	1926	9288	Gillett	Mary J.	d
		[1883-1884]	1331	Gillette	R. M.	d
Jan.	26	1951	20765	Gillette	Wallace J.	d
Jan.	16	1950	19458	Gilliam	Luellen	m
		1882	1257	Gilliam	Mitchel	d
		1920	7591	Gilliam	Samuel J.	d
July		1908	4472	Gillies	James A.	d
		1854	45	Gilliland	John M.	d
July	15	1951	20442	Gilliland	William	d
Mar.	17	1955	23062	Gillingham	Joseph Eddy, etc.	d
Mar.	28	1957	24560	Gillis	Alexander S., etc.	d
June	12	1958	25697	Gillis	John Edwin	d
Mar.	27	1951	20237	Gillmore	Everett E.	d
Nov.	27	1942	15121	Gilloaly	Mary E.	d
		[1902-1903]	3485	Gillooly	Cornelius A.	d

Month	Day	Year	File No.	Surname	Given Name	Type
Nov.	25	1948	18692	Gillooly	James Patrick	d
		[1903-1905]	3746	Gillooly	John P.	d
June		1923	8367	Gillooly	Mary A.	d
July	26	1936	12692	Gillooly	Mary H.	m
Feb.	29	1912	5442	Gilman	L. J.	d
July	3	1917	6477	Gilman	Rebecca	d
June	11	1927	9625	Gilmer	John M.	d
Jan.	11	1943	15222	Gilmor	Quincy S. et al	d
Dec.	30	1944	16297	Gilmore	Percy	d
June	17	1958	25709	Gilolin ?	Patrick H.	m
Sept.	13	1945	16692	Gilooly	Clara H.	d
Oct.	25	1945	16734	Gimbal	Louis, etc.	d
Apr.	31	1940	14320	Ginbergin	John B.	d
Apr.	10	1941	14392	Ginesi	Pietro, etc.	d
		[1917-1918]	6635	Gingery	Joseph	d
May	8	1947	17733	Ginsberg	Reva, etc.	d
		1922	8172	Ginter	Mary A.	m
Nov.	27	1922	8172	Ginter	Richard O.	m
		[1889-1890]	1872	Giolin	Sarah	d
Feb.	15	1930	10813	Giolitti	Antonio	d
May	15	1935	12272	Gione	Alice May	m
Apr.	15	1935	12272	Gione	Dora Eleanor	m
June	15	1935	12272	Gione	Hazel	m
Apr.	15	1935	12272	Gione	Ray	m
May	10	1940	14026	Giorgetti	A., etc.	d
		1935	12320	Giorgetti	Emma	inc
		[1919-1920]	7523	Giorgi	Achille	d
		1922	8040	Giorgi	Elvira	m
Sept.	7	1932	11329	Giorgi	Giacomo	d
June		1917	6467	Giorgi	Giovanni	d
		1937	12899	Giorgi	Giovanni	d
May	7	1941	14930	Giorgi	Giuseppina	d
Dec.	3	1942	15175	Giorgi	Luigi	d
Aug.	16	1949	19217	Giorgi	Regina Sabadins, etc.	d
		1922	8040	Giorgi	Yolanda	m
		1871	477	Giovanari	P.	d
		[1910-1911]	4942	Giovannini	Angelo	d
Mar.	6	1944	15872	Giovannini	Antonio, etc.	d
Mar.	7	1936	12544	Giovannini	D.	d
Apr.	19	1940	13966	Giovannini	George	inc
Feb.	23	1946	16958	Giovannini	George D.	d
May	2	1938	13308	Giovannini	Laura	d

Month	Day	Year	File No.	Surname	Given Name	Type
June	13	1939	13699	Giovannini	Luigi	d
Jan.	24	1948	18776	Giovannini	Philomina, etc.	d
Sept.	3	1953	22043	Giovannini	Pietro, etc.	d
May	27	1937	12975	Giovannini	Theresa	d
July	17	1940	14113	Giovannoni	Edward	d
		1922	7917	Giovannoni	Marino, etc.	d
Jan.	6	1922	7917	Giovannoni	Martino, etc.	d
Dec.	24	1948	18796	Giovannoni	Philomina	d
Nov.	8	1928	10107	Girard	Julica	d
		[1860-1865]	166	Gird	Henry S.	ins.
		[1907-1908]	4266	Gird	Henry S.	d
May	22	1952	21082	Girolo	Emilia	d
Jan.	4	1949	18812	Girolo	James	d
Sept.	15	1949	19261	Girolo	Lorenzo	d
Aug.	11	1950	19866	Girolo	Peter	d
Mar.	11	1944	15834	Gist	Jeannette L.	d
Sept.	11	1941	14634	Gist	John L.	d
Mar.	20	1945	16482	Giudetti	Domenico	d
June	1	1951	20422	Giudici	Ben, etc.	d
Feb.	6	1939	13525	Giugai	Anderson	d
Feb.	27	1913	5682	Giuliani	Filippo, etc.	d
July	7	1930	10670	Giulieri	Benjamin, etc.	d
Mar.	15	1946	17005	Giuntali	Amedeo	d
July	8	1936	12668	Giussani	Gregorio	d
Aug.	31	1940	14127	Giuste	Antone, etc.	inc
June	18	1955	23248	Giusti	Albert J., etc.	d
Mar.		1953	21798	Giusti	Antonio	d
Feb.	15	1944	15781	Giusti	Cherubina	d
Jan.	18	1944	15780	Giusti	Eliseo	d
Aug.	9	1937	13028	Giusti	Elizabeth	d
		1928	9896	Given	John M.	d
		1887	1644	Givens	Ada	m
		1891	2206	Givens	Ada	m
		1887	1644	Givens	Anna J.	m
		1887	1644	Givens	George	m
		1887	1644	Givens	Grace M.	m
		1891	2197	Givens	R. R.	d
Apr.	5	1949	18999	Gladden	Letitia, etc.	d
June	21	1913	5513	Glading	Lawton C. (aka L. C.)	d
		[1903-1905]	3884	Glaister	Thomas Skelton	d
July	15	1948	18455	Glakrow	Lorena Stanto, etc.	d
Sept.	4	1944	16113	Glando	Luis	d

Month	Day	Year	File No.	Surname	Given Name	Type
Sept.	19	1954	22647	Glantz	Alfred A.	d
Apr.	4	1944	15909	Glantz	George C.	d
Feb.	17	1957	24462	Glascock	Audrey G.	d
		[1869-1870]	408	Glascock	Wm.	d
Mar.	20	1930	10558	Glasford	Jasper	d
June	6	1952	21169	Glass	Katherine A.	d
		[1906-1907]	4130	Glass	Marguerite	d
July	7	1957	24722	Glass	Monte	d
Apr.	13	1956	23861	Glatfelder	Alta I.	d
Nov.	15	1951	20736	Glazier	Frank Le Roy	M
July	27	1951	20458	Glazier	Joseph Benjamin, etc.	d
Oct.	28	1951	20643	Glazier	Mabel	d
Sept.	3	1940	14166	Gleasan	David P.	d
Sept.		1924	8730	Gleason	Bridget, etc.	d
Feb.	11	1944	16316	Gleason	Caster R.	d
Nov.	18	1932	11412	Gleason	Charles M.	d
Sept.	20	1928	10040	Gleason	George John	d
Sept.	8	1950	19921	Gleason	Joseph W., etc.	d
Nov.	10	1941	14701	Gleason	Lillian	d
Nov.	10	1941	14706	Gleason	Lillian	d
		1905	3977	Gleason	William	d
Oct.	11	1957	25081	Gleeson	Mary W.	d
June	7	1947	17838	Gleffe	Sylvia	d
Sept.	6	1956	24196	Gleisner	LeRoy B., etc.	d
Oct.	21	1955	23550	Gleissle	Flora, etc.	d
July	16	1932	11197	Glendenin	Laura, etc.	d
		1891	2094	Glendening	Robert	d
Jan.	12	1939	13863	Glenn	James	d
		[1883-1884]	1374	Glenn	John	d
		[1895-1897]	2520	Glenn	Margaret	d
Jan.	28	1913	5680	Glockner	Charles	d
Sept.	12	1947	17993	Gloe	Pearl May	d
		[1876-1878]	850	Glover	A. B.	ins
		[1881-1882]	1198	Glover	Albert B.	m
		[1881-1882]	1198	Glover	Josephine M.	m
Sept.	6	1951	20588	Glover	M. H.	d
Aug.	12	1938	13374	Glpver	Norman C.	d
		1879	994	Glynn	Michael	d
Feb.	25	1912	5248	Glynn	Patrick	inc
July	22	1912	5328	Glynn	Patrick	d
Mar.	10	1948	18222	Gnecco	John, etc.	d
		1909	4622	Gnesa	Edith	m

Month	Day	Year	File No.	Surname	Given Name	Type
		1909	4622	Gnesa	Geraldine	m
July	24	1943	15490	Gnesa	Louis	d
		1909	4622	Gnesa	Louis G.	m
		1909	4622	Gnesa	Maria	m
June	23	1946	17217	Gnesdiloff	Alexander N.	d
May	1	1957	24709	Gnos	Anna Maria, etc.	d
May	1	1957	24708	Gnos	Franz, etc.	d
		[1903-1905]	3793	Goatley	Armsted	d
Feb.	4	1944	15818	Goatley	Ruth K.	d
Sept.	11	1936	12728	Gobbi	Anastasia	inc
May	6	1940	14020	Gobbi	Annastasia, etc.	d
Aug.	16	1938	13321	Gobbi	Ernest J.	ins
May	22	1940	14007	Gobbi	Ethel	ins
Sept.	5	1952	21317	Gobbi	Joe`	d
		1935	12447	Gobbi	John A.	d
May	4	1915	5953	Gobbi	John L.	m
Jan.	10	1949	19410	Gobbi	John L.	inc
		1924	8705	Gobbi	Julius	d
		1898	2866	Gobbi	Julius James	d
Mar.	13	1957	24584	Gobbi	Lena	d
June	18	1942	14951	Gobbi	Raymond Allen, etc.	d
Apr.	4	1915	5953	Gobbi	William V.	m
Oct.	31	1955	23471	Gober	Birdie Joyce	m
Oct.	31	1955	23471	Gober	Bonnie Joan	m
		[1898-1899]	2889	Gobetti	John	d
Dec.	24	1954	22886	Godard	Minnie L.	d
Nov.	21	1927	9750	Goddard	A. D.	d
Feb.	12	1958	26141	Goddard	Arthur L.	d
May	23	1940	14045	Goddard	Daniel N., etc.	d
Mar.	19	1943	15313	Goddard	Edith R.	d
Feb.	27	1956	23757	Goddard	Elmer F.	d
July	22	1931	11012	Goddard	H. S.	d
Jan.	14	1945	16882	Goddard	Jacob H., etc.	d
Feb.	7	1956	23781	Goddard	James A.	d
Apr.	21	1915	6159	Goddard	Jane M.	d
		1876	795	Goddard	Jesse P. et al	m
Apr.	1	1947	17722	Goddard	Lorraine Christine	m
Apr.	1	1947	17722	Goddard	Lucille Elizabeth	m
Feb.	16	1958	26152	Goddard	Nora Lee, etc.	d
July	22	1931	11013	Goddard	Sam L.	d
Apr.	1	1947	17722	Goddard	William Roger	m
		[1869-1870]	411	Goddard	Wm. B.	d

Month	Day	Year	File No.	Surname	Given Name	Type
Feb.	2	1945	16394	Godfretsen	Albert	d
Dec.	4	1945	16858	Godfretsen	Maurice J.	m
Mar.	7	1935	12186	Godfrey	Mary E. Ritchie	d
Mar.	5	1956	23833	Goding	Mina L.	d
		[1875-1876]	770 1/2	Godwin	F. O. et al (no papers)	m
Mar.	31	1912	5256	Goeller	Louise	d
July	13	1948	18513	Goering	John M.	d
Apr.	20	1936	12595	Goeth	Marie M.	d
June	13	1946	17199	Goetzfried	Elizabeth	d
Feb.	22	1948	18179	Goetzfried	Elizabeth	d
Oct.	9	1951	20657	Goewey	James W.	d
July	3	1951	20468	Goewey	Olivet, etc.	d
Nov.	16	1935	12359	Goff	William S.	d
		[1900-1902]	3204	Goforth	Elizabeth A. R.	d
Sept.	15	1950	19874	Gogmins	Carrie Frances	d
Apr.	14	1952	21057	Gold	Eva	d
Mar.	15	1949	18903	Goldbeck	Edna E.	d
Feb.	14	1949	18835	Goldbeck	Fredrich	d
		[1899-1900]	2986	Goldberg	Nathan	d
Apr.	18	1931	10916	Golden	Doro C.	d
		[1902-1903]	3519	Golden	James	m
Mar.	27	1957	24557	Golden	James, etc.	d
		1925	9056	Golden	Joseph, etc.	d
		[1878-1879]	982	Golden	Thomas	d
Sept.	27	1943	15531	Golden	Thomas	d
		1897	2722	Goldstun	Henry	d
May	6	1952	21103	Golla	Valentin	d
Jan.	11	1945	16875	Golladay	Floyd W.	d
Jan.	9	1920	7605	Goller/Goeller	John	d
		1919	7262	Golliah/Goul	John, etc.	d
June	26	1949	19099	Golly	Alice Ann	m
Apr.	25	1940	13972	Golton	Louis H.	d
July	2	1943	15503	Gomes	Antonio E.	d
Nov.	3	1937	13117	Gomes	John F.	d
Jan.	23	1957	25234	Gomez	Donald L.	d
Feb.	23	1953	21601	Gomez	Jessie M., etc.	inc
		1953	21703	Gomez	Jessie M., etc.	d
June	26	1928	9956	Gomez	M. J.	d
		[1880-1881]	1088	Gomley	Berdie	d
Dec.	15	1930	10774	Gondola	George	m
Jan.	18	1943	15739	Gondola	Giuseppe	inc
Dec.	15	1930	10774	Gondola	Joseph	m

Month	Day	Year	File No.	Surname	Given Name	Type
Apr.	21	1949	18969	Gonella	John	d
June	6	1936	12665	Gonis	Mary Vincent	inc
July	2	1917	6519	Gonnella	Amerigo	d
Jan.	17	1956	23731	Gonnella	Eleanor	d
Oct.	8	1956	24261	Gonnella	John W., etc.	d
Apr.	4	1935	12258	Gonsalves	Francisco Silverio	d
Mar.	22	1948	18297	Gonsalves	John Silveria	d
Jan.	3	1958	25253	Gonsalves	Joseph, etc.	d
Aug.	18	1950	19823	Gonsalves	Manuel Jude, etc.	d
Feb.	16	1951	20216	Gonzales	Anton F., etc.	d
Mar.	16	1951	20216	Gonzales	Katrina, etc.	d
Feb.	15	1951	20212	Gonzales	Saturn. etc.	d
Feb.	12	1938	13503	Gonzalez	Viola Viloa	d
Aug.	15	1938	13406	Gonzalves	Richard Alfred	m
Jan.	21	1911	5225	Good	Harry Carlton	d
		1891	2222	Good	John	d
		1937	12881	Good	Richard	d
		1900	3200	Good	Walter C.	d
May	22	1958	25569	Goodall	Charles F., etc.	d
June	8	1953	21828	Goodbrake	John J., etc.	d
		1926	9181	Goodburn	William R.	d
Nov.		1928	10092	Goode	James F.	d
Sept.	11	1951	20595	Goodell	Anna M.	d
Aug.	23	1940	14122	Gooderts	Levien John, etc.	d
Feb.	3	1931	10858	Goodfellow	King, etc.	d
Sept.	12	1956	24204	Goodfellow	Mary	d
Oct.	29	1950	19951	Goodhue	Gilbert H., etc.	ins
Feb.	26	1951	20181	Goodhue	Gilbert H., etc.	d
Nov.		1915	6112	Goodloe	Mary Susanne	d
		1910	4834	Goodman	Allen	d
		1923	8427	Goodman	Bridget	d
		[1894-1895]	2400	Goodman	David	m
July	11	1913	5557	Goodman	David	d
June	10	1914	5563	Goodman	David	d
June	22	1953	21902	Goodman	Emma	d
Aug.	15	1946	17295	Goodman	Frank W.	d
July	15	1946	17296	Goodman	Frank W.	d
		1935	12381	Goodman	Fred S.	d
Jan.	25	1950	19479	Goodman	Harold W., etc.	d
Nov.	11	1932	11409	Goodman	James Edwin	d
		1924	8613	Goodman	James Wesley	d
		1924	8723	Goodman	Margaret	d

Month	Day	Year	File No.	Surname	Given Name	Type
May	14	1940	14031	Goodman	Mattie B.	d
		[1917-1918]	6631	Goodman	Nellie M.	d
		[1894-1895]	2400	Goodman	S. F.	m
		1886	1527	Goodman	Thomas M.	d
Sept.	11	1925	9054	Goodman	Walter W.	m
		[1889-1890]	1886	Goodman	William T.	d
Dec.	5	1956	24370	Goodrich	Dennis Neal	m
Nov.	24	1947	18057	Goodrich	Elizabeth, etc.	d
Feb.	7	1949	18890	Goodrich	Irwin C., etc.	d
Mar.	10	1947	17688	Goodrich	M. P., etc.	d
Nov.	8	1946	17472	Goodrich	Nettie Frances	d
		1880	1068½	Goodspeed	Charles	m
Nov.	28	1936	12739	Goodspeed	Orville Charles Pratt	d
		1880	1068½	Goodspeed	Wilston F.	m
Nov.	15	1931	11078	Goodstein	David, etc.	d
		1918	6711	Goodwin	D. B.	d
Mar.	29	1924	8556	Goodwin	Ellen M.	d
May	20	1928	9945	Goodwin	James	d
Feb.	21	1928	10153	Goodwin	Peter F.	d
May	13	1940	14028	Goodwin	Victoria M.	d
		1918	6810	Goodwin	William J.	d
May	9	1948	18329	Gordon	Cynthia E., etc.	d
June	29	1952	21148	Gordon	Duane	m
Oct.	11	1957	25082	Gordon	Elvira A.	d
Nov.	16	1931	11133	Gordon	Francis Jackson, etc.	d
		1919	7059	Gordon	Frank	d
June	30	1956	23958	Gordon	Fred	d
Feb.	30	1958	25337	Gordon	Henry B., etc.	d
Oct.	8	1948	18669	Gordon	James Allen, etc.	d
Mar.	28	1945	16446	Gordon	Lizzie	d
June	3	1955	23290	Gordon	M. Herbert, etc.	d
Mar.	11	1954	22338	Gordon	Margaret	d
Aug.	5	1955	23409	Gordon	Olivia M.	d
		[1903-1905]	3564	Gordon	Rhoda	m
Feb.	8	1954	22269	Gordon	Robert	d
Nov.		1918	6867	Gordon	Rollin, etc.	d
Aug.	16	1912	5362	Gordon	Sarah A.	d
Sept.	9	1929	10278	Gordon	William A.	d
June		1926	9274	Gordon	Winifred F.	d
Feb.	15	1934	11826	Gore	R. F.	d
July	16	1938	13319	Gori	Alfonsa, etc.	d
Feb.	18	1958	25393	Gori	Annunziata	d

Month	Day	Year	File No.	Surname	Given Name	Type
Mar.	9	1949	18943	Gori	Miche Secundo, etc.	d
Apr.	21	1947	17702	Gorie	Garland	d
Apr.	21	1947	17701	Gorie	Jennie	d
Sept.	17	1938	13411	Gorigan	John D., etc.	d
Apr.	21	1952	20939	Gorman	Edward A.	d
Mar.	27	1953	21669	Gorman	Minnie	d
		[1854-1855]	46	Gormly	Martin E.	d
	19	1917	6533	Gorski	Carl	d
Feb.	18	1935	12164	Gorzano	Angelo, etc.	d
	24	1917	6629	Gosch	Henry, etc.	d
Aug.	22	1955	23452	Goslin	Floyd J.	d
Mar.	13	1951	20274	Goss	Alice L.	d
Oct.	1	1956	24244	Goss	Benjamin R., etc.	d
		1891	2101	Goss	Caroline	d
July	25	1948	18478	Gossage	Bert L., etc.	d
		[1903-1905]	3564	Gossage	Carrie	m
Mar.	1	1957	24567	Gossage	Edna, etc.	d
Sept.	24	1928	10043	Gossage	Eliza	d
Apr.	8	1929	10204	Gossage	Fanny	d
Nov.	15	1941	14639	Gossage	H. S.	d
		1887	1697	Gossage	Harry S.	m
		[1886-1887]	1581	Gossage	Jerome B.	d
		1887	1697	Gossage	Jerome B.	m
Nov.	4	1912	5425	Gossage	Rachel A.	d
Nov.	10	1926	9432	Gossage	William S.	d
		1887	1697	Gossage	Winfield S.	m
		[1876-1878]	851	Gossage	Zephaniah	d
Aug.	15	1938	13404	Gossia	Edith	d
Mar.	28	1925	8892	Gossin	Charles S.	d
Mar.	5	1954	22327	Gossner	F. M.	d
July	6	1927	9641	Gott	Michael C.	d
Sept.	30	1937	13077	Gottenberg	Hartley W.	d
June	23	1955	23266	Gottenberg	Ruth Todd, etc.	d
July	29	1914	5799	Gottenberg	Wm. Lewis	d
Dec.	9	1928	10109	Gouagher	James	d
Apr.	2	1917	6384	Gough	John	d
		1921	7786	Gough	Margaret	d
		[1919-1920]	7333	Gough	Michael G.	d
Feb.	3	1930	10797	Gouid	Jennie V.	d
Feb.	17	1914	5717	Gould	Charles A.	d
Mar.	8	1927	9535	Gould	Don	d
Dec.	14	1947	18092	Gould	Ida Wiley	d

Month	Day	Year	File No.	Surname	Given Name	Type
Apr.	28	1957	24618	Gould	Margaret B.	d
		1923	8396	Gould	Mattie A.	d
		1907	4225	Gould	Thomas J.	d
		[1883-1884]	1297	Gourley	Joseph	d
	28	1921	7754	Gourley/Gorley)	Ina	d
Jan.	20	1930	10529	Goussebaille	John Baptist, etc.	d
Nov.	16	1951	20676	Goussline	Harvey E., etc.	d
May	30	1957	24703	Gouygon	Noemie A.	d
Feb.	24	1950	19474	Gow	A. W., etc.	d
Oct.	19	1951	20685	Gowan	Ernest A.	d
Apr.	23	1917	6427	Gowans	Alan Gray	m
Apr.	23	1955	23130	Gowans	Carleene S.	d
May	6	1942	14845	Grable	William Hearst, etc.	d
Apr.	21	1933	11567	Grabomski/Grebbo	John/Joh, etc	d
		1911	5180	Grabtree	Nancy	d
		[1906-1907]	4132	Grace	Catherine	d
May	20	1936	12619	Grace	Catherine L.	d
Apr.	26	1945	16493	Grace	Ethel A., etc.	d
Oct.	16	1940	14185	Grace	Frank P., Jr.	d
Nov.	29	1930	10717	Grace	Frank Patrick, etc.	d
July	12	1943	15510	Grace	Jane C.	d
Nov.	21	1957	25095	Grace	Joseph T., etc.	d
Nov.	27	1956	24349	Grace	Julianne	m
Nov.	27	1956	24349	Grace	Pamela	m
May	19	1939	13677	Grace	Pearl C., etc.	d
Dec.	27	1956	24349	Grace	William Proctor	m
May	24	1931	10952	Grace	William R.	d
Nov.	14	1956	24327	Grace	William R., etc.	d
Sept.	17	1945	16694	Grace	Francis Joseph Morgan, III, e	m
Mar.	1	1944	15864	Gracia	Lucile, etc.	d
Mar.	12	1956	23850	Grady	Walter L.	d
Feb.	8	1923	8496	Graefer	Charles C., etc.	d
		[1900-1902]	3267	Grael	Patrick	d
		1887	1686	Graetzer	Stephan	d
		1925	9146	Graf	Paul	d
Sept.	9	1954	22575	Graff	Edward	d
Jan.	25	1950	20068	Graff	Henry	d
June	29	1939	13684	Graff	Maria	d
June	17	1915	6020	Graham	A. D.	d
		1922	7995	Graham	Andrew Lang	d
		[1871-1873]	637	Graham	Ann	d
		[1880-1881]	1119	Graham	Arthur	m

Month	Day	Year	File No.	Surname	Given Name	Type
		1918	6772	Graham	Eleanor, etc.	d
Aug.	22	1935	12362	Graham	Elmer Max	ins
Nov.		1924	8774	Graham	Elsie O.	d
Oct.	28	1939	13741	Graham	Elver Max	d
June	7	1949	19067	Graham	Emma	d
		1928	10154	Graham	Francis E.	d
May	11	1942	14938	Graham	Fred A., etc.	d
Oct.	8	1957	25067	Graham	George	d
Jan.	3	1951	20782	Graham	Herbert	d
Nov.	29	1944	16194	Graham	Howard	d
Oct.	19	1927	9724	Graham	Ida F., etc.	d
		[1880-1881]	1119	Graham	Ida J.	m
Sept.	29	1930	10715	Graham	J. H.	inc
Nov.		1926	9349	Graham	James H.	d
June		1916	6269	Graham	John	m
Mar.	13	1931	10911	Graham	Jonathan Harvey, etc.	d
July	12	1944	16031	Graham	Mabel	d
July	22	1916	6270	Graham	Mary J.	d
		[1906-1907]	4116	Graham	Patrick	d
July	19	1946	17262	Graham	Promise, etc.	d
July		1916	6269	Graham	Robert	m
Feb.	6	1928	9826	Graham	Roy Arthur	m
		1916	6269	Graham	Teresa	m
May		1921	7732	Graham	Thomas	m
Aug.	23	1957	24976	Graham	William T., etc.	d
Sept.	16	1952	21346	Grahn	William H.	d
Dec.	17	1946	17487	Graillat	Christine Marie	d
Nov.	17	1946	17487	Grallia	Marie, etc.	d
Sept.	7	1943	15547	Gramberg	Frederick August, etc.	d
May	21	1937	13298	Gramberg	John	d
Sept.	28	1944	16104	Gramham	Mabel E.	d
Aug.	8	1938	13397	Grammer	Joseph	d
Feb.	9	1951	20144	Granberg	Anna L.	d
May	31	1936	12602	Granberg	Frank L.	d
Dec.		[1910-1911]	5209	Grand	Frank	m
		[1910-1911]	5123	Grand	Mary Jane	d
June	21	1947	17805	Grande	Maria Teresa	d
Apr.	7	1947	17730	Grandi	Agnes	d
Aug.	30	1957	24917	Grandi	Frank C.	d
Jan.	16	1947	18136	Grandi	Fulvio	inc
May	3	1921	7758	Grandi	Mary F.	d
May	30	1951	20303	Grandola	Constance	d

Month	Day	Year	File No.	Surname	Given Name	Type
Aug.	3	1936	12699	Granella	Giovanni	d
Mar.	19	1948	18245	Granelli	Giovanni, etc.	d
Nov.	10	1947	18045	Granelli	Louis	d
Feb.	6	1915	5931	Granice	Harry Hale	d
Feb.	14	1915	5939	Granice	Kate	d
Apr.	27	1913	5502	Grannel	William A.	d
Dec.	8	1944	16312	Granoli	Battista, etc.	d
Nov.	6	1950	19958	Grant	Addie	d
Apr.	10	1933	11559	Grant	Anita F.	d
Jan.	6	1954	22266	Grant	Edwin A.	d
		1878	914	Grant	Fergus	d
Jan.	18	1933	11769	Grant	Frances C.	d
Apr.	26	1957	24696	Grant	Frank Benjamin	d
		[1894-1895]	2402	Grant	Frederick F.	m
		[1865-1869]	296	Grant	H. D. F.	m
Oct.	15	1951	20671	Grant	Herman A.	d
		[1919-1920]	7413	Grant	Isabel	d
		1893	2300	Grant	Jesse R.	d
July	18	1944	16087	Grant	John D., etc.	d
Sept.	8	1953	22052	Grant	Mary	d
Mar.	19	1949	18967	Granucci	Antonetta, etc.	d
Apr.	19	1949	18968	Granucci	G., etc.	d
June	18	1942	14952	Graper	Herman	d
May	19	1937	12963	Grasler	Dorothea	d
May	14	1918	6736	Grass	Adeline	inc
Sept.	14	1953	22009	Grass	Frank	d
		1916	6235	Grass	Peter	d
June	25	1950	19647	Grasso	Cesare, etc.	d
June	2	1936	12660	Grasso	Joseph	d
		[1894-1895]	2487	Grater	John F.	d
		[1903-1905]	3663	Graven	Gunder L.	d
		[1900-1902]	3359	Graves	B. F.	d
		[1890-1891]	1971	Graves	George W.	d
		1891	2081	Graves	Georgie	m
July		1891	2081	Graves	Hill B.	m
Dec.	5	1953	22162	Graves	John	d
July	24	1940	14078	Graves	Luella B.	d
Jan.	18	1940	13882	Graves	Sarah J.	d
		[1893-1894]	2309	Graves	William H.	d
		[1860-1865]	162	Gray	Anderson	d
		[1919-1920]	7284	Gray	Bertha	m
Feb.		1926	9459	Gray	Cecile, etc.	d

Month	Day	Year	File No.	Surname	Given Name	Type
Aug.	16	1957	24955	Gray	Edward A.	d
Apr.	20	1952	20933	Gray	Edward Willis, etc.	d
July	24	1914	5753	Gray	Eliza A.	d
Apr.	30	1948	18308	Gray	Elizabeth, etc.	d
May		1926	9241	Gray	Frank O.	d
		[1899-1900]	3000	Gray	Garrett M.	d
Sept.	12	1940	14145	Gray	George B., etc.	d
May	24	1950	19585	Gray	George Harvey	d
Oct.	10	1942	15039	Gray	Harold Le Roy	d
Nov.	28	1957	25105	Gray	Henry Charles	d
Jan.	13	1948	18171	Gray	Hugh	d
		[1865-1869]	306	Gray	Hugh	d
Dec.		[1910-1911]	5197	Gray	Isaac	d
Dec.	28	1944	16295	Gray	J. D.	d
Oct.	20	1950	19935	Gray	J. W.	d
Mar.	9	1924	8569	Gray	James H.	d
		[1899-1900]	3006	Gray	John	d
Sept.	9	1935	12374	Gray	John M.	d
June	18	1931	10969	Gray	Kelley, Sarah Z., etc.	d
July	12	1957	24873	Gray	Lilian	d
Feb.	10	1952	20843	Gray	Lillie Haskins	d
Sept.		1918	6819	Gray	Mary	d
July	25	1952	21217	Gray	Robert B., etc.	d
Dec.	3	1953	22157	Gray	Vesta	inc
Apr.	2	1954	22369	Gray	Vesta	d
June	31	1939	13685	Gray	William P., etc.	d
Nov.	15	1954	22811	Graybill	George D.	d
		[1917-1918]	6689	Grayson	Harry	d
		1923	8428	Grayson	Harry W.	d
Aug.		1923	8432	Grayson	Harry W., etc.	d
Sept.	14	1941	14575	Grayson	Margaret, etc.	d
Dec.	20	1939	13845	Grayson	Nathaniel G., etc.	d
Jan.	30	1955	23684	Grayson	William C.	d
		[1879-1880]	1017	Greathouse	George L.	d
		[1910-1911]	4846	Greaver	Sarah Ann	m
July		1946	17250	Gredel	Raymond W., etc.	d
		1909	4713	Greeley	Henry St. Clair	d
Nov.		1917	6579	Greely	Eloise et al	m
		[1870-1871]	462	Green	A. M.	d
Sept.	30	1940	14165	Green	Albena, etc.	inc
Nov.	20	1938	13441	Green	Alex, etc.	d
Aug.	18	1955	22989	Green	Alexander M.	d

Month	Day	Year	File No.	Surname	Given Name	Type
July	7	1917	6504	Green	Anna/Annie	d
		[1910-1911]	4919	Green	B. F.	d
		1918	6840	Green	David J.	d
Nov.	7	1927	9763	Green	Dell D.	d
Aug.	16	1957	24958	Green	Edith	inc
Apr.	26	1954	22417	Green	Edward Dennis, etc.	m
		[1906-1907]	4138	Green	Emily	m
		1909	4658	Green	George	m
July	16	1939	13702	Green	George	inc
		[1890-1891]	1968	Green	George D.	d
		1909	4658	Green	Gertrude	m
		[1855-1857]	48	Green	H. A.	d
June	21	1954	22543	Green	Herman	d
May	22	1955	23191	Green	Ida Juhl	d
May	23	1958	25573	Green	James Lawrence	d
Feb.	2	1935	12177	Green	James W.	d
Nov.	9	1931	11127	Green	Jane Isabel	d
Oct.	1	1927	9687	Green	Jean McBeth	d
		1909	4637	Green	Lillie	d
		[1920-1921]	7610	Green	Margretta	m
Jan.	10	1933	11499	Green	Mary Miriam, etc.	d
Feb.	26	1957	24555	Green	Meda E., etc.	d
Mar.	12	1948	18281	Green	Mettie May	d
		1919	7170	Green	Paul F.	d
		1909	4658	Green	Perry	m
Oct.	10	1957	25004	Green	Robert E.	d
May	30	1943	15356	Green	Rose Hodge	d
		[1910-1911]	5078	Green	Sadie J.	d
Mar.	11	1912	5285	Green	Sarah A.	d
		1909	4734	Green	Sarah J.	d
May	16	1939	13672	Green	Stella Morrison	d
		[1900-1902]	3291	Green	Warren	d
		[1899-1900]	3085	Green	William	d
		1909	4658	Green	William	m
		1909	4718	Green	William S.	d
Nov.	17	1950	20052	Greenberg	David	d
Nov.	24	1946	17413	Greene	Jessie M.	d
Aug.	29	1953	21916	Greene	Kenneth L., etc.	d
Dec.	7	1956	24374	Greene	Lloyd A.	d
Nov.	7	1931	11097	Greene	Maggie G.	d
May	24	1942	14911	Greene	Willis E., etc.	d
Dec.	23	1948	18748	Greene	Wm., etc.	d

Month	Day	Year	File No.		Surname	Given Name	Type
July	18	1914	5826		Greenhagen	Carl J.	m
Sept.	18	1914	5826		Greenhagen	Emily J.	m
Nov.	18	1943	15643		Greenough	Annie	inc
May	29	1946	17174		Greenough	Annie F., etc.	d
		1903	3538		Greenslade	Charles	d
Feb.	1	1950	19487		Greenwald	Rose	d
		1898	2833		Greenwell	S. T.	d
Aug.	3	1945	16563		Greenwood	Alice A., etc.	d
		[1908-1909]	4561		Greenwood	Elizabeth	d
Oct.	4	1957	25060		Greeot	Sarah E.	d
Jan.	14	1942	15191		Greeott	John	d
July	21	1957	24820		Gregg	Charles W.	d
		[1910-1911]	5044		Gregg	Elisabeth A.	d
Oct.	13	1940	14181		Gregg	George N.	d
		[1910-1911]	4992		Gregg	Henry	d
July	25	1958	25729		Gregg	Lottie	inc
Nov.	25	1951	20695		Gregg	Marian	d
		[1908-1909]	4567		Gregg	Narcissus M.	d
Nov.	23	1939	13817		Gregg	Robert Oscar	d
		1921	7836		Gregoire	Frank	d
Dec.		1919	7197		Gregoire	L., etc.	d
		1919	7229		Gregoire	L., etc.	d
		[1900-1902]	3218		Gregori	Celestine	d
		1875	761		Gregory	Ann	d
Sept.	6	1925	8922		Gregory	Catherine, etc.	d
June	29	1952	21152		Gregory	E. S., etc.	d
Nov.	28	1955	23559		Gregory	Edward D., etc.	d
Nov.	28	1955	23559		Gregory	Edward J., etc.	d
		[1887-1888]	1702		Gregory	Henry	d
		[1888-1889]	1796		Gregory	Lulu	m
Mar.	7	1933	11555		Gregory	William, etc.	d
Feb.	7	1958	25365		Gregson	John Westley, etc.	con
July	14	1958	25782		Gregson	John Westley, etc.	d
Apr.	11	1958	25546		Gregson	Lucy N.	d
Dec.	18	1931	11140		Grehe	A. L.	ins
Jan.	23	1932	11449		Greifeld	Albert Carl	d
Mar.	11	1913	5494		Greig	James, Jr.	d
		[1900-1902]	3349		Greiner	Frederick	inc
June	4	1948	18436		Greiner	Joseph	d
Jan.	4	1948	18152		Greiner	Theresia	d
June	21	1948	18404		Greiner	Theresia Rosa	inc
Nov.	29	1953	22143		Greiner	Theresta Rosa	d

Month	Day	Year	File No.	Surname	Given Name	Type
		1889	1877	Greives	Samuel H.	ins
May	28	1954	22501	Grenier	Emaline	d
Aug.	26	1956	24127	Grenier	Walter L.	d
Mar.	5	1958	25434	Greninger	Fletcher Elwood	m
July	27	1948	18538	Greppe	L.	d
Jan.	7	1943	15715	Greppi	Delfina	d
Feb.	3	1956	23772	Greppi	Edward H., etc.	d
Mar.	28	1936	12536	Greppi	Silvestro	d
		[1900-1902]	3293	Grewell	Howard Marshall	d
Feb.	9	1951	20206	Grey	Donald	m
Jan.	24	1933	11774	Grey	Henry W.	d
Dec.	30	1955	23616	Grider	Jessie	inc
May	20	1954	22542	Grider	Loren T.	d
Jan.	25	1938	13230	Grider	Newton J.	d
Oct.	10	1937	13092	Grider	Newton Jackson	d
Oct.	2	1914	5859	Griess	George	d
		1884	1389	Griest	Peter	d
		[1903-1905]	3774	Grieves	Samuel H.	d
		[1903-1905]	3781	Grieves	William Clarence	d
Nov.	9	1943	15670	Griffen	Susan Florence	d
		1865	269	Griffeth	James A.	ins
		1869	402	Griffeth	James A.	d
Apr.	20	1951	20286	Griffin	Carol Jean	m
		[1903-1905]	3815	Griffin	Catherine	inc
		1924	8727	Griffin	Louis	d
Feb.	1	1956	23765	Griffin	William	d
Sept.	8	1958	25909	Griffith	Annie T.	d
Mar.	18	1914	5719	Griffith	Hannah N.	d
Sept.	27	1957	24984	Griffith	Laura W.	d
Nov.	13	1950	20046	Griffith	Lenora Theresa	inc
Feb.	19	1937	12865	Griffith	Ruth E.	d
Jan.	22	1931	11173	Griffith	William V., etc.	d
Oct.		1922	8139	Griffith	Minnie E.	d
Oct.	21	1953	22068	Griffithe	Robert R.	d
Jan.	30	1931	11151	Griffiths	David J.	d
Nov.	15	1933	11715	Griffiths	Mary T., etc.	d
Aug.	15	1947	17952	Griggs	Alvin Stanley, etc.	d
July	27	1948	18540	Griggs	Amy Grace	d
Oct.	20	1948	18634	Griggs	Ann D., etc.	d
		[1897-1898]	2759	Griggs	Joseph H.	d
Feb.	26	1915	6138	Griggs	Smith M.	d
Jan.	24	1954	22942	Grignolo	John, etc.	d

Month	Day	Year	File No.	Surname	Given Name	Type
May	6	1933	11579	Grigsby	R. A.	d
Aug.	17	1953	21954	Grime	Charles, etc.	d
May	18	1954	22539	Grimes	Elizabeth	d
		[1919-1920]	7147	Grimm	Albert	m
Oct.		1922	8113	Grimm	Bruce F.	ins
Mar.	3	1931	10898	Grimm	Bruce F.	d
		[1919-1920]	7147	Grimm	Dorothy	m
Feb.	19	1916	6369	Grimm	Ferdinand J.	d
		1917	6456	Grimm	Frederick	d
		[1919-1920]	7147	Grimm	Kenneth	m
June	19	1921	7766	Grimm	Mary E.	d
Dec.	6	1952	21500	Grimmer	Jesse Charles, etc.	d
		1921	7787	Grimmett	Irena	d
June	14	1953	21838	Grims	Lily	d
Sept.	1	1951	20519	Grings	R. E.	d
Feb.	12	1940	13893	Grinstud	Jean Elizabeth	m
		[1876-1878]	800	Grissom	William	d
Jan.	11	1953	22229	Grist	Mary E.	d
Nov.	16	1956	24334	Griswold	Emma Elizabeth	d
Dec.	10	1948	18771	Grob	Joseph, Sr.	d
		[1883-1884]	1321	Groff	Caroline	m
		[1883-1884]	1304	Groff	John S.	d
		[1883-1884]	1321	Groff	Louis W.	m
		[1883-1884]	1321	Groff	Sarah E.	m
		[1883-1884]	1321	Groff	William S.	m
		1926	9238	Grogan	William L.	d
Nov.		1923	8484	Grogan (aka Gard)	Alice Aldorette	d
May	26	1927	9579	Grohe	Frederich	d
Oct.	20	1931	11035	Grohe	Henry	d
Feb.	1	1957	24507	Groll	George Alfred, etc.	d
June	29	1947	17766	Gromo	Maria	d
Oct.	20	1949	19271	Gromolo	Ernest, etc.	d
July	31	1934	11965	Groner	Lurenia	d
June	26	1915	6010	Groning	Augusta A.	d
		1926	9315	Groning	Hjalmar	d
		[1876-1878]	829	Gropp	Charles	ins
May	3	1937	12981	Groser	John E.	d
May	13	1951	20338	Groskoff	Charles E.	d
June	14	1940	14070	Groskopf	Barbara	d
June	28	1954	22551	Gross	Claire C., etc.	d
Mar.	24	1914	5723	Gross	Eugene A.	d
Jan.	26	1938	13491	Gross	Frances	d

Month	Day	Year	File No.	Surname	Given Name	Type
		1908	4473	Gross	L. L.	d
Nov.	10	1947	18087	Gross	Max	d
Sept.	6	1938	13426	Grosse	Fred, etc.	d
Nov.	22	1938	13443	Grosse	Frederika, etc.	d
		[1907-1908]	4298	Grosse	Guy B.	d
		1883	1292	Grosse	Joseph E.	m
May	6	1934	11916	Grosse	Lizzie Gibbs, etc.	d
Dec.	1	1943	15701	Grossi	Stephen	d
Feb.	30	1948	18193	Grosso	Frank, etc.	d
Feb.	24	1949	18856	Grosso	Rosa, etc.	d
May	30	1957	24704	Grote	Paul E.	d
Mar.	14	1955	23049	Groth	Emiel Otto	d
		1922	8103	Groth	Jacob	d
		[1899-1900]	3093	Grothaus	Ferdinand	d
Oct.	10	1950	19963	Grott	Francentz	d
Jan.	10	1956	23717	Grove	Beryl E., etc.	d
Nov.	19	1954	22878	Grove	Chester Monroe, etc.	d
Oct.	16	1953	22061	Grove	Clarence	d
Jan.	28	1918	6868	Grove	Everett H.	d
		[1919-1920]	7548	Grove	John	d
		1919	7037	Grove	John H.	m
July	11	1913	5556	Grove	Lewis S., etc.	d
Apr.	18	1946	17011	Grove	Lillian A.	d
		1881	1197	Grove	Louis S.	d
May	2	1948	18317	Grove	Mary A., etc.	d
July	29	1953	21915	Grove	Olga E.	d
Dec.	16	1955	23660	Grove	Peder, etc.	d
Jan.	9	1926	9458	Grove	W. G.	d
Apr.	11	1921	7639	Grove	W. H.	g
Mar.		1919	7037	Grove	Ward K.	m
Sept.	15	1950	19875	Grove	William A., etc.	d
		1857	49	Grover	B. F.	d
Feb.	13	1958	25379	Grover	Eleanor M.	d
		1858	127	Grover	James M.	m
Oct.	7	1955	23521	Grover	Ruth I.	d
Dec.	20	1951	20755	Groverman	Bernhard, etc.	d
Dec.		1926	9439	Groves	Edwin H.	d
		[1917-1918]	6680	Groves	Elliott W.	d
Feb.	4	1950	19496	Groves	George N., Jr.	m
Mar.	17	1948	18291	Groves	James Harland	d
Feb.	1	1946	16979	Grozner	Matzes, etc.	d
May	13	1944	15883	Grube	August, etc.	d

Month	Day	Year	File No.	Surname	Given Name	Type
Jan.	9	1957	25202	Gruber	Anna, etc.	d
July	1	1957	24843	Gruber	George, etc.	d
Jan.	22	1958	25316	Grundstrom	Edwin V.	d
		[1878-1879]	945	Grundy	Thomas E.	d
Jan.	28	1927	9787	Grune	Charles J., etc.	d
Oct.	30	1949	19286	Grutgen	Greta Helen	d
Aug.	18	1955	23444	Gruver	James C.	inc
		1898	2857	Gryff	John A.	d
		1899	2961	Gryff	Magdalena	d
Oct.	9	1951	20655	Guadagni	Ida	d
June	15	1933	11640	Guanella	Louis	d
Nov.	21	1936	12760	Guastucci	Paolo	d
Nov.	26	1949	19332	Gubbins	James Byron	d
Feb.	5	1958	25360	Guder	William K.	d
		[1910-1911]	5020	Gueer	Frank, Sr.	d
May	13	1945	16522	Guenza	Alfred L.	d
Feb.	28	1944	15807	Guenza	Cristinn, etc.	d
Jan.	16	1929	10408	Guenza	James	d
Aug.	30	1948	18552	Guenza	Mary	d
Oct.	26	1956	24234	Guerin	Emmett L.	d
Aug.	14	1956	24158	Guerinoni	Charles	d
Sept.	14	1956	24158	Guerinoni	F.	d
Aug.	14	1956	24158	Guerinoni	Fabia F., etc.	d
Aug.	7	1950	19855	Guerinoni	Martha C.	d
Aug.	6	1945	16686	Guerne	Alfred A.	d
		[1890-1891]	2016	Guerne	Henriette	d
Sept.	25	1934	11982	Guerne	Henry Louis, etc.	d
Jan.	30	1940	13911	Guerne	Julia S.	inc
Mar.	9	1940	13929	Guerne	Julia S.	d
June	25	1950	19724	Guerne	Marie	inc
Sept.	7	1950	19915	Guerne	Marie Louise, etc.	d
		1921	7765	Guerne	George	d
Dec.	3	1940	14219	Guernoni	John	d
July	16	1912	5327	Guernsey	Louis E.	m
June	10	1952	21181	Guerra	Angiolina	inc
Nov.	5	1954	22789	Guerra	Angiolina	d
June	14	1949	19123	Guerra	Cosantino, etc.	d
Mar.	24	1943	15331	Guerra	Guido	d
June	27	1958	25652	Guerra	Louie M.	inc
May	23	1939	13618	Guerra	Massima	d
Oct.	10	1939	13804	Guerra	William, etc.	ins
Aug.	20	1947	17859	Guerra	Luigi	d

Month	Day	Year	File No.	Surname	Given Name	Type
Nov.	22	1953	22127	Guerrant	Louisse	d
July	23	1950	19773	Guerrazzi	Attillio, etc.	d
		[1909-1910]	4759	Gugglielmetti	Domenica	inc
Apr.	18	1952	21070	Guglielmetti	Alfred J., etc.	d
June	10	1913	5526	Guglielmetti	Domenica	d
Mar.	20	1936	12591	Guglielmetti	Dora A.	d
		1909	4621	Guglielmetti	Giovanni	d
Apr.	30	1948	18305	Guglielmetti	Henry L.	d
May	7	1948	18380	Guglielmetti	Jennie	inc
June	24	1940	14047	Guglielmetti	Paula M.	d
		1921	7835	Guglielmetti	Peter C., etc.	d
Nov.	26	1926	9444	Guglielmetti	Serafino, etc.	d
Feb.	11	1947	17640	Guglielmini	Alesander, etc.	d
Oct.	27	1956	24235	Guglielmini	Emilio	d
Aug.	25	1944	16096	Guglielmini	Mary, etc.	d
Jan.	28	1950	20072	Guibilo	Pietro, etc.	d
		[1907-1908]	4335	Guidotti	Americo E.	d
Mar.	23	1929	10223	Guidotti	Angelo	d
		[1903-1905]	3686	Guidotti	C.	inc
		[1900-1902]	3395	Guidotti	Francisco	d
Apr.	9	1928	9871	Guidotti	Teresa	d
Sept.	10	1926	9330	Guidotti	Zelinda	d
Mar.	24	1943	15332	Guilfoile	Frank	d
Aug.	25	1949	19146	Guilfon	Martha	d
Aug.		1921	7792	Guillon	Alfred	d
Jan.	7	1925	9133	Guinan	James	d
		[1883-1884]	1336	Guinn	George W.	d
		1855	47	Guinnett	Nancy Ann	d
		1922	7928	Guisler	Edward Thomas	d
		[1907-1908]	4429	Guisti	Angelo	d
May	3	1930	10564	Guisti	Vitale	d
		1915	6027	Gully	Frank J.	d
		1894	2379	Gum	Isaac	d
Feb.	3	1939	13554	Gum	J. F.	d
		[1894-1895]	2488	Gum	Nellie Hazel	m
		1902	3420	Gummer	Frederick	d
Sept.	18	1956	24212	Gunderson	Galen Manuel	m
Apr.	16	1957	24674	Gunderson	John	d
Feb.	4	1958	25350	Gunderson	Melvin, etc.	d
Nov.	10	1952	21445	Gunn	Clayton Edward	m
Dec.	3	1928	10135	Gunn	F. G.	d
		1928	10061	Gunn	Fred G.	inc

Month	Day	Year	File No.	Surname	Given Name	Type
		1922	7923	Gunn	John H.	d
Dec.	10	1952	21445	Gunn	Lana	m
		[1885-1886]	1464	Gunning	Ann	d
June	5	1932	11184	Gunnison	August	d
May	28	1927	9580	Gunnison	Bertha	d
Feb.		1912	5430	Gunstrom	Charles F.	d
Sept.	7	1954	22734	Gunter	Marie	d
		[1922-1923]	8231	Gunter	Wendell G.	d
June	8	1943	15407	Guntly	Andrew, etc.	d
July	13	1931	11028	Guptill	Augusta C., etc.	d
Mar.	11	1957	24581	Guptill	Cecil D.	d
Sept.	21	1944	16182	Guptill	Grace G.	d
		[1919-1920]	7566	Guptill	Grace R.	m
Mar.	16	1956	23798	Guptill	Henry S.	d
		1909	4743	Guptill	James H.	d
		[1919-1920]	7566	Guptill	James H.	m
		[1919-1920]	7455	Guptill	Katie L.	d
		[1919-1920]	7566	Guptill	Maude F.	m
Mar.	18	1958	25394	Guptill	W. H., etc.	d
Apr.	16	1946	17146	Gustafson	Anna	d
June	7	1934	11918	Gustafson	Celine	d
Jan.	25	1935	12208	Gustafson	Charles	d
Jan.	23	1952	21532	Gustafson	Frank	d
Nov.	16	1956	24333	Gustafson	John O.	d
Nov.	20	1950	19995	Gustavsen	Anna Elizabeth, etc.	d
Nov.	20	1945	16828	Gustavsen	Herman	d
May	18	1955	23248	Gusti	Albert, etc.	d
Mar.	6	1944	15876	Gutches	Mary Ann, etc.	d
Aug.	2	1946	17325	Gutermute	Cora	d
May	14	1941	14479	Gutermute	David N., etc.	d
Dec.	10	1928	10144	Gutermute	Etta B.	d
July	30	1958	25746	Gutermute	H. S., etc.	d
Aug.	23	1943	15525	Gutermute	John Marshall, etc.	d
Nov.	12	1957	25138	Guthrie	Horatio N.	d
Oct.	14	1951	20604	Guthrie	Vernon H., etc.	d
June	10	1948	18383	Guthrie	Victor Glancus	d
Dec.	5	1939	13856	Gutridge	Joanna	d
Dec.	26	1945	16835	Gutridge	Joanna	d
Mar.	22	1943	15314	Gutscher	Joseph	d
		[1890-1891]	1957	Gutscheuritter	Domenique	d
Apr.	20	1956	23944	Gutter	Mark M.	d
Dec.	18	1955	23600	Guyer	Nora A.	d

Month	Day	Year	File No.	Surname	Given Name	Type
Feb.	19	1952	20931	Guymon	Anna M., etc.	d
		[1902-1903]	3520	Guyot	Charles A.	d
Aug.	9	1935	12373	Gwin	Cornelia Lapham	d
		[1883-1884]	1333	Gwin	George	d
Jan.		1935	12466	Gwinn	J. H.	d
		1890	1939	Gwinn	John E.	d
Nov.	18	1945	16775	Gwinn	Leo W., etc.	d
Jan.	8	1912	5238	Gwinn	Olny M.	d
		1891	2076	Gwynn	Edward	d
		1891	2091	Gwynn	Eunice	d
		[1910-1911]	4872	Gwynn	Mary E.	d
Sept.	17	1953	22013	Gyger	James T., Sr.	d

Month	Day	Year	File No.	Surname	Given Name	Type
Apr.	6	1954	22439	Haake	A. H.	d
Aug.	15	1913	5575	Haas	John	d
May	14	1957	24736	Haase	Harry H., etc.	d
Jan.	9	1957	24440	Habekotte	Ida	d
Dec.	16	1952	21518	Haberhauer	Mary Ellen	d
Apr.	28	1946	17109	Haberkorn	John	d
Sept.	27	1914	5832	Habinger	Josef	d
Apr.	8	1915	6153	Habinger	Anna	d
Nov.	8	1955	23577	Hackenberg	Margaret Rose	d
Jan.	31	1952	21545	Hacker	Earl L., etc.	d
Apr.	1	1958	25512	Hacker	Helen T.	d
		[1895-1896]	2518	Hacket	John James	d
Apr.	29	1957	24620	Hadden	Charlotte, etc.	d
June	17	1957	24805	Haderman	Carel	d
Dec.	21	1945	16895	Haderman	Carl J., Jr.	d
Mar.	1	1957	24562	Haderman	Carlo	d
May	26	1952	21143	Hadley	James	d
Oct.	24	1956	24223	Hadley	Jessie A., etc.	d
July	4	1928	9989	Hadley	William	d
Nov.	26	1944	16234	Haedler	Amanda	d
		1925	9061	Haegelin	Roscoe F.	d
		[1891-1892]	2011	Haehl	Amy Mary	m
		1890	1927	Haehl	Henry	d
		[1891-1892]	2011	Haehl	Henry L.	m
		1884	1392	Haehl	J. J.	d
Jan.	15	1944	15787	Haekel	Justus	d
Nov.	12	1943	15678	Haekel	Justus A.	d
June	23	1944	15997	Haensch	Oscar	d
		[1887-1888]	1634	Haering	Joseph	d
Nov.	27	1949	19333	Haeseler	Paul C.	d
Mar.	18	1954	22351	Haffner	Nellie	d
		[1899-1900]	3041	Hagan	Henry	d
		1906	4076	Hagan	Robert E.	inc
		1907	4384	Hagan	Robert E.	inc
Nov.	24	1916	6329	Hagans	George W.	d
Mar.	18	1948	18242	Hage	Henry Klaus Diedrich	d
Oct.	19	1935	12337	Hage	Henry W.	d
		[1892-1893]	2272½	Hagedohm	Rena	d
		1893	2337	Hagedohm	William	m
Aug.	10	1936	12725	Hagerdon	Nancy (formerly Nancy Stanf	d
July	17	1952	21253	Hagerman	Irene H.	d
June	16	1933	11615	Hagg	Gloria Virginia	m

Month	Day	Year	File No.	Surname	Given Name	Type
Mar.	20	1953	21709	Haggard	Charles H.	d
		[1883-1884]	1360	Haggard	Ida Mabel	m
May	17	1951	20342	Haggard	Jess	d
July	9	1951	20472	Hagman	Anna	d
Apr.	13	1927	9600	Hagman	Fred	d
Jan.	21	1954	22303	Hagopian	Sylvia R.	d
Mar.	21	1946	17534	Hagston	Carl J.	d
Sept.	22	1943	15519	Hagstrom	Carl Edward, etc.	d
		1906	4078	Haguewood	Margaret J.	d
Sept.	11	1950	19865	Hahman	Harriet B.	d
Aug.	14	1942	15011	Hahman	Paul T., tc.	d
		1924	8688	Hahmann	Clara T.	d
		[1883-1884]	1356	Hahmann	F. G.	d
Dec.	20	1913	5661	Hahmann	Henrietta	m
		1918	6726	Hahmann	Henrietta Ann	d
Feb.	20	1912	5433	Hahmann	Henry G.	d
Nov.	20	1913	5661	Hahmann	Margaret H.	m
Jan.	16	1952	20854	Hahmann	Martha J.	d
Dec.	20	1913	5661	Hahmann	Paul T., Jr.	m
		1924	8641	Hahmann	Pauline M.	d
Feb.	4	1958	25356	Hahn	Fannie	inc
May	22	1952	21079	Hahn	Frederick G.	d
May	7	1954	22522	Hahn	Gertrude M.	d
Oct.	24	1951	20631	Hahn	Milton H.	d
May	1	1944	15905	Haigh	Charles	d
June	6	1939	13691	Haigh	Emma	d
Jan.	3	1955	22957	Haigh	F. R., etc.	d
Apr.	6	1951	20315	Haigh	Florence, etc.	ins
		[1898-1899]	2950	Haigh	Frank	d
July	11	1923	8387	Haigh	George W.	d
		[1880-1881]	1107	Haigh	John B.	d
Jan.	19	1936	12810	Haigh	Julia B.	inc
		[1884-1885]	1412	Haigh	Mary	d
		1911	5088½	Haigh	Robert	d
May	11	1949	19075	Haigh	Verdie J.	inc
June	23	1949	19095	Haigh	Virdie Phillips, etc.	d
Jan.	2	1918	6932	Haigh	William Ramey	d
June	20	1944	16046	Haight	Ella, Mrs.	d
		[1873-1874]	654	Haight	H. M.	d
Apr.	27	1936	12598	Hail	Mattie J.	d
Dec.	28	1952	21482	Haile	Maude	d
		[1887-1888]	1677	Hailman	Jane R.	d

Month	Day	Year	File No.	Surname	Given Name	Type
Nov.	11	1957	25078	Haines	Clara May	inc
Oct.	19	1953	22057	Haines	Margaret H., etc.	d
May	29	1958	25589	Haines	Mary Evelyn	con
Aug.	6	1958	25833	Haines	Mary Evelyn, etc.	d
Mar.	5	1927	9531	Haines	Matilda	d
Mar.	16	1951	20283	Haines	Ridgeway H.	d
May	29	1946	17113	Haines	Wesley J.	d
		1920	7474	Hair	Althea C. E.	d
Apr.	2	1943	15360	Haith	Charles	d
		[1902-1903]	3493	Hakamon	John	d
		1907	4374	Hakes	Dorr	d
		[1888-1889]	1758	Hale	Edward	d
		[1899-1900]	3160	Hale	Marion E.	d
July	6	1913	5555	Hale	Marion Newlon	d
		1904	3765	Hale	Wiley D.	d
Dec.		1922	8218	Hales	Ada, etc.	d
Apr.	13	1951	20339	Haley	Robert E., etc.	d
May	2	1933	11599	Hall	Agnes	d
May	9	1926	9247	Hall	Albert S., etc.	d
Dec.	29	1915	6099	Hall	Alfred C.	d
Dec.		1921	7890	Hall	Alonzo C.	d
Aug.	16	1914	5825	Hall	Amelia	d
Feb.	8	1955	23030	Hall	Annie W., etc.	d
Apr.	8	1958	25528	Hall	Arthur	inc
		1926	9452	Hall	Arthur L.	m
		1922	8063	Hall	August P.	d
July	12	1943	15511	Hall	Ben F.	d
Dec.	19	1953	22183	Hall	C. Persson	d
Feb.	1	1924	8558	Hall	Charles H.	d
Jan.	8	1943	15216	Hall	Charles Page, etc.	d
June	29	1952	21153	Hall	Charles Theron, etc.	d
Mar.	11	1947	17692	Hall	Charlotte, etc.	d
		1926	9373	Hall	Clarence C.	d
May	14	1925	8931	Hall	Clarence Delmar	d
		[1904-1905]	3883	Hall	Daniel R.	d
Feb.	2	1953	21552	Hall	David W., etc.	d
Oct.	15	1951	20674	Hall	Dicey M.	d
Oct.	13	1954	22635	Hall	Donnelle Shelley, etc.	m
Nov.	29	1953	22150	Hall	Edna Lonsway	d
		1923	8394	Hall	Edward W.	inc
		[1908-1909]	4461	Hall	Edward W. W.	m
July	3	1957	24849	Hall	Edwin L.	d

Month	Day	Year	File No.	Surname	Given Name	Type
		[1883-1884]	1306	Hall	Elizabeth P.	d
Sept.	4	1945	16728	Hall	Elsie	d
Apr.	19	1913	5500	Hall	Emily J.	d
May	4	1944	15911	Hall	Eugene Forrest, etc.	d
		1926	9452	Hall	Florence K.	m
July	10	1953	21931	Hall	Florence M.	d
Nov.	22	1955	23608	Hall	Florence M., etc.	d
Nov.	15	1944	16270	Hall	Fred	d
Aug.	1	1936	12721	Hall	George A.	d
Oct.	15	1951	20673	Hall	George A., etc.	d
Mar.	26	1921	7688	Hall	George H., etc.	d
Apr.	15	1914	5765	Hall	Gertrude I.	d
Apr.	7	1941	14467	Hall	Gilbert	d
Nov.	28	1957	25109	Hall	Grace	d
Sept.	22	1934	12058	Hall	H. M.	d
May	1	1950	19661	Hall	Harley A.	d
Mar.	24	1948	18251	Hall	Harry L.	d
		[1887-1888]	1631	Hall	Henry	d
Oct.	8	1933	11708	Hall	Henry	m
Jan.	10	1958	25276	Hall	Herbert	d
		1920	7546	Hall	Howard A.	d
Jan.	13	1919	6944	Hall	James W.	d
Dec.	3	1948	18764	Hall	Joseph A.	d
July	27	1958	25732	Hall	Joseph A.	d
Apr.	8	1947	17732	Hall	Joseph L.	d
Sept.	8	1933	11708	Hall	Josephine	m
June	20	1958	25721	Hall	Josie	d
		1911	5160	Hall	Kate	d
		1912	5160	Hall	Kate	d
		[1883-1884]	1330	Hall	L. B.	d
Mar.	21	1950	19525	Hall	L. J., etc.	d
Sept.	4	1945	16728	Hall	Lewis A.	d
June	20	1944	16045	Hall	Lewis E.	d
Oct.	10	1950	19966	Hall	Lila A.	d
Jan.	31	1935	12505	Hall	Lottie	inc
		1920	7536	Hall	Lou Eva	d
Sept.	2	1947	17947	Hall	Louise M.	d
Feb.	16	1942	14776	Hall	Lulu	d
July	21	1919	7090	Hall	Mahala Olive	d
Apr.		1937	12956	Hall	Maitland	d
Sept.	8	1933	11708	Hall	Malcolm	m
May	25	1940	14011	Hall	Margaret J.	d

Month	Day	Year	File No.	Surname	Given Name	Type
		[1893-1894]	2351	Hall	Maria	d
Dec.		1920	7627	Hall	Mary A.	d
		1932	11374	Hall	Mary L., etc.	d
Aug.	5	1913	5589	Hall	Mildred Eloise	m
		1927	9485	Hall	Minnie May	d
Jan.	20	1923	8523	Hall	Nellie C.	d
Oct.	24	1948	18644	Hall	Nellie G., etc.	d
		[1887-1888]	1669	Hall	Olive Edna	d
Oct.	3	1940	14215	Hall	Oren A.	d
Nov.	4	1943	15666	Hall	Richard B.	d
June		1916	6417	Hall	Robert	d
Apr.	4	1958	25521	Hall	Robert James, etc.	d
		1881	1134	Hall	Samuel	d
Dec.	21	1934	12106	Hall	Sarah	d
July	2	1917	6499	Hall	Thirza Denia	d
June	19	1950	19761	Hall	Virginia Lou	m
June	19	1950	19761	Hall	Vivian Rosa	m
		[1887-1888]	1668	Hall	Winnie Wright	d
Apr.	30	1953	21734	Hall	Verna M.	d
Feb.	3	1956	23776	Hallberg	Mary Elizabeth, etc.	d
May	18	1938	13279	Hallenbarter	John	d
Apr.	2	1954	22429	Hallengren	Linda	d
Nov.	19	1956	24281	Hallengren	Lloyd	d
Oct.	20	1955	23492	Hallengren	Margaret	inc
Mar.	24	1943	15333	Haller	John	d
July	15	1952	21251	Hallett	Fannie B.	d
Sept.	17	1947	18000	Hallett	Henry J.	d
Dec.	25	1955	23611	Halley	Edward	d
Dec.	13	1948	18743	Hallfors	Victor M.	inc
July	5	1917	6520	Hallingren	Marie L.	d
June	24	1945	16547	Hallngren	Lily	d
May	10	1955	23225	Halloway	Herbert C.	d
May	12	1957	24664	Hallowell	William, etc.	d
July	23	1953	21906	Hallyburton	Cora	d
June	17	1938	13332	Halner	Lizzi, etc.	d
Jan.	13	1944	15757	Halonen	Nels	d
		[1898-1899]	2838	Halpin	William	d
		1923	8361	Halsted	Jasper D.	d
May		1927	9602	Halsted	John B.	d
		[1895-1896]	2562	Haltinner	Jacob	d
May	1	1940	13947	Haltor	Emma	m
Mar.	1	1940	13947	Haltor	Joseph	m

Month	Day	Year	File No.	Surname	Given Name	Type
Apr.	1	1940	13947	Haltor	Mary	m
Mar.	1	1940	13947	Haltor	Rose	m
		[1910-1911]	4832	Halverson	Otto	d
Oct.	4	1942	15034	Halverson	Tollef Morris, etc.	d
Oct.	11	1922	8137	Halvorseth	Claus K.	d
		1903	3688	Halvorson	Otto	d
June	9	1918	6735	Ham	James T., etc.	d
Feb.		1924	8536	Ham	Lena	d
May	13	1953	21836	Hamar	Nels, etc.	d
		1911	5198	Hambleton	Geo. W.	d
Aug.	6	1957	24934	Hamby	Jesse F.	d
July	7	1952	21240	Hamel	Louis Joseph	d
Feb.	29	1931	10850	Hamele	Anna, etc.	d
		1903	3666	Hamill	John	m
		[1899-1900]	3081	Hamilton	Alithia B.	m
Sept.	24	1956	24224	Hamilton	Annie R.	d
Jan.	31	1937	13201	Hamilton	Charles S.	d
July	6	1928	10013	Hamilton	Cornelius Young	d
		[1910-1911]	4850	Hamilton	G. S.	d
Mar.	18	1949	18905	Hamilton	Gertrude M.	d
		[1910-1911]	4849	Hamilton	Harriet	d
Dec.	25	1924	8814	Hamilton	Harriett Josephine	d
Dec.	27	1942	15125	Hamilton	Ida	d
		1921	7871	Hamilton	James P.	d
		1922	8045	Hamilton	James W.	d
July	1	1955	23353	Hamilton	Layton G.	d
Nov.	24	1935	12339	Hamilton	Mable M.	m
		1924	8633	Hamilton	Rosella	d
		[1899-1900]	3027	Hamilton	Sarah L.	d
Aug.	20	1944	16089	Hamilton	Lulu	d
May	17	1943	15431	Hamlin	Catherine	d
		1921	7991	Hamlin	Georgia	d
Aug.	10	1950	19861	Hamlin	Margaret J.	d
		1922	8215	Hamlin	Sarah Alethe	m
		[1881-1882]	1157	Hamm	Ellen E.	m
Oct.	28	1949	19283	Hamm	Robert Clymer	inc
		[1880-1881]	1094	Hamm	Wm. H.	d
Mar.	21	1956	23809	Hammack	Myrtle Irene	d
Feb.	15	1955	23053	Hammatt	Lucile M.	d
		1902	3525	Hammeken	Henry F. B.	d
Apr.	16	1934	11891	Hammeken	Louise M.	d
		[1897-1898]	2803	Hammeker	Henry	d

Month	Day	Year	File No.	Surname	Given Name	Type
Oct.	2	1958	25972	Hammell	Fred R.	d
May	7	1913	5523	Hammell	Laurana	d
		1929	10162	Hammell	Lester	g
Jan.	3	1928	9823	Hammell	Walter	d
Jan.	4	1946	16913	Hammer	Jacob	d
May	15	1930	10626	Hammerman	Anita E.	g
Aug.	5	1957	24928	Hammerman	Ella	d
May	15	1930	10626	Hammerman	Hilda M.	g
May	15	1930	10626	Hammerman	Waldemar G.	g
Oct.	11	1954	22690	Hammersley	Garvin	d
Sept.	19	1947	18005	Hammersmith	Louis	d
Oct.	19	1947	18006	Hammersmith	Lucie, etc.	d
		[1895-1896]	2573	Hammill	Grace	d
Apr.	23	1947	17759	Hammond	Alice	d
		[1896-1897]	2694	Hammond	Alvin A.	d
May	27	1927	9616	Hammond	Wibur P., etc.	d
July	21	1943	15482	Hammons	Mary	d
		1893	2320	Hammy	Catherine	d
		[1919-1920]	7403	Hammy	David	ins
Jan.		1919	6953	Hammy	Delphine	inc
Feb.		1919	6982	Hammy	Delphine	d
		1902	3463	Hammy	George	d
Feb.	17	1950	19522	Hampton	Durward B.	d
Oct.	3	1930	10719	Hanain	Mary C., etc.	d
		[1901-1902]	3340	Hand	Ella M.	ins
		1856	53	Hand	Samuel	d
Oct.	23	1931	11088	Handler	Conrad	d
May	15	1958	25627	Handley	Harry E., etc.	d
Oct.	28	1939	13711	Handy	Henriettta	ins
July	15	1938	13377	Handy	R. D.	d
July	23	1954	22612	Handy	Raymond P.	d
Jan.	3	1956	23693	Handy	Royal S.	d
Nov.	20	1922	8166	Haneatty	Mary	d
		1912	5319	Hanele/Hannele	Geo.	d
Dec.	23	1945	16827	Haney/Hull	Mary	inc
Apr.	19	1954	22402	Hanf	Paul L.	d
Feb.	29	1943	15250	Hanger	Clara	d
Dec.	28	1927	9791	Hanisch	Frank	d
Mar.	4	1929	10226	Hank	Frank J.	d
Mar.	18	1928	9882	Hankenson	John B.	inc
Aug.	22	1947	17907	Hanking	Romayne Searle, etc.	d
Nov.	28	1941	14691	Hankins	Miles D.	d

Month	Day	Year	File No.	Surname	Given Name	Type
Mar.	6	1946	17054	Hanlon	John	d
Feb.	11	1958	25376	Hanna	Elizabeth	inc
Feb.	4	1958	25355	Hanna	Mary Ann	inc
Feb.	31	1921	7659	Hanna	Mary Anna	ins
		1923	8442	Hanna	Mary M.	d
Dec.	14	1942	15193	Hannah	Cassius. etc.	d
		1888	1737	Hannah	John	d
Mar.	4	1924	8595	Hannah	William/James William	d
Dec.	29	1948	18756	Hannan	Daniel Francis	d
Dec.	6	1940	14259	Hannan	Mary, etc.	d
Oct.	23	1940	14156	Hannan	Thomas James	d
		1886	1544	Hannath	Eliza	d
Aug.	18	1950	19825	Hanratty	Belinda Cassarote, etc.	d
May	7	1950	19615	Hanratty	Belle, etc.	d
June	12	1945	16608	Hansby	Salome F., etc.	d
Dec.	3	1956	24363	Hansen	Agnes Mary, etc.	d
Jan.	6	1950	19444	Hansen	Andrew, etc.	d
Sept.	27	1957	25042	Hansen	Angela M.	d
Dec.	15	1957	25146	Hansen	Anna L.	d
Sept.	29	1912	5366	Hansen	Anna M.	m
		1912	5302	Hansen	Anna T.	d
Sept.	11	1957	25009	Hansen	Antone M.	d
Feb.	30	1914	5928	Hansen	Bertha P.	d
		1903	3595	Hansen	Carl	d
Mar.	24	1942	14793	Hansen	Carl C.	d
May	30	1928	9960	Hansen	Carl, etc.	d
June	3	1929	10302	Hansen	Carsten	d
		1903	3594	Hansen	Catherine	d
Nov.	26	1931	11090	Hansen	Charles	d
Mar.	27	1953	21667	Hansen	Christina F.	d
May	28	1955	23204	Hansen	Clara J.	d
Nov.	4	1949	19349	Hansen	Clifford Peter	d
Dec.	4	1952	21494	Hansen	Clyde W., etc.	d
Mar.	8	1952	20913	Hansen	Dawn	d
Apr.	8	1958	25529	Hansen	Elizabeth M.	inc
Nov.	10	1947	18044	Hansen	Emma	d
Apr.	20	1952	20997	Hansen	Florence Ida	inc
May	8	1952	21105	Hansen	Florence Ida	inc
		[1908-1909]	4494	Hansen	Florence O. B.	d
July	18	1955	23373	Hansen	Fred H.	d
Mar.	3	1950	19548	Hansen	Fred O.	d
Dec.	7	1934	12121	Hansen	Frederick J., etc.	d

Month	Day	Year	File No.	Surname	Given Name	Type
		1907	4381	Hansen	Hans	d
Apr.	10	1951	20328	Hansen	Hans J.	d
July	6	1937	12988	Hansen	Herbert	ins
Oct.	27	1945	16739	Hansen	Ingeborg	d
Nov.	9	1949	19357	Hansen	Iver J.	d
May	4	1942	14924	Hansen	Jens Peter	d
June	19	1953	21896	Hansen	Johannah Marie	d
Sept.	24	1948	18593	Hansen	Jorgine Peter	d
Aug.	13	1950	19819	Hansen	Kathrina	inc
Aug.	24	1953	21970	Hansen	Kathrine	d
Nov.	15	1943	15640	Hansen	Marie	d
June	9	1950	19748	Hansen	Marinin J.	d
Jan.	12	1949	19411	Hansen	Martha V.	d
Mar.	1	1957	24565	Hansen	Michal Yager	inc
July	28	1957	24838	Hansen	Michal Yager	d
Feb.	20	1957	24545	Hansen	Patrina K.	d
May	23	1943	15399	Hansen	Peter	d
		1911	5159	Hansen	Peter E.	d
Apr.	3	1953	21746	Hansen	Peter Petersen	d
Oct.	27	1952	21422	Hansen	Ralph A.	d
Nov.	6	1950	20025	Hansen	Stanton A., etc.	d
		1921	7799	Hansen	William	d
		1924	8690	Hansen	William	d
Sept.	4	1929	10397	Hansen	William	d
Aug.		1919	7140	Hansen	S., etc.	d
Dec.	29	1957	25181	Hanson	Angela Mabel, etc.	d
Dec.	1	1924	8821	Hanson	Bonita E.	d
		1924	8639	Hanson	Carl O.	ins
Feb.	7	1936	12519	Hanson	Edmond P., etc.	d
May	14	1953	21841	Hanson	Ella A.	d
		1923	8349	Hanson	F. H.	d
May	20	1958	25642	Hanson	Frank W.	d
May	21	1948	18403	Hanson	Hans, Jr.	d
		1924	8728	Hanson	Henry B.	d
July	10	1940	14024	Hanson	Joseph	d
Sept.	15	1958	25925	Hanson	Lois E.	d
Sept.	5	1917	6523	Hanson	Olaf, etc.	d
Sept.	4	1930	10698	Hanson	Oscar	d
June	7	1923	8349	Hanson	Thomas Howard	d
Mar.	1	1955	23089	Hanson	Walter W.	d
		1907	4270	Hanto	J. P.	d
Sept.	11	1936	12727	Haran	Anna	d

Month	Day	Year	File No.	Surname	Given Name	Type
Nov.	3	1927	9761	Haran	Owen	d
		1888	1731	Haraszthy	Attila F.	d
		[1902-1903]	3507	Haraszthy	Eleonora	d
		[1877-1879]	983	Haraszthy	Frances	d
Nov.		1913	5605	Haraszthy	Natalia V., Mrs.	d
		[1910-1911]	5016	Harbine	Elizabeth	d
		1885	1477	Harbine	Hardy Ralson	m
Feb.		1929	10195	Harbine	Nathan W.	d
July	17	1930	10656	Harbine	Sadie G.	d
		[1887-1888]	1659	Harbins	Leander	d
Nov.	11	1954	22805	Harbold	Lena W.	d
May	29	1947	17764	Hardcastle	Eaten	d
		1874	698	Hardcastle	Job N.	ins
		1911	5141	Hardegen	August	d
Jan.	22	1924	8831	Harden	Ephriam	d
June	14	1935	12303	Harden	Nannie I.	d
Feb.	27	1955	23001	Hardenbergh	Edward J., etc.	d
		[1890-1891]	1932	Hardermann	Herman	d
Mar.	28	1933	11550	Hardigger	John, etc.	d
June	16	1939	13700	Hardin	Barbara Louise	m
Nov.	28	1952	21426	Hardin	Clarence E	d
		1865	283	Hardin	George M.	m
July	29	1933	11653	Hardin	George Milton	d
		1885	1479	Hardin	George W.	m
		[1895-1896]	2509	Hardin	George W.	d
Nov.	21	1952	21471	Hardin	Harold J.	d
		1859	149	Hardin	Henry	d
		1885	1479	Hardin	Henry	m
June	21	1946	17211	Hardin	Henry, etc.	d
		1905	3925	Hardin	James A.	d
May	2	1944	15952	Hardin	Jefferson Rolla	d
Jan.	6	1936	12514	Hardin	John Marcus	d
Feb.	2	1956	23769	Hardin	Joseph C., etc.	d
		1921	7838	Hardin	L. A.	d
Apr.	23	1928	9915	Hardin	Lester B.	d
		1937	12928	Hardin	Lulu G., etc.	d
Jan.	10	1956	23718	Hardin	Mattie	inc
Sept.	26	1958	25884	Hardin	Mattie	d
May	18	1941	14485	Hardin	Mildred Croiuther	d
May	8	1922	8038	Hardin	Rebecca F.	d
		1865	283	Hardin	S. J.	m
Jan.	21	1925	9151	Hardin	Sarah Jane	d

Month	Day	Year	File No.	Surname	Given Name	Type
Feb.	14	1950	19159	Hardin	Victoria R., etc.	d
		[1864-1865]	256	Hardin	William J.	d
		1900	3178	Hardin	Wm. Jefferson	d
Sept.	22	1912	5380	Hardin	Nannie C.	d
June	6	1931	10935	Hardina	James	d
May	13	1957	24734	Harding	George John, etc.	d
Mar.	8	1946	17056	Harding	Richard H.	d
		1888	1707	Harding	William A.	d
Nov.	5	1924	8797	Hardisty	Charles W.	d
		1903	3661	Hardisty	Cibbly Ray	d
Mar.	27	1942	14835	Hardisty	Lee E., etc.	d
Jan.	6	1941	14333	Hardisty	Lois	m
Sept.	10	1928	10017	Hardisty	Mildred	d
		1906	4147	Hardt	Henry W.	d
Aug.	19	1952	21298	Hardy	Edward	inc
Sept.	19	1952	21298	Hardy	Edward, Mrs.	inc
July		1923	8409	Hardy	Jonathan	d
Oct.	22	1958	26026	Hardy	Max Lee	d
Jan.	15	1954	22284	Hardy	Nick	d
		[1904-1905]	3841	Harford	Mary E.	d
Feb.	3	1944	15817	Hargrave	H. A.	d
Mar.		1921	7701	Hargreaves	Emma M.	d
Feb.	23	1928	9851	Hargreaves	Thomas W.	d
Apr.	9	1947	17737	Harkraber	Elizabeth	d
Jan.	19	1952	20863	Harkrader	Albert Leroy, etc.	d
Feb.	10	1955	23038	Harlamoff	Julia	d
May	1	1958	25590	Harlan	James W.	d
Nov.	24	1943	15611	Harlan	Nancy Ree	m
Aug.	6	1957	24933	Harlan	Olive I.	d
Apr.	9	1954	22442	Harlan	Thelma Georgia	d
		1882	1212	Harlow	James	d
Dec.	17	1956	24399	Harlow	Jane B.	d
Dec.	15	1928	10091	Harman	Floyd	g
Sept.	25	1945	16735	Harman	Grant	d
July	28	1928	9983	Harman	Jean Margaret	d
Aug.	15	1947	17891	Harman	John Frederich	d
Feb.	10	1927	9489	Harman/Harmon	H. F.	d
Dec.	8	1941	14700	Harmeson	Prudence Lewis	d
Nov.	4	1935	12425	Harmmell	Belle	d
		1920	7543	Harmon	Delia C.	d
Apr.	6	1958	25435	Harmon	Edward D., etc.	d
Oct.	8	1951	20654	Harmon	Grace J., etc.	d

Month	Day	Year	File No.	Surname	Given Name	Type
Nov.	9	1956	24323	Harmon	Jesse B.	d
		1880	1060	Harmon	Luther N.	d
		1862	209	Harmon	Martha	d
Nov.	2	1945	16800	Harmon	Mary C., etc.	d
		[1883-1884]	1375	Harmon	Owen	m
Mar.	3	1947	17675	Harmon	Owen Edger	d
		1921	7867	Harmon	Peter A.	d
		1920	7545	Harmon	Ralph	d
		1916	6234	Harmon	Sarah J.	inc
Jan.		1918	6637	Harmon	Sarah J.	d
July		1911	5095	Harms	August	d
		[1900-1901]	3236	Harms	Bonney F.	d
		1907	4297	Harms	Bonney H. P.	d
		[1901-1902]	3326	Harms	Charles M.	m
		[1901-1902]	3326	Harms	Clarence	m
Oct.	24	1952	21417	Harms	Clarence H.	d
		[1901-1902]	3326	Harms	Frederick K.	m
		[1901-1902]	3326	Harms	Leland	m
Aug.	2	1926	9351	Harne	Egbert	d
Jan.	29	1941	14753	Harneson	David C.	m
Apr.	21	1955	23127	Haroldson	Andrew	inc
May	6	1955	23220	Haroldson	Andrew	d
June	13	1935	12332	Harow	Tom	d
Nov.	4	1943	15664	Harper	Anna Walsh	d
Aug.	4	1934	12015	Harper	Donald	m
Feb.	5	1941	14380	Harper	Donald	m
Mar.	12	1946	17066	Harper	Jean B.	d
		[1894-1895]	2440	Harper	John	d
Feb.	5	1941	14380	Harper	John F., Jr.	m
Aug.	4	1934	12015	Harper	John, Jr.	m
Feb.	21	1946	16952	Harper	Judith Elisabeth	m
		[1899-1900]	3165	Harper	Maggie A.	m
		[1858-1859]	102	Harper	Reuben R.	d
		1902	3442	Harper	Sarah	m
Mar.	16	1951	20218	Harrell	U. G., etc.	d
May	7	1933	11553	Harria	Philo W.	d
		1911	5084	Harriman	C. P.	d
		1903	3616	Harrington	Alfred B.	m
		[1886-1887]	1559	Harrington	Anthony S.	d
		1902	3467	Harrington	Benjamin	d
Dec.	25	1938	13467	Harrington	Daniel	d
		1903	3616	Harrington	Florence E.	m

Month	Day	Year	File No.	Surname	Given Name	Type
Dec.	8	1950	20094	Harrington	Harry	d
June	5	1958	25671	Harrington	Harry	d
July	18	1945	16652	Harrington	Harry	d
Sept.	7	1946	17388	Harrington	James Warner	d
Aug.	22	1950	19884	Harrington	Jennie	d
Mar.	27	1956	23889	Harrington	John A.	d
		1903	3616	Harrington	John O.	m
		1919	6988	Harrington	John O.	d
		1903	3616	Harrington	Mabel E.	m
Apr.	10	1941	14472	Harrington	Max, etc.	d
June	14	1957	24798	Harrington	Nellie R.	d
		1903	3616	Harrington	Ralph I.	m
		1923	8420	Harrington	Ralph Irving	inc
Aug.	4	1948	18560	Harrington	Warner, etc.	d
		1903	3616	Harrington	William B.	m
Jan.	21	1956	24412	Harriott	Herbert S., etc.	d
Apr.	24	1950	19586	Harris	Annie	inc
June	21	1957	24747	Harris	Annie	d
Feb.	20	1921	7649	Harris	Benjamin Henry	d
Jan.	3	1918	6636	Harris	Catherine A.	d
July	7	1934	11948	Harris	Charley T., etc.	d
Nov.	8	1950	20030	Harris	Clara L.	inc
Jan.	18	1955	22986	Harris	Clara L.	d
Aug.	17	1956	24103	Harris	Claude W., etc.	d
Feb.	2	1956	23770	Harris	Delilah A.	d
		[1865-1866]	303	Harris	E. D.	d
Aug.	10	1950	19860	Harris	Eli Raymond	d
Dec.	23	1952	21529	Harris	Florence, etc.	d
May	4	1953	21819	Harris	Frank W.	inc
Oct.	1	1954	22781	Harris	Gertrude D.	d
Aug.	24	1953	21971	Harris	Granville S.	d
		1903	3718	Harris	Henry	d
		1903	3618	Harris	John W.	d
Dec.		1925	9097	Harris	Joseph	inc
July	23	1938	13361	Harris	Katherine E., etc.	d
		1921	7857	Harris	Laura A. Y.	d
May	17	1949	19082	Harris	Lowell J.	d
June	14	1913	5527	Harris	Martha Belle	d
June	5	1928	9965	Harris	Mary A.	d
		1927	9650	Harris	Mirren, etc.	d
Sept.	24	1934	12032	Harris	Nettie M.	d
Mar.	11	1957	24580	Harris	Olga, etc.	d

Month	Day	Year	File No.	Surname	Given Name	Type
May	12	1915	5994	Harris	R. V.	d
May	13	1930	10621	Harris	Ralph	d
		[1892-1893]	2223	Harris	Richard	d
Mar.	14	1939	13643	Harris	Richard James, etc.	d
Oct.	14	1919	7216	Harris	Riley	m
		1924	8732	Harris	Samuel Gillespie	m
		[1886-1887]	1551	Harris	Sarah E.	d
May	13	1915	6019	Harris	Stella Arnold	d
June	27	1939	13710	Harris	Sylvester	d
		1855	52	Harris	Thomas	d
Oct.	19	1938	13412	Harris	Thomas	d
Oct.	10	1949	19312	Harris	Thomas A.	d
Jan.	8	1953	22221	Harris	Wiley H.	d
July	2	1923	8405	Harris	Dee, etc.	d
Jan.	7	1955	23637	Harrison	Albert C.	d
Jan.	7	1955	23636	Harrison	Clyde C.	d
Apr.	31	1941	14456	Harrison	Dice V., etc.	d
Nov.	11	1945	16756	Harrison	Evangeline Pearl, etc.	d
		[1904-1905]	3850	Harrison	Frank M.	d
Feb.	26	1912	5439	Harrison	George	d
		1879	997	Harrison	Johanna	d
Nov.	16	1945	16767	Harrison	Lionel James	m
Sept.	2	1944	16114	Harrison	Myrtle	inc
Dec.	2	1939	13831	Harrison	True	d
May	28	1956	23895	Harrs	Edward J.	d
		[1897-1898]	2797	Hart	Charles E.	m
		[1890-1891]	1993	Hart	E.	d
		1916	6372	Hart	Ernest	d
		[1881-1882]	1154	Hart	George R.	d
Oct.	3	1940	14216	Hart	George W.	d
Sept.	23	1947	17970	Hart	James Francis	d
Feb.	20	1945	16429	Hart	James Malcolm, etc.	d
May	30	1923	8343	Hart	Laura A.	d
		[1897-1898]	2801	Hart	Lottie	d
Apr.	28	1923	8293	Hart	Louisa A.	inc
Jan.	17	1935	12495	Hart	Mabel A.	d
Mar.	28	1923	8293	Hart	Marion	inc
Nov.	20	1941	14680	Hart	Mary V.	d
Jan.	13	1928	9834	Hart	Sarah P.	d
Jan.	10	1950	19453	Harter	A. L.	d
Nov.	31	1950	20017	Hartley	Max	d
May	3	1943	15408	Hartley	Samuel	d

Month	Day	Year	File No.	Surname	Given Name	Type
Jan.	7	1946	16914	Hartley/Harley	Jessarch/Samuel, Mrs.)	d
Dec.	2	1942	15131	Hartman	Anna	d
Feb.		1932	11453	Hartman	Elizabeth A.	d
Jan.	3	1945	16348	Hartman	Frances, etc.	d
Feb.	2	1928	9867	Hartman	Mary	inc
		[1890-1891]	1945	Hartman	W. D.	d
Nov.	13	1950	19980	Hartmann	Emma	d
May	5	1953	21822	Hartmann	Frank	d
		1885	1481	Hartsock	A.	d
		1894	2390	Hartsock	Bonnie	m
May	30	1952	21093	Hartsock	Florence A.	inc
Aug.	1	1952	21279	Hartsock	Florence A.	d
		1894	2390	Hartsock	Freedom	m
Apr.	10	1942	14853	Hartsock	Freedom E., etc.	d
		[1893-1894]	2339	Hartsock	Isabel M.	d
June	24	1948	18408	Hartson	William R.	d
July	11	1950	19806	Hartung	Ann T., etc.	d
Oct.	22	1951	20689	Hartung	Ann T., etc.	d
Aug.	14	1956	24161	Hartwick	John Seward	inc
Aug.	14	1956	24162	Hartwick	Rose	inc
Oct.	28	1956	24241	Hartwick	Rose	d
Nov.	3	1912	5408	Harty	Edward	d
Jan.	10	1950	19454	Hartzog	John T.	d
Dec.	18	1947	18096	Harvell	Robert H., etc.	d
		1872	554	Harvey	Alex A.	d
		1919	7163	Harvey	Annie	d
Mar.	4	1948	18265	Harvey	Annie Lei	d
		[1891-1892]	2132	Harvey	Calvin A.	m
		[1880-1881]	1096	Harvey	Charles A.	m
Feb.	4	1941	14377	Harvey	Colby Leroy	d
		1924	8592	Harvey	D. C.	d
Aug.	16	1941	14612	Harvey	Elizabeth W.	d
		[1891-1892]	2132	Harvey	Elmer R.	m
Dec.	18	1957	25227	Harvey	Elmer Rosen, etc.	d
Aug.	13	1932	11296	Harvey	Harold A.	d
Aug.	14	1957	24949	Harvey	Huldah Bell, etc.	d
Aug.	2	1957	24925	Harvey	Ida May	d
		[1873-1874]	644	Harvey	Joel	d
		[1877-1879]	916	Harvey	L. B.	d
		1892	2166	Harvey	Lilian	d
Oct.	29	1945	16743	Harvey	Lowell N.	d
Feb.	14	1941	14401	Harvey	Mabel	d

Month	Day	Year	File No.	Surname	Given Name	Type
Mar.	27	1939	13587	Harvey	Mary Matilda, etc.	d
Apr.	8	1958	25532	Harvey	Regina G.	inc
Oct.	3	1958	25977	Harvey	Regina G., etc.	d
Nov.	30	1939	13826	Harvey	Robert L.	d
		[1880-1881]	1096	Harvey	Sarah V.	m
Mar.	23	1958	26177	Harwood	Marshall L.	m
Aug.		1937	13086	Haryes	R. R.	d
		1924	8699	Hasbrouck	Ed	d
		[1910-1911]	4994	Hasbrouck	Hiram B.	d
		[1910-1911]	4936	Hasbrouck	Sherman	inc
Oct.	26	1927	9713	Hasck	Frank	d
Feb.	10	1958	25281	Hasek	Ladislav F.	d
Jan.	10	1958	25281	Hasek	Ladislav F., etc.	d
May	9	1954	22443	Haselden	Grace Eliza	d
		1879	1033	Hashronck	Acelia	d
Mar.	10	1936	12523	Haskall	Emma A., etc.	d
		[1884-1885]	1393	Haskell	Abigail	d
		1887	1610	Haskell	Barnabus	d
		[1888-1889]	1749	Haskell	Emma G.	m
Jan.	19	1950	20111	Haskell	George E.	d
Feb.	21	1944	15848	Haskell	H. J.	d
Dec.	8	1953	22219	Haskell	Hiram A.	d
Feb.	28	1944	15808	Haskell	Virginia	d
Jan.	29	1957	24497	Haskell	William Burton, etc.	d
Nov.	14	1914	5867	Haskell	Wm. B.	d
Aug.	26	1948	18537	Haskett	Elizabeth, etc.	d
July		1914	5812	Hasking	Mary Jane Elizabeth	d
Mar.	15	1946	17003	Haskins	Francis L.	d
Feb.	8	1951	20140	Haskins	Pearl	d
Mar.	3	1953	21676	Haslehurst	William E., etc.	d
Aug.	18	1938	13378	Hasper	Bertha	d
Dec.	22	1947	18103	Hasper	Cora May, etc.	d
Nov.	19	1956	24279	Hasper	Henry, etc.	d
Dec.		1905	4016	Hasper	William	d
Oct.	10	1929	10430	Hasper	William	m
Sept.	31	1945	16703	Hass	Marie	d
		[1892-1893]	2252	Hassett	Aaron	d
Oct.	5	1956	24257	Hassett	Byron W.	d
		[1892-1893]	2283	Hassett	Carrie Josephine	m
		[1887-1888]	1650	Hassett	John	d
		[1899-1900]	3087	Hassett	M. L. J.	d
		[1908-1909]	4445	Hassett	Sarah E.	d

Month	Day	Year	File No.		Surname	Given Name	Type
		[1909-1910]	4787		Hasting	W. R.	d
Sept.	15	1950	19876		Hastings	Alice M.	d
Mar.	24	1953	21721		Hastings	Allison W., etc.	d
Jan.	29	1957	24496		Hastings	Cynthia J.	m
		1872	536		Hastings	Isaac	d
Jan.	28	1927	9792		Hastings	J. M., Mrs., etc.	d
Feb.	29	1957	24496		Hastings	Judith A.	m
Nov.	4	1930	10752		Hastings	Mary C., etc.	d
July	18	1953	21958		Hastings	Maude Leslie	d
Mar.	19	1956	23874		Hastings	W. W., etc.	d
Feb.	29	1957	24496		Hastings	William Walton II	m
		1893	2299		Hatch	C. P.	d
		[1892-1893]	2253		Hatch	Chester P. (1)	inc
		[1892-1893]	2256		Hatch	Chester P. (2)	inc
Dec.		1920	7619		Hatch	J. F.	d
Nov.	5	1914	5894		Hatch	Mary Jane	d
Jan.	14	1949	19366		Hatch	Emma T.	d
Dec.	1	1950	20077		Hatch	Gilbert Edward	d
Feb.	26	1924	8554		Hatcher	George J., etc.	d
Jan.	8	1938	13212		Hatcher	Mary	d
		1873	596		Hatfield	Francis J.	m
		[1881-1882]	1146		Hatfield	Francis J.	m
		1873	596		Hatfield	Joseph A.	m
		[1881-1882]	1146		Hatfield	Joseph A.	m
		1873	596		Hatfield	Rebecca	m
		[1881-1882]	1146		Hatfield	Rebecca	m
		1873	596		Hatfield	William P.	m
		[1881-1882]	1146		Hatfield	Wm. C.	m
Oct.	12	1914	5839		Hathaway	Edward L.	d
Jan.	14	1928	9835		Hathaway	Emily	d
Sept.	28	1931	11063		Hathaway	Harriet K. E.	d
Dec.	6	1923	8473		Hathaway	Rulief D.	d
Dec.	3	1917	6575		Hathway	Deloir George	d
Nov.	15	1952	21456		Hattam	David A.	m
Nov.	15	1952	21456		Hattam	Edward A., Jr.	m
Nov.	15	1952	21456		Hattam	Paul L.	m
		[1908-1909]	4431		Hattie	George	m
		[1908-1909]	4431		Hattie	John	m
		[1908-1909]	4431		Hattie	Minnie	m
		[1908-1909]	4431		Hattie	Sadie	m
Nov.		1924	8781		Hatton	David	d
June	7	1954	22572		Hatton	Hermina, etc.	d

Month	Day	Year	File No.		Surname	Given Name	Type
		1916	6359		Hatton	James Ellis	d
Jan.	28	1918	6653		Hatton	Richard Earl	d
Jan.	15	1954	22284		Hattua	Nicholas Andrew	d
Feb.	2	1943	15256		Haub	Charles F.	d
		[1900-1901]	3229		Haubrich	Peter	d
		1906	4043		Haubrich	Sarah	d
		[1910-1911]	4991		Haun	James W.	d
		1903	3624		Haupt	Charles	d
		[1919-1920]	7261		Haupt	Charles William	d
Aug.	7	1931	10936		Haupt	Freda	m
June	18	1936	12618		Haupt	Julia	d
Aug.	7	1931	10936		Haupt	Mary Eleanor	m
Sept.	21	1934	12028		Haurat	Frank	d
Dec.	24	1952	21535		Hauri	Martha Bradley	d
		[1873-1874]	635		Hausch	Anna B.	m
		[1873-1874]	635		Hausch	Charles H.	m
		[1873-1874]	635		Hausch	Elsey	m
		[1873-1874]	635		Hausch	Flora	m
		[1873-1874]	635		Hausch	Hannah M.	m
		[1873-1874]	635		Hausch	Henrietta	m
		[1873-1874]	635		Hausch	Joseph	m
July	5	1957	24855		Hauser	Edith May	d
June	25	1958	25727		Hauser	Mary F.	d
May	18	1932	11277		Hausmann	John	d
Oct.	12	1950	19924		Hausmann	John M., etc.	d
		1899	2970		Haustman	Ernest A.	d
		1907	4344		Hauto	Anna	m
		1907	4344		Hauto	Dora	m
		1907	4344		Hauto	Edward	m
		1907	4344		Hauto	Elsa	m
		1907	4344		Hauto	Ernest	m
		1907	4344		Hauto	Marie	m
		1907	4344		Hauto	Olga	m
		[1904-1905]	3858		Haven	Elsie E.	m
May		1918	6705		Haven	Maud Irene	d
Feb.	28	1952	20884		Haven	Ida C.	d
Mar.	21	1950	19527		Havenstrite	Rose A., etc.	d
Feb.	18	1944	15844		Havenstrite	Walter B., etc.	d
Nov.	25	1927	9756		Hawes	Henry	d
May	16	1915	5961		Hawk	Annie	d
Mar.	21	1955	23072		Hawk	Ethel J.	d
July	12	1955	23368		Hawk	Russell J., etc.	d

Month	Day	Year	File No.	Surname	Given Name	Type
Apr.	17	1958	25559	Hawkes	Joseph	d
June	1	1951	20374	Hawkins	Alfred T.	d
Jan.	2	1933	11734	Hawkins	Arthur O., etc.	d
Feb.	23	1931	11175	Hawkins	Clifton Worth, etc.	d
May	23	1958	25645	Hawkins	Edith, etc.	d
		1918	6864	Hawkins	Helen Anthony	m
July	21	1953	21965	Hawkins	James, etc.	m
		[1866-1868]	342	Hawkins	Jesse	d
		1891	2074	Hawkins	Joseph	d
		1888	1719	Hawkins	L. J.	d
		1888	1717	Hawkins	Mamie	m
		1888	1717	Hawkins	Mark	m
		1888	1717	Hawkins	Maud	m
Mar.	24	1943	15334	Hawkins	Oliver	d
Feb.	10	1950	19455	Hawkins	Wrena, etc.	d
Mar.	27	1953	21666	Hawkinson	Harry A.	d
July	16	1948	18525	Hawthorn	Clara A.	d
July	16	1948	18525	Hawthorn	Oliver B.	d
Nov.	15	1927	9744	Hawthorne	Mary E.	inc
Nov.	25	1955	23551	Hawthorne	Walter B., etc.	d
		1903	3626	Hayden	Birdie	m
		1921	7804	Hayden	Catherine P.	d
		1903	3626	Hayden	Richard	m
		1903	3626	Hayden	Rodney	m
May	24	1934	11933	Haydn	Stephen	d
Feb.	24	1945	16437	Hayes	Annie G.	d
Sept.	22	1956	24178	Hayes	Clara May	inc
July	18	1956	24051	Hayes	Hazel Lenora	m
Apr.		1925	8875	Hayes	Henry Lawrence, etc.	d
Feb.	27	1956	23756	Hayes	James	d
		1938	13269	Hayes	Julian	d
July	17	1933	11666	Hayes	Martin	d
		[1888-1889]	1815	Hayes	Rosa	m
		[1883-1884]	1367	Hayes	Thomas	d
		[1892-1893]	2204	Hayes	Thomas	d
Apr.	24	1944	15851	Hayes	Thomas	d
July	13	1947	17849	Hayg	Joseph	d
Feb.	18	1922	8224	Hayishi	Kyosuke	d
		[1908-1909]	4480	Hayme	Joseph	d
Aug.		1924	8719	Haymond	Edward Oer	m
Feb.	26	1953	21664	Hayner	A. Eldred	d
Dec.	4	1935	12453	Hayner	Lydia	inc

Month	Day	Year	File No.	Surname	Given Name	Type
Jan.	3	1936	12510	Hayner	Lydia	d
Apr.	2	1952	21026	Haynes	Albin Anthony, etc.	d
		1919	7190	Haynes	Charlotte Grace	g
Mar.	12	1956	23848	Haynes	Clarence Asa, etc.	d
July	15	1942	14985	Haynes	Walter H., etc.	d
		[1908-1909]	4443	Haynes	William H.	d
July	28	1919	7070	Haynie	Bella May	m
Mar.	6	1945	16458	Hays	Albert, Jr.	m
Mar.	6	1945	16459	Hays	Albert, Sr.	d
Mar.	6	1956	23837	Hays	Gertrude Adams, etc.	d
		[1909-1910]	4691	Hays	Harriet I.	d
		[1886-1887]	1582	Hays	Mary Jane	d
Jan.	24	1945	16898	Hays	Pauline C.	d
		1871	481	Hays	S. M.	d
Sept.	29	1940	14124	Hays	W. T., etc.	d
		1924	8605	Hays	Wilfred B.	d
		[1894-1895]	2415	Hayselden	Catherine	d
Dec.	30	1956	24358	Hayward	Addie May	d
Nov.		1926	9409	Hayward	Celia A.	d
May	8	1946	17129	Hayward	Florence T.	d
Oct.	26	1912	5404	Hayward	Harry Lewis & Martin George	m
		1924	8647	Hayward	Martin George	inc
Oct.	11	1925	9053	Hayward	Martin George	d
		[1884-1885]	1427	Hayward	Mary	d
Apr.	9	1914	5735	Hayward	Sallie P.	d
Apr.	6	1936	12574	Haywood	Etta May	inc
May	16	1936	12614	Haywood	Etta May	d
Apr.	19	1951	20284	Haywood	Freida Olivia	m
Feb.	9	1943	15271	Hazen	Myra	inc
Apr.	10	1943	15375	Hazen	Myra	inc
Apr.	22	1947	17758	Hazen	Myra F.	inc
Nov.	4	1949	19346	Hazen	Myra F.	d
Mar.	26	1945	16443	Head	Eva M., etc.	inc
May	9	1930	10596	Head	R. May, etc.	d
Sept.	10	1951	20535	Heagney	W. D.	d
		[1897-1898]	2807	Heald	Daniel G.	d
Aug.	3	1934	12014	Heald	Edwin D.	d
		[1856-1858]	54	Heald	Elizabeth	d
Apr.	9	1923	8305	Heald	Elizabeth	d
		1861	196	Heald	George W.	m
		[1858-1859]	134	Heald	Harmon G.	d
Oct.	15	1952	21340	Heald	Henrietta E.	d

Month	Day	Year	File No.	Surname	Given Name	Type
		[1895-1896]	2572	Heald	Jacob G.	d
		[1873-1874]	599	Heald	John E.	m
Jan.	31	1957	25245	Heald	Marjorie Elsie	inc
Aug.	22	1955	23380	Heald	Mary L., etc.	d
		1904	3736	Heald	Rachel	d
Sept.		1925	9029	Heald	Thomas T.	d
Sept.	14	1937	13124	Healey	Claire	m
		1922	8198	Healey	Dennis J.	d
Nov.	9	1956	24324	Healey	Julia H./J. H., Mrs./Julia E./W	d
Sept.	14	1937	13124	Healey	Katherine	m
Mar.	5	1929	10199	Healey	Margaret Elsie, etc.	d
Oct.	14	1952	21399	Healey	William E., etc.	d
Feb.	20	1945	16365	Healy	Letta	d
Apr.	16	1945	16475	Healy	Thomas M.	d
May	5	1959	26185	Heaney	Pauline J.	d
Sept.	1	1944	16110	Heantugsen	Johanna	d
Apr.	15	1935	12159	Heard	Jessie	d
Nov.		1926	9421	Heard	Roland	d
Oct.	6	1941	14667	Hearn	William	d
		[1910-1911]	4909	Hearne	Fred E.	d
		1911	5174	Hearne	Thomas J.	d
July	18	1945	16654	Hearns	Charles	d
Apr.	30	1951	20299	Hearon	Oliver	inc
Nov.	30	1951	20706	Hearon	Oliver	d
		[1885-1886]	1514	Heath	Barbara M.	d
		1924	8768	Heath	Clarence	d
Oct.	21	1927	9676	Heath	E. F.	d
Oct.	5	1950	19911	Heath	Mary Rogene	d
Nov.	4	1944	16200	Heatly	Emily	d
		[1919-1920]	7402	Heaton	Charles C.	d
May	25	1925	8917	Heaton	Robert Bruce	d
		[1909-1910]	4700	Heaton	S. O.	d
		[1903-1904]	3721	Hebard	Charles	d
June	25	1917	6473	Heberling	Leonard L.	d
Oct.	24	1951	20630	Hebert	Ernest Joseph, etc.	d
		1922	8051	Hebert	John B.	d
		[1898-1899]	2898	Hebron	Henry	d
Apr.	22	1958	25572	Hechtle	Eugene	d
Feb.	16	1928	9838	Hedge	John W.	d
		1907	4334	Hedges	Nellie L.	d
Mar.	20	1931	10886	Hediger	Emily	m
May	26	1941	14530	Hediger	Emily, etc.	d

Month	Day	Year	File No.	Surname	Given Name	Type
Mar.	15	1924	8572	Hediger	G. A. Eugene	d
Apr.	20	1931	10886	Hediger	Hilda	m
Mar.	9	1955	23107	Hedrick	Donald E., etc.	d
Apr.	18	1955	23181	Hedrick	Lela M., etc.	d
		1919	7172	Hedrick	Richard Wayne	g
		[1877-1879]	865	Heffel	Robert	d
Mar.	17	1952	20989	Heflen	Barbara	m
June	16	1953	21892	Heflin	Barbara Jean	d
June	13	1955	23314	Heflin	Brenda	m
Mar.	3	1955	23098	Heflin	Junior C.	d
June	13	1955	23314	Heflin	Linda	m
Dec.		1920	7557	Hefti	John, etc.	d
Feb.	22	1919	6965	Hefty	Anna M.	d
Dec.	11	1937	13156	Hefty	Fred, etc.	d
Nov.	13	1917	6562	Hefty	Lydia	d
Oct.	14	1918	6808	Hefty	Walter John	m
Dec.	20	1939	13847	Hegel	John H.	d
		[1873-1874]	627	Hegeler	Gerhard et al	m
		[1873-1874]	612	Hegeler	J. H. J.	d
		[1873-1874]	611	Hegeler	Maria del Carmen	d
Mar.	5	1951	20252	Heggie	Gabrielle F.	d
Feb.	17	1958	25295	Heggie	Norman John, etc.	d
		1882	1220	Hegler	Gerhard, Sr.	d
		[1901-1902]	3352	Hegmann	Gustaf	d
		[1910-1911]	4941	Heidorn	Claus	d
Oct.	14	1933	11714	Heidorn	Henry	d
May	23	1955	23267	Heilmann	Lena, etc.	d
Dec.	1	1942	15173	Heim	Mabel I.	d
June	23	1953	21904	Hein	Dawson Peter, etc.	d
Feb.	25	1954	22306	Hein	Fred G.	d
Jan.	20	1957	25232	Hein	Henry B.	d
Dec.	20	1957	25232	Hein	Mark, etc.	d
		1907	4376	Hein	Peter C.	d
Aug.	11	1929	10350	Heine	Bertha	d
Mar.	27	1946	17106	Heine	Frederich Ferdinand	d
Sept.	5	1947	17984	Heinemann	Oluf John, etc.	d
Mar.	7	1933	11535	Heinke	Horst	d
Sept.	3	1953	21990	Heinrich	Albert Gustave, etc.	d
Mar.	22	1935	12237	Heinrich	Bruno	d
Mar.	7	1927	9532	Heinrich	Dorette	d
Aug.	2	1946	17322	Heinsen	George Edlef	d
Feb.	30	1931	10852	Heinsen	Henry	d

Month	Day	Year	File No.	Surname	Given Name	Type
	7	1913	5593	Heintz	A.	d
Oct.	10	1940	14176	Heintz	Albert (terminate joint tenanc	d
May	23	1942	14908	Heintz	Charlotte	d
July	14	1951	20438	Heintz	Lena	d
Oct.	25	1953	22080	Heintz	Leston T.	d
Nov.	8	1912	5427	Heintz	Marie E. C.	d
Dec.	1	1955	23619	Heise	Martha C.	d
		[1890-1891]	1966	Heisel	Caroline	m
Nov.		1913	5643	Heisel	Ellen	d
		[1890-1891]	1966	Heisel	John	m
June	5	1958	25674	Heisel	John E., etc.	d
		[1890-1891]	1966	Heisel	Nellie	m
		[1890-1891]	1937	Heisel	Paul	d
		[1890-1891]	1966	Heisel	Paul	m
June	27	1958	25653	Heisil	John	con
		1901	3301	Heitmann	Bernhard	d
		[1901-1902]	3397	Heitmann	William	m
Nov.	4	1935	12452	Heitz	Louis	d
Sept.	21	1951	20625	Heitz	Margaret	ins
July	17	1953	21955	Heitz	Patricia	m
July	17	1953	21955	Heitz	Richard	m
July	21	1953	21962	Heitz	Wilbur, etc.	d
July	17	1953	21955	Heitz	William	m
June	28	1936	12651	Heitz	Frederick, Sr.	d
Sept.	20	1928	10023	Helberg	Fred/Jan F.	d
Sept.	21	1933	11671	Helberg	Frederick	d
		1926	9433	Helberg	Lulu Agnes	d
June	20	1913	5544	Helberg	Meta C.	d
		1926	9374	Helberg	Wm. O., etc.	d
		[1875-1876]	750	Held	Henrietta G.	m
Sept.	21	1933	11669	Held	Marie A.	d
July	2	1949	19112	Held	Robert Jeffry	m
Sept.	3	1948	18608	Helden	Ted E.	d
Nov.	7	1955	23576	Heller	Lloyd S., etc.	d
Jan.	4	1944	15747	Heller	Nancy J., etc.	d
Nov.	7	1955	23576	Heller	Sam, etc.	d
		1918	6702	Heller	Wilhelmina	d
June	2	1951	20376	Hellgren	Tobias R., etc.	d
Dec.	4	1944	16301	Helliard	H .P.	d
		[1877-1879]	915	Hellsten	Charles	d
Jan.	28	1957	24491	Helm	Lena	inc
Aug.	11	1919	7158	Helm	Magdalena	d

Month	Day	Year	File No.	Surname	Given Name	Type
		[1897-1898]	2733	Helm	Mary E.	d
Mar.	21	1947	17703	Helman	A. S. Grant, etc.	d
June		1912	5338	Helman	Edwin	d
Dec.	24	1958	26034	Helman	Lula	d
Dec.		1923	8464	Helman	Minnie, etc.	d
May	12	1949	19077	Helman	T. Evelyn	d
		[1908-1909]	4486	Helman	William	d
Nov.	24	1958	26033	Helman	William C., etc.	d
Dec.	30	1956	24359	Helmke	Edward Christian	d
Mar.	4	1946	17046	Helterline	George	d
		[1873-1874]	657	Hembree	A. F.	d
Jan.	7	1933	11494	Hembree	Andrew J.	d
June	8	1942	14933	Hembree	Atlas T., etc.	d
Aug.	15	1957	24952	Hembree	Clara C.	d
Feb.	7	1933	11495	Hembree	Mary E.	d
Mar.	17	1955	23119	Hemenover	F. Hadley	d
		1902	3414	Hemenway	George	d
		1903	3632	Hemker	Henry	d
Feb.	21	1944	15849	Hemminger	Cyril	d
	22	1919	6962	Hemphill	David	d
Feb.	28	1923	8292	Hemphill	Isabella	d
Feb.	16	1923	8282	Hemphill	Robert	d
July	13	1953	21938	Hemstalk	Kenneth George	m
Jan.	16	1937	13191	Hend	Thomas	d
		1907	4330	Henderlong	John E.	d
July	16	1943	15516	Henderlong	William R.	d
Jan.	24	1924	8835	Henderson	Alexander O.	d
May	23	1955	23265	Henderson	Frank Orville, etc.	d
Aug.	14	1913	5572	Henderson	John	d
Nov.	28	1952	21427	Henderson	Katherin A., etc.	d
		1911	5195	Henderson	Mary	d
Jan.	26	1955	22999	Henderson	Maude F., etc.	d
May	26	1952	21139	Henderson	Priscillia, etc.	d
Aug.	23	1923	8419	Henderson	Alice J.	d
Mar.	25	1957	24550	Hendler	Fred A.	d
		1911	5168	Hendley	Charles B.	d
		1885	1465	Hendley	Frank P.	m
		1911	5167	Hendley	George W.	d
		1885	1461	Hendley	Harriet E.	d
		1875	736	Hendley	John	d
Sept.	1	1929	10367	Hendley	Lucy B.	d
		1885	1465	Hendley	William G.	m

Month	Day	Year	File No.	Surname	Given Name	Type
Nov.	1	1955	23568	Hendreckson	James B.	d
Aug.	9	1937	13089	Hendren	James A.	d
May	15	1948	18347	Hendren	Margaret Isabelle, etc.	d
Mar.	22	1937	12869	Hendren	Olive M.	d
Sept.	9	1937	13089	Hendren	V. Marshall	d
Aug.	5	1957	24929	Hendricks	Beatrice	inc
Feb.	20	1956	23740	Hendricks	Beatrice E.	inc
Jan.	5	1938	13209	Hendricks	Elizabeth W.	d
Feb.	10	1930	10519	Hendricks	J. M.	d
		1903	3643	Hendricks	Leon	m
		[1899-1900]	3128	Hendricks	M. C.	d
		[1902-1903]	3513	Hendricks	Maud Rea	d
		[1908-1909]	4602	Hendricks	Whitley F.	d
Aug.	15	1957	24879	Hendricks	William Thomas, etc.	d
		[1897-1898]	2740	Hendricksen	Henry	m
		[1897-1898]	2740	Hendricksen	Mary	m
		[1897-1898]	2740	Hendricksen	Nicholas	m
		1911	5185	Hendrickson	Arthur	d
Apr.	17	1958	25467	Hendrickson	Henry P.	d
Sept.	8	1952	21326	Hendrickson	Mary Elizabeth, etc.	d
Aug.	6	1934	11989	Hendrix	Frank M.	d
Feb.	18	1938	13221	Hendrix	Granville Lloyd	d
		[1899-1900]	2980	Hendrix	Lewis	d
Dec.	25	1955	23612	Hendrix	William A., etc.	d
Mar.	24	1943	15335	Hendryx	Ben	d
Sept.	12	1930	10703	Heneghan	Anthony J.	d
	4	1913	5586	Henelly	Ellen	d
May	23	1928	9952	Henelly	John F., etc.	d
Jan.	12	1917	6595	Henelly	Mary C.	d
		[1908-1909]	4609	Henelly	Patrick	d
May	27	1933	11570	Henke	Gerhardt S., etc.	d
Sept.	28	1957	24986	Henke	John T.	d
Sept.	8	1958	25905	Henley	Ellen A.	d
		[1890-1891]	1998	Henley	Jonathan S.	d
Jan.	22	1944	16337	Hennard	Christinn	d
Dec.	3	1956	24365	Hennenhofer	Peter Silas, etc	d
		[1866-1868]	325	Hennessey	Daniel	d
July	18	1951	20496	Hennessy	James	d
Aug.	12	1955	23430	Henning	Margaret A.	inc
Mar.	23	1943	15286	Henninger	Dora	d
July	30	1952	21227	Henninger	Henry	d
		1937	12924	Henninger	Marvelle L.	d

Month	Day	Year	File No.		Surname	Given Name	Type
Feb.	5	1952	20899		Henningsen	Andres C.	d
Aug.	20	1944	16092		Henny	Emily, etc.	d
Apr.	2	1951	20304		Henricks	Albertina K., etc.	d
Feb.	1	1943	15253		Henricksen	Theresa Esmeralda	d
Oct.		1921	7865		Henrickson	Charles F.	d
Oct.	3	1958	25978		Henry	Eve Hughey, etc.	d
		1870	453		Henry	James, Sr.	d
Apr.	6	1951	20319		Henry	Pat O.	d
June	10	1954	22538		Hensler	Joseph R.	d
July	28	1950	19786		Hensler	Walter Henry, etc.	d
		1905	3991		Hensley	Jennie A.	d
June	23	1953	21857		Hensley	P. C., Mrs.	d
Jan.	13	1951	20798		Henze	Nancy Eliza	d
Sept.	19	1958	25941		Henzi	William	d
June	29	1956	24022		Herbert	Abbie C., etc.	d
Aug.	22	1942	14989		Herbert	Abbie Mary, etc.	d
		[1890-1891]	2005		Herbert	Alexander	d
Jan.	4	1936	12512		Herbert	Lewis	d
Nov.	27	1912	5405		Herbst	Theresa	inc
Oct.	5	1922	8156		Herbst	Theresa	d
July	19	1948	18527		Herburger	Burene	m
Aug.	15	1930	10679		Hereford	Thomas	d
May		1937	12966		Hereman	Allie	d
		[1897-1898]	2721		Herges	Mary E.	m
Sept.	26	1945	16737		Herkley	Olive D.	d
Mar.	20	1958	25398		Herlihy	Patrick T., etc.	d
		1903	3693		Herlin	Charles	d
May	30	1943	15389		Herman	Albert	d
		1921	7841		Herman	Allie	d
Mar.	15	1940	13962		Herman	Ezra A.	d
Feb.	15	1915	6130		Herman	Joseph	d
Aug.	23	1915	6057		Herman	Julius F.	d
Sept.	14	1937	13105		Herman	Mary Katharine	d
Apr.	24	1953	21720		Hermann	Albert	d
Dec.	24	1944	16290		Hermann	Margaretha B.	inc
Feb.	22	1945	16367		Hermann	Margaretha B.	d
Oct.	6	1941	14668		Hermansen	Herman Christian, etc.	d
Feb.	18	1955	23068		Hermansen	Sine	d
Jan.	5	1947	18120		Hermanson	Gustaf Adolf	d
Apr.	20	1914	5769		Hermer	Jochim	d
July	27	1914	5776		Hermer	Mary E.	inc
Sept.	4	1925	9047		Hermer	Mary E.	d

Month	Day	Year	File No.	Surname	Given Name	Type
		[1883-1884]	1319	Hermon	Maud Blench	a
Apr.	4	1950	19611	Hern	Lloyd	d
Sept.	14	1958	25854	Hernandez	Melburgo Ocampo, etc.	d
Apr.		1924	8626	Herne	Agnes	d
July	30	1933	11654	Herold	Harry	d
Aug.	4	1950	19850	Herold	Katy, etc.	d
July	28	1944	16058	Herr	A. G., etc.	d
July	20	1955	23327	Herr	Gail	m
Aug.	24	1955	23458	Herr	Jane B.	d
July	20	1955	23327	Herr	Jonathan Guthrie	m
		1870	455	Herren	William G.	d
Aug.	26	1948	18535	Herrick	Albert Benjamin, Jr.	d
May	9	1940	14023	Herrick	Albert Benjamin, III	m
Nov.	26	1948	18701	Herring	Edward H.	d
Aug.	18	1934	12026	Herrmann	Anton, etc.	d
		[1891-1892]	2134	Herrmann	Christopher	d
		1876	790	Herron	Amy	m
		1876	790	Herron	Bell	m
July	18	1951	20494	Herron	Mellie Frances C.	inc
Oct.	20	1951	20687	Hersch	Harold S.	inc
Apr.	21	1952	21003	Hersch	Harold S.	d
		[1877-1879]	947	Hershberger	Charles	m
		[1877-1879]	947	Hershberger	Frank	m
Aug.	25	1955	23384	Hertert	Agnes	d
		[1891-1892]	2130	Herth	W. G. A.	d
Mar.	29	1936	12568	Hertz	Anna	ins
Nov.	13	1936	12774	Hertz	Anna	d
Feb.	22	1946	16956	Hertz	Franklin Joseph, etc.	d
Mar.	20	1958	25401	Hertz	Hilma	inc
		1910	4807	Hervey	Alice Ann	d
		[1875-1876]	748 1/2	Hervey	Ella	m
		1905	3973	Hervey	Nelson B.	d
Sept.	30	1943	15535	Heryford	Daisy C.	d
Jan.	19	1931	11168	Heryford	Josie	d
Dec.	28	1916	6356	Herzog	Frank	d
Apr.	6	1951	20314	Heselschwerdt	Katie Lee	inc
Nov.	19	1951	20751	Heselschwerdt	Katie Lee	d
May	1	1950	19663	Heselschwerdt	O. F.	d
Oct.	1	1948	18654	Hesing	Harriet June	d
Aug.	8	1956	24152	Heske	Ernest	d
		[1896-1897]	2633	Hesketh	William M.	d
		1863	223	Hesler	Phillip	d

Month	Day	Year	File No.	Surname	Given Name	Type
Aug.	14	1946	17345	Hespe	Amy E., etc.	d
Jan.	4	1957	24432	Hess	Carl	d
		1911	5157	Hess	E. J.	d
Jan.	29	1952	21539	Hess	Emma	d
Apr.	27	1956	23891	Hess	Frank G.	d
		[1888-1889]	1757	Hess	Frederick	d
		1912	5299	Hess	John	d
Aug.	30	1941	14566	Hess	John R.	d
		[1910-1911]	5012	Hess	Louisa	d
		1918	6758	Hess	Sophie, etc.	d
Aug.	26	1935	12387	Hesse	George William	m
Nov.	31	1947	18074	Hesse	Louis	d
Feb.		1932	11375	Hesse	Milton	m
Aug.	18	1936	12684	Hesse	Milton	d
Oct.	26	1935	12387	Hesse	Nancy Ann	m
Mar.	13	1952	20978	Hesse	Peter C., etc.	d
Oct.	26	1935	12387	Hesse	Richard Henry	m
Aug.	21	1934	12027	Hesse	Walter E.	d
Mar.		1919	7000	Hessel	Andrew	d
Oct.	13	1950	19976	Hessel	Anna Amelia	d
Jan.	26	1950	20121	Hessel	Bertha	d
Nov.	20	1944	16278	Hessel	Elizabeth K., etc.	d
Dec.	7	1942	15181	Hessel	Eva Margaret, etc.	d
Jan.	29	1954	22949	Hessell	Herbert W., etc.	d
Jan.	19	1940	14285	Hesseltine	Edward K., etc.	d
		1926	9300	Hesseltine	Ralph Hampton	d
Aug.	31	1952	21277	Hessler	Francis K.	d
Feb.	4	1938	13238	Hessler	Francis Kilian	m
Feb.	4	1938	13238	Hessler	Francis Killian	m
Feb.	4	1938	13238	Hessler	Rose Catherine	m
Feb.	4	1938	13238	Hessler	Rose Catherine	m
Apr.		1916	6407	Hesson	Jacob	d
		[1881-1882]	1156	Hester	John H.	d
		1912	5236	Hetchings	Mary	d
Oct.	15	1953	22117	Heublein	Minnie M.	d
		1918	6855	Heugit	John	d
Aug.		1918	6755	Heugitt	Jennie	d
		1955	23003	Heumader	Frances B.	d
Jan.	15	1955	22984	Heumader	Frances B., etc.	d
Feb.	6	1939	13526	Heushaw	Mary E.	d
Aug.	27	1956	24133	Hevel	Elmer	inc
June	8	1956	24036	Hevel	Persis A.	d

Month	Day	Year	File No.	Surname	Given Name	Type
Feb.	25	1952	20877	Heverin	Margaret J.	d
Sept.	31	1955	23472	Hewelcke	Louisa M., etc.	d
Sept.	31	1955	23472	Hewelke	Louisa M. Hart, etc.	d
Feb.	8	1948	18160	Hewelke	William A., etc.	d
May	22	1948	18406	Hewett	Dorothea S.	d
May	5	1949	19060	Hewett	Edith Cordelia, etc.	d
		[1910-1911]	5007	Hewitt	Chasel F.	d
Apr.	31	1930	10589	Hewitt	Emma, etc.	d
Nov.	10	1930	10755	Hewitt	Frances E.	ins
Sept.	21	1931	11058	Hewitt	Frances E.	d
Jan.	4	1951	20126	Hewitt	Helen C.	d
July	22	1945	16623	Hewitt	Henry Grant, etc.	d
June	16	1933	11614	Heyen	Henry B.	d
June	2	1947	17820	Heyward	Aaron	d
May	20	1951	20350	Heyward	Elaine	d
Feb.	29	1933	11801	Heyward	Frank	d
July	4	1951	20424	Heyward	Minnie C.	inc
July	18	1952	21203	Heyward	Minnie C.	d
Jan.	8	1952	20839	Hiatt	Effa M., etc.	d
		1916	6304	Hiatt	Franklin Lloyd	m
Jan.	23	1938	13519	Hiatt	Joseph G.	d
Dec.	19	1914	5903	Hiatt	L. N.	d
May	10	1957	24728	Hiatt	Miranda	d
Oct.	16	1937	13126	Hiatt	Robert N.	d
Jan.	25	1945	16903	Hiatt	Rovella I.	d
Oct.		1916	6304	Hiatt	Thomas Effa	m
Feb.	11	1949	18825	Hiatt	Wellington E.	d
Nov.		1922	8165	Hiatt	William Hardin	d
		1916	6304	Hiatt	William Shelford	m
Nov.	23	1924	8786	Hibbard	Nellie	d
		1914	5732	Hibbard	Summer C.	inc
Apr.	23	1914	5773	Hibbard	Summer C.	d
Nov.	28	1946	17410	Hibberd	Frederick F.	d
July	26	1915	6023	Hick	John	d
Dec.	9	1958	26134	Hickey	Charles Andrew	d
Mar.	21	1930	10559	Hickey	Jeremiah D.	ins
Nov.		1919	7204	Hickey	Mary Ann	d
Dec.	13	1957	25218	Hickey	May, etc.	d
May	14	1941	14478	Hickey	Patrick J.	d
May	5	1950	19671	Hickin	Benjamin	d
Nov.	28	1949	19337	Hickle	Frederic	d
		[1894-1895]	2459	Hicklin	Georgie	m

Month	Day	Year	File No.	Surname	Given Name	Type
		[1894-1895]	2459	Hicklin	Mable E.	m
Aug.	15	1957	24951	Hicklin	Roy N.	d
Feb.	23	1951	20175	Hickman	Bessie C.	d
May	9	1958	25613	Hickman	Enoch	d
Apr.	18	1926	9205	Hickman	Henry	d
Aug.	18	1952	21260	Hickman	Horace A.	inc
June	8	1953	21883	Hickman	Horace A.	d
Feb.	1	1930	10540	Hickman	J. G.	d
		[1910-1911]	4889	Hickok	Anna E.	d
Feb.	28	1948	18803	Hickox	Fred	d
Mar.	3	1949	18928	Hickox	Fred	d
Feb.	17	1956	23799	Hicks	Alvin L.	m
Oct.	17	1952	21407	Hicks	Archibald L., etc.	d
Feb.	17	1956	23799	Hicks	Archie L.	m
Feb.	17	1956	23799	Hicks	Audra L.	m
Mar.	31	1939	13629	Hicks	Ethel E.	d
Feb.	28	1944	15806	Hicks	George M.	d
Nov.	18	1927	9780	Hicks	Lucy B.	d
Dec.	24	1933	11773	Hicks	Margaret Phillis, etc.	d
Jan.	14	1952	20850	Hicks	Mary J.	d
		[1910-1911]	4847	Hicks	Moses C.	inc
Sept.	23	1925	8966	Hicks	Odia Valentine	d
		[1908-1909]	4591	Hicks	Sally	d
		[1897-1898]	2804	Hickson	Clarence	m
		[1897-1898]	2804	Hickson	Mabel	m
		[1897-1898]	2804	Hickson	Willie	m
		1872	541	Hiett	George	d
		[1854-1855]	51	Higara	Nicholas	d
Feb.	31	1936	12848	Higbee	Julia A., etc.	d
June	20	1929	10311	Higbie	Alfred H.	d
		[1887-1888]	1700	Higby	William	d
		[1904-1905]	3892	Higgins	Archibald Brown	d
		1901	3268	Higgins	Asa	d
Jan.	2	1940	14295	Higgins	Charles F. (terminate joint ten	d
Sept.	5	1958	25900	Higgins	Hubert C., etc.	d
Apr.	18	1928	9942	Higgins	Hubert Preston	m
		1901	3315	Higgins	Percy C.	m
Aug.	30	1958	25744	Higgins	Sandra Kay	m
		1896	2612	Higgins	Walter B.	d
Apr.	7	1954	22440	Higgs	Edwin T.	d
		[1919-1920]	7435	Higgs	Mary	d
July	17	1929	10342	Higgs	William T.	d

Month	Day	Year	File No.	Surname	Given Name	Type
Mar.	9	1937	12919	High	Alfred G., etc.	d
June	18	1945	16615	High	Rosalie	d
May	21	1942	14907	High	Rosalie, etc.	d
Sept.	19	1944	16181	Hilber	Julius	d
		[1895-1896]	2550	Hilberer	Marie A.	d
		1909	4681	Hilbrant	James A.	d
		[1871-1872]	488	Hilby	A.	m
		[1871-1872]	488	Hilby	F.	m
		[1861-1862]	204	Hilby	Francis M.	d
July	23	1950	19772	Hildebrand	W., etc.	d
Jan.	26	1939	13875	Hildebrandt	Albert M., etc.	d
		1927	9521	Hildebrandt	John	d
Sept.	8	1951	20593	Hilderbrandt	Norva	d
May	22	1954	22476	Hildreth	Olivia	d
Mar.	15	1952	20922	Hilgerloh	Mildred	d
May	9	1944	15973	Hilgerloh	Sierich	d
Jan.	21	1944	16335	Hilkerbannen	John W., etc.	d
Sept.		1922	8076	Hill	Alexander B.	d
Aug.	10	1948	18571	Hill	Alice M.	d
		[1876-1877]	821	Hill	Amos	ins
Oct.	1	1922	8130	Hill	Amos	d
		[1875-1876]	772	Hill	Anita	m
Dec.	20	1931	11112	Hill	Charles	d
June	28	1954	22554	Hill	Chester H.	d
Nov.	7	1927	9766	Hill	Dolph B., Jr.	m
	6	1923	8426	Hill	Dorothy Mae	g
Nov.	5	1948	18716	Hill	Elaine Maurice	m
	26	1926	9443	Hill	Elizabeth F.	d
Nov.	7	1927	9767	Hill	Elizabeth Higbee	m
Mar.	20	1951	20229	Hill	Ella, etc.	d
		[1895-1896]	2569	Hill	Emily	inc
		1922	8203	Hill	George	d
Dec.		1925	9136	Hill	Harriett Louise, etc.	d
Apr.	2	1952	21029	Hill	James Curtis	d
Apr.		1914	5763	Hill	James T.	d
Apr.	24	1955	23132	Hill	John W., etc.	d
May	6	1925	8952	Hill	John Wayne	inc
Nov.	2	1937	13134	Hill	John Wentworth	d
		1879	1040	Hill	Joshua G.	d
Jan.	15	1918	6644	Hill	Josie P.	d
Dec.	28	1952	21488	Hill	Kate Donohue	d
Nov.	7	1927	9766	Hill	Lewis Maney	m

Month	Day	Year	File No.	Surname	Given Name	Type
Oct.	30	1939	13713	Hill	Lillie T.	d
Jan.	21	1932	11483	Hill	Mary Z.	d
Nov.	18	1952	21462	Hill	Norman R.	d
Nov.	8	1957	25132	Hill	Olga Elizabeth	d
Apr.	25	1930	10561	Hill	Otis	d
Nov.	7	1927	9767	Hill	Raymond M., Jr.	m
		[1895-1896]	2587	Hill	Raymond P.	d
Mar.	18	1927	9568	Hill	Robert Cotter	d
		1916	6251	Hill	Samuel R.	d
		[1894-1895]	2472	Hill	Sarah	d
Aug.	1	1927	9663	Hill	Violet May	m
Nov.	7	1927	9766	Hill	William Fairbanks	m
Dec.	12	1944	16319	Hill	William J.	d
		[1897-1898]	2814	Hill	Wm. McPherson	d
May	10	1950	19687	Hillard	George Edwin	d
May	10	1950	19678	Hillard	George Edwin, etc.	d
Aug.	21	1946	17213	Hiller	Joseph C.	d
June	28	1958	25654	Hillhouse	Daisy M.	d
Mar.	28	1946	17034	Hilligso	Peter	d
July	20	1938	13354	Hillis	Louise	d
Apr.	15	1952	21058	Hillis	William	d
Nov.	4	1948	18657	Hillman	R. E.	d
Mar.	23	1946	17099	Hilloyd	Lizzie A.	d
Oct.	30	1955	23508	Hills	Percy J., etc.	d
		1907	4315	Hilmer	Louis	d
		[1910-1911]	4876	Hilmer	Louis, Jr.	d
		1924	8776	Himebauck	Jacob Denton	d
Jan.	30	1920	7634	Himes	Harmon	d
Apr.	28	1924	8620	Himes	Lydia Esther	d
Jan.		1918	6895	Himley	Edwin T.	d
Apr.	28	1929	10262	Himsbauch	Joseph Henry, etc.	d
Jan.	4	1929	10452	Hinchey	C. H.	ins
		1919	6995	Hinds	Edgar W.	d
June	6	1944	16025	Hinds	William S.	d
July	28	1932	11289	Hines	Frank B., etc.	d
Sept.	19	1957	24965	Hinis	Harry Kent, etc.	d
Mar.	26	1945	16442	Hinkelman	Auguste, etc.	d
July	17	1947	17853	Hinkelman	Clara Cecilia, etc.	d
Jan.	20	1946	17488	Hinkelman	Elizabeth	d
June	12	1947	17789	Hinkilman	Gustav A., etc.	d
		[1892-1893]	2171	Hinkston	Greenbury	d
		[1881-1882]	1142	Hinkston	Harlow	d

Month	Day	Year	File No.	Surname	Given Name	Type
		[1891-1892]	2096	Hinkston	Joseph R.	d
		[1900-1901]	3248	Hinkston	M. A. E.	d
		[1877-1879]	918	Hinkston	Nancy	inc
		[1884-1885]	1441	Hinkston	Nancy	d
		[1897-1898]	2755	Hinman	Miles	d
		[1887-1888]	1693	Hinrichs	Carl	ins
Dec.	3	1958	26053	Hinrichs	Herman F.	d
May	10	1935	12266	Hinrichsen	P. F., etc.	d
May	7	1935	12295	Hinrichsen	P. M., etc	d
Jan.	3	1958	25254	Hinricksen	Helena, etc.	d
Aug.	24	1946	17266	Hinshau	Albert Lee	d
June	6	1956	24030	Hinshaw	B. B., etc.	inc
Mar.	2	1956	23828	Hinshaw	Florence C.	inc
		1916	6287	Hinshaw	Harold A. et al	m
Jan.		1926	9467	Hinshaw	John David	d
		[1907-1908]	4393	Hinshaw	M. Lou	d
Mar.	29	1924	8589	Hinshaw	Rebecca E.	d
		1916	6287	Hinshaw	Roy F.	m
Dec.	16	1914	5899	Hinshaw	Sibry A.	d
		[1893-1894]	2362	Hinshaw	William Carter	d
		[1900-1901]	3232	Hinshaw	Wm. Petis	d
Jan.	13	1931	10836	Hinshey	C. H.	d
Dec.	1	1933	11778	Hinson	William Harmon	m
		[1881-1882]	1139	Hinton	Ann	m
Feb.	17	1948	18239	Hinton	Malonia M.	d
		[1881-1882]	1139	Hinton	Mary	m
June	7	1955	23300	Hinton	Melvin Vernon, etc.	d
		1865	280	Hinton	Otho	d
June	7	1955	23301	Hintze	Leo	d
May	7	1946	17192	Hintze	Sophia D.	d
Jan.	30	1954	22896	Hipkins	Charles L.	d
Dec.	25	1941	14714	Hippert	Florence	d
June	24	1943	15446	Hiram	Herbert	d
		1916	6287	Hirnhaw	Walter E.	m
		[1899-1900]	3018	Hirth	Albrecht	m
		1903	3533	Hirth	Frederick	d
		[1898-1899]	2915	Hirth	George	d
July	19	1913	5560	Hirth	Susanna, etc.	d
Jan.		1918	6929	Hisen	William Jackson	d
Aug.	2	1936	12659	Hiser	Nellie F.	d
		1927	9530	Hitchcock	Hiram	d
		1896	2599	Hitchcock	Hollis	d

Month	Day	Year	File No.	Surname	Given Name	Type
		1905	3910	Hitchcock	Leroy V.	d
Feb.	21	1938	13228	Hitchcock	Nellie N.	d
Oct.	21	1934	12057	Hiura	Asao	m
Oct.	21	1934	12057	Hiura	Toshiaki	m
Oct.	16	1956	24273	Hively	Emma A., etc.	d
Dec.	10	1948	18770	Hively	Norma L.	d
Dec.	30	1945	16855	Hixson	Jennie	d
Nov.	10	1939	13805	Hixson	John	d
July	15	1952	21250	Hixson	John, Jr.	d
Dec.	23	1953	22193	Hixson	Nellie F.	d
July	22	1955	23379	Hjort	Hans Petersen, etc.	d
Dec.	28	1951	20776	Hjort	Marie	d
Nov.	18	1927	9781	Hjort	Olaf Rye Petersen	d
Feb.	23	1953	21604	Hnningsen	Jans	d
Oct.	22	1936	12761	Hnson	Mary	d
		[1891-1892]	2121	Hoadley	George H.	m
Apr.	6	1915	5929	Hoadley	Harriet C.	d
		[1891-1892]	2109	Hoadley	J. F., Sr.	d
Sept.	7	1956	24200	Hoadley	Linda N., etc.	d
Mar.	25	1955	23088	Hoag	Edith Lillian, etc.	d
		1879	1039	Hoag	Hannah A.	d
Dec.	28	1931	11148	Hoaglund	Jonas	d
Dec.	10	1948	18773	Hoar	Emma	d
		1925	9078	Hoar	Jennie	d
		[1877-1879]	970	Hoar	Martin	d
Jan.	30	1941	14754	Hobbie	Annie G.	d
May	28	1950	19657	Hobbie	Ernest, etc.	d
Aug.		1921	7800	Hobbie	Johann Gerhard	d
Feb.	29	1943	15251	Hobbie	John	d
July	10	1956	24092	Hobbs	Dora	inc
Mar.	19	1929	10213	Hobbs	William H.	d
		[1897-1898]	2793	Hobson	Alfred D.	d
June	21	1943	15480	Hobson	Elida F.	d
June	24	1944	16000	Hobson	J. C., etc.	d
June	8	1948	18444	Hochelt	Beida E.	d
Oct.	19	1947	18007	Hochwarter	Joseph	inc
June	8	1947	17840	Hochwarter	Mary	d
Oct.	17	1946	17402	Hochwarter	John	d
June	24	1941	14528	Hockensmith	Thomas R.	d
Aug.	12	1919	7159	Hockin	William	d
June	27	1949	19103	Hocking	Edith Cordelia	d
Nov.	20	1951	20752	Hocking	Francis Albert, etc.	d

Month	Day	Year	File No.	Surname	Given Name	Type
June	18	1945	16615	Hocking	Minnie et al	d
Dec.	16	1934	12079	Hockman	Margaret P.	d
Mar.	17	1940	13935	Hockman	Theodore P.	d
Apr.	8	1945	16463	Hockstra	Jacob D.	d
Feb.	13	1948	18227	Hockwarter	Joseph, etc.	d
Oct.	9	1934	12074	Hodapp	Forrest W., etc.	d
Aug.	13	1937	13061	Hoddinott	Harry H.	d
		[1899-1900]	3013	Hodgdon	Matilda C.	d
		[1909-1910]	4703	Hodge	A. L.	d
		1922	8223	Hodge	Elizabeth G.	d
		1916	6197	Hodge	Levi F.	d
Mar.	16	1927	9563	Hodge	Robert	d
Mar.	23	1947	17689	Hodges	Anna Bassett, etc.	d
July	25	1948	18481	Hodges	C. R.	d
Aug.	6	1956	24146	Hodges	Elois F.	d
Apr.	26	1957	24614	Hodges	Elora F.	d
Dec.	10	1949	19360	Hodges	John B.	d
Jan.	11	1928	9833	Hodges	Mary Bassett	d
Jan.	10	1941	14341	Hodges	William M.	d
Apr.	13	1932	11227	Hodgson	David R.	d
		[1883-1884]	1358	Hodgson	Eunice	d
Apr.	2	1954	22313	Hodgson	Leticia A., etc.	d
		1905	4027	Hodgson	Richard	d
Jan.	26	1939	13876	Hoeckele	Amy	m
May	27	1937	12976	Hoeh	Fred	d
		1885	1493	Hoen	Berthold	d
Jan.	9	1929	10490	Hoen	Bertholda/Bertha, etc.	d
		[1898-1899]	2875	Hoen	Ernest	d
		[1891-1892]	2150	Hoen	Mary A.	d
July	13	1956	24097	Hoen	Mary Elizabeth, etc.	d
June	15	1956	24046	Hoffecker	Ralph W.	d
		1921	7831	Hoffer	Charles	d
		1882	1277	Hoffer	Christina	d
Jan.	2	1919	6931	Hoffer	Frederick	d
Dec.	29	1929	10450	Hoffer	Virgil	inc
Dec.	4	1947	18117	Hoffer	Virgil	d
Apr.	28	1932	11264	Hoffinan	Joseph E., etc.	d
		1903	3658	Hoffman	Catherine	d
Mar.	17	1949	18804	Hoffman	Dora	d
Dec.	3	1937	13184	Hoffman	Fred	d
Jan.	9	1925	8843	Hoffman	Frederick	d
Sept.	14	1936	12748	Hoffman	Howe C.	m

Month	Day	Year	File No.	Surname	Given Name	Type
June	29	1947	17770	Hoffman	Howe C.	d
Oct.	14	1936	12748	Hoffman	Jara	m
Sept.	10	1936	12726	Hoffman	Jean M. C.	d
July	29	1953	21913	Hoffman	Jemella	d
Sept.	14	1936	12748	Hoffman	Martha I.	m
Sept.	14	1936	12748	Hoffman	Martin	m
June	31	1955	23284	Hoffman	Norman Edward, etc.	d
Sept.	14	1936	12748	Hoffman	Sargent S., Jr.	m
June	31	1950	19733	Hoffmann	Charles Theodore	d
Feb.	19	1940	13898	Hoffmann	John (terminate joint tenancy)	d
July	16	1948	18523	Hoffmeyer	Howard	d
Sept.	26	1945	16738	Hoffschneider	William	m
		1885	1451	Hoffstetter	Eleanora	m
		1885	1451	Hoffstetter	Jeanne	m
		[1884-1885]	1409	Hofgaard	Charles	d
Aug.	17	1956	24167	Hofland	Theresa, etc.	d
Jan.	25	1952	20873	Hofmann	Anna	inc
Jan.	14	1955	22974	Hofmann	Anna	d
Jan.	18	1952	20857	Hofmann	Franz	d
May	17	1956	23931	Hofmann	Gene Leon, etc.	m
Feb.	8	1949	18895	Hofmann	N. W., etc.	d
Aug.	4	1950	19849	Hofmann	Otto	d
May	22	1949	19033	Hofmeister	Laura Jane	ins
Dec.	3	1932	11464	Hofmeyer	Frank	d
		[1894-1895]	2479	Hofstetter	B.	d
		[1895-1896]	2523	Hofstetter	Eleanore	m
		[1895-1896]	2523	Hofstetter	Jeanne	m
		[1889-1890]	1895	Hogan	Alice F.	d
Mar.	3	1945	16455	Hogan	Jack	d
		1921	7678	Hogan	Walter	d
Feb.	7	1935	12149	Hogue	Edward W., etc.	d
Mar.	15	1943	15276	Hogue	Helen, etc.	d
Dec.	21	1933	11772	Hohansen	Anders Martin	d
Nov.	7	1927	9765	Hohenshell	Jesse	d
Apr.	24	1943	15336	Hohnsee	James	d
May		1938	13305	Hohven	Charles Heylwood	d
Jan.	30	1920	7629	Holden	Josiah N.	d
Jan.	22	1927	9812	Holden	Sarah C.	d
Jan.	23	1948	18795	Holden	William Simon, etc.	d
		[1890-1891]	2008	Holivan	James	d
		[1899-1900]	3131	Holland	Annie F.	m
		1893	2307	Holland	Eliza C.	d

Month	Day	Year	File No.	Surname	Given Name	Type
		[1875-1876]	781	Holland	H. L.	d
Apr.	27	1942	14871	Holland	John A., etc.	d
		[1899-1900]	3131	Holland	Maggie M.	m
Mar.	2	1934	11847	Holland	May Gertrude, etc.	d
		[1899-1900]	3131	Holland	Michael H.	m
		[1898-1899]	2880	Holland	Samuel	d
June	16	1944	16044	Hollenbeak	Ralph	d
June	2	1958	25662	Holley	Benjamin L., etc.	d
		1864	253	Hollgrene	Henry	d
Jan.	10	1933	11740	Holliday	Albert	d
		[1866-1868]	360	Holliday	Joseph	d
May	24	1950	19723	Hollingsworth	Alice	d
Apr.	7	1958	25525	Hollingsworth	Frank	inc
May	12	1958	25615	Hollingsworth	Frank Wm.	d
Apr.	7	1958	25526	Hollingsworth	Mary Anna	inc
Sept.	10	1936	12745	Hollingsworth	Perry S.	d
July	11	1948	18449	Hollis	John	d
June	27	1930	10636	Hollister	John Wilson	d
		[1876-1877]	823	Hollister	S. E.	d
Oct.	26	1944	16188	Hollivan	James Thomas	d
Oct.	26	1944	16187	Hollivan	Margaret	d
Nov.	16	1951	20743	Hollmann	Mabel	inc
Aug.	11	1926	9310	Holloway	Addie M.	inc
July	21	1927	9634	Holloway	Charles	d
		1903	3592	Holloway	Cornelia	d
		1916	6294	Holloway	J. C.	d
Dec.	21	1924	8809	Holloway	J. W.	d
		1922	8202	Holloway	John, etc.	d
Dec.	24	1954	22887	Holloway	Mary	d
Mar.	3	1937	12912	Holloway	Mary A., etc.	d
May	28	1948	18366	Holm	Adolph A.	d
July	7	1953	21929	Holm	Chris F.	d
Nov.	27	1914	5889	Holm	George	d
		[1883-1884]	1300	Holm	John P.	d
June		1912	5329	Holm	Richard Erick	m
		[1901-1902]	3362	Holman	Alice	d
Nov.	4	1949	19348	Holman	Ben, etc.	d
		[1888-1889]	1791	Holman	Caroline N.	d
July	18	1943	15476	Holman	Ellen Mary/Mrs. Walter	d
		1860	164	Holman	Isaac A.	d
		[1904-1905]	3830	Holman	J. H. J.	d
Dec.	11	1942	15189	Holman	Nellie Isabel	d

Month	Day	Year	File No.	Surname	Given Name	Type
		[1890-1891]	2038	Holman	Wm. O.	d
Sept.		1922	8081	Holmboe	Even M.	d
May	27	1938	13332	Holmer	Lizzi, etc.	d
		1917	6615	Holmer	Jep	d
May	5	1952	21100	Holmes	Anna E.	d
		1907	4238	Holmes	Anna M.	d
May	17	1926	9257	Holmes	Charles Hazelwood, etc.	d
		[1899-1900]	3126	Holmes	Edward M.	d
		1872	565	Holmes	Elizabeth	d
		1908	4417	Holmes	Elvira E.	d
		1907	4372	Holmes	Estelle	m
Jan.	15	1943	15680	Holmes	Frank A.	d
July	24	1945	16662	Holmes	Hattie Austin, etc.	d
		[1888-1889]	1810	Holmes	Henry	d
		1906	4202	Holmes	Henry	d
Oct.	30	1958	25964	Holmes	James Stuart	m
Mar.	19	1929	10250	Holmes	Jasper, etc.	d
May	11	1948	18384	Holmes	John	d
		1882	1219	Holmes	Lucy F.	d
		1907	4372	Holmes	Neva	m
		[1897-1898]	2748	Holmes	Rebecca M.	d
		[1904-1905]	3773	Holmes	Sarah A.	d
July	2	1948	18411	Holmes	Stephen, etc.	d
		1904	3752	Holmes	William	d
Mar.	8	1940	13928	Holmes	William F.	d
		1858	99	Holoway	A. D.	d
		[1858-1859]	129	Holoway	George	m
		[1858-1859]	129	Holoway	Henrietta	m
		[1858-1859]	129	Holoway	Mary	m
		1922	8190	Holper	Ferdinand	d
May	6	1933	11604	Holpin	Nancy E., etc.	d
		1866	320	Holser	Conrad	d
Dec.	12	1944	16320	Holst	Henry	d
Feb.	8	1938	13241	Holst	Joseph A.	d
Apr.	18	1928	9940	Holst	Peter N.	d
		[1901-1902]	3376	Holstead	Robert	d
Apr.	18	1928	9939	Holstl	Caroline M.	d
		1926	9279	Holt	Annie, etc.	d
Feb.	7	1948	18212	Holt	Bert	d
Mar.	23	1946	17096	Holt	Clifford	d
Mar.	3	1947	17674	Holt	Helene C., etc.	d
Apr.	14	1947	17746	Holt	Henrietta Jane, etc.	d

Month	Day	Year	File No.	Surname	Given Name	Type
Nov.	10	1955	23583	Holt	Herbert R., etc.	d
June	6	1958	25677	Holt	John	d
		1893	2321	Holton	P. H.	d
Nov.	14	1929	10434	Holtorf	Hans J.	d
Nov.	3	1940	14218	Holtz	Antonne	d
Feb.	17	1940	13896	Holtzer	George	d
		[1895-1896]	2585	Holtzmann	Ben	d
Feb.	6	1933	11532	Homain	Patrick	d
Dec.	7	1946	17470	Homana	Alfred J.	d
Feb.	28	1941	14364	Hombery	Martin J.	d
		[1883-1884]	1325	Homes	Albert	d
		1902	3458	Homes	Carrie Edna	m
Mar.	15	1949	18902	Homes	Guy R.	d
Jan.	31	1956	24424	Homick	Mary	d
		1919	7125	Hommel	Ervine	d
Dec.	21	1950	20057	Hong	Sue Lai	d
Mar.	3	1939	13556	Honor	Henry	d
Mar.	26	1954	22362	Hons	Frances Martha	d
		[1885-1886]	1495	Hons	Hermann	d
June	8	1942	14935	Honsa	Joseph, etc.	d
Mar.	21	1949	18970	Honsmekin	George L.	d
Sept.	15	1949	19174	Honzik	Fanny	d
Aug.	22	1930	10689	Hood	Alonzo Abel, etc.	d
Jan.	16	1932	11477	Hood	Benjamin Henry, etc.	d
		[1877-1879]	888	Hood	Blancha	m
Mar.	20	1941	14406	Hood	Florence	d
		[1898-1899]	2821	Hood	George	d
Oct.		1923	8444	Hood	Isabella M.	d
		1921	7870	Hood	James G.	d
Oct.	27	1929	10422	Hood	Jennie	d
June	1	1939	13593	Hood	Laura Frances	d
June	1	1939	13593	Hood	Leonidas E,	d
Apr.	9	1931	10906	Hood	Margaret A.	d
Mar.	8	1937	12882	Hood	Neva Y.	d
Dec.	19	1936	12778	Hood	Nora Y.	inc
		1893	2331	Hood	Robert	d
		[1876-1877]	843	Hood	Sarah et al	m
		1902	3440	Hood	William	inc
		1903	3604	Hood	William	d
June	29	1950	19732	Hook	Cleo S.	d
Mar.	25	1944	15852	Hooker	Eric Theron	m
Feb.	25	1944	15853	Hooker	Eric Theron	m

Month	Day	Year	File No.	Surname	Given Name	Type
June	30	1934	11940	Hooper	Carrie I.	d
		1879	1007	Hooper	Frances M.	d
May	28	1955	23205	Hooper	Homer H., etc.	d
		[1908-1909]	4612	Hooper	J. N.	d
		[1908-1909]	4613	Hooper	Marlin Cedric	m
June	14	1956	24045	Hooper	Rowena	m
Sept.	4	1912	5390	Hooper	Edna E.	d
Oct.	17	1943	15600	Hooper	George	d
		[1862-1863]	212	Hooser	Jose	d
		[1899-1900]	3017	Hooten	Elizabeth	d
		[1868-1869]	385	Hooten	Jessee	d
		1918	6822	Hooton	M. N.	d
Oct.	7	1954	22794	Hoover	Elmer G.	d
May	31	1953	21791	Hoover	Flora V.	d
Dec.	5	1941	14734	Hoover	George L.	d
June	13	1952	21191	Hoover	George S.	d
Nov.	18	1952	21464	Hoover	Henry F.	d
Sept.	27	1946	17367	Hoover	Walter, etc.	d
June	28	1926	9294	Hopcroft	Charles	d
May	20	1923	8337	Hope	Adelaide	d
June	18	1927	9630	Hope	Anna D., etc.	d
May	4	1937	12984	Hope	Halver	d
		[1888-1889]	1756	Hope	Valentine	d
Mar.	11	1927	9559	Hopke	August Frederick	d
Dec.	14	1938	13481	Hopke	Louise, etc.	d
May	2	1957	24638	Hopkin	Susan Ellen, etc.	d
July	18	1940	14116	Hopkin	Thomas	d
		[1897-1898]	2730	Hopkins	Alica	d
		1922	8211	Hopkins	Alice A.	m
Nov.	4	1954	22844	Hopkins	Charles	d
Dec.		1922	8210	Hopkins	Elvira C.	d
June	16	1944	16038	Hopkins	Gladys V., etc.	d
		[1897-1898]	2779	Hopkins	Hiram	m
June	3	1947	17824	Hopkins	Jessie	d
Feb.	15	1957	24535	Hopkins	John	d
Aug.	4	1924	8725	Hopkins	Lois W.	d
		[1897-1898]	2779	Hopkins	Lottie	m
May	10	1953	21758	Hopkins	Mabel V.	d
May	16	1957	24739	Hopkins	Margaret	m
June	16	1957	24739	Hopkins	Mary	m
Dec.	7	1950	20092	Hopkins	Mary Louise, etc.	d
Nov.	1	1940	14255	Hopkins	Oliver Clay, etc.	d

Month	Day	Year	File No.	Surname	Given Name	Type
May	16	1957	24739	Hopkins	Robert Emmet	m
		1919	7244	Hopkins	S. J.	inc
May	16	1957	24739	Hopkins	Susan	m
Oct.	17	1958	26014	Hopkins	Walter Herbert, etc.	d
		[1897-1898]	2779	Hopkins	Willett	m
Nov.	23	1942	15115	Hoppe	Anton F. H.	d
Sept.	29	1929	10368	Hoppe	Joseph E.	d
Jan.	12	1958	26145	Hoppe	William A.	d
		[1892-1893]	2280	Hoppe	Henry William	d
		1914	5774	Hopper	Belitha	d
Jan.	19	1877	863	Hopper	Climama	m
July	13	1914	5819	Hopper	Clyde Mc.	m
		1907	4388	Hopper	David	d
Sept.	10	1912	5393	Hopper	Dicie	d
Oct.	24	1957	25035	Hopper	Donald K.	d
Jan.	19	1877	863	Hopper	Emma Bell	m
Jan.	19	1877	863	Hopper	Eugene	m
Jan.	19	1877	863	Hopper	Eward	m
Feb.	7	1958	25366	Hopper	George T.	d
Sept.	3	1930	10766	Hopper	Grace A.	d
July	13	1914	5819	Hopper	Hazel C.	m
Aug.	29	1934	11985	Hopper	I. D.	d
		[1891-1892]	2083	Hopper	Jacob	d
		[1900-1901]	3217	Hopper	Margaret Ann	d
July	13	1914	5819	Hopper	Ruby H.	m
July	13	1912	5339	Hopper	Thomas	d
Jan.	19	1877	863	Hopper	Thomas B.	d
July	13	1914	5819	Hopper	Walter E.	m
May		1921	8035	Hopper	Wesley Lee	d
Oct.	24	1957	25036	Hopper	William Larkin	d
		1912	5269	Hopper	Wm. T.	d
Sept.	31	1951	20514	Hoppers	Blanche I., etc.	d
		1916	6277	Horgan	Eugene	d
Oct.	3	1940	14217	Hormmel	Margaret	d
		1921	7985	Horn	Annie F.	d
		[1908-1909]	4521	Horn	B. E.	d
		[1909-1910]	4751	Horn	E. D.	d
		1918	6655	Horn	Edith Winifred	m
May	13	1948	18387	Horn	Frank C	inc
June	24	1948	18407	Horn	Frank C.	d
Jan.	28	1918	6655	Horn	Herbert John et al	m
Jan.	28	1918	6654	Horn	J. W.	d

Month	Day	Year	File No.	Surname	Given Name	Type
Apr.	1	1957	24629	Horn	Margaret A.	d
		1918	6655	Horn	Marjorie Ethel	m
May	8	1944	15971	Horne	Anna C.	d
		[1910-1911]	4976	Horne	Archie	m
		[1910-1911]	4976	Horne	David	m
Apr.	17	1939	13613	Horne	David William, etc.	d
		[1902-1903]	3472	Horne	Edwin A.	d
		[1910-1911]	4887	Horne	Elizabeth H.	d
Nov.	8	1944	16248	Horne	Henry	d
Jan.	13	1938	13218	Horne	Jacob	d
		1921	7862	Horne	Robert	d
Nov.	22	1938	13442	Horne	William Jacob	mp
Nov.	9	1944	16253	Horne	William Jacob	mp
Nov.	4	1928	10084	Hornes	Elizabeth	d
Sept.	7	1951	20592	Hornick	John	d
Nov.	19	1954	22872	Hornick	William Virgil	d
Mar.	16	1951	20281	Horrall	Florence C.	d
Apr.	10	1936	12611	Horst	Joseph	d
July	29	1940	14051	Horstmann	William	d
		[1887-1888]	1675	Horton	Smith	d
June	25	1930	10788	Horvath	Louis	d
Jan.	30	1942	15205	Horvath	Vendel	d
Mar.	5	1956	23832	Horvatis	Mathilda	d
		1898	2820	Hosatte	Jean Baptiste	d
		[1898-1899]	2839	Hosatte	Jean Baptiste	d
		1925	8956	Hose	Orville	d
June	27	1955	23274	Hosford	Lyle O.	d
		[1897-1898]	2714	Hosking	Elizabeth	d
		[1897-1898]	2726	Hosking	Elizabeth	d
		[1897-1898]	2715	Hosking	Mary Jane E.	ins
		1919	7260	Hosmer	Gilman F. S.	d
		1923	8441	Hosmer	Harry D., etc.	d
		1911	5116	Hosmer	Mary M.	d
July	30	1944	16062	Hosmer	Maybell D.	d
Dec.	7	1945	16865	Hosner	Stanley	d
Nov.	17	1944	16273	Hosts	Raymond	d
		[1866-1868]	332	Hotell	David	d
Aug.		1924	8716	Hotell	Winston Orren	m
Dec.	16	1914	5915	Hotle	Charles E.	d
Jan.	23	1914	5921	Hotle	Harold L.	m
		[1919-1920]	7386	Hotle	Julia A.	d
Dec.	23	1914	5921	Hotle	Mabel D.	m

Month	Day	Year	File No.	Surname	Given Name	Type
		[1890-1891]	1999	Hotle	Peter	d
		[1919-1920]	7385	Hotle	Zachariah F.	d
Aug.	12	1915	6053	Hottinger	Dorothy B.	m
Aug.	12	1915	6053	Hottinger	Dorothy B.	m
Jan.	15	1954	22284	Hottua	Nicholas Andrew	d
Feb.	26	1954	22308	Hottua	Nicholas Andrew, etc.	d
Apr.	12	1948	18278	Hotz	Emma A.	d
Jan.	21	1934	12135	Hotz	G. H.	d
June		1924	8686	Hotz	Lloyd, Jr.	g
		1924	8686	Hotz	Rosewell	g
Oct.	7	1949	19309	Hourguet	Frank	d
May	6	1944	15961	Hourigan	Frank M.	d
Jan.	19	1942	15198	Hourquet	Frank	d
Oct.	7	1949	19307	Hourtquet	Frank	d
Apr.	8	1958	25531	House	Agnes O'Niel	inc
May	8	1944	15969	Houser	Charles Edward, etc.	d
June	29	1930	10641	Housinger	Nicholas	d
Oct.	13	1927	9737	Housmann	Irene E.	d
Feb.	14	1953	21646	Houston	Beatrice Beathous, etc.	d
Feb.	3	1948	18201	Houston	John D., etc.	d
July	9	1948	18503	Houts	Orrie Leonard	d
Mar.	25	1941	14413	Houx	Henry C., etc.	d
		1904	3749	Houx	John W.	d
May	5	1942	14929	Houx	Martha J.	d
June	24	1945	16548	Houx	Robert	d
June	3	1943	15457	Hover	Arvid W.	d
May	30	1929	10265	Hovey	Alice A.	d
Apr.	23	1949	18975	Howard	Alvin A.	d
Nov.	22	1954	22822	Howard	Arthur	inc
Nov.	27	1956	24347	Howard	Arthur Kelly, etc.	d
Jan.	9	1952	20842	Howard	Bonita Jane	m
		1929	10175	Howard	C. B.	inc
Feb.	8	1938	13261	Howard	Charles Ellsworth	d
Oct.	23	1952	21360	Howard	Charles F.	d
Aug.	16	1958	25789	Howard	Clyda, etc.	d
Sept.	14	1953	22004	Howard	Edith L., etc.	d
June	5	1933	11629	Howard	Emma	d
Mar.	17	1956	23800	Howard	Etoile E.	d
May	22	1929	10292	Howard	Fannie F.	d
		[1908-1909]	4491	Howard	George	d
June	18	1956	24053	Howard	Isabel H., etc.	d
		1912	5288	Howard	James	d

Month	Day	Year	File No.	Surname	Given Name	Type
Jan.	9	1952	20842	Howard	James Laurence	m
		[1899-1900]	3032	Howard	John James	m
		1902	3446	Howard	Julia A.	d
Apr.	10	1952	21047	Howard	Kimberly	m
Nov.	5	1914	5892	Howard	Lena Russell	d
July	10	1941	14573	Howard	Leonard C. (terminate joint te	d
		1926	9446	Howard	Martha Amada	d
Jan.	9	1952	20842	Howard	Mary Lou	m
Mar.	5	1956	23832	Howard	Mathilda	d
Dec.	20	1948	18791	Howard	Nellie H.	d
Sept.	26	1958	25953	Howard	Paulina	d
Jan.	7	1958	25271	Howard	Pauline	d
June	28	1953	21871	Howard	Pearl K.	d
Jan.	9	1952	20842	Howard	Phillip Glenn	m
		[1899-1900]	3102	Howard	Square D.	d
		[1908-1909]	4588	Howard	W. M.	d
		[1909-1910]	4791	Howard	Wallace Franklin	d
		1911	5063	Howard	Warren	d
		[1909-1910]	4721	Howard	William L.	d
Feb.	3	1958	25346	Howard	William T.	d
Oct.	6	1942	15102	Howard	Thomas R.	d
May	15	1930	10628	Howarth	Leonard	d
Mar.	5	1956	23832	Howartis	Mathilda	d
Nov.	14	1946	17438	Howe	Alfred O.	d
Jan.	17	1928	10149	Howe	Babe	d
		[1908-1909]	4652	Howe	Charles J.	d
Dec.	4	1944	16302	Howe	Ella, etc.	d
		1893	2323	Howe	George G.	d
July	21	1945	16658	Howe	Joseph	d
Feb.	27	1939	13547	Howe	Maude N., etc.	d
Aug.	13	1937	12997	Howe	Ross	d
Oct.	10	1942	15043	Howe	Stephen	d
		1869	431	Howell	A. E. L.	d
May	4	1953	21818	Howell	Arthur S., etc.	d
Jan.	10	1930	10517	Howell	Elizabeth F.	d
Dec.	23	1937	13170	Howell	Fred S.	d
May	6	1935	12185	Howell	L. V. H.	d
		1925	8857	Howell	Mabel Emily	d
Oct.	13	1949	19258	Howell	Marie A., etc.	d
Apr.	25	1947	17712	Howell	T. Flass, etc.	d
		1879	1048	Howes	Wm. F.	d
Oct.	10	1917	6527	Howie	Margaret A. C.	d

Month	Day	Year	File No.	Surname	Given Name	Type
June	4	1930	10546	Howsare	John	d
May	5	1944	15958	Hoy	Sid	d
Sept.	10	1929	10404	Hoyle	George Dunn	m
July	10	1929	10334	Hoyle	George Wilson	d
Sept.	10	1929	10404	Hoyle	Irene Lydia	m
Oct.	10	1929	10404	Hoyle	Leora Margaret	m
		1906	4038	Hoyle	Sarah J.	d
Nov.	8	1935	12433	Hoyt	Allen E.	d
		[1896-1897]	2691	Hoyt	F. C.	d
July	25	1945	16669	Hoyt	Louella C.	d
Aug.		1945	16667	Hoyt	Louella F. C.	d
		[1877-1879]	903	Hrotis	Nicholas	d
Aug.	17	1912	5340	Hrusa	John	d
Aug.	8	1926	9307	Hubbard	Addie M.	d
		[1888-1889]	1816	Hubbard	Charles N.	d
		1906	4167	Hubbard	Charles W.	d
Aug.	22	1957	24899	Hubbard	Charles, etc.	d
Jan.	18	1944	15790	Hubbard	Ebert O.	d
Jan.	18	1944	15790	Hubbard	Fannie E.	d
		[1908-1909]	4539	Hubbard	Henry	d
July	21	1956	24066	Hubbard	Mary R.	d
Oct.	20	1958	26020	Hubbard	Rose	d
		1930	10521	Hubbell	Kathleen Virginia	d
Sept.	21	1931	11084	Hubbul	George R.	d
July	15	1914	5820	Hubell	Orton	d
May	24	1956	24013	Huber	Crystal J., etc.	d
		1905	4034	Huber	Frank	d
Apr.	21	1947	17755	Hubert	Alfred	d
Apr.	25	1947	17711	Hubert	Fred W.	d
Sept.	19	1938	13381	Hubert	Joseph, etc.	d
Jan.	23	1931	10845	Hubler	Ernest F.	d
Oct.	26	1958	25957	Hubner	James, etc.	d
Sept.	27	1956	24184	Huchler	Annie G., etc.	d
		[1919-1920]	7370	Huckabay	Samuel S., etc.	d
Mar.	5	1914	5689	Huddark	Henry	m
Feb.	11	1944	15836	Huddleson	Florence A.	d
Jan.	15	1925	8855	Hudsfeth	William Walter, etc.	d
		1872	538	Hudson	Ann	d
		[1876-1877]	847	Hudson	C. E.	d
		1879	1013	Hudson	David A.	d
Nov.	25	1915	6078	Hudson	Dulcenia	d
		[1888-1889]	1764	Hudson	Elizabeth M.	d

Month	Day	Year	File No.	Surname	Given Name	Type
Sept.	15	1937	13125	Hudson	Eugene	d
Jan.	30	1943	15699	Hudson	George R.	d
Mar.	1	1954	22364	Hudson	George R., etc.	d
		1888	1706	Hudson	Henry F.	d
		1872	529	Hudson	Henry W.	m
		[1877-1879]	964	Hudson	M. J. M.	m
Feb.	8	1947	18126	Hudson	Martha E.	d
		1872	517	Hudson	Martin	d
		[1875-1876]	747	Hudson	Samuel	m
Oct.	1	1951	20648	Hudson	Serenia Ann Faber	d
Nov.	16	1927	9778	Hudson	W. H.	d
Nov.	11	1940	14236	Hudspeth	Mary Addie	d
July	7	1917	6502	Hudspeth	William W.	inc
June	18	1958	25711	Huebner	Fred	inc
July	25	1957	24830	Huerby	Albert Lawrence, Jr.	m
Feb.	16	1954	22346	Huerby	N. Beatrice, etc.	d
Mar.	5	1951	20253	Huey	Robert C.	d
		1906	4087	Huffine	Henry C.	inc
Feb.	29	1941	14367	Huffine	Laura G.	d
Nov.	28	1937	13132	Huffman	Dan	d
Mar.	3	1950	19544	Huffman	Georgina	d
May	26	1930	10634	Huffman	J. W., etc.	d
Apr.	16	1948	18287	Huffman	Jacob	d
Jan.	15	1954	22282	Huffman	Louella M.	d
		1926	9468	Huffman	Ralph W.	d
Dec.	12	1957	25213	Hufft	L. V., etc.	d
Apr.	20	1928	9885	Hugentobler	Jacob	ins
Oct.	27	1928	10079	Hugentobler	Jacob	d
		1912	5229	Huggins	Burrell	d
Sept.	11	1934	12046	Hughes	Ada	d
Mar.	4	1947	17571	Hughes	Cecile G.	d
Jan.	14	1953	22231	Hughes	Curtis	d
Mar.	23	1925	8863	Hughes	David	d
June	13	1938	13317	Hughes	David	d
Sept.	11	1948	18576	Hughes	Frank Dexter, etc.	d
Mar.	4	1947	17678	Hughes	Gary Norman	d
June	12	1956	24041	Hughes	Gary W.	inc
Aug.	8	1958	25841	Hughes	Gary W.	d
Feb.	4	1955	23025	Hughes	James Joseph, etc.	d
		1854	50	Hughes	John C.	d
		[1871-1872]	489	Hughes	Josephine	m
July	24	1930	10662	Hughes	Joshua	d

Month	Day	Year	File No.	Surname	Given Name	Type
Dec.	12	1919	7241	Hughes	Margaret	inc
		[1919-1920]	7423	Hughes	Margaret	d
July	24	1921	7717	Hughes	Mary Jane	d
Apr.		1919	7052	Hughes	Minnie	d
June	12	1956	24042	Hughes	Nellie	inc
Nov.	3	1955	23571	Hughes	Nellie Arena	inc
		1921	7906	Hughes	Rennette E., etc.	d
		1921	7718	Hughes	Rowland	d
Jan.	6	1925	8841	Hughes	T. M.	d
		[1881-1882]	1192	Hugues	Balthazar	d
Sept.		1882	1230	Hugues	Francis Josephine	d
Oct.	2	1958	25971	Hugus	Walter W.	d
Dec.	21	1944	16281	Huhtolo	Elis	d
Sept.	26	1952	21306	Huitfeldt	William	d
Oct.	10	1957	25075	Hukee	Andrew	d
		[1904-1905]	3856	Hulbert	Harry Edmond	d
July	19	1915	6021	Hulbut	Edwin Taft Monroe	d
May	8	1925	8953	Hull	Ace Lorreen	g
Feb.	22	1933	11797	Hull	Cephas Clay	d
May		1921	8007	Hull	Gertrude Elizabeth	d
Nov.	16	1953	22118	Hull	John R., etc.	d
Sept.	24	1949	19140	Huller	Prescott Bernard	ins
May	22	1956	24006	Hulslander	Phillip LeRoy, etc.	d
		1919	7206	Hultman	Hulda E.	d
Aug.	19	1955	23446	Humbert	Charles Emile	d
		[1894-1895]	2420	Humbert	Elmira	d
May	13	1930	10623	Humbert	George H.	d
May	22	1950	19715	Humbert	Ida Louisa	d
Jan.	3	1951	20780	Hume	Robert M.	m
Jan.	9	1928	9828	Hummel	Lois	d
June	27	1952	21144	Humphrey	Earl Lawrence, etc.	d
		1926	9428	Humphrey	J. L.	d
Sept.	10	1929	10401	Humphrey	J. N.	d
Aug.	10	1948	18575	Humphrey	Oroville Clarke/Jack	d
		[1888-1889]	1750	Humphreys	R. J.	d
		1865	291	Humphries	William	d
		1916	6315	Huneke	Wayne Henry	m
Mar.	21	1957	24546	Hunger	Elmer	d
		[1894-1895]	2476	Hunger	Felix	d
		[1899-1900]	3106	Hungerbuhler	Ulrich	d
		[1899-1900]	3044	Huni	Otto	ins
May	10	1954	22524	Hunsicker	Clyde L, etc.	d

Month	Day	Year	File No.	Surname	Given Name	Type
		1905	3968	Hunt	Alice L.	d
		1902	3453	Hunt	B. W.	d
		[1872-1873]	580	Hunt	Charles W.	d
June	11	1957	24788	Hunt	Grace	d
		[1919-1920]	7356	Hunt	H. J., etc.	d
		1907	4253	Hunt	Hazel Berna	m
		[1883-1884]	1293	Hunt	Jane Doe	m
Aug.	9	1956	24154	Hunt	Jessie Viola	d
		1882	1265	Hunt	Katie	inc
June	5	1953	21881	Hunt	Lou A.	d
June	25	1956	24016	Hunt	Mabel A.	d
		1882	1261	Hunt	Manassah	d
May	28	1958	25580	Hunt	Marvin L., etc.	d
		[1883-1884]	1335	Hunt	Phoebe	d
Oct.	28	1948	18650	Hunt	Ralph M.	d
Sept.	12	1915	6067	Hunt	Sarah A.	d
		[1900-1901]	3222	Hunt	Thomas Rowland	d
		[1919-1920]	7309	Hunt	Warren E.	d
		1872	564	Hunt	Charles W.	m
		1872	564	Hunt	Francis W.	m
		1872	564	Hunt	James B.	m
		1872	564	Hunt	Lottie E.	m
		1872	564	Hunt	Sarah C.	m
Jan.	5	1938	13495	Hunter	Edward J., etc.	d
		1872	525	Hunter	Elizabeth A.	d
Sept.	28	1945	16670	Hunter	Ethel E.	d
		1916	6343	Hunter	Henry A.	d
June	1	1953	21875	Hunter	Ida May	d
		1868	380	Hunter	James	d
Sept.	2	1952	21314	Hunter	James Stanley	m
		[1910-1911]	5061	Hunter	John & Lizie (his wife)	d
		1906	4161	Hunter	Joseph E.	d
Feb.		1929	10185	Hunter	Pearle	d
		1932	11335	Hunter	Rea Barron	d
Jan.	17	1913	5678	Hunter	William	d
Feb.	30	1925	9155	Huntington	Annie E.	inc
Apr.	7	1926	9162	Huntington	Annie E.	d
Nov.	7	1949	19352	Huntington	Arthur E., etc.	d
Dec.		1920	7573	Huntington	Horace D.	d
Mar.	10	1943	15304	Huntington	L. Glenn	d
		1907	4301	Huntley	Albert	d
Feb.	4	1958	25357	Huntley	Emma	inc

Month	Day	Year	File No.	Surname	Given Name	Type
		1918	6870	Huntley	Garfield	d
		1912	5291	Huntley	Geo. H.	d
		1888	1745	Huntley	John Stanley	m
Jan.	15	1919	6952	Huntley	Mary	d
May	28	1949	18983	Huntley	Richard	d
Jan.	15	1919	6951	Huntley	Vincent J.	d
Apr.	27	1913	5503	Huntoon	Laura Maria Nelson	d
		1927	9581	Huntoon	Sarah L.	d
Jan.	25	1944	15801	Huntringer	David E.	d
Oct.	19	1930	10741	Huntsinger	Alma L., etc.	d
Feb.	23	1933	11514	Huntz	Josephine, etc.	d
Aug.	25	1954	22615	Hupp	Edgar	d
Dec.	20	1951	20753	Hupp	Zadie	d
May	3	1930	10592	Hurd	Anna M.	d
		1875	738	Hurd	Charlotte P.	m
Mar.	12	1951	20269	Hurd	Clara E.	d
Dec.	8	1920	7602	Hurd	Estella	d
June	15	1954	22593	Hurd	G. Lansing	d
		1875	738	Hurd	George H.	m
		[1874-1875]	702	Hurd	Isabella	d
Aug.		1919	7138	Hurd	John	d
		1875	738	Hurd	Lizzie J.	m
		1897	2699	Hurd	Mattie	d
Nov.	13	1933	11741	Hurgren	Alma	ins
June	31	1935	12319	Hurgren	Alma	d
Nov.	9	1927	9771	Hurgren	E. N.	d
Aug.	10	1926	9355	Hurley	Gerald Baynton	m
Aug.	10	1926	9355	Hurley	Margaret Louise	m
Aug.	10	1926	9355	Hurley	Phyliss Anna	m
Jan.	19	1928	10117	Hurn	Georgia	d
		1865	278	Hurn	John F.	m
		1865	278	Hurn	Seth R.	m
		1865	278	Hurn	Sibbie E.	m
		1865	278	Hurn	Solomon F.	m
		1865	278	Hurn	Wm. M.	m
May	3	1919	7041	Hurst	Sarah A., etc.	d
May	3	1935	12290	Hurt	Emma R.	d
Sept.	29	1933	11727	Hurt	Jean	m
Mar.	9	1932	11190	Hurt	William T.	d
Apr.	21	1927	9575	Huse	Minna	d
Jan.	6	1923	8514	Husehlar	Charles	d
		1919	7126	Huslen	Magdalene	d

Month	Day	Year	File No.		Surname	Given Name	Type
Dec.	7	1956	24375		Husler	Dora	inc
Oct.	10	1958	25993		Husler	Dora M., etc.	d
		[1887-1888]	1691		Hussey	Edward	d
Dec.	8	1944	16310		Hussey	Louise B.	d
Feb.	8	1941	14386		Hussey	Mary E.	d
		[1881-1882]	1188		Hutchens	Horatio	d
Sept.	10	1952	21327		Hutchin	Bessie C., etc.	d
		1895	2510		Hutchins	Edrick F.	d
		1875	742		Hutchinson	Abel F.	d
Sept.	18	1946	17347		Hutchinson	Benjamin F.	d
Apr.	16	1950	19564		Hutchinson	Edwin L.	d
		[1908-1909]	4617		Hutchinson	Elizabeth	d
June	14	1955	23317		Hutchinson	Francis A.	d
		1912	5294		Hutchinson	Frank	d
		1912	5295		Hutchinson	Harold	m
		[1900-1901]	3205		Hutchinson	Henry H.	d
Oct.		1924	8777		Hutchinson	James F.	d
Feb.	14	1958	25390		Hutchinson	John Walter, etc.	d
		1905	3954		Hutchinson	Lymon	d
June	14	1955	23318		Hutchinson	Lynus W., etc.	d
May	5	1955	23216		Hutchinson	Martin B., etc.	d
Apr.	13	1951	20337		Hutchinson	Mary J.	d
Nov.	7	1955	23520		Hutchinson	Maud	d
		[1922-1923]	8252		Hutchinson	May E.	d
Aug.	23	1951	20503		Hutchinson	Melissa A.	d
		1927	9523		Hutchinson	Rachel	d
Apr.	19	1934	11873		Hutchinson	Samuel John, etc.	d
Aug.	23	1940	14118		Hutchinson	Thomas J., etc.	d
Mar.		1921	7894		Hutchinson	Helen	d
Jan.	22	1934	12138		Hutchison	Eva	d
Sept.	21	1926	9363		Hutchison	Lawrence	d
Mar.	13	1914	5695		Hute	H.	d
Jan.	7	1958	25266		Hutson	Gladys F.	d
Oct.	28	1941	14589		Hutson	Nell B.	d
Apr.	25	1941	14453		Hutton	Asa L.	d
Mar.	14	1949	18950		Hutton	Billie, etc.	d
May	15	1944	15986		Hutton	Elizabeth (aka Hutton, Lizzie)	d
Jan.	18	1944	15791		Hutton	Elizbeth, etc.	inc
Dec.	8	1950	20031		Hutton	Lyle M.	d
July	14	1944	16081		Hutton	Samuel J., etc.	d
		1877	861		Hutton	Sarah L.	d
Apr.	9	1952	21044		Hyatt	Clifford	d

Month	Day	Year	File No.	Surname	Given Name	Type
Jan.	30	1913	5685	Hyatt	Emily G.	d
		[1895-1896]	2567	Hyatt	John B.	d
Feb.	8	1954	22331	Hyde	Darwin Shay	inc
		1896	2634	Hyde	James	d
		[1908-1909]	4616	Hyde	Loretta	m
Feb.	16	1955	23054	Hyde	Olga B., etc.	d
		[1908-1909]	4517	Hyde	Philip F.	d
Apr.	27	1943	15353	Hyde	Walter S.	d
		[1908-1909]	4616	Hyde	William B.	m
		[1910-1911]	4953	Hyde	William H.	d
		1905	3974	Hydorn	J. W. W.	d
		[1889-1890]	1899	Hydt	Louis	d
Sept.	12	1957	25014	Hyland	Nellie A.	inc
Jan.	18	1952	20862	Hyland	Thomas R.	d
Mar.	14	1947	17695	Hyman	Edward J., etc.	d
Oct.	6	1928	10052	Hynding	Morris	d
		1912	5261	Hyndman	Alexander	d
		1882	1225	Hynes	James	d
		1882	1247	Hynes	John P.	m
		1883	1283	Hynes	Laura A.	m
		1883	1283	Hynes	Wildrick F.	m

Month	Day	Year	File No.	Surname	Given Name	Type
Apr.	1	1954	22428	Iaccheri	Joseph, etc.	d
Mar.	2	1952	21312	Ianni	Francesco	d
July	5	1945	16562	Ianni	Maria, etc.	d
Jan.	26	1948	18537	Ibach	Elizabeth Boyd Haskett, etc.	d
Feb.	11	1931	11161	Ielmorini	Komilda G.	d
Nov.	29	1945	16594	Ihrcke	John W.	d
May	26	1934	11936	Ijichi	Kosuke	m
July	13	1937	12961	Ijichi	Tomoki.	d
		[1920-1924]	8250	Iles	Alfred	d
Dec.	13	1919	7085	Iles	Alonzo Thomas	d
Mar.	22	1953	21796	Illia	Helena, etc.	d
Sept.	11	1955	23114	Illia	Michael, etc.	d
Apr.	27	1950	19590	Illia	Stephen I.	d
Mar.	20	1949	19327	Illias	Mildred Mabell, etc.	d
Apr.	16	1951	20278	Illig	Gus	d
		[1912-1916]	5588	Illingworth	William	d
		1941	14529	Imato	Mike	m
Apr.	4	1935	12427	Imoto	Itano	m
Nov.	26	1934	11961	Imoto	Kiyorni	m
Nov.	26	1934	11961	Imoto	Masashi	m
Sept.	28	1949	19151	Imwalle	Joseph J.	d
Sept.	8	1956	23841	Imwalle	Mary M.	d
Apr.	26	1952	21365	Inells	Anne F.	d
		1899	2999	Ingalls	Chester A.	m
		[1896-1897]	2666	Ingalls	Chester A.	d
		1903	3672	Ingalls	Jane A.	d
		[1920-1924]	8348	Ingalls	John C.	d
Sept.	16	1934	12102	Ingalls	Laura C.	d
Mar.	7	1956	24198	Ingalls	Mary	d
June	16	1934	12101	Ingalls	Myron	d
Oct.	25	1947	17662	Ingebrigtson?	Ingebrigh B.	d
Mar.	31	1958	25339	Ingensoll	Lee R.	inc
Jan.	31	1939	13742	Ingersen	Ella M.	d
Apr.	21	1942	15017	Ingerson	Lawrence K.	d
Dec.	25	1946	17454	Ingeversen	Johanna M.	d
Mar.	21	1951	20404	Ingham	Arthur C.	d
Dec.	16	1955	23490	Ingham	Hattie J.	d
		1908	4441	Ingham	William	d
Sept.	7	1930	10595	Ingle	Fanny C.	d
Feb.		1912	5426	Ingle	Robert	d
June	21	1949	18846	Ingle	Jesse Albert, etc.	d
Apr.	15	1948	18283	Ingledew	Charles H., etc.	d

Month	Day	Year	File No.	Surname	Given Name	Type
		1896	2657	Ingmansen	John	d
Dec.	12	1931	10999	Ingmersen	Diedrick, etc.	d
		1878	968	Ingoldsky	Charles	d
Sept.	14	1952	21293	Ingols	Lyle P.	d
Apr.	21	1954	22471	Ingram	Charles E.	d
Sept.	1	1949	19109	Ingram	George V.	d
Feb.	16	1958	26153	Ingram	Guy M., etc.	d
		1871	500	Ingram	J. S.	d
Mar.		1917	6442	Ingram	James L.	d
		1877	891	Ingram	John	d
Feb.	7	1936	12609	Ingram	Josephine Virginia	d
Jan.	16	1957	24953	Ingram	Katherine Throop	d
		[1908-1912]	4753	Ingram	Mary	d
June	21	1954	22472	Ingram	Nellie	d
July	15	1954	22596	Ingwersen	Carl	d
Dec.	25	1958	25808	Ingwersen	Catherine	d
Apr.	9	1943	15373	Ingwersen	Thomas	d
Mar.		1903	3620	Ink	Hannah	d
		[1899-1903]	3024	Ink	Walter P.	d
		1884	1404	Inman	Aaron C.	d
Apr.		1942	14979	Inman	Gladys	d
Aug.	1	1943	15359	Inman	Gladys	d
		1882	1262	Inman	H. K.	d
	29	1919	7034	Inman	Maitland A.	d
Mar.	24	1919	7034	Inman	Maitland H.	d
Dec.	13	1924	8682	Innes	Cyrus, etc.	d
Oct.	16	1925	9087	Intemann	Adelheid	g
Dec.	19	1920	7421	Intemann	D. H., etc.	d
Aug.	8	1925	8977	Intemann	Jessie	d
		[1920-1924]	7519	Internizzi	Domenico	d
Oct.	20	1949	19272	Inwood	Donna Lee	m
		1941	14399	Inwood	Geneva W.	d
Mar.	6	1956	24147	Inwood	Jennie Soernsen, etc.	d
		1916	6204	Inwood	William A.	d
Jan.	1	1948	18710	Inwood	William A., etc.	d
Feb.	10	1958	25992	Ioas	Arthur C., Sr., etc.	d
Dec.	29	1944	16006	Ioub	Minnie	d
Nov.	8	1948	18326	Iragawa	Kiyiko	d
Nov.	12	1945	16817	Ireland	Johnston	d
July	9	1958	25764	Irons	George H.	d
June	23	1930	10742	Irons	William H.	d
Feb.	1	1946	17462	Irvin	Dell	d

Month	Day	Year	File No.		Surname	Given Name	Type
Mar.	24	1950	19582		Irving	Arthur Edward, etc.	d
May	17	1944	16276		Irving	Grace H.	d
Mar.	12	1947	17848		Irving	John J.. etc.	d
July	29	1958	25587		Irving	M. Louise	con
		1872	573		Irwin	Archibald B.	d
Dec.		1919	7222		Irwin	Charles H.	d
May	11	1919	7267		Irwin	Florence Anna	m
Dec.	11	1919	7267		Irwin	Frederick	m
June	3	1949	18809		Irwin	Hilda J.	d
May		1917	6909		Irwin	Joseph W.	d
Dec.	11	1919	7267		Irwin	Mildred	m
		[1899-1903]	3438		Irwin	Newton Cannon	d
		1919	7267		Irwin	Perry Louis	m
July	7	1948	18325		Irwin	Richard H.	d
		1892	2277		Irwin	T. J.	d
		[1899-1903]	3037		Irwin	Thomas N.	d
		1941	14627		Irwin	Thomas, etc.	d
Apr.	10	1958	25446		Isaacs	Delbert Russell	d
		[1920-1924]	7903		Isaacs	Delbert Russell	inc
Dec.	31	1953	21737		Isaacs	Ernest A., etc.	d
Aug.	13	1957	24589		Isaacs	Harriett	inc
Apr.	21	1958	25485		Isaacs	Harriett	con
		[1877-1878]	919		Isaacs	Louis	m
		[1877-1878]	919		Isaacs	Marks	m
		1916	6298		Isaacs	Sarah A.	d
May	21	1934	11958		Isaak	Christian	d
May	29	1932	11372		Isaakson	Minnie I.	d
July	10	1929	10431		Isackson	Albin	d
Nov.	1	1938	13236		Isaia	Giovanini	ins
Nov.	11	1944	15921		Isakson	Erika, etc.	d
Nov.	25	1957	24612		Isley	Sarna, etc.	d
June	10	1946	17524		Ismael	Quintin Audan, etc.	d
Sept.	14	1952	20982		Issalis	Adrien	d
		1897	2757		Itin	John	d
Apr.	25	1930	10692		Itjen	Frederick	d
July		1942	14897		Itjen	Richard	d
Apr.	21	1932	11281		Ito	Fazuo	m
Oct.	19	1955	23251		Ito	Kazuo	d
Aug.	21	1932	11281		Ito	Terico	m
July	16	1958	25557		Itono	Toshivo, etc.	d
		1912	5249		Ivaldi	Marcelina	d
		1940	13879		Ivancovich	Clara Belle	d

Month	Day	Year	File No.		Surname	Given Name	Type
June	21	1924	8784		Ivancovich	George	inc
Oct.	1	1924	8818		Ivancovich	George	d
		1954	22481		Ivanetich	Mary A.	d
Feb.	19	1931	11008		Ivarson	Magdalena	d
Mar.	26	1949	19276		Iversen	Vera A.	d
Apr.	20	1928	10042		Iverson	Anders Gustav	d
May	6	1943	15545		Iverson	Chris	d
Sept.	14	1951	20340		Iverson	George	d
Apr.	8	1947	18039		Iverson	Hans	d
May	30	1944	16345		Iverson	Johanne	d
Mar.	15	1957	25144		Iverson	Karen, etc.	d
Oct.	10	1945	16638		Ives	Alfred	d
Aug.	6	1955	23631		Ives	Edwin H., etc.	d
		1939	13832		Ives	Katherine L.	d
Mar.	11	1955	23530		Ives	Lucille J.	d
Apr.	3	1954	22375		Ivy	Hazel G.	d
Apr.	13	1932	11228		Iwaoka	Aiko	m
Feb.	13	1932	11228		Iwaoka	Aline	m
Feb.	13	1932	11228		Iwaoka	Ben	m
Apr.	13	1932	11228		Iwaoka	Jo	m
Aug.	28	1951	20644		Izard	Edith C., etc.	d
Oct.	21	1958	25798		Izard	Tommie James, etc.	d
Apr.	31	1953	22261		Izzett	George W.	d

Month	Day	Year	File No.	Surname	Given Name	Type
Mar.	12	1956	23849	Jabin	Nicholas	d
Jan.	12	1953	21567	Jabin	William John	d
June	24	1939	13656	Jachter	Barney J.	d
May	28	1956	23892	Jacinto aka Jones	Etta A., etc.	d
Dec.	13	1944	16261	Jack	Ellen E., etc.	d
Jan.	17	1915	6070	Jack	Harry A.	inc
Mar.	12	1916	6171	Jack	Harry A.	d
June	23	1911	5017	Jack	Ailleen	m
Jan.	23	1911	5017	Jack	Harold	m
Jan.	23	1911	5017	Jack	Ruppert	m
Mar.	2	1929	10481	Jacks	Josephine B.	d
Mar.	28	1952	20950	Jacks	Rocy, Jr.	d
		[1872-1873]	587	Jackson	Abraham J.	m
Jan.	12	1951	20154	Jackson	Annie	inc
May	11	1947	17691	Jackson	Arthur	d
		1894	2457	Jackson	Beatrice A.	m
		1857	55	Jackson	Charity	d
July	4	1953	21820	Jackson	Claire M.	d
		[1890-1891]	1982	Jackson	Eunice	d
		[1872-1873]	587	Jackson	Fanny Vic	m
Sept.	1	1933	11704	Jackson	George C.	d
		[1872-1873]	587	Jackson	Gidean	m
May	13	1956	23923	Jackson	Granville Lambert	d
Jan.	8	1951	20141	Jackson	Howard C.	d
		[1896-1901]	2753	Jackson	James H.	d
		1914	5715	Jackson	James L.	d
Mar.	26	1945	16833	Jackson	John P., etc.	d
Jan.	25	1943	15246	Jackson	John W.	d
		1867	340	Jackson	L.	d
		[1872-1873]	587	Jackson	Margaret	m
		[1891-1894]	2189	Jackson	Martha Jane	d
		[1872-1873]	587	Jackson	Mary Ann	m
May	7	1957	24721	Jackson	Maud M.	d
June	9	1952	21109	Jackson	Odessa	d
		[1872-1873]	585	Jackson	Robert	d
Nov.	27	1934	12034	Jackson	Roy, etc.	d
		1894	2457	Jackson	Ward Sutliff	m
		[1868-1869]	379	Jackson	William	d
Apr.	22	1929	10256	Jacob	John	d
		[1922-1924]	8240	Jacobi	Ludwig	d
Dec.	24	1954	22885	Jacobs	A. Neal, etc.	d
Dec.	10	1950	20042	Jacobs	Alice	d
		1921	7802	Jacobs	Ann Maria	d

Jan.	4	1928	10141		Jacobs	Annie H.	d
Jan.	4	1940	13878		Jacobs	Charles (terminate joint tenan	d
Aug.	15	1957	24950		Jacobs	Edward E.	d
May	18	1946	17152		Jacobs	Edwin S.	inc
Jan.	2	1946	17505		Jacobs	Edwin S.	d
May	21	1944	15895		Jacobs	Emma	d
Apr.	25	1942	14870		Jacobs	George (joint tenancy), etc.	d
Dec.	8	1916	6190		Jacobs	George H.	d
Apr.	20	1942	14904		Jacobs	George, etc.	d
Nov.	25	1953	22082		Jacobs	Hazel Eldredge	d
Sept.	31	1938	13334		Jacobs	James	d
June	27	1939	13682		Jacobs	Joseph	d
Jan.	6	1941	14694		Jacobs	Joseph	d
Aug.	31	1957	24762		Jacobs	Lulu E., etc.	d
Mar.	27	1956	23818		Jacobs	Ray G.	d
Aug.	3	1931	10988		Jacobs	William	d
		1890	1928		Jacobs	Eli	d
Feb.	19	1936	12839		Jacobs	Marie	d
Sept.	24	1952	21264		Jacobsen	Albert H.	d
Mar.	27	1953	21668		Jacobsen	Albert H., etc.	d
		1934	11811		Jacobsen	Ch.	d
Apr.	14	1957	24591		Jacobsen	Christian	inc
		[1917-1921]	7014		Jacobsen	Dagmar Andrea	d
		1926	9387		Jacobsen	Emily	d
Aug.		1921	7778		Jacobsen	Ernest, etc.	d
Feb.	9	1955	23642		Jacobsen	Harold Alfred	d
		[1917-1921]	6847		Jacobsen	Harold Alfred	m
		[1917-1921]	7620		Jacobsen	Harold Alfred	d
Dec.	25	1952	21480		Jacobsen	Harry M., etc.	d
Jan.	6	1937	12957		Jacobsen	Ingvald Teresius	d
		[1922-1924]	8317		Jacobsen	Irene & Frances	m
Oct.	31	1953	21986		Jacobsen	Jacob W.	d
Sept.	21	1928	9978		Jacobsen	Jens Christian, etc.	d
Nov.	21	1955	23546		Jacobsen	Joseph Leslie	m
May	26	1951	20182		Jacobsen	Mathilda A., etc.	d
Oct.	21	1955	23545		Jacobsen	Michael Stuart	m
Nov.	13	1936	12801		Jacobsen	Nellie	m
Nov.	21	1917	6424		Jacobsen	Niels L.	d
Jan.	13	1953	21573		Jacobsen	Sine	d
Jan.	13	1953	21586		Jacobsen	Sine Hoirup	d
Dec.	21	1955	23548		Jacobsen	William M., etc.	d
		1917	6546		Jacobsen	Jacob E.	d
Sept.	22	1957	24975		Jacobson	Edwin Oscar, etc.	d

		[1885-1887]	1478		Jacobson	Jacob	d
Feb.	9	1927	9803		Jacobson	Mike	d
Nov.	26	1956	24233		Jacobson	Oscar E.	d
		[1896-1901]	2963		Jacobson	Rosalie	d
Aug.	16	1948	18526		Jacquemin	Danny Glen	d
		1922	7971		Jaeger	Annie	d
		1922	8077		Jaeger	Pualulani Walter	m
Mar.	7	1929	10167		Jaeger	Rudolph	d
Mar.	20	1922	7931		Jaeger	Samuel Allen	g
Sept.	28	1927	9636		Jaeger	Samuel Allen	d
June	25	1930	10586		Jaffe	Joseph L., Jr.	m
Feb.	18	1953	22244		Jagla	Walter G., etc.	d
Oct.	17	1943	15566		Jahnke	Theresia	d
Mar.	27	1948	18801		Jahoda	Louis J, etc..	d
		[1922-1924]	8386		Jain	Miles	inc
Sept.	12	1933	11636		Jakoher	Matilda	d
Dec.	17	1954	22922		Jamart	Angela	inc
Dec.	12	1958	26073		Jamart	Angela	d
Nov.	7	1946	17427		James	Andrew T.	m
May		1943	15337		James	Annie	d
Sept.	27	1944	16189		James	Arnold Chester	m
		[1917-1921]	6697		James	Asa L. P.	d
Jan.	25	1913	5663		James	Carl C.	m
Sept.	27	1944	16189		James	Carol Joyce	m
		[1876-1877]	793		James	Charles A.	d
		[1888-1889]	1781		James	Charles G.	d
Dec.	23	1926	9390		James	Clarence H., etc.	m
Sept.	27	1944	16189		James	Donald Norman	m
Feb.	25	1913	5663		James	Elsie L.	m
Feb.	11	1955	23043		James	Ethel Mae, etc.	d
Sept.	27	1944	16189		James	Gerald Lee	m
Nov.	10	1947	18089		James	Gussie	d
Sept.	27	1944	16189		James	Lawrence A.	m
July	11	1950	19809		James	Maud S.	inc
Jan.	30	1951	20186		James	Maud S.	d
Nov.	27	1944	16189		James	Nadine Alice	m
Nov.	17	1950	19984		James	Oril Edward	d
Nov.	27	1944	16189		James	Shirley Mae	m
		[1922-1924]	8471		James	Zachariah D.	d
		[1904-1907]	4101		Jameson	Sarah J.	d
May	3	1953	21574		Jameson	Verna M., etc.	d
July	3	1953	21922		Jameson	Verna M., etc.	d
		1891	2100		Jamison	Anne J. (restoration to capacity	p

Oct.	17	1913	5638	Jamison	J. H.	d
Apr.	13	1937	12891	Jamison	James M.	d
		[1904-1907]	3836	Jamison	James M.	m
Aug.	4	1942	15031	Jamison	Margaret M.	d
		[1904-1907]	3834	Jamison	Rachel	inc
		[1907-1908]	4390	Jamison	Rachel	d
Jan.	3	1921	7858	Jamtegaard	O.	d
Feb.	10	1958	25279	Janes	S. J.	d
Mar.	18	1957	24466	Janes/Jaynes	Fred, etc.	d
Oct.	27	1955	23502	Janik	Anastazie	inc
June	10	1954	22526	Janke	Maude A., etc.	d
Apr.	28	1958	25503	Jankwitz	Anthony F., etc.	inc
Aug.	6	1958	25601	Jankwitz	Anthony F., etc.	d
Apr.	28	1958	25502	Jankwitz	Augusta B., etc.	inc
		[1922-1924]	8571	Jansen	Ernie Anton	d
July	10	1944	15976	Janson	Erik	d
		[1917-1921]	7254	Janson	Matilda	d
Mar.	14	1951	20803	Janson	Richard Ludwig	d
Mar.	15	1954	22342	Janssen	Ihno P.	d
Nov.	12	1954	22693	Janssen	James C.	d
Feb.	11	1938	13244	Janssen	Lillian	d
Dec.	19	1930	10710	Janssen	Oliver E.	inc
Aug.	23	1927	9613	Jaques	Rosa B.	d
Aug.	11	1944	15989	Jarbal	Viola L.	d
Mar.	24	1945	16492	Jardine	Ida	d
Mar.	20	1938	13510	Jarr	John	d
Nov.	2	1945	16679	Jarvis	Amlia F. G., etc.	d
Apr.	2	1933	11526	Jarvis	Beatrice	inc
Mar.	3	1934	12116	Jarvis	Donald A.	d
July	19	1955	23252	Jarvis	E. B.	d
June		1922	8025	Jarvis	Edward	d
		[1917-1921]	6885	Jarvis	Hansini H.	d
Mar.	28	1944	15857	Jarvis	Julia	d
		[1922-1924]	8486	Jarvis	Miles	d
Feb.	5	1949	19402	Jarvis	Rose	d
Apr.	21	1950	19527	Jarvis	Rose A., etc.	d
		[1868-1869]	393	Jarvis	William	ins
June	5	1958	25595	Jasmann	Mary Traub	d
Dec.	24	1938	13465	Jaso	Alice	m
Oct.	6	1938	13425	Jaso	Domingo	d
Nov.	24	1938	13465	Jaso	Emilio	m
Feb.	8	1930	10805	Jaso	Mauricia	ins
Nov.	20	1943	15570	Jason	Antone, etc.	d

Sept.	11	1914	5739		Jason	Mary	d
Oct.	21	1941	14614		Jasper	Freda	d
Oct.	21	1941	14615		Jasper	George Alexander	d
Mar.	8	1945	16395		Jay	E. C., etc.	d
Aug.	29	1943	15501		Jay	Esther	d
Oct.	14	1938	13459		Jefferds	Wallace Vincent	d
July	29	1942	14918		Jefferson	Jesse	d
		[1917-1921]	7223		Jefferson	Jesse J., etc.	ins
Mar.	4	1936	12540		Jeffery	Clarence	m
July	4	1955	23154		Jeffery	Edward J., etc.	d
Sept.	18	1944	16129		Jeffery	Edward Julian	d
Feb.	15	1954	22340		Jeffery	Ernest M.	d
		[1922-1924]	8302		Jeffery	Helen, Richard & Julian	m
Feb.	4	1936	12540		Jeffery	Richard	m
Nov.	4	1941	14673		Jeffrey	George Riley, etc.	d
Apr.	23	1934	11932		Jeffrey	Myra, etc.	d
Jan.	15	1950	20106		Jeffrey	Rush	d
Oct.	25	1958	25880		Jenck	James A.	m
Oct.	25	1958	25880		Jenck	Timothy	m
		[1904-1907]	4105		Jenkines	Anna W.	d
July	11	1929	10280		Jenkins	Arthur George	d
		1954	22941		Jenkins	Carrie D., etc.	d
		[1917-1921]	7397		Jenkins	Charlotte Carlyon	d
June	14	1933	11541		Jenkins	Edgar William, etc.	d
Sept.	13	1951	20543		Jenkins	Joseph W., etc.	d
Nov.	4	1948	18563		Jenkins	Leo B. F.	d
Apr.	4	1940	13984		Jenkins	Martha H. Morton	d
Nov.		1936	12770		Jenkins	Richard	d
Aug.	15	1958	25856		Jenkins	Rolla D.	d
		[1876-1877]	796		Jenne	David	d
Sept.	20	1951	20554		Jenness	Idella Mary, etc.	d
Aug.	10	1914	5863		Jenni	Fritz	d
		1925	9048		Jennings	Charles	d
Feb.	19	1940	13897		Jennings	Gotfred	d
Aug.	27	1939	13709		Jennings	James Goodman	m
Aug.	24	1936	12717		Jennings	Jennie	d
Feb.	12	1958	26147		Jennings	Julia	d
Dec.	9	1954	22853		Jensen	Alfred J. P.	d
May	18	1927	9607		Jensen	Anders	d
Apr.	13	1953	21694		Jensen	Anna	d
Dec.	27	1953	22198		Jensen	Annie E.	d
		1925	8959		Jensen	August	d
Oct.	11	1938	13372		Jensen	Christ	d

Nov.	2	1945	16660	Jensen	Christen F.	inc
		[1922-1924]	8581	Jensen	Evelyn J.	m
Apr.	16	1945	16478	Jensen	Fred	d
Dec.	10	1929	10403	Jensen	Fred N., etc.	d
Dec.	15	1930	10706	Jensen	Fred P.	d
Apr.	21	1938	13226	Jensen	George	d
		[1922-1924]	8581	Jensen	Grace E.	m
Mar.	12	1942	14856	Jensen	Hans Carl	inc
July	3	1941	14536	Jensen	Harry C.	d
		[1917-1921]	7243	Jensen	Hilmer W.	d
Aug.		1891	2097	Jensen	Jacob Wilhelm	d
Mar.	15	1954	22341	Jensen	Jena J.	d
Jan.	3	1940	14214	Jensen	Jens C.	d
Aug.	10	1942	15009	Jensen	Jens W.	d
Aug.	15	1931	11003	Jensen	John C.	d
July	27	1945	16593	Jensen	John L.	d
Apr.	27	1937	12874	Jensen	Knud	inc
Jan.	8	1940	14267	Jensen	Kristine	d
Nov.	24	1958	26029	Jensen	Lena A.	inc
Jan.	28	1952	21484	Jensen	Lena C.	d
		[1908-1909]	4570	Jensen	Loren F.	d
Aug.	23	1951	20502	Jensen	Louise	d
		1904	3745	Jensen	Louise M.	d
July	30	1954	22950	Jensen	Louise M.	d
Sept.	7	1931	11048	Jensen	N. M.	d
Nov.		1936	12753	Jensen	Nellie	d
Sept.	12	1929	10355	Jensen	Ovc Gunhard	d
Aug.	14	1958	25853	Jensen	Patrick	d
Jan.	28	1928	10131	Jensen	Peter	d
Jan.	15	1933	11790	Jensen	Peter C.	d
Oct.	15	1949	19171	Jensen	Peter James, etc.	d
		[1922-1924]	8581	Jensen	Ruth C.	m
		[1908-1909]	4571	Jensen	S. F.	d
Sept.	2	1936	12733	Jensen	Sallie, etc.	d
July	13	1946	17251	Jensen	Walter	d
May	9	1944	15975	Jenson	Frances	d
Nov.	12	1928	10058	Jeramanos	Katherine, etc.	d
Sept.	26	1955	23389	Jerauld	W. W., etc.	inc
Nov.	10	1956	24262	Jerauld	Woodson William, etc.	d
Aug.	7	1949	19115	Jespersen	Lalonga S.	m
May		1926	9429	Jesse	James William	d
Aug.	22	1912	5435	Jesse	Mary E.	d
May	10	1941	14512	Jessen	C. B., etc.	d

Oct.	5	1945	16727	Jessen	Christian F.	d
Aug.	16	1936	12616	Jessen	Haus C., Sr.	d
May	11	1956	23986	Jessen	Julius T., etc.	d
Nov.	24	1952	21419	Jessmer	Gordon B.	d
Mar.	28	1939	13591	Jessup	Margaret M., etc.	d
May	21	1941	14355	Jessup	Charlie Wright	d
		1869	430	Jett	John	d
Apr.	8	1957	24652	Jewell	Carolina Bale	d
May	27	1934	11938	Jewell	Carrie	d
		1863	230	Jewell	George C.	d
		[1888-1889]	1772	Jewell	George W.	m
		[1888-1889]	1772	Jewell	Ida N.	m
		1891	2061	Jewell	Isaac R.	d
		1872	516	Jewell	Jesse	d
June	1	1943	15425	Jewell	Jesse I.	d
		1874	715	Jewell	Mary	d
		1909	4776	Jewell	Mary M.	d
		[1917-1921]	7560	Jewell	Petrea	d
		[1888-1889]	1772	Jewell	Ruby Grace	m
Oct.	30	1932	11397	Jewell	Samuel M., etc.	d
Nov.	19	1911	5120	Jewett	John H.	d
Nov.	27	1913	5628	Jewett	Mary A.	d
Aug.	9	1954	22629	Jillson	Debra Ann	m
Mar.	21	1955	23070	Jillson	Ernest H., etc.	d
Aug.	9	1954	22628	Jillson	Harlan S.	m
Apr.	21	1955	23071	Jillson	Norma Elizabeth, etc.	d
Dec.	10	1934	12076	Jobbins	Alphaeus	d
Oct.	14	1951	20606	Jobe	Thomas Fredrick, etc.	d
Feb.	14	1947	17565	Johannessen	Karl Gustav	d
May		1914	5757	Johannsen	L. M.	d
		[1908-1909]	4587	Johannsen	Ludwig Matthias	d
July	23	1938	13323	Johannsen	Nils	d
Mar.	13	1958	25460	Johannson	Robert	d
Nov.	1	1944	16240	Johansen	Andreas	d
Jan.	1	1933	11772	Johansen	Andris Martin	d
May	28	1939	13625	Johansen	Hanna	d
Jan.	9	1951	20143	Johansen	Hans Carl	d
Aug.	21	1947	17904	Johanson	Alexander	d
Oct.	10	1957	25006	Johns	Pearl Margaret Ann, etc.	d
		[1896-1901]	3046	Johnson	A.	d
Oct.	22	1950	19886	Johnson	Aileen H.	d
Sept.	23	1929	10387	Johnson	Aina	d
Apr.	1	1926	9455	Johnson	Albert	d

Feb.	6	1931	10863		Johnson	Albert	d
Oct.	12	1950	19812		Johnson	Alice Alvira	d
Mar.	2	1930	10581		Johnson	Alice Lillian	m
Jan.		1910	4997		Johnson	Alma	inc
		[1896-1901]	2988		Johnson	Almon T.	d
		[1917-1921]	7498		Johnson	Amanda	d
Mar.	17	1941	14351		Johnson	Andrew	d
		1908	4505		Johnson	Andrew C.	m
Sept.		1925	8987		Johnson	Anna	d
Oct.	3	1955	23405		Johnson	Anna A., etc.	d
Apr.		1925	9215		Johnson	Anna M.	d
Aug.	27	1946	17277		Johnson	Archabild M., etc.	d
		1882	1236		Johnson	Bertha	d
		[1880-1882]	1126		Johnson	Bertha	m
		1901	3123		Johnson	Catherine	d
Apr.	22	1934	11832		Johnson	Catherine Frances	m
Jan.		1910	4972		Johnson	Charles	d
May	13	1954	22456		Johnson	Charles	d
		[1858-1863]	122		Johnson	Charles	m
		[1904-1907]	3924		Johnson	Charles	d
		1925	9060		Johnson	Charles A.	d
Oct.	28	1927	9728		Johnson	Charles A.	d
Feb.	30	1948	18191		Johnson	Charles A.	d
Mar.	22	1942	14788		Johnson	Charles Axel	d
May	25	1946	17170		Johnson	Charles D.	d
Mar.	18	1931	10884		Johnson	Charles D., etc.	d
		1943	15305		Johnson	Charles W.	d
Jan.	16	1922	7926		Johnson	Charlotte May	d
Apr.	15	1929	10243		Johnson	Chester	m inc
June	30	1954	22507		Johnson	Christine, etc.	d
Aug.	29	1942	14962		Johnson	Claude E.	d
Apr.		1908	4447		Johnson	Claus J.	d
		[1917-1921]	7720		Johnson	Conrad	m
Dec.	9	1958	26136		Johnson	Cornelia V.	d
Aug.	12	1950	19811		Johnson	Cornelius Marion	d
		1896	2649		Johnson	D. W.	d
Mar.	9	1956	23842		Johnson	Danny Raymond	m
Nov.	12	1953	22172		Johnson	David	m
Oct.	4	1947	17926		Johnson	David E.	d
Mar.	14	1958	25463		Johnson	Donald Leslie, etc.	d
Mar.	11	1935	12222		Johnson	Earl	m
Jan.	31	1935	12370		Johnson	Edith R.	d
Feb.	31	1930	10826		Johnson	Edward	d

		1922	7929		Johnson	Edwin V. D.	d
		1888	1709		Johnson	Eleanor	d
		[1904-1907]	3811		Johnson	Elizabeth	d
		[1917-1921]	7030		Johnson	Elizabeth R.	d
Jan.	6	1945	16803		Johnson	Elmer K., etc.	d
Aug.	10	1952	21183		Johnson	Elsie (aka Mrs. Martin C.), etc	d
May	11	1941	14435		Johnson	Emma	inc
Mar.	14	1956	23786		Johnson	Emma A.	d
May	7	1928	9869		Johnson	Emma G.	d
Mar.	15	1929	10243		Johnson	Ernest	m inc
Nov.	3	1941	14693		Johnson	Ernest	d
Feb.	13	1943	15677		Johnson	Ethel E., etc.	d
Apr.	2	1930	10581		Johnson	Ethel Maria	m
Jan.	29	1957	25180		Johnson	Eugene Evans	d
Mar.	9	1956	23842		Johnson	Frances Elizabeth	m
		[1890-1891]	1988		Johnson	Francis John	d
May	11	1957	24658		Johnson	Frank	d
		[1907-1908]	4258		Johnson	Frank	d
Aug.	25	1945	16624		Johnson	Frank E.	d
		1926	9250		Johnson	Fred	d
		[1917-1921]	7441		Johnson	Frederick	d
Apr.		1934	11832		Johnson	Frederick Robert	m
Mar.	16	1956	24337		Johnson	Geoffrey Steven	m
		1917	6610		Johnson	George	m
June	15	1952	21062		Johnson	George V.	d
		[1857-1858]	56		Johnson	George W.	d
Nov.	27	1957	25045		Johnson	Gladys W.	d
Oct.	2	1934	11943		Johnson	Grace	d
June	21	1943	15481		Johnson	Gus	d
Sept.	31	1944	16108		Johnson	Gustav, etc.	d
		1921	7744		Johnson	Hans, etc.	d
Jan.	16	1956	24337		Johnson	Harriet Andrea	m
Apr.	1	1940	13913		Johnson	Harriet E.	d
Apr.	11	1935	12223		Johnson	Henning	d
Mar.	22	1914	5701		Johnson	Hester C.	d
Dec.	24	1951	20692		Johnson	Ida	d
Dec.	18	1958	26086		Johnson	Ida F.	d
Mar.	8	1944	15826		Johnson	Irene V.	d
		[1895-1896]	2571		Johnson	Isabella H.	d
Dec.	24	1954	22940		Johnson	J. A.	d
Nov.	19	1932	11414		Johnson	J. E.	inc
Apr.	13	1957	24587		Johnson	J. Harold, Jr., etc.	d
July		1947	17786		Johnson	James	d

Nov.	12	1953	22172	Johnson	James	m
May	15	1955	23117	Johnson	James E.	d
		1879	1010	Johnson	James G.	d
Apr.	8	1946	17128	Johnson	James M., etc.	d
Nov.	2	1958	25975	Johnson	Janice Ellen	m
Sept.	6	1924	8674	Johnson	Jeanette A.	d
Mar.	11	1935	12222	Johnson	Joan	m
Oct.	3	1958	25975	Johnson	Joann Caroline	m
July	24	1947	17864	Johnson	Johanna	d
Nov.	16	1943	15642	Johnson	John	d
Dec.	1	1946	17461	Johnson	John	d
		1942	15113	Johnson	John Alvin	d
Jan.	2	1934	11809	Johnson	John E.	d
		[1917-1921]	7425	Johnson	John E.	d
Dec.	7	1927	9800	Johnson	John Eber	d
July	9	1957	24862	Johnson	John I.	d
Jan.	13	1921	7924	Johnson	John Oliver	d
Dec.	4	1932	11434	Johnson	John R., etc.	d
		[1888-1889]	1754	Johnson	John Z.	d
Sept.	16	1957	24959	Johnson	Johnnie Mae	m
		1935	12355	Johnson	Jonas Edward	d
Mar.	3	1944	15867	Johnson	Josephine	d
Jan.	19	1953	21589	Johnson	Julius H.	d
Aug.	30	1928	9921	Johnson	Katherine	d
Jan.	15	1939	13757	Johnson	L. Chris, etc.	d
Feb.	9	1932	11471	Johnson	L. J., etc.	d
June	21	1945	16576	Johnson	Lena	d
Aug.	30	1941	14567	Johnson	Leonide B.	d
		1876	787	Johnson	Levi	d
Sept.	17	1913	5497	Johnson	Loraine S.	m
May	28	1942	14916	Johnson	Lucien H.	d
Feb.	16	1958	26154	Johnson	Mae Ellen	d
June		1943	15396	Johnson	Magdalena	d
May	14	1950	19628	Johnson	Maggie E., etc.	d
Jan.	6	1958	25263	Johnson	Malcolm	d
Oct.	7	1913	5596	Johnson	Malinda	d
Apr.	26	1948	18254	Johnson	Malinda C., etc.	d
July	3	1948	18318	Johnson	Malinda C., etc.	d
Aug.	14	1930	10601	Johnson	Marshall N.	d
Dec.	18	1925	9145	Johnson	Martha L.	d
July	14	1936	12550	Johnson	Martin	d
July	7	1947	17879	Johnson	Martin	d
Dec.	27	1948	18600	Johnson	Martin C., etc.	d

May	22	1958	25568	Johnson	Martin O., etc.	d
		1889	1870	Johnson	Mary	inc
July	18	1935	12230	Johnson	Mary	d
July	29	1951	20417	Johnson	Mary	d
Apr.	8	1954	22383	Johnson	Mary	d
Dec.	27	1927	9758	Johnson	Mary A.	d
Mar.	2	1930	10581	Johnson	Mary Julia	m
		1921	7855	Johnson	Mary R.	d
Aug.	22	1931	11086	Johnson	Mathilda	d
Sept.	15	1925	8961	Johnson	May S.	d
		1877	886	Johnson	Melville	d
Mar.	3	1944	15870	Johnson	Minnie O.	d
June		1926	9252	Johnson	Nellie	d
June	16	1941	14521	Johnson	Oliva	d
Aug.		1911	5018	Johnson	Olive B.	d
		1921	7748	Johnson	Oliver	inc
Apr.	12	1940	13957	Johnson	Oliver	d
May	7	1950	19616	Johnson	Oscar A.	d
Apr.	4	1939	13633	Johnson	Oscar E., etc.	d
Nov.	21	1951	20626	Johnson	Oscar H.	d
		[1901-1904]	3477	Johnson	Otto	d
		1922	7968	Johnson	P. A., etc.	d
Jan.	5	1952	21495	Johnson	Patricia M.	m
		[1880-1882]	1125	Johnson	Peter	d
May	26	1938	13252	Johnson	Rasmus	d
Jan.	19	1935	12380	Johnson	Ray	d
July	9	1954	22577	Johnson	Reins, etc.	d
Nov.	25	1949	19331	Johnson	Richard	d
		[1908-1909]	4685	Johnson	Robert F.	d
Jan.	14	1939	13789	Johnson	Rose	d
Jan.	9	1934	12095	Johnson	Roy A.	d
Mar.	11	1935	12222	Johnson	Ruth	m
		1930	10645	Johnson	Sam, etc.	d
Feb.	7	1915	6087	Johnson	Samuel B.	d
Mar.	24	1947	17597	Johnson	Sidney A., etc.	d
Nov.	7	1949	19239	Johnson	Spencer, etc.	d
		1870	465	Johnson	T. J.	d
		1895	2517	Johnson	Temperance M.	d
		[1887-1888]	1658	Johnson	Thomas	d
Aug.	27	1929	10298	Johnson	Thomas H.	d
		1907	4235	Johnson	Thos. J.	d
May	7	1952	21040	Johnson	Virginia M.	m
Apr.	17	1946	17151	Johnson	Walter	d

July	26	1953	21866	Johnson	Walter S.	d
		1880	1071	Johnson	William	d
		[1879-1880]	1053	Johnson	William	d
		[1908-1909]	4767	Johnson	William	d
June	11	1931	10964	Johnson	William J.	d
		1908	4505	Johnson	William M.	m
Feb.	25	1936	12533	Johnson	William Mc Kinley	d
Nov.	12	1953	22172	Johnson	William R.	m
Apr.	3	1942	14883	Johnson	Winifred, etc.	d
		[1858-1863]	122	Johnson	Wm. A.	m
		1858	94	Johnson	Wm. B.	d
Mar.	14	1931	11052	Johnston	C. J.	d
Dec.		1925	9117	Johnston	Carrie, Mrs., etc.	d
June		1922	8049	Johnston	Charles A., etc.	d
Sept.	2	1922	8058	Johnston	Eva	d
Sept.	5	1933	11577	Johnston	Evaline	d
June	17	1931	10915	Johnston	Ida R.	d
June	2	1950	19668	Johnston	John W.	d
Aug.	24	1957	24751	Johnston	John W. R.	inc
Jan.	4	1938	13204	Johnston	John William	d
		1922	8143	Johnston	Julius	d
Feb.	4	1938	13205	Johnston	M.	d
		1891	2099	Johnston	Mary	d
Apr.	23	1956	23881	Johnston	Mary Eleanor	d
Feb.	4	1916	6361	Johnston	Robert L.	d
June	10	1946	17196	Johnston	Samuel	d
Oct.	4	1952	21283	Johnstone	Henry S.	d
Jan.	17	1957	25223	Johnstone	Richard W.	d
		[1907-1908]	4382	Jonas	Noah	d
		1868	372	Jones	A. J.	d
May	4	1938	13282	Jones	Addie, etc.	d
June	19	1940	14002	Jones	Alfred	inc
Aug.	19	1940	14003	Jones	Alfred	ins
Nov.	3	1941	14665	Jones	Alfred	d
July	22	1935	12276	Jones	Alice B., etc.	d
July	6	1948	18500	Jones	Alice R.	d
Mar.	26	1958	25423	Jones	Alvie N., etc.	d
Dec.	28	1932	11426	Jones	Amanda	d
		[1917-1921]	6760	Jones	Annie J.	d
Jan.	30	1937	13199	Jones	Bertha Fay	d
Jan.	16	1936	12804	Jones	Bertha L.	d
July	12	1948	18282	Jones	Betha A., etc.	d
May	12	1945	16523	Jones	Brainerd	d

		[1917-1921]	7074	Jones	Cellie	d
July	6	1939	13687	Jones	Charles A.	d
Aug.	27	1934	11939	Jones	Charles Leroy	d
Apr.	22	1924	8834	Jones	Charles M.	d
Feb.	21	1911	5154	Jones	Clarence D.	m
		[1896-1901]	3039	Jones	Cordelia	d
		[1891-1894]	2286	Jones	David W.	d
Jan.		1921	7896	Jones	Dora A.	d
Apr.	31	1949	19433	Jones	Earl P., etc.	d
Feb.	23	1943	15688	Jones	Edward Lewis	d
Mar.	27	1958	25329	Jones	Edward M.	inc
Aug.	27	1947	17912	Jones	Edward W.	d
		[1917-1921]	7508	Jones	Edwin	d
Aug.	11	1930	10702	Jones	Eliza Ellen	d
Apr.	21	1952	21004	Jones	Elizabeth C.	d
Sept.		1926	9265	Jones	Elizabeth, etc.	d
May	15	1956	23990	Jones	Elmo Edwin, etc.	d
Nov.	9	1954	22685	Jones	Eloisa	d
Mar.	25	1935	12170	Jones	Emma A.	inc
June	1	1935	12346	Jones	Emma A.	d
		[1904-1907]	4148	Jones	Everett	m
May	20	1957	24745	Jones	Fern A.	d
		[1873-1874]	623	Jones	Fred	m
Nov.	14	1941	14706	Jones	Fred Lee, etc.	d
July	1	1951	20420	Jones	Fred Wilton, etc.	d
Mar.	23	1940	13905	Jones	Fred, etc.	d
Apr.	15	1946	17076	Jones	Frieda M.	d
Nov.	5	1940	14134	Jones	H. W., etc.	d
Oct.	25	1956	24017	Jones	Harold	d
Mar.	4	1946	17044	Jones	Harry	d
Aug.	11	1955	23363	Jones	Harry C.	d
Aug.	24	1941	14586	Jones	Harry Oliver, etc.	ins
Mar.	23	1946	16959	Jones	Henrico, A. M.	d
Oct.	12	1942	15038	Jones	Herbert James, etc.	d
Mar.	6	1944	15875	Jones	Hugh L.	d
July	6	1952	21171	Jones	J. A.	d
		[1917-1921]	7325	Jones	James H.	d
Apr.	30	1942	14875	Jones	Jeanette S.	d
Mar.	9	1948	18216	Jones	Joe	d
May	18	1944	15890	Jones	John H.	d
Feb.	18	1944	16271	Jones	John L.	d
Apr.	15	1946	17077	Jones	John L.	d
Oct.	13	1921	7829	Jones	John Robert	d

Dec.	27	1950	20012	Jones	John Wayne	m
Aug.	6	1958	25832	Jones	Jonah	d
June	12	1941	14513	Jones	Joseph Franklin, etc.	d
Mar.	18	1952	20990	Jones	Josie, etc.	d
Nov.	10	1952	21396	Jones	Kate E.	inc
Oct.	5	1927	9693	Jones	Lewis S.	g
Sept.	5	1924	8747	Jones	Lizzie Armstrong	inc
		1924	8750	Jones	Lizzie Armstrong	d
Mar.	4	1929	10163	Jones	Martha	d
Nov.	6	1913	5655	Jones	Martha Marian	m
		[1877-1878]	890	Jones	Mary	d
May	10	1925	8929	Jones	Mary P.	d
Apr.	9	1954	22447	Jones	Mary Sarah, etc.	d
Mar.	16	1929	10410	Jones	Mayme	d
		[1904-1907]	4148	Jones	Melvin	m
June	2	1946	17182	Jones	Milton H.	ins
Nov.	12	1946	17338	Jones	Milton H.	d
		[1873-1874]	623	Jones	Minnie	m
		[1917-1921]	6668	Jones	Patrick Carrole	d
		[1917-1921]	7449	Jones	Raford W.	m
Feb.	29	1916	6223	Jones	Rebecca Ann	d
Sept.	11	1915	6024	Jones	Richard Hugh	d
		1901	3371	Jones	Robert	d
		[1901-1904]	3372	Jones	Robert R.	m
July	25	1954	22616	Jones	Rosa, etc.	d
May	21	1958	25567	Jones	Roxie	d
Sept.	17	1926	9314	Jones	Smith P.	d
Dec.	20	1933	11720	Jones	Smith P., Jr.	m
Jan.		1924	8787	Jones	Suzanne	d
Dec.	2	1932	11458	Jones	Theodore K.	d
		1884	1403	Jones	Thomas	d
Feb.	19	1932	11480	Jones	Thomas A., etc.	d
Mar.	12	1927	9806	Jones	Thomas B.	d
		1887	1627	Jones	Thomas J.	d
		1873	613	Jones	W. D.	d
June	7	1946	17233	Jones	Wanda	m
Oct.	23	1946	17307	Jones	Warren M.	d
Feb.	6	1951	20720	Jones	William H.	d
May	26	1957	24693	Jones	William J.	inc
May	12	1925	8854	Jones	William L., etc.	d
		[1908-1909]	4595	Jones	William Ladd	d
		[1889-1890]	1883	Jones	William M.	d
		[1858-1863]	119	Jones	Wm.	d

		[1896-1901]	3098	Jones	Wm. D.	d
Dec.	24	1924	8761	Joos	Placide	d
		1901	3251	Joost	Carl & Anna	m
Aug.	20	1951	20499	Joost	Catharine	d
Apr.	30	1925	9156	Joost	Frank, etc.	d
		1901	3251	Joost	Harry	m
		[1904-1907]	4002	Joost	Jacob	d
		1878	948	Joost	John	d
		1901	3251	Joost	Nettie	m
		1901	3251	Joost	Rudolph	m
Dec.		1925	9114	Joosten	Frederich W.	d
		1943	15319	Joosten	Helene A., etc.	d
Dec.	10	1954	22910	Jordan	Arthur L.	d
May	15	1949	18956	Jordan	H. Lloyd	d
Nov.	13	1933	11711	Jordan	Harvey O'Mena	d
Dec.	15	1949	19374	Jordan	Hattie	d
		[1873-1874]	642	Jordan	Joshua	d
Mar.	4	1952	20962	Jordan	Julia O'Meara	d
Apr.	18	1952	20991	Jordan	Julia O'Meara	d
June	22	1949	18973	Jordan	Viroqua	d
		1875	785	Jordan	W. H.	d
June	12	1947	17752	Jordan	William	d
Sept.	23	1956	24009	Jordan	William R., etc.	d
		[1901-1904]	3502	Jorg	Crescenz et al	m
Apr.	3	1947	17671	Jorgansen	Ellen Marie, etc.	d
Sept.	14	1939	13724	Jorgensen	Arleen	m
Mar.	8	1944	16311	Jorgensen	Clara	inc
Jan.	27	1947	18064	Jorgensen	Clara M.	d
May	13	1931	10910	Jorgensen	George	d
Aug.	23	1943	15489	Jorgensen	George P.	d
Dec.	6	1927	9734	Jorgensen	Harry	d
Sept.	11	1928	10055	Jorgensen	Harry I.	d
Mar.	11	1958	25454	Jorgensen	Henry B.	d
Jan.	12	1940	13892	Jorgensen	L. C.	d
Sept.	11	1932	11251	Jorgensen	Maria Christine, etc.	d
Apr.	6	1929	10273	Jorgensen	Niels, etc.	d
Oct.	9	1932	11355	Jorgensen	Vernon Peter	m
July	31	1950	19734	Jorgensen	Virgil W., etc.	d
Sept.	1	1928	10050	Jorgensen	Wilhelm	d
Oct.	22	1952	21358	Jorgensen	William A., etc.	d
		[1888-1889]	1748	Jory	Benjamin	d
		[1888-1889]	1739	Jose	Louisa	m
		[1888-1889]	1739	Jose	Paul Henry	m

		[1888-1889]	1739		Jose	Sophia	m
Dec.	30	1953	22203		Joseph	Alfred P.	d
Feb.	7	1936	12518		Joseph	Gloria	m
Sept.	28	1953	21977		Joseph	J. W., etc.	d
Dec.	10	1949	19358		Joseph	Mary	inc
July	19	1950	19760		Joseph	Mary	d
Aug.	9	1948	18505		Josephs	Paul, Sr.	d
Sept.	21	1918	6838		Joslin	Jason W.	d
Dec.	9	1957	25072		Josue	Arthur H.	d
July	7	1950	19800		Journey	G. W.	d
Oct.	28	1940	14085		Joy	Annie M.	d
Dec.	1	1955	23566		Joy	Lillian F., etc.	d
		[1904-1907]	3750		Joy	Sarah N.	d
Feb.	28	1938	13493		Joy	Thomas Benjamin, etc.	d
Sept.	4	1936	12740		Joy	William H.	d
		[1873-1874]	618		Joyce	Ann	d
		[1877-1878]	920		Joyce	Thomas	d
Mar.	11	1947	17637		Judd	Margart H.	d
Nov.	12	1947	17942		Judge	William	d
		[1858-1863]	100		Judkins	L. M.	d
Sept.	27	1928	10044		Juell	Nila	d
Dec.	28	1928	10081		Juhl	Luis P.	inc
		[1917-1921]	7145		Juilliard	Louis W.	d
Aug.	13	1958	25702		Juler	Olive M.	d
Mar.	26	1931	10891		Julin	Adolf	d
Mar.	27	1948	18755		Jung	Jakob, etc.	d
		[1922-1924]	8404		Junkin	Polla D.	d
		1942	15055		Junqueir	J. J.	d
Jan.	4	1950	20083		Junqueiro	Albert, etc.	d
Mar.	23	1953	21601		Jurado	Jessie M., etc.	inc
May	17	1953	21703		Jurado	Jessie M., etc.	d
		1917	6413		Jurgens	Cora Inez	d
Feb.	31	1953	22260		Jurgensen	C. M.	d
July	17	1949	19085		Jurgenson	Fred P.	d
Feb.	8	1955	23639		Jurgewitz	Charlyne C.	d
Mar.	7	1957	24574		Jury	Maude A.	d
Jan.	6	1946	17468		Juste	Leopold	d
		1885	1488		Justi	Charles	d
		1925	9147		Justi	Hulda I.	d
		[1896-1901]	3031		Justi	Marie C.	d
May	22	1956	24005		Justice	Lewis William	m
Nov.	22	1953	22129		Justis	Harry W.	d
Apr.	8	1927	9488		Jutting	Louis	d

Month	Day	Year	File No.	Surname	Given Name	Type
May	8	1937	12885	Kaartinen	Ida	d
June	5	1936	12664	Kabler	Harry A.	d
Feb.	31	1934	11846	Kachler	Wannetta	d
Apr.	31	1950	19606	Kaclin	Edward	d
Aug.	4	1922	8107	Kaelinke	George	d
Oct.	14	1938	13350	Kagan	Joseph, etc.	d
Mar.	2	1943	15294	Kage	Henry	d
Dec.	21	1952	21474	Kahdemann	Paul	d
Oct.	23	1940	14120	Kahle	Antone	d
Feb.	13	1948	18229	Kahlke	Christine, etc.	d
		1922	8164	Kahn	Achille	d
Dec.	10	1919	7265	Kahn	Moise	d
Feb.	29	1927	9685	Kahn	Rosa	d
		[1910-1911]	4907	Kahrs	Augusta Annchen	d
Jan.	12	1943	15221	Kahrs	Ibie L.	d
Apr.	28	1953	21673	Kahrs	Leander, etc.	d
Feb.	12	1932	11193	Kai	Kiknge	m
Apr.	12	1932	11193	Kai	Kimiko	m
June	13	1936	12583	Kaiser	Anton	d
Apr.	10	1955	23108	Kaiser	June C.	inc
Feb.	14	1949	18834	Kaiser	Lena K., etc.	d
July	21	1957	24824	Kaithley	James W., etc.	d
		1924	8742	Kalich	William G., etc.	d
Jan.	22	1954	22936	Kalin	Benedict	d
Nov.	8	1952	21393	Kalipolis	Peter J.	d
May	4	1948	18372	Kalipolis	William, etc.	d
July	10	1958	25768	Kalish	Lena Husler, etc.	d
July	5	1929	10332	Kalkbrenner	Mary	d
Oct.	12	1930	10729	Kalklbrenner	Martin	d
Sept.	29	1948	18544	Kallman	Arthur E.	d
Dec.	18	1936	12835	Kalquest	Alfred	d
Dec.	18	1936	12836	Kalquest	Mary	d
		1923	8535	Kalthoff	William	d
Feb.	16	1934	11867	Kamabata	Alice	m
Apr.	16	1934	11867	Kamabata	Earl Hiroshi, etc.	m
Mar.	16	1934	11867	Kamabata	Margaret Shizerl, etc.	m
Feb.	29	1932	11456	Kamabata	Roy, etc.	d
Oct.	24	1932	11394	Kamahara	Toshimasa	m
July		1936	12688	Kamahara	Yoshito	m
Sept.	24	1932	11394	Kamahara	Yoslito	m
		1921	7715	Kamp	Julia	d
		[1883-1884]	1305	Kamp	Julia	m

Month	Day	Year	File No.	Surname	Given Name	Type
Sept.	10	1954	22745	Kanduth	Rosa	inc
Apr.	23	1954	22485	Kane	Charles E.	d
Nov.	21	1936	12712	Kane	Donald Lee	m
May	7	1933	11536	Kane	E. J.	d
Jan.	31	1938	13522	Kane	George, etc.	d
Sept.	11	1937	12994	Kane	Mary A.	d
Aug.	21	1936	12712	Kane	Robert James	m
May	7	1945	16564	Kanihan	John	d
Sept.	21	1950	19937	Kanihan	Michael J.	d
Sept.	7	1923	8350	Kanode	Charles P.	d
Dec.	24	1915	6137	Kaplan	Ella M.	d
Nov.	10	1957	25076	Kaplan	Nathan	inc
June	28	1952	21146	Kaponat	Florence Estelle, etc.	d
Aug.	29	1948	18491	Karas	Forest Elwood, etc.	d
Aug.	15	1951	20546	Karas	Tom J., etc.	d
Mar.	3	1950	19546	Karcher	William	d
June	28	1919	7098	Karidis	Harry Nicolaou	d
Feb.	12	1953	21568	Karkov	Alexander	d
Sept.	18	1930	10708	Karls	Michael	d
Oct.	27	1939	13794	Karlson	Axel E., etc.	d
May	15	1942	14899	Karn	Walter W., etc.	d
Feb.	15	1943	15226	Karn	E. M.	d
Oct.	17	1930	10733	Karne	Hubert	m
May	22	1947	17754	Karnes	J. E.	d
Jan.	8	1932	11187	Karr	Bert M.	d
Jan.	18	1955	23597	Karras	George	d
Oct.	25	1955	23462	Karras	Olga	d
Aug.	19	1930	10604	Karrell	Chris	d
June	25	1932	11283	Karsama	Niklas J., etc.	d
Feb.	11	1925	9052	Karsten	Anna	d
Nov.		1925	9041	Karsten	Christian, etc.	d
Aug.	4	1955	23406	Karsten	Emily A.	d
		[1907-1910]	4673	Kasel	J. B.	d
		[1900-1901]	3162	Kaselan	John C.	d
Feb.	9	1915	5933	Kaster	James	d
		1891	2111	Katen	Annie et al	m
July	18	1951	20399	Katen	Frank A.	d
Mar.	20	1934	12007	Katen	Frank, etc.	d
		[1921-1922]	7945	Katen	John	d
Dec.	19	1944	16179	Katen	Louis	d
Nov.	23	1953	22134	Katen	Marian A.	d
Mar.	11	1955	23040	Katen	Mary	d

Month	Day	Year	File No.	Surname	Given Name	Type
Jan.	21	1951	20814	Katen	Anna	d
Sept.	28	1945	16671	Kathriner	Josephine	d
June	9	1950	19682	Katler	Robert H., etc.	d
		1915	6006	Kattrup	Thorvald	d
Aug.	21	1950	19829	Katzer	Marie T., etc.	d
		[1894-1895]	2409	Kauffman	Frank	d
		[1881-1882]	1185	Kauffman	Frank Antone	d
Aug.	19	1929	10359	Kauffman	Hazel Mary	g
Oct.	17	1928	10021	Kauffman	Melvin C.	d
Oct.	19	1929	10359	Kauffman	Zelma I.	g
		1884	1406	Kauffmann	Catherine	d
July	17	1934	11952	Kaufmann	Max	d
June	15	1936	12635	Kauppi	John Kristian	d
June	8	1951	20389	Kausek	Joseph	d
		1923	8468	Kawaoka	Hideo	m
		1923	8468	Kawaoka	Itsico	m
		1923	8468	Kawaoka	Mitsuto	m
Mar.	30	1940	14316	Kaware	Hatua, etc.	m
		[1894-1895]	2446	Kay	Ah	d
Dec.	2	1940	14293	Kay	Teresa, etc.	d
Aug.	30	1926	9268	Kayser	A. H.	inc
July	17	1928	9974	Kayser	A. H.	d
Mar.	30	1952	20891	Kayser	Harry	d
Feb.	26	1934	11838	Keachler	Joseph	d
Apr.	16	1935	12273	Keachler	Joseph	d
Dec.	3	1940	14213	Keane	John	d
Oct.	30	1935	12393	Kearas	Thomas	inc
Nov.	13	1935	12402	Kearas	Thomas	d
June	11	1938	13292	Kearn	James J.	d
		[1894-1895]	2471	Kearney	Alice	m
Apr.	29	1956	23896	Kearney	Alice G., etc.	d
Mar.	9	1943	15269	Kearney	Emily C.	d
Dec.	23	1956	24346	Kearney	James Clark	d
		[1894-1895]	2471	Kearney	Louis Phillip	m
Apr.	5	1935	12218	Kearney	Mary	d
		[1880-1881]	1077	Kearney	Patrick	d
Jan.	24	1950	20006	Kearney	Susan J.	d
Oct.	22	1950	19885	Kearney	William J., etc.	d
		[1886-1887]	1602	Kearns	James	inc
		1903	3548	Kearny	Dennis H.	d
Apr.	22	1954	22479	Keast	Caroline	d
Mar.	31	1940	14318	Keating	Gilbert Kennedy, etc.	d

Month	Day	Year	File No.	Surname	Given Name	Type
Apr.	21	1937	13129	Keating	William	inc
Sept.	19	1939	13790	Keaton	Harriett, etc.	d
		[1889-1890]	1887	Keck	Fred	d
Oct.		1924	8731	Keck	John	d
Jan.	9	1946	17521	Kecskemeti	John, Jr.	d
June	3	1941	14460	Kee	David S.	d
Apr.	17	1913	5498	Kee	James	d
Jan.	8	1943	15663	Kee	Mary A.	d
July	15	1954	22591	Kee	Robert T.	inc
		1921	7864	Keechler	Bernice Katherine	m
Oct.	17	1921	7864	Keechler	Bertha Catherine	m
Oct.	17	1921	7864	Keechler	Helen Eunice	m
Oct.		1920	7535	Keechler	Joseph Peter	d
Oct.	17	1921	7864	Keechler	Josephine Rose	m
		1921	7864	Keechler	Loraine Margaret	m
Apr.	16	1954	22394	Keeder	Edgar, etc.	d
		1925	8969	Keefe	Aileen E.	m
		1925	8969	Keefe	Bernice V.	m
Apr.	2	1926	9228	Keefe	Helen, etc.	m
Feb.	23	1940	13906	Keefe	John H., etc.	d
Apr.		1926	9228	Keefe	Katherine, etc.	m
		1925	8969	Keefe	Lucille F.	m
Mar.		1924	8830	Keefe	Thome	d
Apr.	19	1940	13968	Keefer	Irvin R.	d
		1898	2790	Keegan	Daisy	m
Dec.	15	1917	6547	Keegan	Elizabeth	d
Sept.	30	1932	11327	Keegan	Ellen	d
		1898	2791	Keegan	Frank D.	d
Dec.	13	1929	10379	Keegan	Harry J.	d
		1898	2790	Keegan	James	m
		1898	2790	Keegan	Lilly A.	m
		1911	5152	Keegan	Thomas P.	inc
Oct.	2	1915	6029	Keegan	Thos. P.	d
Apr.	3	1926	9423	Keeler	Clarence G.	d
Dec.	18	1947	18097	Keeling	Arthur F.	d
Dec.	4	1947	18080	Keeling	Bill A.	d
Feb.	7	1948	18211	Keenan	Edward	d
		1907	4215	Keene	Jacob C.	d
Nov.	29	1937	13174	Kees	Marion A.	d
Nov.	29	1937	13174	Kees	Marion H.	d
Mar.	13	1953	21645	Kegan	Adelia. etc.	d
June		1952	21135	Kehoe	Robert F.	d

Month	Day	Year	File No.	Surname	Given Name	Type
May	31	1952	21155	Kehoe	Robert F.	d
		1911	5189	Keig	Harriet Belle	d
		[1907-1910]	4425	Keil	George P.	d
		1922	8235	Keil	Peter	d
Feb.	6	1939	13833	Kein	William G.	d
Apr.	13	1945	16526	Keinast	Konrad	d
Feb.	21	1958	26096	Keiser	Amanda	inc
July	1	1958	25748	Keiser	Amanda Jane	inc
May	2	1939	13630	Keiser	Antone	inc
June	25	1939	13651	Keiser	Antone	d
Dec.	24	1936	12816	Keiser	Dora	ins
Feb.	17	1947	17574	Keiser	Engelbert B., etc.	d
June	12	1950	19691	Keiser	Eva A.	m
Apr.	5	1935	12220	Keiser	Francesca	d
Mar.	17	1950	19565	Keiser	Joseph	d
Sept.	12	1939	13697	Keiser	Theodore A.	d
Dec.	5	1948	18720	Keith	Eileen M., etc.	d
		[1875-1880]	763	Keithley	Jacob	d
Apr.	31	1954	22423	Keizar	Martha A.	d
July	12	1936	12677	Kekuchi	Tomouyuki	m
Sept.	2	1932	11378	Kellan	Alexander	d
Jan.	27	1943	15694	Kelleher	Elizabeth T.	inc
July	28	1934	11962	Kelleher	Timothy	d
		1952	21014	Keller	Charles C.	d
Feb.	20	1947	17585	Keller	Edward A.	d
Aug.	19	1924	8685	Keller	Edwin Paul	ins
May	29	1929	10299	Keller	Edwin Paul	d
Jan.	3	1941	14664	Keller	Helene	d
July	11	1933	11661	Keller	Ida J.	d
		1905	3900	Keller	J. S.	d
Feb.	8	1928	10087	Keller	Jacob	d
Oct.	17	1945	16722	Keller	Jacob, etc.	d
Nov.	19	1955	23542	Keller	John	d
Mar.	24	1944	15799	Keller	Phillip L.	d
Mar.	10	1950	19514	Keller	Schuyler Colfax	d
July	3	1950	19793	Keller	Schuyler Colfax	d
Oct.	14	1921	7846	Keller	William	d
		1923	8550	Kelley	Charles A., etc.	d
Dec.	20	1958	26093	Kelley	Charles, etc.	d
		1904	3757	Kelley	Eddie	m
May	13	1936	12581	Kelley	Emma F.	d
Apr.	17	1947	17696	Kelley	Frank	inc

Month	Day	Year	File No.	Surname	Given Name	Type
May	21	1952	20936	Kelley	Frank	d
		1904	3757	Kelley	Gertie	m
Feb.	26	1952	20881	Kelley	Howard H.	d
May	26	1935	12285	Kelley	James Joseph	d
Jan.	8	1932	11189	Kelley	Jane	d
June	17	1915	5964	Kelley	John	d
		1915	6142	Kelley	John	d
Sept.	28	1951	20569	Kelley	Laura Bell	d
June	29	1949	19042	Kelley	Lillus A.	d
		1904	3757	Kelley	Maud	m
		1872	528	Kelley	Michael	d
Nov.	22	1951	20688	Kelley	Peter J., etc.	d
June	18	1931	10969	Kelley	Sarah, etc.	d
Mar.		1916	6211	Kelley	Thomas H.	d
		1904	3757	Kelley	Willie	m
Feb.	2	1958	26121	Kellogg	Edna	d
Apr.	2	1957	24635	Kellogg	Fred H.	d
June	18	1958	25468	Kellogg	Hattie M.	d
		1873	619	Kellogg	Warren S.	d
		1911	5003	Kelly	Charles	d
Apr.	31	1950	19605	Kelly	David C.	d
Jan.	7	1944	15751	Kelly	Edith	d
May	24	1956	23948	Kelly	Edward J.	d
Mar.	31	1950	19604	Kelly	Elizabeth	d
Jan.	15	1955	22984	Kelly	Frances B., etc.	d
		[1900-1901]	3237	Kelly	Francis Peter	d
May	16	1943	15386	Kelly	Frank	d
		1892	2226	Kelly	J. C.	d
Aug.	24	1956	24122	Kelly	James L.	d
Sept.	13	1945	16645	Kelly	James P., etc.	d
Mar.	17	1913	5496	Kelly	James Russell	m
Nov.	15	1947	17951	Kelly	James Russell, etc.	d
		1917	6557	Kelly	James W.	d
Dec.	20	1915	6110	Kelly	James William	inc
May	17	1944	15886	Kelly	Jane	d
Apr.	24	1939	13544	Kelly	John	inc
Dec.	23	1950	20002	Kelly	John	d
Feb.	5	1943	15261	Kelly	John F.	d
Sept.	10	1954	22741	Kelly	Joseph	d
Feb.	17	1913	5496	Kelly	Lillian M.	m
		1880	1059	Kelly	Mark	d
Apr.	10	1928	10120	Kelly	Mark P.	d

Month	Day	Year	File No.	Surname	Given Name	Type
		1912	5245	Kelly	Mary C.	d
		[1900-1901]	3235	Kelly	Mary C.	d
		1923	8452	Kelly	Michael T.	d
May	16	1932	11478	Kelly	Michael, etc.	d
Feb.	29	1954	22312	Kelly	Paul B.	d
July	12	1944	16030	Kelly	Prudence A.	d
Oct.	12	1958	25918	Kelly	Shawn Kay	m
Sept.	12	1958	25918	Kelly	Steven Kay	m
Jan.	11	1954	22276	Kelly	Thomas Roy, etc.	d
Mar.	4	1954	22377	Kelly	Thomas Roy, etc.	d
Aug.	19	1957	24889	Kelly	Violet Nelson, etc.	d
June	2	1948	18427	Kelly	William Heny	d
		1911	5148	Kelly	William S.	d
		1890	1933	Kelsey	Alice F.	m
		1922	8009	Kelsey	Alice F.	inc
		1922	8148	Kelsey	Alice F., etc.	d
		1890	1933	Kelsey	Annie R.	m
Sept.	14	1922	8115	Kelsey	Annie R.	d
		1890	1933	Kelsey	Daniel M.	m
		1890	1933	Kelsey	Edwin J.	m
July	10	1949	19130	Kelsey	Edwin J., etc.	d
May	25	1946	17026	Kelsey	Harold E.	d
		1855	57	Kelsey	Joseph	m
		1889	1845	Kelsey	Richard	d
		1922	8116	Kelsey	Richard J., etc.	d
Sept.		1921	7808	Kelsey	Sarah V.	d
		1890	1933	Kelsey	Thomas H.	m
		1855	57	Kelsey	William	m
		[1883-1884]	1372	Kelsey	William	d
Oct.	7	1950	19913	Kelting	Henry C.	d
Jan.	2	1952	20833	Keltner	Archie E., etc.	d
		1875	729	Kelty	A. L.	m
Jan.	10	1950	19451	Kemlierk	Edward W.	d
Nov.	21	1938	13463	Kemp	Alice L.	d
		1919	7307	Kemp	Emily R.	d
July	17	1958	25706	Kemp	Freeman Bird, etc.	d
Nov.	24	1943	15606	Kemp	Herbert L.	d
		[1876-1877]	831	Kemp	Thomas	d
		[1907-1910]	4333	Kemper	J. H.	d
Mar.	20	1941	14445	Kempf	Henry B., etc.	d
Sept.		1925	9005	Kench	Frank G.	d
Mar.	26	1951	20226	Kendall	Ada, etc.	d

Month	Day	Year	File No.	Surname	Given Name	Type
		[1888-1889]	1736	Kendall	Arthur	m
Oct.	27	1953	22032	Kendall	Courtney Leon, etc.	d
Feb.	9	1910	4916	Kendall	Enoch	d
Apr.	6	1945	16511	Kendall	F. W.	d
		[1888-1889]	1736	Kendall	Homer	m
Jan.	9	1910	4915	Kendall	Thomas	d
May	17	1956	23932	Kendall	Walter L.	d
Oct.	22	1954	22769	Kendig	Burrel B.	d
Mar.	1	1955	23090	Kenduth	Rosa	d
Aug.	31	1931	11040	Kenealey	Irma Margaret	m
Sept.	31	1931	11040	Kenealey	Robert Alfred	m
Jan.	21	1938	13487	Kenlay	Newton B.	d
Nov.	4	1952	21382	Kennaly	Robert John	d
Jan.	18	1920	7581	Kennard	Jack	d
July	7	1949	19119	Kenne	Rose	inc
Jan.	7	1919	6934	Kenneally	Frances	m
Aug.	21	1942	15056	Kenneally	J. M., etc.	d
		[1884-1885[	1442	Kenneally	James	d
		1919	6934	Kenneally	William	m
Aug.		1912	5316	Kennedy	Byron D.	d
Jan.	9	1946	16921	Kennedy	Carolyn Sue	m
May	23	1945	16538	Kennedy	Charles	d
Jan.	9	1946	16921	Kennedy	Edna Mae	m
Sept.	26	1950	19837	Kennedy	George A., etc.	d
Jan.	10	1956	23716	Kennedy	Herbert C.	d
		[1875-1880]	751	Kennedy	Hugh C.	d
		[1880-1881]	1062	Kennedy	James (No. 1)	d
		1885	1503	Kennedy	James (No. 2)	d
Nov.	28	1949	19335	Kennedy	John Preston, etc.	d
Nov.	15	1955	23591	Kennedy	Joseph D.	d
June	10	1938	13345	Kennedy	Julia E.	m
Apr.	24	1919	7009	Kennedy	Margaret	d
		1886	1539	Kennedy	Mariah	d
Oct.	30	1932	11398	Kennedy	Martin	d
Jan.	15	1955	23592	Kennedy	Mary A., etc.	d
June	10	1938	13345	Kennedy	Mary Ellen	m
Feb.	9	1928	9872	Kennedy	Patrick	d
Jan.	9	1946	16921	Kennedy	Rita Joan	m
Aug.	16	1944	16043	Kennedy	Robert D.	d
Nov.	23	1945	16781	Kennedy	Roger J.	d
Oct.	15	1940	14107	Kennedy	Samantha A.	d
July	23	1943	15512	Kennedy	Samantha Harriett	d

Month	Day	Year	File No.	Surname	Given Name	Type
Jan.	21	1949	19379	Kennedy	Sonia Alice	m
Oct.	15	1944	16166	Kennel	Daniel	d
Jan.	6	1946	17518	Kenneslly	William J.	d
June	27	1931	10893	Kenney	J. O., etc.	d
May	7	1918	6639	Kenney	James	d
Oct.	27	1941	14623	Kenney	Martha C.	d
May	3	1932	11211	Kenney	Mary Ann, etc.	d
Sept.	21	1944	16092	Kenny	Emily R., etc.	d
		1903	3685	Kenny	James (petition to alienate homes	p
		[1881-1882]	1193	Kenny	Julia	d
Oct.	1	1941	14661	Kenny	Laurence J., etc.	d
		[1900-1901]	3190	Kenny	Margaret	d
		[1878-1880]	979	Kenny	Patrick	inc
		[1900-1901]	3186	Kenny	Patrick	d
Oct.	12	1931	11076	Kent	Roannah L.	d
Dec.	18	1957	25152	Kenyon	Carl	d
July		1936	12709	Kenyon	Emma Sheldon	d
Apr.	16	1934	11892	Keough	Elizabeth	d
Aug.		1921	7751	Keough	Michael	d
		1920	7463	Keough	Phillip	d
Feb.	18	1943	15235	Keown	Fred Lestel	d
Aug.	9	1939	13695	Keown	James Lestle	m
May		1917	6471	Kerbey	Sarah A.	d
		[1921-1922]	7918	Kerby	Ida L.	d
Oct.	16	1955	23441	Kerby	James F., etc.	d
		1857	59	Kern	George	d
June	8	1942	14971	Kern	Mae Ducy et al	d
Feb.	21	1958	25309	Kernen	Victor	d
July	31	1935	12318	Kerner	Albert	d
Dec.	2	1940	14296	Kerner	Henry R.	d
		[1887-1888]	1619	Kerns	James	d
Aug.	6	1942	15037	Kerr	Matthew	d
Aug.	21	1930	10688	Kerridge	Frederick John, etc.	d
May	28	1944	15902	Kerrigan	Mary Agnes	d
Aug.	26	1951	20507	Kerrigan	Martin	d
		[1907-1910]	4614	Kerrison	Caroline Eliza	d
Aug.	8	1917	6506	Kerrison	George Alfred	d
Aug.	31	1951	20516	Kerrison	Sarah M., etc.	d
May	25	1948	18411	Kerrison	Stephen Markham, etc.	d
May	13	1944	15981	Kerry	George	d
Nov.	17	1958	26083	kersey	Harold C.	d
June	5	1955	23218	Kersh	Frances	inc

Month	Day	Year	File No.		Surname	Given Name	Type
Jan.	8	1933	11786		Kerstan	Wilhelm	d
Dec.	23	1940	14315		Keser	Alma M.	d
		[1895-1896]	2563		Keser	Louis, Sr.	d
		[1907-1910]	4290		Keser	Pauline	d
Dec.	22	1930	10761		Kessack	Juanita	m
Jan.	6	1956	23701		Kester	Susan Gertrude	d
June	21	1957	24748		Ketcham	Claude O., etc.	d
May	26	1948	18361		Ketcham	Clifton Alton, etc.	d
		1911	5175		Ketcham	D. M.	d
Apr.	20	1945	16428		Ketcham	Ivy	d
Feb.	26	1935	12474		Ketcham	Julia	d
Sept.	27	1954	22716		Ketcham	O. C.	d
Apr.	19	1945	16536		Ketcham	Paul	d
July	4	1930	10594		Ketils	Gus, etc.	d
Jan.	21	1931	11113		Ketils	Harold	m
Oct.	24	1942	15061		Ketterlin	Augustine M.	d
Mar.	13	1939	13529		Ketterlin	William F.	d
June	1	1939	13658		Kettlewell	Edith S.	d
Mar.	21	1949	18909		Kettlewell	Idell L.	d
Mar.	28	1950	19539		Kevertt	Clarence M.	d
Dec.	21	1932	11418		Keviston	J. F.	d
Oct.	21	1948	18638		Keyes	Delphine Jennings	d
Dec.	10	1948	18727		Keyes	Delphine Jennings	d
Mar.	12	1921	7640		Keyes	Elma Bessie	g
Feb.	1	1949	18875		Keyes	George Pardon	d
Sept.	27	1935	12368		Keyes	James E.	d
		[1889-1890]	1900		Keyes	Marshall M.	d
Nov.		1915	6106		Keyes	William A., etc.	d
		1888	1704		Keyes	William S.	d
Apr.	6	1916	6226		Keyser	Lucie Ellerson	d
Oct.	20	1934	12006		Keyt	Edwin N.	d
Jan.	2	1947	18113		Khan	Dalel, etc.	d
Mar.	18	1956	24407		Kianduth	Sophie, etc.	d
July	4	1927	9590		Kibbee	Eva G.	d
June	8	1948	18442		Kibbee	Martin B.	d
		1925	9106		Kibbee	Thomas W.	d
		1898	2931		Kidd	Daisy	d
Dec.	19	1920	7553		Kidd	Elizabeth	d
		[1892-1893]	2242		Kidd	Elizabeth	d
Sept.	30	1916	6215		Kidd	Grayce	m
		[1865-1871]	277		Kidd	Peter	d
		[1888-1889]	1765		Kiddey	Mary	d

Month	Day	Year	File No.		Surname	Given Name	Type
Nov.	10	1957	25007		Kidwell	Amelia L.	d
Oct.	25	1941	14617		Kidwell	Charles W.	d
May		1922	8182		Kidwell	George W.	d
June	28	1948	18423		Kidwell	H. C.	d
Jan.	27	1944	16236		Kidwell	William Franklin	d
May	1	1929	10200		Kiechler	Joseph	d
Apr.	12	1955	23171		Kiedaisch	G. Arthur J.	m
Apr.	2	1954	22432		Kiedaisch	Laura Lee	d
Feb.	13	1956	23726		Kiefer	Mary, etc.	d
Jan.	13	1956	23725		Kiefer	William J., etc.	d
		[1896-1897]	2729		Kiegan	Nettie K.	d
Mar.	11	1958	25373		Kiely	John, etc.	d
Aug.		1922	8071		Kiely	Norah	d
		[1901-1902]	3392		Kier	Hans Henry	d
Oct.	19	1949	19176		Kiernan	Clarence E.	d
		[1907-1910]	4498		Kiernan	Gesa	d
		1874	664		Kiernan	Michael	d
Apr.		1917	6454		Kiesbuye	Jacob	d
May	19	1934	11927		Kiessling	Edmund F., etc.	d
Feb.	17	1945	16414		Kikuchi	Chizuyo	m
Mar.	6	1940	13922		Kikuchi	Chizuzo	m
June	20	1944	15994		Kikuchi	Chyuyo	m
Dec.	8	1954	22905		Kikuchi	Joe Yonigo, etc.	d
Feb.	20	1945	16364		Kikuchi	Les Tomoyuki	d
		1942	14851		Kikuchi	Matoyuki	m
May	20	1944	15994		Kikuchi	Matoyuki	m
Feb.	17	1945	16414		Kikuchi	Matoyuki	m
Apr.		1942	14851		Kikuchi	Satsuyo	m
May	20	1944	15994		Kikuchi	Satsuyo	m
Feb.	17	1945	16414		Kikuchi	Satsuyo	m
Feb.	6	1940	13922		Kikuchi	Shizuzo	m
May		1942	14851		Kikuchi	Tazuyo	m
June	20	1944	15994		Kikuchi	Tazuyo	m
Feb.	17	1945	16414		Kikuchi	Tazuyo	m
Dec.	14	1933	11764		Killeen	Patrick J.	d
		1923	8582		Kim	Herman E.	d
		1877	922		Kimball	Ada P.	m
		1910	4873		Kimball	C. L.	d
		[1876-1877]	845		Kimball	G. W.	d
		1877	922		Kimball	Georgie	m
		1877	922		Kimball	Helen M.	m
		[1865-1871]	287		Kimball	J. T.	d

Month	Day	Year	File No.	Surname	Given Name	Type
		1877	922	Kimball	Leila A.	m
Feb.	24	1913	5621	Kimball	Margaret V.`	d
		1877	921	Kimball	Sarah A.	d
July	27	1947	17765	Kimble	Arthur E.	d
Nov.		1920	7544	Kimble	Frank L.	d
		[1893-1894]	2353	Kimble	Harrison	d
		[1900-1901]	3179	Kimble	Mary Ann	d
Mar.	8	1949	18942	Kimes	Walter H.	d
Feb.	4	1930	10512	Kimwia	Kamano	d
June	8	1933	11608	Kincaid	Genevieve	d
		1876	789	Kincaid	Oscar F.	m
Aug.	27	1954	22662	Kinder	Ward H.	d
July	19	1951	20449	Kindig	Alice A.	d
Jan.	21	1941	14682	Kindig	Theodore	d
June	18	1948	18463	Kindle	E. A.	d
Jan.	10	1949	18822	Kindred	Mary Ann	d
Aug.	11	1943	15472	Kinest	Gustav	d
Aug.	27	1914	5855	King	Alfred	m
		1877	924	King	Alice	m
		1926	9302	King	Anna J.	d
Jan.		1917	6618	King	Annie L.	d
May	23	1928	9949	King	Annie M.	d
July	16	1935	12360	King	Bertha	d
June	29	1958	25659	King	Bertha	d
Aug.	25	1914	5806	King	Carl	d
Jan.	15	1915	6157	King	Charles	d
Nov.	19	1956	24288	King	Charlotte Ann	d
Jan.	27	1956	24350	King	Charlotte Ann	d
Jan.	11	1953	22228	King	Connie May	m
Dec.	8	1957	25133	King	Dana Maureen	m
May	23	1928	9948	King	David	d
		1920	7514	King	Dorothea	m
Aug.	27	1914	5855	King	Edna	m
Aug.	27	1914	5855	King	Edward	m
Sept.	11	1958	25774	King	Elnor Eloys, etc.	d
		1920	7514	King	Elsie	m
Jan.	18	1949	19377	King	Frances	d
July	30	1933	11655	King	Frank C.	d
		1918	6749	King	Fred	d
Feb.	16	1930	10815	King	George Franklin, etc.	d
Aug.	24	1954	22712	King	Gertrude M., etc.	d
		[1883-1884]	1308	King	Henry Haight	m

Month	Day	Year	File No.	Surname	Given Name	Type
Aug.		1914	5844	King	Henry, Jr.	ins
Mar.	18	1949	18960	King	Howard C.	d
Feb.	10	1930	10770	King	Ida M.	d
Mar.	16	1951	20215	King	Ida M.	d
Feb.	19	1949	18845	King	Isabella Winifred, etc.	d
Aug.	16	1955	23323	King	Iva, etc.	d
Feb.	26	1927	9712	King	J. T.	d
Mar.	25	1936	12564	King	J. W.	d
May	6	1918	6732	King	James V.	m
		[1910-1911]	4944	King	Jesse	d
		1877	923	King	Jessie	d
Mar.		1926	9202	King	John	inc
Nov.	22	1928	10073	King	John David	g
		1919	7108	King	John T.	d
		[1906-1907]	4176	King	John/Jno Joaquin Coello	d
Mar.	8	1954	22330	King	Joseph Bell, Jr.	d
May	15	1940	13996	King	Julia A.	inc
July	27	1940	14050	King	Julia A.	d
Feb.	11	1935	12436	King	Lora Z.	d
Aug.	12	1947	17889	King	Loren W., etc.	d
		1920	7514	King	Mabel	m
Aug.	27	1914	5854	King	Manuel J.	d
		[1910-1911]	4917	King	Margaret D.	d
		1913	5521	King	Mary C.	d
		[1893-1894]	2324	King	Mathew Wallace	d
		[1899-1900]	3094	King	Mathew Wallace	m
Mar.	2	1955	23094	King	Minnie B.	d
June	21	1948	18466	King	Myra	d
May	2	1919	7048	King	Philip	d
		1877	924	King	Samuel	m
July	26	1920	7432	King	Samuel	g
Dec.	27	1914	5855	King	Stanley	m
Oct.	25	1943	15493	King	T. G.	d
	27	1919	7122	King	Thomas	d
Mar.		1921	7647	King	W. B.	d
		[1889-1890]	1896	King	William F.	m
Jan.	31	1945	16909	King	William H.	d
Oct.	16	1953	22119	King	William John	m
June	26	1954	22490	Kingsburg	Milton L.	d
		1917	6476	Kingsbury	A. L.	d
Apr.	27	1946	16973	Kingsly	Henrietta F.	d
Nov.	16	1926	9359	Kinley	Barnabas C., etc.	d

Month	Day	Year	File No.	Surname	Given Name	Type
May	26	1942	14959	Kinley	Fred J., etc.	d
July	10	1958	25766	Kinley	Mabel aka	d
		1923	8458	Kinley	Mary C.	d
Oct.	20	1951	20621	Kinnaird	Lester	d
Aug.	11	1922	8096	Kinnaman	Victor	inc
Nov.	3	1932	11402	Kinne	Edward A, etc.	d
		1902	3448	Kinne	Ethel S.	m
		1902	3448	Kinne	G. Newton	m
		1902	3448	Kinne	Mary F.	m
Oct.	18	1950	19989	Kinne	Rose	d
Feb.	6	1950	19499	Kinsey	Jesse	d
July	5	1931	10996	Kinslow	Imelda	inc
Nov.	13	1937	13094	Kinslow	James C.	d
Oct.	18	1939	13811	Kinslow	John F.	d
Aug.	16	1953	21948	Kinst	John P.	d
July	25	1948	18482	Kinyon	Dianne Cecelia	m
Oct.	30	1951	20572	Kinzy	Carl	d
June	12	1948	18451	Kipsey	A. S. (trustee)	t
Apr.	1	1927	9585	Kirby	Augustina Haynes	d
		[1899-1900]	3003	Kirby	E. C.	inc
Nov.	16	1956	24274	Kirby	Edith A., etc.	d
		1920	7529	Kirby	Harriet B.	d
June	25	1945	16550	Kirby	Jeanette	m
Aug.	22	1956	24004	Kirby	Rollie Claude, etc.	d
Mar.	1	1921	7690	Kirch	Helen A.	d
Jan.	21	1929	10500	Kirch	Julius	d
Mar.	28	1949	18921	Kirch	Leonard	d
Dec.	22	1933	11695	Kirch	William	d
Nov.	20	1958	26092	Kirk	Albert Wellington	m
		1858	112	Kirk	Alice J.	m
Nov.	20	1958	26092	Kirk	Richard Fox Hammatt	m
Apr.	6	1951	20261	Kirkpatrick	Francis, etc.	d
Aug.	8	1942	15006	Kirkpatrick	Howat R.	d
Jan.	31	1942	15129	Kirkpatrick	Wilma	d
Feb.	3	1958	25251	Kirpatrick	Beryl	inc
Mar.	18	1944	15792	Kirs	Rudolf	d
		[1900-1901]	3310	Kirsch	Eliza	d
		1896	2623	Kirsch	Joseph	d
Apr.	22	1921	7710	Kirschenhisher	Frank	d
Nov.	13	1953	22176	Kirwan	Patrick Achitle, etc.	d
Aug.		1912	5293	Kise	Samuel Cooper	d
		1880	776	Kiser	A. Cooper	m

Month	Day	Year	File No.		Surname	Given Name	Type
Dec.	3	1919	7257		Kiser	Albert D.	d
		1894	2380		Kiser	Anton	d
		1897	2780		Kiser	Anton	m
Apr.	11	1955	23112		Kiser	Conrad J.	d
		1880	776		Kiser	John	d
		1880	776		Kiser	John	m
		1897	2780		Kiser	Joseph	m
		1916	6305		Kiser	Meinrad`	d
		1897	2780		Kiser	Theodore	m
		[1906-1907]	4160		Kiser/Keser	Peter	d
		[1883-1884]	1353		Kissack	Margaret E.	d
		[1883-1884]	1359		Kissack	Margaret S.	d
Sept.	20	1946	17361		Kissock	Golde C., etc.	d
Aug.	14	1946	17302		Kissock	Lewin D., etc.	d
Mar.	3	1926	9186		Kistler	Amandus C., etc.	d
July	21	1945	16619		Kitterman	Grace M., etc.	d
July	3	1958	25757		Kittredge	Ina M.	d
		1892	2151		Kittredge	William T.	d
May	10	1929	10305		Kivett	Amy	m
May	10	1929	10305		Kivett	Elma	m
May	10	1929	10305		Kivett	Warren	m
Aug.	19	1955	23249		Kjellmann	Mary M.	d
May	7	1950	19619		Klagperick	Louis H.	d
Feb.	9	1948	18219		Klass	David	d
June	24	1946	17169		Klebanoff	Frank	d
Jan.	30	1945	16851		Klebanoff	Sarah	d
May	27	1955	23201		Klebe	Bert J.	d
Feb.	26	1947	18147		Klebsnoff	David, etc.	d
Jan.	6	1948	18769		Klecker	Peter J., etc.	d
Mar.	25	1958	25414		Klein	Arthur L.	d
July	18	1950	19822		Klein	Barbara	d
Dec.	21	1919	7247		Klein	Francis	d
Jan.	25	1952	20875		Klein	Harry	d
		1920	7467		Klein	Margaretha	d
July	11	1956	23985		Klein	Marie A.	inc
Feb.	19	1953	21587		Kleinworth	Albert F.	d
Nov.	4	1947	17927		Klemax	Bertha I.	d
Sept.	17	1956	24166		Klemenok	Paul	d
May		1943	15382		Klimansky	Jeanne	d
Dec.	30	1951	20703		Klimansky	Katie	inc
Oct.	13	1954	22749		Klimax	Bertha, etc.	d
Sept.	25	1948	18596		Kline	Irvin, etc.	d

Month	Day	Year	File No.	Surname	Given Name	Type
		[1881-1882]	1196	Kline	Jacob	d
June	2	1935	12288	Kline	Minnie	d
		[1906-1907]	4198	Klinge	Charles	d
Oct.	2	1940	14197	Klingel	Elise	d
		1871	499	Klink	George E.	m
		1871	499	Klink	Margaret J.	m
		1871	499	Klink	Nicholas W.	m
		1900	3105	Kloppenburg	Charles W.	d
Aug.	1	1952	21278	Klostermeyer	Max J.	d
Oct.	1	1952	21298	Klostermeyer	May J.	d
Aug.	22	1916	6184	Klotz	Gustave	d
Apr.	16	1948	18289	Klotz	Lizzie	d
		[1899-1900]	3005	Klotz	Mollie A.	d
Aug.	14	1947	17791	Kluge	Bertha	d
		[1893-1894]	2310	Kluit	Adriaan Provo	d
		[1894-1895]	2441	Kluit	Adriana J. L. Provo	m
		[1894-1895]	2441	Kluit	Henriette Provo	m
July		1923	8649	Klusing	Herman	d
Feb.	31	1919	6978	Klusing	Herman W.	g
Apr.		1919	7008	Klusing	Sophie	d
		[1884-1885[	1426	Klute	Henry	d
Nov.	2	1956	24303	Klutz	Georgette, etc.	d
		[1876-1877]	853	Knaak	August	d
May		1935	12276	Knapp	Alice B., etc.	d
		[1896-1897]	2637	Knapp	G. W.	d
		[1896-1897]	2732	Knapp	Hope Irene	m
		[1896-1897]	2732	Knapp	Ida Lulu	m
Mar.	10	1956	23785	Knapp	Jennie E.	d
		[1913-1914]	5760	Kneale	John	d
Dec.	28	1940	14249	Knecht	John, etc.	d
Apr.	5	1930	10547	Kneeland	Herman M.	d
June	11	1958	25692	Knego	James	d
Jan.	6	1948	18766	Kneller	Elizabeth	d
Nov.	5	1948	18662	Kneller	Elizabeth M.	d
		1901	3363	Kneller	George W.	d
Jan.	27	1953	22201	Kneller	Walter E.	inc
Aug.	6	1954	22625	Kneller	Walter Edwin, etc.	d
		[1892-1893]	2260	Knick	Albert D.	d
Sept.	27	1954	22717	Knight	Clara E.	d
June	10	1926	9249	Knight	Edward J.	d
		1878	967	Knight	George	m
		1893	2305	Knight	George W.	m

Month	Day	Year	File No.		Surname	Given Name	Type
		1906	4066		Knight	Honora	d
		[1893-1894]	2350		Knight	Luther	d
July	13	1951	20481		Knight	Mack F.	d
June	5	1950	19743		Knight	Otis L., etc.	d
Sept.	20	1956	24172		Knight	Sherwood S.	inc
Dec.	4	1957	25188		Knight	Sherwood S., etc.	d
Apr.	14	1915	5940		Knittel	Lorene	d
Nov.	8	1954	22802		Knittl	Betty, etc.	d
Aug.	20	1954	22708		Knittl	Max	inc
May	26	1949	19036		Knoff	Alette Mc Minn, etc.	d
		1912	5237		Knoles	Mamie	inc
July	12	1929	10356		Knolle	Charlotte W.	d
June	10	1928	9969		Knolle	Frans L.	d
		1911	5009		Knolty	Margaret (minor)	g
		[1907-1910]	4785		Knolty	Moses	d
Nov.	9	1956	24320		Knopp	Alfred John	inc
Dec.	31	1942	15070		Knopp	Fred C.	ins
Sept.	18	1958	25795		Knopp	Fred C.	d
Nov.	10	1953	22170		Knops	Henry John, etc.	d
Nov.	15	1956	24328		Knops	Lillian Lange	d
		1885	1462		Knorr	Martin P.	d
May	1	1957	24708		Knoss	Frank, etc.	d
June	1	1957	24709		Knoss	Mary, etc.	d
Mar.	3	1944	15869		Knott	Frank N.	d
Dec.	4	1954	22846		Knott	Henry M., etc.	d
		1883	1299		Knowles	Charles	d
		1911	5233		Knowles	Clairesa A.	d
		[1891-1892]	2129		Knowles	Clarence E.	inc
		1895	2552		Knowles	J. H.	d
		1911	5170		Knowles	Stephen W.	d
Aug.	3	1956	24140		Knowlton	Cyrus	d
Jan.	27	1914	5866		Knox	Edith	m
June	22	1948	18470		Knox	Florence M.	ins
Feb.	31	1913	5483		Knox	Mary E.	d
		1920	7318		Knude	Kurt Goethe	d
July	8	1957	24859		Knudsen	Niels Peter, etc.	d
May	16	1951	20282		Knudson	Asle	d
Jan.	12	1953	21566		Knudson	Mathilda Johanna	d
Oct.	24	1938	13362		Knudson	Nicholas T.	d
Nov.	12	1940	14271		Knudtsen	Conrad N.	d
		1925	8911		Kober	Charles Bernard	d
Apr.	5	1943	15361		Koberg	Laura M.	d

Month	Day	Year	File No.	Surname	Given Name	Type
Jan.	4	1924	8769	Koberg	Louis C.	d
May	5	1950	19673	Kobler	August	d
May	6	1950	19614	Kobler	Millie S., etc.	d
June	29	1938	13306	Koboyoshi	I.	d
Aug.	6	1952	21168	Koch	Charles, etc.	d
		[1913-1914]	5619	Koch	Edward	d
Jan.		1918	6922	Koch	Edward C., etc.	d
		[1881-1882]	1183	Koch	Franz	d
		1911	5122	Koch	Gustav	d
		[1881-1882]	1184	Koch	Ida	m
		[1907-1910]	4370	Koch	John	d
Mar.	14	1921	7703	Koch	Jurgen M.	d
Dec.	10	1945	16808	Koch	Lillian Edith	d
Apr.	18	1955	23183	Koch	Lillian Edith, etc.	d
Sept.	28	1928	10009	Koch	Minnie	d
		[1881-1882]	1184	Koch	Minnie	m
		[1907-1910]	4234	Koch	Minnie, etc.	d
Mar.	17	1950	19566	Koch	Morris	d
		1904	3889	Koch	Nicholas R. S.	d
		[1913-1914]	5618	Koch	Reuben	d
Nov.	1	1958	25967	Koch	Valentine	d
Sept.	10	1946	17339	Koch	William Behler, etc.	d
Aug.		1917	6498	Kockores	John	d
Mar.	4	1949	18930	Koebelen	Louis F.	d
		1914	5809	Koebeli	Rudolph	d
May	19	1917	6627	Koeboom	John H.	d
May		1920	7336	Koehnke	Behrend	d
Aug.		1914	6843	Koenig	Antonio Josephine	m
		1918	6843	Koenig	Antonio Josephine	m
Jan.		1918	6917	Koenig	Elizabeth	d
Aug.	20	1927	9609	Koenig	Sophie	inc
June	30	1954	22503	Koepke	Welsch Victor	d
June	24	1935	12338	Koerner	Henry	d
Sept.	25	1939	13767	Koerner	Louise	d
July	5	1957	24768	Koet	William J.	d
		1856	58	Koger	William	d
		1923	8371	Kohl	Frank	d
		1882	1249	Kohle	Augustina	m
		1885	1470	Kohle	Catherine	d
Dec.	2	1919	7256	Kohler	Johanna	d
Dec.	20	1954	22815	Kohler	Margaret	d
July	25	1958	25728	Kohler	Maxwell J., etc.	d

Month	Day	Year	File No.	Surname	Given Name	Type
July	13	1950	19757	Kolar	John C., etc.	d
Feb.	17	1956	23732	Kolb	Henry John, etc.	d
Nov.	17	1951	20744	Kolk	Lempi E.	inc
Jan.	14	1944	15769	Kolkmeyer	H. F.	d
Jan.	14	1944	15769	Kolkmeyer	Olga E.	d
		1898	2823	Kolmer	John	d
		1865	274	Kolmer	Josefa	d
Feb.	25	1950	19478	Kolnes	Adolf I.	d
May	25	1940	13971	Kolnes	Annie I.	d
Nov.	28	1953	22146	Konietzki	Delia	d
Apr.	4	1947	17729	Konstman	Andrew	d
Jan.	5	1942	14757	Konvalenka	Glenn J.	d
Feb.	5	1951	20131	Koonce	Katherine Agnes, etc.	d
Mar.	31	1936	12849	Koopman	Bertha	d
Nov.	23	1949	19225	Koopman	Peter Piers, etc.	d
		[1907-1910]	4711	Kopf	A. J.	d
		[1921-1922]	7898	Kopf	Adolph Albert	d
		1892	2203	Kopf	Bertram	d
		1916	6293	Kopf	Carl Ludwig	d
July	2	1931	11023	Kopf	Emma Marie	d
Apr.	13	1957	24585	Kopf	Hans	d
		1914	5835	Kopiske	Lewis William	m
Jan.	28	1952	21485	Kopp	Marie	d
Oct.	27	1956	24236	Kopper	Richard F.	d
Dec.	9	1957	25199	Kopriva	James Douglas, etc.	m
Jan.	9	1957	25199	Kopriva	Paul Jay, etc.	m
Oct.	28	1957	24985	Korbel	Leo V., etc.	d
June	10	1929	10306	Korn	Bertha	d
July	19	1929	10343	Korn	Bertha	d
June	12	1929	10307	Korn	Sidney P.	d
Feb.	8	1951	20136	Korsmoe	Oscar E.	d
Oct.	4	1921	7821	Kose	George, etc.	inc
Mar.	22	1941	14448	Koseman	Arthur Allan	m
Apr.	22	1941	14448	Koseman	Betty Mae	m
May	22	1941	14448	Koseman	Sarah Ann	m
Nov.	16	1939	13808	Kosh	Minnie Lena	ins
		1912	5247	Kossack	Andrew	d
Apr.		1926	9397	Kost	Delia Clough	d
Oct.	15	1951	20672	Koster	Albert C.	d
June	2	1944	16010	Koster	Alma E./James, Mrs.	d
		[1913-1914]	5714	Koster	John H.	d
Mar.	11	1947	17634	Kostitch	Josephine	d

Month	Day	Year	File No.	Surname	Given Name	Type
Nov.	17	1945	16725	Kotch	John	d
Jan.	14	1955	22979	Kotzman	Stephen W.	inc
June	11	1942	14939	Kouchi	Gunichi, etc.	d
Aug.	18	1933	11668	Koval	Augusta	d
Nov.	18	1933	11668	Koval	Etel, etc.	d
Oct.	16	1931	11077	Koval	Sucher, etc.	d
		1914	5711	Kowalsky	Kate	d
Apr.		1915	6182	Kowell	Emily	d
Apr.	18	1949	18964	Kraft	Florence E.	d
		1887	1604	Kraft	Rosamond	d
		[1887-1888]	1611	Kraft	Violet	m
		[1900-1901]	3155	Kraft	Violet E.	d
Mar.	20	1948	18248	Kraft	W. R.	d
Aug.	15	1941	14580	Krager	Vina (terminate joint tenancy)	d
June	24	1940	14046	Krahn	Christine	inc
July	3	1940	14057	Krahn	Joseph	d
Jan.	9	1931	11100	Krakela	John, etc.	d
May	16	1925	8910	Kramer	Andreas	d
Apr.	21	1928	9886	Kramer	Henry	m
Feb.	1	1943	15255	Kramer	Lena	d
Apr.	21	1928	9886	Kramer	Louie	m
Apr.	26	1948	18253	Kramer	Noble	inc
May	20	1948	18356	Kramer	Noble	d
Feb.	7	1951	20204	Kramer	John	d
		1942	14791	Kranskopf	Charles	d
May	23	1951	20354	Krasny	Emil, etc.	d
Jan.	7	1942	15183	Krause	Evelyn Bough/Oliver J., Mrs., etc	d
Jan.	12	1957	25211	Krause	Leo Robert, etc.	d
		[1900-1901]	3115	Krause	Wm. H.	d
Aug.	8	1946	17239	Krausse	Emma	d
Sept.	10	1946	17391	Krausse	J. C. H.	d
		1905	4006	Krawetzki	John J.	d
Apr.	7	1930	10570	Kraxberger	Grace Ellen	m
		1916	6335	Kreh	Christine	d
Sept.	24	1931	11060	Kreh	Jacob	d
Nov.	10	1955	23525	Kreiss	William Henry, etc.	d
Sept.	18	1944	16127	Kresge	Laura E.	d
Oct.	13	1952	21190	Kresky	J. E., etc.	d
		1892	2181	Kreuz	Catherina	inc
June	16	1917	6486	Kriche	August	d
		1905	4017	Kricke	Ernest	d
Apr.	7	1948	18334	Krieg	Bertha Annie, etc.	d

Month	Day	Year	File No.	Surname	Given Name	Type
Apr.	7	1948	18333	Krieg	Fred	d
Sept.	8	1930	10724	Kripiak	Hilary A.	d
Aug.	26	1937	12943	Kristiansen	Sigurd R., etc.	d
Jan.	26	1950	20119	Krisymel	Josephine Reyes Maldini, etc.	d
Dec.	24	1929	10442	Kritzer	Janie	d
Nov.	2	1945	16801	Kroll	Walter	d
July	13	1933	11610	Kron	Cora A.	d
Mar.	23	1943	15285	Kron	Cora Alma	d
Apr.	28	1945	16445	Kron	Elbert W.	d
		1899	2969	Kron	Elizabeth	d
Apr.	19	1943	15311	Kron	Frithiaf John, etc.	d
Nov.	18	1946	17403	Kron	Grace F.	d
		1877	862	Kron	John	d
June	25	1943	15449	Kronch	Frederick, etc.	d
Dec.	8	1946	17471	Kronche	Ada	d
July	11	1946	17198	Kroncke	Anna, etc.	d
Nov.		1919	7188	Kroncke	Peter H.	d
July	9	1950	19751	Krone	Lena	d
Aug.	28	1955	23005	Krone	Lena	d
Jan.	3	1929	10483	Kronz	Wallace	d
Dec.	18	1946	17481	Krotser	Ella L.	d
May	17	1953	21783	Krouse	Samuel E.	d
Mar.	7	1941	14426	Kroyer	John F., etc.	d
		1922	8019	Krugh	Daisy, Mrs., etc.	d
		1920	7343	Krupich	Frank	d
Nov.	7	1949	19350	Kruschwitz	Emil	d
Nov.	15	1949	19373	Kruschwitz	Emil	d
		[1894-1895]	2463	Kruse	August	m
Dec.	19	1936	12731	Kruse	Carrie M.	d
Mar.	2	1926	9217	Kruse	Charles G.	d
Feb.	23	1948	18181	Kruse	Clara Elsie, etc.	d
Sept.	25	1930	10714	Kruse	Fred	d
Jan.	17	1954	22924	Kruse	Fred Paul, etc.	d
June	20	1949	19091	Kruse	George W.	d
June	5	1953	21823	Kruse	Henry A., etc.	d
		1885	1510	Kruse	James	d
Apr.	30	1953	21733	Kruse	Lena	d
	22	1913	5771	Kruse	Mary A.	d
Apr.	25	1949	18981	Kruse	Minna	d
		[1913-1914]	5627	Kruse	Nellie M.	d
Jan.	17	1914	5917	Kruse	Nelson H.	m
		[1910-1911]	4964	Kruse	Walter H., etc.	d

Month	Day	Year	File No.	Surname	Given Name	Type
Aug.	12	1949	19164	Kruse	William, etc.	d
		[1899-1900]	3099	Kruse	Wm. H.	inc
		[1906-1907]	4067	Krusemarck	Nanny	d
Jan.	20	1933	11794	Kryger	Aaron	d
Mar.	31	1930	10536	Kuake	Paul C., etc.	d
Feb.	15	1954	22285	Kubbernus	William J., etc.	d
Dec.	27	1953	22196	Kucera	Joseph	inc
Apr.	13	1954	22451	Kucera	Joseph	d
Aug.	13	1930	10705	Kuchel	Henry	d
		[1900-1901]	3170	Kuchel	Jacob	d
		[1889-1890]	1874	Kuchler	Blasius	m
		[1889-1890]	1874	Kuchler	Joseph	m
		[1889-1890]	1874	Kuchler	Josephine	m
		[1889-1890]	1874	Kuchler	Rosalie	m
		1918	6734	Kuck	Henry	d
Mar.	11	1957	24446	Kuechler	Henry Norbury, etc.	d
		1942	14831	Kuehl	Herman	d
Mar.	18	1936	12557	Kuehn	Helen	d
Oct.	20	1956	24215	Kuehn	Sarah L.	d
Apr.	7	1957	24573	Kuehn	Wallace William	d
July	29	1931	11020	Kuemmerle	Emil G.	d
Apr.	15	1914	5515	Kuffel	Isaac	inc
Apr.	1	1914	5518	Kuffel	Isaac	d
		1914	5519	Kuffel	Wilma	inc
Dec.		1922	8167	Kuffel	Wilma	d
May	14	1958	25624	Kuhale	Perry	d
Mar.	29	1934	12086	Kuhlcke	Albert K.	inc
July	9	1954	22576	Kuhlcke	Albert K.	inc
Nov.	5	1956	24310	Kuhlcke	Albert K.	d
Nov.	18	1946	17404	Kuhlmann	Thelma, Miss, etc.	d
May	12	1934	11922	Kuhlmeyer	Mary Elizabeth	m
Oct.	28	1938	13471	Kuhn	Lena, etc.	d
June	22	1907	4325	Kuhnle	Fred	d
		1920	7612	Kulberg	Andrew J., etc.	d
Apr.	5	1943	15298	Kulberg	Sarah Jane	d
Jan.	5	1952	21498	Kulenkamp	Lenora G.	d
Aug.	14	1953	22008	Kullberg	A., etc.	d
		1912	5262	Kulper	Henry	d
Nov.	23	1943	15575	Kumert	Florence R.	d
		1881	1133	Kumli	Jacob	d
Nov.	16	1958	25932	Kummer	Homer B., etc.	d
Sept.	23	1932	11306	Kummer	Margaret, etc.	d

Month	Day	Year	File No.	Surname	Given Name	Type
Nov.	28	1948	18651	Kumsik	Frank, etc.	d
Oct.	18	1922	8144	Kunde	Charles Louis	d
		1921	7731	Kunde	Eleanor Marie	m
Feb.	27	1944	16344	Kunde	Marie	d
May	15	1957	24666	Kunde	Richard Morris	m
Feb.		1919	7285	Kundtsen	Conrad N.	d
Apr.	5	1926	9237	Kunkel	Genevieve	m
Apr.	5	1926	9237	Kunkel	Helen	m
Apr.	26	1947	17665	Kuntz	Hurlie C., etc.	d
Aug.	9	1941	14572	Kurhler	Blass F.	d
Feb.	11	1946	16931	Kurlander	Frank B.	d
May	17	1931	10880	Kurlander	Hulda L.	d
Oct.	19	1953	22020	Kurlander	Irving Sal	inc
Sept.	25	1957	24909	Kurlander	Irving Sol, etc.	d
Mar.	5	1925	8840	Kurlander	Joseph	d
Sept.	10	1932	11386	Kurlander	Lyda V.	d
June	5	1952	21165	Kurlander	Maurice A., etc.	d
June	10	1958	25685	Kurlander	Sidney, etc.	d
Apr.	24	1956	23814	Kursteiner	Ruth W.	d
		[1907-1910]	4786	Kurtz	Emily C.	d
		1919	7058	Kuster	Emma H.	d
Mar.	9	1955	23034	Kustzhal	Hannah Northrup	d
May	10	1958	25447	Kutschmar	Elizabeth	d
Feb.	30	1936	12846	Kutschmar	Julius	d
June	17	1943	15433	Kutschmse	Paul	d
July	21	1941	14525	Kuykendall	Dolly, etc.	d
Nov.	16	1930	10757	Kuykendall	James O.	d
May	22	1955	23187	Kyle	Frances Florence, etc.	d
Mar.	9	1954	22333	Kyle	George Ernest	d
Aug.	8	1953	21882	Kyle	Harry T.	d
Dec.		1919	7230	Kyle	John G.	d
May	5	1957	24651	Kyle	Sharon Diane	m
		1898	2863	Kyle	Thomas	d
Mar.	19	1940	13937	Kyle	Thomas	d
June	28	1953	21813	Kynoch	Abbie W.	d
July		1922	8027	Kynoch	Alonzo, etc.	d

Heritage Books by the Sonoma County Genealogical Society, Inc.:

CD: *Sonoma County [California] Records, Volume 1*

Early School Attendance Records of Sonoma County, California, Beginning 1858

Early School Attendance Records of Sonoma County, California, Volume II: 1874–1932

Homestead Declarations: Amended Index, Sonoma County, California, Second Edition

Index and Abstracts of Wills, Sonoma County, California: 1850–1900

Index to Naturalization Records in Sonoma County, California, Volume 1: 1841–1906

Naturalization Records in Sonoma County, California, Volume II: 1906–1930

Index to The Sonoma Searcher*: Volume 16, No. 1 to Volume 28, No. 3*
(Including Index to The Sonoma Searcher*: Volume 1, No. 1 to Volume 15, No. 4, SCGS, August 1993)*

Index to Vital Data in Local Newspapers of Sonoma County, California, Volume 1: 1855–1875

Index to Vital Data in Local Newspapers of Sonoma County, California, Volume 2: 1876–1880

Index to Vital Data in Local Newspapers of Sonoma County, California, Volume 3: 1881–1885

Index to Vital Data in Local Newspapers of Sonoma County, California, Volume 4: 1886–1890

Index to Vital Data in Local Newspapers of Sonoma County, California, Volume 5: 1891–1899

Index to Vital Data in Local Newspapers of Sonoma County, California, Volume 6: 1900–1903

Index to Vital Data in Local Newspapers of Sonoma County, California, Volume 7: 1904–1906

Index to Vital Data in Local Newspapers of Sonoma County, California, Volume 8: 1907–1909

Index to Vital Data in Local Newspapers of Sonoma County, California, Volume 9: 1910–1912

Index to Vital Data in Local Newspapers of Sonoma County, California, Volume 10: 1913–1915

Index to Vital Data in Local Newspapers of Sonoma County, California, Volume 11: 1916–1918

Indigent Records in Sonoma County, California 1878 to 1926, Volume 1: The Indigents

Indigent Records in Sonoma County, California 1878 to 1926, Volume 2: Taxpayers Who Certified Indigent Need

Militia Lists of Sonoma County, California, 1846 to 1900

Probate Records, Sonoma County, California Index for 1847 to 1959

Santa Rosa Rural Cemetery, 1853–1997

Sonoma County, California Cemetery Records, 1846–1921, Third Edition

Sonoma County, California Death Records, 1873–1905, Second Edition

Sonoma County California Reconstructed 1890 Census

The 1930 School Census of Sonoma County, California